13.50

15⁰⁰ EC

Lenin and Leninism

Lenin and Leninism

State, Law, and Society

Edited by
Bernard W. Eissenstat
Oklahoma State University

Lexington Books
D.C. Heath and Company
Lexington, Massachusetts
Toronto   London

Table of Contents

Foreword

The significance of Lenin's impact on world developments in the twentieth century is an essential exercise in awareness given the numbers in the world, states, movements and individuals, claiming to be adherents or followers of Lenin and Leninism. To further this understanding, a major scholarly conference marking the centenary of Lenin's birth was held in Stillwater, Oklahoma at Oklahoma State University from April 20 through April 22, 1970, under the cosponsorship of the university's History Department and the American Bar Association's Committee on Education About Communism and Its Contrast With Liberty Under Law.

The theme of the conference was the Leninist approach to state, law, and society. The importance of Lenin's work in these areas is that he structured on the Marxist past a theory of revolution, seizure of power, and postrevolutionary government which has influenced, and continues to influence, subsequent revolutionary movements.

The conference was not an exercise in scholarly inbreeding. In keeping with its charter to educate about communism, the cosponsoring ABA Committee arranged for an audience of lawyers and law students who participated in the formal postpresentation discussions and, in what proved to be the most challenging and exciting encounters, the informal talk fests which were encouraged wherever and whenever a scholar was present. For instance, every afternoon the scholars met with the law students to discuss the problems of society as seen by the students. The most stimulating aspect of the conference was the exposure of the scholars both to one another and to the lawyers and law students in the audience—there was no refuge behind the podium or the prepared text.

The Conference was a successful exercise in scholarship and education and it is only fitting that its work receive wider dissemination. This collection of papers, therefore, is a welcome and significant addition to the literature in the field.

Bernard A. Ramundo
American Bar Association

Preface

April 22, 1970 marked the one hundredth year of the birth of Vladimir Ilyich Lenin, a centenary event noted throughout the world. Official celebrations occurred in all communist countries, and nowhere was there more enthusiasm than in the Soviet Union. There official preparations for this centenary celebration had been planned for some two years. Songs and plays were written about Lenin; television and radio blared forth documentaries and accolades; newspapers and journals featured articles about his life; and scholarly periodicals devoted entire issues to his contributions and continuing influence. Chocolate replicas of Lenin could be purchased in the stores of Moscow and the dictum "Lenin Lives" was heard throughout the nation. For the scholar, the celebration reached its peak with a number of scholarly conferences devoted to Lenin's life and influence. In the so-called Western World, the only major scholarly conference marking the centenary of Lenin's birth was held in Stillwater, Oklahoma, at Oklahoma State University, and the chapters in the book are a result of that conference.

The Conference at Oklahoma State University was an attempt to review and reinterpret Lenin's diverse roles during his lifetime and his lingering influence after his death. In short, the Conference was an attempt to place Lenin's varied roles and influence in historical continuity and ideological perspective. The invitations to participants were based only on scholarly credentials, not on ideological leanings, and thus the chapters in this volume represent an enormously wide spectrum of political opinion and national origin.

Scholars from five nations have contributed chapters to this volume. Unfortunately my invitation to a representative of the Soviet Union was rejected. Consequently a contribution by a Soviet scholar does not appear in this volume. In addition, because of the limitations of space and at the request of some of the conference participants, four of the papers presented have been omitted. I should also add that because of the number of Lenin scholars at the Conference, we took advantage of this rare occasion to make six educational television tapes based on the theme "Lenin and Leninism: Some Myths and Realties," in which eighteen of our twenty-one scholars participated. The titles of these programs are "The Influence of Lenin on Our Times"; "Lenin and Ideology"; "Lenin, Leninism and Law"; "The Consequences of Lenin and Leninism on Economics and Political Legality"; "Lenin on Agitation and Propaganda"; and "Lenin on Nationalities, Religion and Dictatorship."

No matter what one may think about the effect of Lenin and Leninism on history, everyone will concede that it was enormous. If greatness is defined as substantially influencing the course of historical development, then it must be conceded that V.I. Lenin was one of the greatest men of our times. While he was not the universal genius his hagiographers make him out to be, neither was he the evil genius his detractors describe. He was, however, unselfishly devoted to achieving revolutionary goals; and while he seemed to lack ambition for personal gain, the evidence indicates that he was vain enough to believe that the coming of the revolution could be expedited and accelerated only under his leadership. He was a man of seeming contradictions who was capable of great extremes. At times he would be extremely kind and solicitous and on other occasions he would be arbitrary and ruthless. Generally, his actions seemed to be determined by his goals. He was a man who not only had a great ideological and political impact in Russia and the Soviet Union, but also has had and continues to have an enormous ideological and philosophical impact on revolutionary movements, both successful and unsuccessful, in other nations. Curiously his revolutionary and ideological influence even extends to some of the diverse elements of the so-called New Left, albeit at times unacknowledged and unrecognized. In the areas of tactics and strategy, and in these areas he did possess genius, he also influenced the Fascist movement.

In general, however, Lenin's contributions to the Revolution and its transition to the final stage of historical development were not in theory, but rather in practical application within the broad framework of Marxism. It must also be noted that Lenin's practical solutions to everyday problems later became an important part of the ideological rationales for excesses undertaken under the all-encompassing term of "Leninism."

Whereas a number of Marxist disciples in Europe, such as Karl Kautsky, looked on the Dictatorship of the Proletariat as a deviation from Marxism, Lenin argued that it was the "very essence" of the teaching of Marx. Consequently, it is no surprise to find that he constantly inveighed against parliamentary democracy as a bourgeois manifestation. He believed, with Marx, that political parties are reflections of class struggle and therefore he created a one Party system in which the Party was superior to the government and from which all basic decisions stemmed.

In his economic program, Lenin was ambiguous and unclear, and his administrative theories were somewhat naive. He argued, as did Marx, that the bourgeoisie had created such a strong, viable, simple system of economics that any charwoman could manage an administrative position. He eventually discovered that he needed well-trained and capable personnel to run the state and thus began the creation of a special bureaucracy in the Soviet Union. It is ironic that the very man who argued that the state was an instrument of exploitation created a system of government which was stronger and more encompassing than any of the Tsars had dreamed of. And in this system of government the party emerged as the major policy-making body.

Democratic centralism, the core of the Party discipline, was adopted in July 1917. This meant that the organization of the Party was of enormous importance. The Party members must be people who could be trusted. Initially, Lenin did not expect the Party to take control of the government after the Revolution, but merely to advise it. However, he did lay the basis for the later control of the state by the Party.

Lenin also contributed the idea of united front tactics to the problem of Communist party cooperation with a noncommunist government. He drew a distinction between united front tactics from above, in which a deal is made with the head of the native Communist party, and united front tactics from below, in which there are no formal overtures, but rather an appeal over the heads of the non-Communist government to the general population and infiltration into subsidiary non-Communist organizations.

Perhaps among the more lasting of Lenin's ideas are his teachings on imperialism. For Lenin the latter part of the capitalist formation was that stage of development in which the domination of monopoly and finance capital had taken place; in which the export of finance capital had taken decisive importance; in which the division of the world by international trusts had begun; and in which the partition of all the territories of the earth had been completed. He argued that capitalists bought raw materials cheap and sold the finished product dear. He anticipated that capitalist nations would eventually fight over markets and this would subsequently lead to a collapse of the entire system. He believed that agitation and revolutionary activities in underdeveloped areas would have great effect on capitalist countries. In his law of uneven development he asserted that because of the export of capital it was possible for underdeveloped countries to affect the economies of the developed countries and to more rapidly undergo the development of capitalism themselves. Consequently, the most advanced countries would approach revolution more quickly.

It is no surprise to find that Lenin's thoughts on capitalism became an important concomitant of communist ideology and that "anti-imperialism" became an important part of the Communist program. As long as capitalism lasted, Lenin maintained the USSR could never be safe, so that to ensure its security, the Communists would have to ferment revolutions around the world.

That Lenin was not always a clear thinker is reflected in his writings, but one must also note that he was willing to admit his mistakes. There is no question that he was the architect of successful Bolshevik revolution in Russia and laid the strong foundation of the Soviet regime, and consequently no matter what one may think about the effect that Lenin had on history, it must be conceded that the effect was enormous.

In this volume an attempt has been made to keep the system of transliteration consistent within each individual chapter. Throughout the volume the only inconsistencies which exist should be in the use of i and y; ia and ya; and iu and yu.

In the broadest sense this volume is an historiographical study of Lenin and Leninism. It is an attempt by some of our most distinguished scholars to discuss a number of diverse subjects concerning Lenin and Leninism, which have had and continue to have an influence on our times. The fact is, that while these papers were written in 1970, their impact should have a continuing influence on the study of Lenin and Leninism for a good many years to come.

**Part I
Lenin,
Philosophy and Ideology**

1

Peter Tkachev:
The Forerunner of Lenin

ALBERT L. WEEKS

One of Peter Tkachev's most characteristic complaints was not aimed at his opponents within the Russian Populist movement, at the semifeudal society of
Russia, or at the Tsarist state—but concerned his own troubled state of mind:

Vechno nosit' v ume idei, kotopym nikogde ne suzhdeno periti v delo, eto uzhe
samo po sebe pytka, i strashno muchitel'naiia pytka.

Carrying about in one's head ideas which have no chance of being put into effect
is agony, sheer, unmitigated torture.[1]

This intense feeling of anguish was not peculiar to Tkachev alone. It was a
typically Russian form of suffering and frustration, the fate of uncompromising
revolutionists and idealists within the ranks of the nineteenth-century Russian
Populists. Aggravating this frustration for Tkachev and other radicals was not
only the lonely extremism of their revolutionary tactics and strategy, but their
status as members of the intelligentsia.

Like the majority of Populists, Tkachev was an *intelligent*, a member of the
miniscule brain-worker minority in Russia, at the same time a member of the
still more microcosmic stratum within the intelligentsia made up of intellectual
proletarians, radicals, and "thinking realists."[a] These partly- or well-educated
and frequently guilt-ridden *intelligenty* were completely isolated and alienated.
Isolated in a double sense: from the bureaucratic Establishment, which was
obedient to the Tsar; isolated also from the inaccessible, inarticulate, illiterate
Russian peasant masses. The separation from the masses was particularly intolerable since it was in their behalf that the revolutionaries exerted all their efforts,
often at great personal danger and sacrifice. The fact was that the socialist intelligentsia had to be content with talking to itself! And this was not only, as
Tkachev put it, an excruciating agony, but often resulted in hopelessly elaborate
utopian schemes, esoteric arguments and counterarguments, extreme and often
fruitless intellectualization of contemporary social and political problems and
means to the solution. George V. Plekhanov summed up this intellectualization
as a form of Russian "scholasticism." The scholasticism sometimes resulted in
cerebral Frankensteins. "The abuse of intellectual power," wrote John Stuart

---

[a]This term was coined by Dmitri Pisarev, who greatly influenced the young Tkachev in the
early 1860s.

Mill in 1865, "is only to be dreaded when society is divided between a few highly cultivated intellects and an ignorant and stupid multitude."[2]

The isolation and the alienation, the attendant frustrations and the feelings of pent-up unrelieved guilt, produced a variety of effects upon the diversified intellects, characters, and temperaments of the various Populists, and as many various ideologies. Tkachev's own ideology of Jacobinism-Blanquism was, of course, only one of many types of populism.[3]

One species of Populists, for example, is of a more moderate temperament and with fewer intellectual pretensions and less metaphysical arrogance than their more radical opponents. Moreover, they regarded isolation within the closed circle of Populist essayists (or *"publitsisty"*), or underground seclusion among dynamiters and political assassins, as a type of totally unsatisfactory dedication to the Cause. To the moderates, bullets and bombs were not only inhumane but, perhaps even more important, were ineffective and self-destructive means for reaching the humanitarian goals of socialism. These Lavrovist socialists of the 1870s advised the socially-conscious *intelligenty* to "go to the people" (*"khodit' v narod"*). The *Mikhailovtsi* and the *Chaikovtsi* believed in the desirability of carrying enlightenment down to the very grassroots—a kind of socialist Peace Corps, if you will, in which literacy, education, science, and, of course, socialism would be spread to the masses. These go-to-the-people *Narodniki* hoped that out of the primitive, "collectivistic instincts" of the Russian peasantry (as symbolized by the commune or *obshchina*) would evolve socialism. The democratic motif of this earliest species of *Narodnichestvo* was quite obvious: educate the masses so that the people themselves could regenerate society. Violence in a nationwide revolution followed by dictatorial methods, or *ukaz*-socialism after the revolution was anathema to most of these Populists. As Lavrov himself put it:

History shows, and psychology convinces us, that any unlimited power, any dictatorship, corrupts even the best people. Could it be possible that our revolutionary youth would agree to the accession to the throne of certain dictators who, even for the best of intentions, would only become new sources of social evils and who, more than likely, would not be dedicated fanatics as much as passionately ambitious men thirsting for power for the sake of power.[4]

And Bakunin, too, shortly after he had thrown off his shortlived flirtation with Jacobinism, warned contemporary revolutionists as early as 1862: "Authoritarian communism . . . can end only with the workers being used once more as an instrument against themselves and being turned over again to bourgeois exploitation."[5] Furthermore, added Bakunin, authoritarianism "awakens within the masses a rebellious spirit, a legitimate counteraction."[6]

Democratic-minded populism, then, put the stress on political democracy (in the form of a democratically-elected Constituent Assembly and a subsequent National Assembly based on universal suffrage) and on local autonomy rather than dictatorship and centralism.[b]

But certain other Populists, who undoubtedly were in a minority during the whole period from the mid-nineteenth century and into the twentieth, could not abide the peaceful, gradualistic road to reform in Russia.[7] Radical injustices lying deep within the old society, they insisted, demanded radical solutions. The coercive Tsarist state demanded equally coercive and violent means to do away with it. These hybrid Populists were obviously possessed of more radical and impatient temperaments than most of their Populist colleagues. Moreover, they regarded the enlightener-Populists, at best, as so many optimistic fools who misapplied Darwinism and/or Comtism to Russian society; at worst, as reactionary continuators of the Old Order. These hot-blooded *intelligenty* promoted entirely different tactics and strategy from that of the other Populists, to whom the ultras addressed countless letters and essays. In essence, theirs was a strikingly different philosophical outlook (*mirosotsersaniye* or *mirovozzreniye*). Violent revolution, not peaceful evolution, was the only answer, they said; only by means of revolutionary violence followed by force applied to society by the new revolutionary state could the old encrusted way of life be smashed through and the equally crustaceous acquisitive psychology of Russian society be plowed over. Thereafter, the seeds of altruistic socialism could be sown in the new furrows, and at the end of the regenerative process would come the New Order. A socialist society of the type, say, depicted in Chernyshevsky's *What Is to Be Done?* or in the classical projections of Cabet, Saint-Simon, or even of Sir Thomas More and old Plato, with his Philosopher-Kings and Nocturnal Council of censors and high-priests.[8]

To this second, more uncompromisingly radical, and also more thoroughgoing brand of Russian socialist ideology belonged Peter Nikitich Tkachev (1844-1886), the most precocious, articulate and widely known of the Russian Jacobins and Blanquists in the whole of the nineteenth century.[9]

Before dealing with Tkachevism in itself and as a proto-Bolshevist ideology, it is important to remember that Tkachev, besides being a forerunner, had himself

---

[b]In reference to a Constituent Assembly, Tkachev evidently agreed with the point of view expressed in *Young Russia*, the Russian Jacobin proclamation of 1862, that "elections for a national assembly must take place under the surveillance of the [revolutionary] government which will at once make sure that no partisans of the old order—that is, if they are alive—make up the composition of this new assembly." The problem of the Constituent Assembly, which was permitted to hold only a one-day meeting in January 1918, Lenin said, had been solved "forcibly" by the Bolsheviks because the Bolsheviks had established their dictatorship *before* the Assembly convened and that, in any case, the bourgeois peasant masses could only be "won over" to socialism through the *power* of the Bolshevik dictatorship and not by tabulating votes. Tkachev had a similar distaste for "arithmetic democracy," since the people themselves do not understand what their best interests are. In any case, Tkachev said he believed in one-party government, if it were socialist, because he had observed that under parliamentary, multi-party government, "polyarchy" reigned. See discussion in Albert L. Weeks, *The First Bolshevik—A Political Biography of Peter Tkachev* (New York, 1968), pp. 99-102.

a few forerunners; a Jacobin tradition had long since set into the Russian revolutionary movement before our Jacobin of the 1860s and 1870s.

Colonel Pavel Pestel', the Decembrist of the 1820s, represented one of the earliest Russian Jacobins. Pestel' called for the radical-nobleman minority, of which he was a member, to make a palace revolution in 1825, a "preventive" coup, in fact, which would preclude the outbreak of a runaway mass peasant revolution. Such a revolution, predicted the Decembrists, was bound to come and would dangerously weaken the nation, economically and militarily. A provisional dictatorship, said Pestel' and his followers, should be established after the coup to complete the parcelization of the land and to institute a National Assembly, and so on.

Until the 1860s, no other outstanding Russian Jacobin appeared. But with the formation of the Petrashevsky revolutionary socialist circle (to which the young Dostoyevsky belonged for a time, much to his dismay later) appeared the strong-minded nobleman Nikolai Speshnev. Speshnev, who had been educated in a French lycée where he was strongly influenced by French utopian socialism, built an imposing structure for Jacobin-style revolution and reconstruction of Russia; however, as in the case of the Russian Jacobins and Blanquists to follow, Speshnev's ideology won few adherents among his colleagues. In brief, the *Petrashevets* Speshnev's program was as follows:

1. A Central Committee *[tsentral'nii komitet]* should be formed in which centralized leadership of all revolutionary groups and revolutionary activity could be organized, led and coordinated;

2. The revolutionary program per se should be avowedly conspiratorial and Babeuvian-communist;
   Revolutionary tactics should be Machiavellian, in terms of the ends justifying the means;
   A postrevolutionary dictatorship *[diktatorstvo]* should be established;
   Collectivization of Russian agriculture should be encouraged.

Speshnev and his colleagues set off some interesting debates, between Jacobins and their critics within the Petrashevsky circle, including Petrashevsky himself, who answered Speshnev by saying that he, Petrashevsky, "would be the first to raise my hand against a dictator." The debates between the Petrashevets—between moderate and radical socialists—foreshadow later controversies revolving about the issue of moderation, gradualism, democracy vs. etatism, the coup revolutionary tactic, and so on—controversies which were to beset both Russian populism and Social Democracy in the nineteenth and twentieth centuries.

Among other Jacobins near the time of Tkachev, one should not overlook Peter Zaichnevsky (1842-1896). In Zaichnevsky's case, however, the predecessor-successor relationship to Tkachev should be reversed: Zaichnevsky was very likely the pupil of Tkachev, not the other way around. Zaichnevsky's most famous Jacobin writing was *Young Russia*, a proclamation drafted in 1862. *Young Russia* was written ostensibly to oppose the views found in most other proclamations of the time, notably that of the *Great Russian*, which was distributed from July to September 1861, evidently under the authorship of Chernyshevsky. M.N. Pokrovsky, the Bolshevik historian, notes the "Menshevist tone" of the *Great Russian* versus the "Bolshevist tone" of the *Young Russia*.

Indeed, by contrast, *Young Russia* displays more "Bolshevism" than "Menshevism." Issued in May 1862, Zaichnevsky's proclamation, a product of what he called "The Revolutionary Committee," stated the following:

We have not studied Western European history for nothing. It was studied for a definite reason. We will henceforth not be the pitiful revolutionaries of 1848, but rather the great terrorists of 1792. We are not afraid if we see that for the overturning of the contemporary social order it will prove necessary to expend twice as much blood as was expended by the Jacobins of the 1790's. We firmly maintain that the revolutionary party, which will stand at the head of the government if the movement will only prove successful, must retain the present centralization of government—beyond all doubt politically centralized and not merely administratively centralized. By this centralized power it can lay the foundations for economic and social life in as short a time as possible. It must take the dictatorship into its own hands and not stop at anything. Elections for a National Assembly must take place *under the surveillance of the [revolutionary] government* which will at once make sure that no partisans of the Old Order—that is if they are still alive—make up the composition of this new Assembly [italics mine—A.L.W.].[10]

On the tasks of the revolutionary-dictatorship government, the proclamation states:

We demand establishment of socialized factories, the administration of which must be elected from society and be held responsible for a prescribed length of time to give a total accounting of things [to the public]. We demand the establishment of shops in which goods will be sold at prices which insure to the seller the quickest possible profit.... We demand the complete liberation of women, the awarding to them of all those political and civil rights enjoyed by men.... The properties of all churches must be confiscated on behalf of the state for the payment of foreign and domestic debt.

And so on.

Among the Petersburg youth, wrote L.F. Pantaleyev, a contemporary, *Young Russia* did not meet with great enthusiasm or sympathy. True, it was disseminated, "but only because the youth at that time considered it their duty to distribute any proclamation."[11] B.P. Kozmin has noted that both Herzen and

Chernyshevsky were also hostile to Zaichnevsky's theories on revolution and a postrevolutionary dictatorship.

Peter Tkachev grew to maturity in an era of "thaw" and talk of reform; talk of revolution was also in the air. By the time he was of college age in 1860, or eighteen years old, two terrible periods in nineteenth century Russian history had ended: the thirty-year reign of Nicholas I (1825-1855) and the nearly disastrous Crimean War (1854-1856), while a promising new tsar, Alexander II, had taken the throne (his reign was 1855-1881). Publicistic activity, frustrated during the thirty years of reaction under Nicholas I, especially in the autocrat's last "seven mad years," burst out in the spring-like intellectual atmosphere which blanketed Petersburg, not unlike that of the post-Stalin year of 1956 a hundred years later.[12]

Of course, much of the old repression remained. The Russian masses could be said, according to Mikhail Speransky, adviser to Alexander II, to be divided into two classes: "slaves of the autocrat and slaves of the landowner. . . . There are no free men in Russia except beggars and philosophers."[13] Tkachev described the regimen within Petersburg Gymnaziya No. 2, in which he was matriculating in 1860-1861, as consisting of "crude despotism, ignorance, and pigheadedness on the part of both teachers and administrators; floggings day after day; senseless learning by rote; arbitrary and oppressive despotism of younger students by upperclassmen."[14]

Creeping disillusionment with the new Tsar Alexander II also gripped the radical intelligentsia of the late 1850s and early 1860s. When, in the pages of Herzen's *Tamizdat* (published abroad, in current Sovietese), *The Bell* and in the Aesopian-worded Russian journal *The Contemporary*, to which Chernyshevsky contributed critical articles at this time, came the news that the tsar's emancipation plans were far less ambitious than what liberals and radicals wanted, the radical youth were up in arms. First, this young generation of intelligenty of the 1860s, or at least the more radical among them, resented the slowness with which the emancipation scheme was being discussed and drawn up. Second, they saw that the nobles were going to hang on to the best, most arable land, and that the peasants were going to be driven into debt with redemption payments for second-class land that would be assigned them.

Tkachev, who was born of modest landowning parents in Velikie-Luki, when he observed peasant conditions, joined those who wished to attack the Tsarist Establishment and the old Russian way of life and who envisioned the avoidance of capitalism and a socialist future for Russia if only the state and society could be entirely made over.[15]

Once in Petersburg University, matriculating for a law degree, Tkachev soon got himself involved in radical student movements on the campus. By the spring of 1861, the university was nearly engulfed with student unrest; the grievances ranged all the way from protests against the overly severe regimen and curtailment of civil liberties to the basic evils of tsarism and the stagnated semifeudal, retarded Russian society. For his role in campus demonstrations and agitation, Tkachev was arrested in the fall of 1861, along with a hundred other persons (some of them nonstudents), after the new semester had begun with greatly stiffened campus regulations. Later in the fall another 300 were rounded up and the university had to close intermittently. Tkachev's term in jail lasted two months; in Kronstadt Prison, however, he received a real "education" by meeting older revolutionaries, reading newspapers and journals, participating in group discussions, writing and reading aloud revolutionary poetry—all of this on the prison grounds! And the same unbelievably lax conditions prevailed at the time at Petropavlovsk Fortress. As B.P. Kozmin has observed: "Young people, who were earlier little interested in the political affairs of the nation, came out of Peter and Paul Fortress, or Kronstadt, dedicated opponents of the contemporary order."[16]

With his two-months' imprisonment, Tkachev's formal university education came to an end. Tkachev had been allowed to take his final examinations for admission into law school and had passed them, but for him, as for Vladimir Ulyanov, practicing law was tantamount to upholding the law. He now dedicated himself to the profession of full-time agitator and revolutionary. At this turning point in his life, too, Tkachev began his extensive publicistic activity which would eventually bring him into close contact and mutual intellectual stimulation with Pisarev and Zaichnevsky, Nechayev and Bakunin, Ogarev and Lavrov—as motley a group of revolutionists as one could imagine! But as the 1860s went on, Tkachev began to work out his own unique ideology of Russian Blanquism, *before*, by the way, he had read a word of the master himself, Louis Auguste Blanqui. Tkachev's ideology, in many respects, anticipated the Bolshevism of Vladimir Ilyich Ulyanov (Lenin). Several Western scholars have noted this connection. E.g., Leonard Schapiro, in *The Communist Party of the Soviet Union*:

An ideology for revolutionary activity was evolved by P.N. Tkachev . . . , the first Russian to teach that the revolution should be made by a small conspiratorial body of professionals, acting in the name of the people . . . It is with justice that Tkachev has often been described as the originator of many of Lenin's ideas.

Adam Ulam, in *The Bolsheviks*:

Peter Tkachev was the only representative of the conspiratorial tradition who was a thinker of distinction and of an original turn of mind . . . Less than thirty years [after Tkachev], V.I. Lenin was to use similar words in describing the revolutionary organization needed by the Russian socialists.

Stefan Possony, in *Lenin—the Compulsive Revolutionary*:

It is evident that Tkachev's ideas impressed Lenin; he later required his followers to read Tkachev carefully. We do not know at what time Lenin himself read

Tkachev, but he may have done so while in Switzerland. When he returned to Russia he possessed a clearer vision of the tasks ahead.

To this list of Western specialists—and I have quoted only a small number of them—could be added countless Russian émigré specialists: B.D. Kofmin, M.N. Pokrovsky, Prof. Mikhail Karpovich, B.I. Gorev, Boris Ivanovich Nikolayevsky, Theodore Dan, Valentinov (Volsky). And as we shall see later, even some Soviet historians have found "proto-Bolshevism" within the ideology of Tkachevism.

Tkachev's theories of history, society, revolution, and the postrevolutionary New Order harmonized rather well.

History

To Tkachev, history should not be examined on the basis of Hegelian determinism, or any other kind of determinism—Spencerian, Comtian, Marxian, etc. There was no dialectic operating in so-called historical "process." Of Hegel, Tkachev writes bitterly: "We have not the slightest reason nor a single rational basis for embracing Hegelian philosophy . . . It is so much nonsense."[17] But Tkachev did not go to the other extreme, either. He did not accept the Carlyleian point of view capsulized by the expression that history consists of the biographies of its greatest men. Not even the most powerful leaders in the world could do whatever they wished, said Tkachev; they would have to base their actions upon an intelligent assessment of a whole range of facts—social, political, psychological, economic, military, and so on. Furthermore, the indeterministic *non*-process of history was full of accidents, maintained Tkachev. Still, Tkachev believed that where political power was maximized, where strong political (read: revolutionary) leaders with realistic ideologies were determined to implant their concepts into society, then history would have a good chance of being driven by men rather than men being driven and enslaved by history. Forward-looking leaders, although called "utopian" by their contemporaries, might prove to be more realistic than their falsely "realistic" critics. Thomas Müntzer was one of these leaders, said Tkachev, referring to the sixteenth-century leader of the peasant revolts in Germany. In his interpretation of the peasant revolts, which was the direct opposite of the one offered by Marx and Engels (the latter of whom Tkachev rebutted, in his famous correspondence with Engels in 1874), Tkachev asserted that he did not think Müntzer's defeat had been the result of historical necessity. Just the opposite. Müntzer had failed for a number of subjective and accidental factors; had he won, said Tkachev, Germany could have been saved from the evils of capitalist development, which came later.[18]

"The radical minority cannot wait for the people; the uncivilized mob is too crude and ignorant to discern knowingly the causes of its hardpressed condition or to find the means of its amelioration."[19] Nor can the radical minority wait for alleged historical process to work itself out, à la Marxist philosophy. Thus, the necessity of making an "*istoricheskii skachok*," an historical jump.

The historical-jump theory was Tkachev's substitute for the Hegelian-Marxist dialectic.[20] The radical socialist revolutionaries, equipped with a forward-looking ideology and ethical principle, simply jump Russian society ahead over bourgeois and other types of unnecessary phases of social and economic development. Not to make the *skachok* means to delay. "Circumstances are now in our favor," wrote Tkachev in the early 1870s. "Within ten or fifteen years, they will be acting against us. Isn't this obvious? Don't you now understand our true reason for making haste and for our impatience?"[21] The Tsarist state now "hangs in the air," but if the *skachok* is not made, the state will have sunk roots into the fast-developing bourgeois life of the country.[22]

The Tkachevian concept of historical jump was, of course, a substitute for delay or for ideologies, like Lavrovism and Bakuninism, which emphasized the popular base and support for revolution and, in short, displayed certain democratic tendencies. For Tkachev, "spontaneity" (*stikhiye*) of the masses was by no means equitable with the advanced socialist "consciousness" (*soznatel'nost'*) of the revolutionary minority.[23]

Society

Tkachev's social theory had in it elements of economic determinism, minus the dialectic found in historical materialism or dialectical materialism of the Marxists. While, for Tkachev, history advances or retreats because of factors both objective and subjective, the essence of any given society will be found in the way the economic life of the people is organized, especially upon what ethical principles. "I assert," wrote Tkachev, who was one of the earliest popularizers of Marx in Russia, "that all phenomena of a political, moral, or intellectual nature, in the last analysis, are the result of causal phenomena in the economic sphere and the 'economic structure' of society, as expressed by Marx . . . This does not mean," continued Tkachev, "that I deny the historical importance of ideas, or intellectual progress of all kinds . . . An idea is always an embodiment, a reflection if you wish, of a certain economic interest . . . The accuracy of this concept may be tested against the history of the philosophy of the 18th century."[24] In an interesting passage which follows, Tkachev then introduced his voluntaristic point of view by way of discussion of the economic causes for women's inequality. While women's inequality—and prostitution, too, for that matter—had an economic basis, the women's liberation movement depended strictly on the women's intelligentsia. Tkachev wrote:

Material force in society means by and large the majority of people who are naive, unreflective, and incapable of strict, efficient organization. Therefore, for the victory of this or that social element, it must have on its side a part of the intellectual minority. This intellectual minority gives to the material force its needed organization and directs it to a conscious goal. From this it is obvious how important it is for social progress in general to have the victory of this or that idea [possibly "ideal"—A.L.W.], the dissemination of this or that philosophy among the intelligentsia . . . From this it must also be obvious what role ideas play in the history of mankind.[25]

For women's liberation, then, said Tkachev, all attention must be given to the creation of a socialist-minded women's intelligentsia.

At all times, Tkachev is after the ethos, the basic moral principle upon which a society bases itself. Western bourgeois society is established upon the principle of acquisitiveness, selfishness, and *homo homini lupus est* (*chelovek cheloveku volk*—man is wolf to man). With all the idealism of a Herzen or a Chernyshevsky, Tkachev weighed competitive and inegalitarian bourgeois society of the West in the mid-nineteenth century against socialist principles, and found the former wanted in the balance.

Furthermore, with regard to *Russian* society, Tkachev placed little hope in the so-called "collectivistic instincts" of the Russian peasant, which he ridiculed, at least by the time he took up residence abroad after 1873 and until he died in 1886. The *obshchina*, or peasant commune, said Tkachev, in 1874, was fast being corrupted by "Kulachestvo," his term for the development of capitalist-like psychology and inequality among the peasants.[26] If the peasants were left to themselves, competition between the village poor and the kulaks (or middle and rich peasants) would intensify. The acquisitive psychology would simply sink deeper and deeper roots; already, in fact, the *obshchina* was flawed. (Tkachev bitterly attacked those Bakuninists, or *obshchinisty*, and the Lavrovists for holding out hopes for regeneration of Russian peasant society on the basis of the "romanticized" Russian *obshchina*.)

Much of Tkachev's famous disagreement with Engels revolved about the question of the *obshchina*, the nature of Russian society as Tkachev viewed it, and the way in which Tkachev regarded bourgeois "progress" in his largest nondeterminist view of history.

For one thing, the "German Marxists," as Tkachev called Marx, Engels, and their colleagues, were too fond of Hegel and of applying Hegel's "reactionary" theories to Russia. The bourgeoisation (*embourgeoisement*) of Russia was not inevitable, Tkachev argued in his polemic with Engels. In fact, he said, if so-called bourgeois progress were permitted to continue, or were underwritten by bourgeois policies of the state, the only result would be the very opposite of progress: more powerful weapons placed in the hands of the exploiters than before by a dictatorial bourgeois state firmly backing a bourgeois social and economic order. Engels was wrong, he said, to cast aspersions upon Russian revolutionaries, whether in Russia or living as "temporary" émigrés in the West.

If it were not for the fact that all your wisdom and naiveté were directed to the discrediting of the Russian revolutionary émigrés and for the fact that the German public might believe in your facts, I would not bother you with my letter . . . I consider it my duty to come to the aid of your naiveté and restrain your cockiness.[27]

Tkachev, meanwhile, thought he knew the Russian people's psychology much better than foreigners or Marx's International.

The average representative of the people is an apathetic person; this is particularly true of the Russians. Slave-like impulses have been implanted in them by centuries' old enslavement. Secretiveness, untrustworthiness, servility . . . have all served to atrophy their energies. They are phlegmatic by nature, and it is impossible to place any hope in their enthusiasm. Their stoical passivity is, in fact, like the encrusted shell of a snail.[28]

He further wrote, "If you leave the people to themselves, they will build nothing new. They will only spread the old way of life to which they are already accustomed."[29]

Tkachev introduced the interesting concept of *"rutina"* (routine) into his discussion of the ignorant workers. The masses, he wrote, are hopelessly caught up in the daily routine of life, meaning about all acquisitive economic behavior and competition.[c] Tkachev strongly suggested that bourgeois *rutina* takes the mass-man away from reason and his own true interests; surely far away from society's true interests.[30] In fact, the characters populating Dostoyevsky's novels are not only poor; they are either maniacs or melancholics. In any case, Dostoyevsky's "egoism" and naturalistic "romanticism" provides no exit from *rutina* for the impoverished masses; to Dostoyevsky, revolutionaries are "sick people." This is a view, he said, which is deeply "harmful" to the Cause.[31] When the revolutionary intelligentsia breaks the vicious circle of routine, by means of violent revolution, mass-man will be able to find his true self. He may even be able to unearth what Tkachev calls "the laws of the secret mechanism of our mental life . . . the true causes and basic laws of our psychic life." By psychological knowledge, continued Tkachev, "we do not mean knowledge which is raw, merely empirical, unclassified and uncategorized (which may well suit the taste of certain pedagogues like Leo Tolstoy), but scientific, rational knowledge, which will come as the result of long, thorough study within the science of psychology."[32] After the revolution, he continued, "psychological specialists will . . . reveal to us this secret mechanism . . . Meanwhile, the method of psychology . . . will be weighted down with metaphysics."

In short, if the unenlightened and unregenerate masses are left to their own designs and pleasures, the old encrusted routine will continue indefinitely, because the principle of individualistic egoism aims only at its own satisfaction, not at any higher, loftier intellectual or ethical principle. Moreover, base, unarticulated, "unconscious" motivations and forces ("the secret mechanism"), in individuals and society, will continue to alienate mass-man from himself. The self-awareness and socialist consciousness already attained by the revolutionary intel-

[c]Tkachev states, "One can imagine how quickly and successfully we could carry out our socialist principles if the program depended on the one-sided, local wishes and capricious arbitrariness of the routine-ridden majority," Tkachev, III, p. 256.

ligentsia will remain lost to the masses unless and until mass-man can be reconstructed by that intellectual minority.

Revolution

Quite obviously, Tkachev's social theories, particularly his ideas about Russian society, have a direct connection with his theories on revolution. If the people, when left to themselves, "will build nothing new," by what means, then, can an entirely new principle of life, the new ethos of altruistic socialism, be made to replace the old principle?

Both in his theories of history (in which he rejected determinism) and in his social theory, Tkachev had maintained that what the Marxists call "progress" is actually reaction. To be truly progressive, said Tkachev, is to *exploit* the adversities produced by the alleged bourgeois "progress" discernible in Russian society. Moreover, a *nastoyashchii* (or authentic) progressive, he said, should work toward destroying the power of the present Tsarist state as soon as possible before that state sinks roots within the increasingly bourgeois society. The Tsarist state, said Tkachev in a frequently quoted and rebutted (by Russian Marxists) passage in his works, "hangs in the air." But, eventually, it will surely send down roots into the economic life of the country; when that happens, true socialist progress and the implanting of the new ethos of socialist altruism and utilitarianism will become nearly hopeless. Thus, what is needed is a "pre-emptive" revolution, aimed at the present state, and not even "minutes" should be wasted in making such a political revolution: "A revolutionary minority is no longer willing to wait but must take upon itself the *forcing of consciousness upon the people* [my emphasis–A.L.W.]." The "socialist outlook" of the intellectual minority of radical revolutionaries guarantees, said Tkachev, that the revolution will be pure, will not be a selfishly-motivated strangulation of the tsar with an officer's scarf; guarantees moreover, that the postrevolutionary order will not degenerate into a Thermidor of reaction, or a turning away from the socialist ethos. Describing the relationship between his revolutionary minority–"the civilized group"–and the boorish masses–the "uncivilized mob"–Tkachev wrote:

The relationship of the revolutionary minority to the people and the participation of the latter in revolution may be described in the following terms. The revolutionary minority, freeing the people from the oppressive terror and fear of their present rulers, opens the way for the people to apply their destructive revolutionary force. Relying on this force, the revolutionary minority skillfully [*iskusstvenno*] directs this violence for the destruction of the immediate enemies of the revolution.[33]

Past and contemporary–including today's Soviet–critics of Tkachev have seen in his recommendations for a minority-led revolution–could *any* planned revolution be led by any other than a minority?—an advocacy of a garden-variety palace coup, infantile, left-wing *buntarstvo* and *putschism*. Soviet critics of Tkachevism detect "petty-bourgeois Blanquism" in these views and indict its alleged inattention to a "popular base" for revolution.

In the light of this criticism, it is important to acquaint oneself with Tkachev's own explanations of the manner in which revolution was to be organized and consummated.

An attack at the *center of power* and seizure of power in revolutionary hands, without at the same time a popular uprising (even if merely local) could lead to positive, lasting results *only under the most favorable of conditions*. [My emphases—A.L.W.] [34]

Thus, "only under the most favorable of conditions" could a coup directed at the "center of power" (say, in Petersburg and Moscow) "lead to lasting results," unless the coup were accompanied by popular uprisings. Incidently, Blanqui's position was essentially similar to Tkachev's on this point.[d]

Furthermore, Tkachev was sensitive about what effect this or that programmatic goal or tactic would have on the prerevolutionary psychology of the masses, and, thereby, revealed his concern for the attitude of those masses once the various programs were disseminated throughout the population.

Finally, in the way in which Tkachev conceived of the precise organization of revolution, it is clear that he never for a moment excluded the destructive force of the masses; interestingly, however, he was quite ready to accept as a compromise, as it were, passive acquiescence on the part of the masses. Also Tkachev's sense of social psychology led him to believe that even an illusory feeling of strength among the masses—"the feeling of united force"—should be instilled in the people by the revolutionary minority: "The masses must feel that effective force has been gathered in the name of their cause . . . Only this assurance can unite them and once united, they will be able to sense the force they have in themselves."[35]

In his discussion of revolutionary ideology, Tkachev comes out with the interesting—one might even say, twentieth century—notion that an ideology, especially agitation (rather than propaganda aspects), is good or bad depending upon how useful it is to the revolutionary cause. Thus, Tkachev spoke of the "great practical importance" of economic materialism; such materialism, he said, "concentrates the energy and activity of those men who are sincerely devoted to social causes on the truly essential questions: namely, the vital interests of the people. Economic materialism guarantees that [the revolutionaries] will gain the support of the most indispensable forces in society . . . It is a spur inspiring direct activism."[36] In other words, Tkachev seems to suggest a Machiavellian exploitation of revolutionary theory, agitation, and/or propaganda "not for the

[d]Wrote Blanqui: "If we seize power by an audacious *coup de main*, like robbers in the shadows of the night, who will answer for the duration of our power?" Quoted in Alan B. Spitzer, *The Revolutionary Theories of Louis Auguste Blanqui* (New York, 1957), p. 146.

sake of whatever truth may be embodied in it," as Mannheim said, "as much as for the political ends for which it can be used."

So far as his organizational principles were concerned, it is perhaps no surprise to learn that Tkachev favored the strictest discipline among his revolutionaries, whom he regarded as "professional revolutionaries," recruitment and an elitist policy in which organizations were definitely not open to everyone.

> The success of revolution depends on the formation and organized unity of the scattered revolutionary elements into a living body [*zhivoye telo*] which is able to act according to a single, common plan of action and be subordinated to a single, common leadership—an organization based on centralization of power and decentralization of function.[37]

The revolutionary organizations, Tkachev added, must act like a "revolutionary army."

As to the members:

> He is no revolutionary who pities anything in contemporary society . . . It is even worse for him if he has any kindred, intimate, or amorous ties. He is no revolutionary if relationships are able to check his hand . . . The necessity of attachment to females, for the completeness of life's happiness and harmony, is only complete rubbish, invented by those medieval mourners over the heavenly Virgin, by those same perverse knights who were themselves tied to women like work horses . . . The revolutionaries know all too well how warm and beautiful a woman's body is. But no matter how sweet the music of her voice or how heavenly the look in her eyes, they will not tolerate even the slightest competition with the irresistible strength of that ideal which fills their lives and actions. So much joy and grief are in their memories, so many hopes and plans, so many other thoughts and considerations that to renounce the ideal in the slightest would mean suicide. This ideal is *that* closely bound to their whole internal being.[38]

Postrevolutionary New Order

Quite consistently, Tkachev held that the superior intellects and political know-how of his professional revolutionaries should not be cast aside the day after the revolution. On the contrary. Their highly centralized authority is put into action in behalf of the reconstruction of Russian society.

> The [revolutionary] minority proceeds with the destruction of the enemies of the revolution. It deprives the enemies of all means of resistance and counter-attack. Then, by making use of its force and its own authority, proceeds with the introduction of new, progressively-communist elements into the conditions of national existence, freeing the people from their age-old chains and breathing life into society's cold and dead forms.[39]

After the passage of the first or "destructive" phase of the socialist revolution, the socialist authorities should be able to count on at least "passive support" of the people as the "constructive" phase was begun.

Putting revolutionary ideals into effect not only does not contradict the true needs of the people, but engenders them with the spirit of communal solidarity which, in turn, interpenetrates the whole social structure. This will occur in such a way that there will not be the slightest basis for assuming that the people would refuse to give their passive support to the revolutionaries.[40]

But in case they don't, there was, Tkachev said, the K.O.B. [*Komissiva obshchestvennoi bezopasnosti*] , or Commission for Public Security, established in order to root out hostile elements, particularly those among the older generation.[41]

Tkachev used rather interesting—and prophetic—language with which to describe his new revolutionary state: *avtoritarno-diktatorskoye gosudarstvo; revolyutsionnoye gosudarstvo; postoyanno-revolyutsionnoye gosudarstvo* (authoritarian-dictatorship state; revolutionary state; permanently-revolutionary state).

This formula, Tkachev said tersely, "is a logical necessity derived from an evaluation made by us of the character and extent of true revolutionary force lodged in our people at the present time." And further: "The uncivilized crowd [the *muzhik*] is too crude and ignorant to discern consciously the causes of its hard-pressed condition." Or interpolating a famous phrase from Rousseau's *Social Contract*: the people "must be forced to be free." Through the compulsive power of the permanently-revolutionary state, such reforms and institutions as the following would be implanted in society:

1. state rearing of children;
2. state-owned and -administered economic life with enforced economic equality;
3. scientific points of view in education, literature, and literary criticism; Tkachev called this "sociological realism";
4. political dictatorship; Tkachev, at one point, used the interesting expression of *"kollektivnoye diktatorstvo"* (collective dictatorship);
5. the state security apparatus.

And so on.

Vladimir Ilyich read through and examined most carefully of all this old revolutionary literature [of the 19th century] paying particular attention [*osoboye vnimaniye*] to Tkachev, remarking that this writer was closer to our point of view than any of the others . . . Not only did V.I. himself read these works of Tkachev; he also recommended that all of us familiarize ourselves with the valuable writings of this original thinker. More than once, he asked newly-arrived comrades [in Geneva] that if they wanted to study the illegal literature, "Begin," V.I. would advise, "by reading and familiarizing yourself with Tkachev's *Nabat [Alarm Bell*, Tkachev's émigré journal] . . . It is basic and will give you tremendous knowledge" . . . I think Vladimir Ilyich's research [into the old Russian revolutionary tradition] helped him when the proletariat seized power and our Party took over the administration of the country.[42]

Indeed, as Bonch-Bruyevich indicated in his memoirs just quoted, many of Lenin's ideas bore a striking resemblance to Tkachevism. It should be noted that Lenin's reading of this type of literature, and of Tkachev's in particular, was not only confined to the library of revolutionary literature in Geneva, Switzerland in the early 1900s. He is known to have thoroughly familiarized himself with Tkachev's and Zaichnevsky's ideas already when he was in Kazan and Samara, in the late 1880s.[43] In his memoirs, Bonch-Bruyevich even went so far as to compare the course of the Bolshevik coup d'état, or "revolution," with the concepts of Tkachev:

It is an irrefutable fact that the Russian Revolution proceeded to a significant degree according to the ideas of Tkachev. The seizure of power was made at a time which was determined in advance by a revolutionary party organized on the principle of strict centralization and discipline. And this party, having seized power, operates in many respects as Tkachev advised.[44]

The first pro-Tkachev/Lenin-kinship article in the immediate post-1917 period was written by Sergie Ivanovich Mitskevich (1869-1944), former head of the Moscow city department of education and one of the organizers, later director, of the Museum of Revolution in Moscow. In the article entitled "The Russian Jacobins" and published in *Proletarskaya Revolyutsiya* in 1923, Mitskevich singled out one idea after the other which, he said, "had entered into the basic fund of Bolshevik ideology": ideas like the formation of a band or party of déclassé intellectual-conspirators who would teach socialism to the masses; seizure of power by this small group amid mass unrest and a weakened state power and in military fashion in the urban power centers of Russia; extreme centralization within the single ruling political party; establishment of a powerful post-revolutionary "socialist dictatorship" headed by those same déclassé "people-of-a-special-mould" who had made the revolution; the carrying out of a "permanent revolution" remaking the old society into a new socialist order; postponement, or lack of definition, of the eventual withering away of the state; nonpermission of political opposition after the revolution; scorn for "liberal" bourgeois democracy; Russia as a special case, as an especially suitable "weak link" in the bourgeois chain where revolution could be made and socialism undertaken.[45]

Mitskevich made a particularly fascinating list of Russia's special characteristics which, he said, led Tkachev and Lenin to the same conclusions as to the proper revolutionary tactics and strategy to employ in Russia:[46]

1. Russia exceeded the West European countries in the "intensity" of its class contradictions and class struggles;

2. The dictatorship of the Tsarist ruling circles ("Tsarist absolutism") caused much popular dissatisfaction and frequent uprisings and *Pugachevshchina*;
3. The conditions of poverty under which the intelligentsia lived and labored;
4. Absence of any possible legal expression for political opposition or the grievances of the working masses;
5. The "retarded" development of capitalism in Russia;
6. The active interference of the state in what little industry there was "[creating] the illusion of the artificiality and lack of any roots [of capitalism in the society]," therefore the overall weak development of Russian capitalism, which facilitated its overthrow.

Mitskevich strongly implied that these six Russian peculiarities were just as true of the Russia of Tkachev's time as they were of Lenin's, some thirty years later.

Tkachev, and Lenin, were right, Mitskevich indicated, in their estimate of the weakness of Russian capitalism and of the Tsarist state (meaning *government*, Mitskevich said explicitly). Also, the Tsarist state, unlike states in the bourgeois West, and Russian capitalism had not sunk roots deep into Russian society. The state was thus artificial; it hung in the air, you might say, following Tkachev; it would be easy to topple it at its heart and center in the capital. (For Lenin, the Provisional Government of Kerensky, a bourgeois regime, was just as weak and vulnerable as the Tsarist government, the weakest link, in fact, in the whole bourgeois chain of states.) Retarded development of capitalism in Russia, Mitskevich maintained, was thus an advantage to the proletarian cause, an advantage, however, which would not last long if the revolutionaries delayed their coup (the same point that was made by Lenin late in 1917). Mitskevich further pointed out that the Tsarist regime had set a precedent of sorts for the etatization of the Russian industry; this would in turn facilitate the etatization of the whole economy by the "worker's half-state" (Lenin's term, in *State and Revolution*) in the period of the worker's dictatorship.

Mitskevich also had some interesting things to say about the origins of Russian socialism:

1. The influence of the European socialist movement on the Russians;
2. Development of large Russian industry;
3. Absence of any deep-rooted or extensive "petty-bourgeois" land ownership by the peasants (Stolypin's reform did not have time to work any major changes in Russian peasant life);
4. Lack of experience which could have been gained from a rapidly-developing working class;
5. Close ties between the Russian working class and the peasantry which nourished the idea that their aims were indistinguishable in the Russian revolutionary movement—that is, indistinguishable from Tkachev's and Lenin's point of view, certainly not from the orthodox Marxist position assumed by Plekhanov or the updated *Narodnik* views of the Socialist-Revolutionaries.[e]

---

[e]Besides Baturin, M.S. Ol'minsky, and someone signing his name "Sineira," an allusion to Tacitus' phrase, *"sine ira et studio"* (without anger or passion). Some half-dozen articles, written between 1923-25, appeared in the pages of *Proletarskaya Revolyutsiya* and *Katorga i Ssylka*. Baturin (Nikolai Nikolayovich) (Zamyatin) (1887-1927) was a writer on the newspaper *Pravda* and later a lecturer in history at Sverdlovsk University.

But the majority of Bolshevik historians and party hacks were distinctly dissatisfied with Mitskevich's ideas on a Tkachevist-Leninist link-up. N.N. Baturin and others accused what they called the "minority of historians" who traced Bolshevism back to Tkachev of being guilty of "blindness" and a "petty-bourgeois attitude." Whatever similarities allegedly existed between Tkachevism and Bolshevism were purely accidental; Mitskevich had erred, wrote one of these partified historians, because he himself was not a pure or orthodox Marxist-Leninist.

By the end of the 1920s, the party line had triumphed in the dispute over Tkachev's contribution to Bolshevism. The debates ended, except for occasionally expressed "erroneous positions," and these were promptly exposed and denounced by the Central Committee's Marx-Engels-Lenin (later -Stalin) Institute. With the promulgation of Stalin's famous letter to Soviet historians in 1931, "anti-Leninist historiography" was given its final *coup de grace* within the U.S.S.R.[47]

Today in the Soviet Union Tkachev continues to be treated—when he is mentioned at all—as a "Blanquist . . . *zagovorshchik* . . . *putschist*," at best as a misguided *Narodnik* and petit-bourgeois "revolutionary-democrat." The Lenin Library today, as this author found out when he worked in it in the summer of 1966, lists only one Tkachev work—not *by* him but *about* him: a pamphlet written by B.P. Kozmin. Lenin's personal library contained only a little more Tkacheviana. The Lenin Library catalog contains hundreds of entries for dozens of other books and pamphlets by countless other revolutionaries of nineteenth century Russia, many of whom deserve less study than Tkachev. But the six volumes of Tkachev's works, published in limited edition in the U.S.S.R. between 1932 and 1937, are not listed among the 22 million titles in the library, nor are the dozens of *Soviet* works about Tkachev (although they are available in libraries in the United States, and probably elsewhere outside of Russia). The latest book dealing with Lenin and Lenin's attitude toward the whole nineteenth century revolutionary tradition in Russia—*V.I. Lenin i russkaya obshchestvenno-politicheskaya mysl'XIX-nachala XXv.*, published under the auspices of the "Nauka" publishing house in Leningrad, in 1969—disputes both Bonch-Bruyevich and Mitskevich on Lenin's indebtedness to Tkachev.[48] But the discussion runs only a few lines and in two footnotes. Among other things, it warns scholars to approach memoir literature with utmost caution, since it is frequently of doubtful authenticity. Not only Mitskevich but also Kozmin is taken to task in the new book, which supports the arguments against them in the 1920s mounted by Baturin and one M.S. Ol'minsky, both of whom, it says, "penetratingly disputed attempts at modernization which the said authors themselves later abandoned when they had become convinced of their worthlessness."[49]

The hoopla surrounding the glorification of Lenin on his one hundredth birthday in 1970 makes a striking contrast to the obscurity into which the promising Jacobin of the 1870s has fallen. An ironic fate to befall the man who may have so strongly influenced Lenin. The story has elements of tragedy.

In 1883, Tkachev was picked up by the Paris police when he was seen behaving oddly in the street. He had fallen victim to some sort of cerebral or neuroparalytic disease at the age of 43. When taken to a nearby hospital in Montparnasse, l'Hôpital Psychiatrique Ste. Anne, Tkachev at first refused to divulge his name, until a Russian doctor was summoned to the hospital. He remained under a doctor's care for three years, during which he was visited by friends of the Russian émigrés and two or three relatives. Three weeks before he died, he was described as a "living corpse"; he could scarcely move his lips or his body. He died at 12:15 a.m. on January 5, 1886. The next day a funeral was held at which friends and acquaintances paid their last respects. An attempt was made to postpone the burial so that time could be found to inform all those who would be interested in attending the funeral. But French hospital regulations pertaining to persons dying on hospital premises, prevented an extension of time. As a result, a pitifully small group of people trailed out of the hospital on the morning of January 6, as the wooden casket was borne to a waiting carriage and taken to the cemetery in Ivry on the southeastern outskirts of Paris (*Cimetiere Parisien d'Ivry*). The day of the funeral was cold and damp, the horse-drawn cortege moving over the cobblestone streets in the rain. Waiting at graveside were two floral displays of *immortelles* bearing a red ribbon with the words "Ancienne redaction du Tocsin," donated by the editors of *Nabat*. Lavrov, his old opponent, delivered a short eulogy in French; he spoke of Tkachev's earlier literary activity in Russia (from 1861-1873) before he went abroad, and of the influence which he had had over the young generation of the time. Another eulogy was delivered by the well-known French Blanquist, Eduard Vaillant.

A burial plot was rented for a period of five years. Over the temporary grave was placed a small plaque made of wood on which was inscribed "Pierre Tkatscheff." According to Tkachev's obituary in the Russian émigré newspaper, *Obshcheye Delo*, an attempt was made to collect the sum of 500 francs for the purchase of a permanent plot in the cemetery; this grave was to be marked with a marble stone capped with a sculptured crown of thorns, suitable, said the obituary, "for an émigré."[50] The fact was, however, that the grave and the stone were never purchased; no one came forward with the 500 francs. Records of the cemetery show that Tkachev's remains were then exhumed in 1892, after expiration of the five-year period. They were then thrown into the ossuary along with the bones of nameless paupers. Today, there is not the slightest trace that Tkachev was ever buried in the cemetery. There is, on the other hand, a very large tomb in Red Square.

Notes

1. B.P. Kozmin, *P.N. Tkachev i revolyutsionnoye dvizhenive 1860-kh godov* (Moscow, 1922), p. 70.

2. J.S. Mill, *Auguste Comte and Positivism* (Ann Arbor, 1961), p. 171.

3. A considerably far-ranging dispute still concerns the precise definition of "Russian Populism." For an interesting and recent discussion of this problem, see A. Walicki, *The Controversy over Capitalism: Studies in the Social Philosophy of the Russian Populists* (Oxford, 1969), pp. 1-2, and Richard Pipes, "Narodnichestvo: A Semantic Inquiry," *Slavic Review*, XXIII (September, 1964).

4. P.N. Tkachev, *Izbranniye sochineniya*, ed. Boris P. Kozmin (Moscow, 1932-1937), III, 92. Henceforth citations from this work will bear only Tkachev's name, the Roman numeral of the volume cited and the page number.

5. G.P. Maximoff, *The Political Philosophy of Bakunin—Selected Writings of Bakunin* (New York, 1953), pp. 293-94.

6. Ibid., p. 398.

7. A recent Soviet book states that the "great majority of Populists were inclined toward anarchism or semi-anarchist point of view." S.N. Valk and V.S. Dyakin, *V.I. Lenin i russkaya obshchestvenno-politcheskaya mysl' XIX-nachala XX v* (Leningrad, 1969), p. 189.

8. For an interesting discussion of the influence of classical utopian projections on Russian revolutionaries, see B.I. Gorev, *Na ideologicheskom fronte* (Moscow-Petrograd, 1923).

9. Besides my book, already cited, the reader is advised to consult Ranco Ventur, *Roots of Revolution: A History of the Populist and Socialist Movements in Nineteenth Century Russia* (New York, 1960), ch. 16, and Walicki, pp. 39-46, 96-99, and 140-44, et passim.

10. Reproduced in G.A. Kuklin, *Itogi revolyutsionnovo dvizheniya v Rossii* (Geneva, 1903), pp. 2-3.

11. B.P. Kozmin, *P.G. Zaichnevsky i "Molodaya Rossiva"* (Moscow, 1932), p. 31.

12. Francis B. Randall, *N.G. Chernyshevskii* (New York, 1967), pp. 88-89.

13. E. Lampert, *Sons Against Fathers: Studies in Russian Radicalism and Revolution* (Oxford, 1965), p. 1.

14. Kozmin, *P.N. Tkachev*, p. 11; quoted from Tkachev's "Unthinkable Thoughts," *Delo*, No. 2, 1872.

15. See the discussion of the avoidance-of-capitalism concept in Walicki.

16. Kozmin, *P.N. Tkachev*, p. 20.

17. Tkachev, III, p. 473.

18. Tkachev, I, pp. 260-62.

19. Tkachev, III, pp. 491-92. Ernesto (Che) Guevara wrote in his diary: "They [the Bolivian peasants] are as impervious as stones; when you talk to them it is as if in the depth of their eyes they were mocking you." Tkachev used the word "God-the-people" in a derogatory way.

20. Kozmin, *P.N. Tkachev*, pp. 67-69.

21. Tkachev, III, pp. 69-70. In his letter to N.K. Mikhailovsky in 1877, Marx

expressed the same impatience, warning that "if Russia continues to move in the path followed up to 1861, it will lose the finest occasion that history has ever offered a people not to undergo all the sudden turns of fortune of the capitalist system." For a discussion of Marx's attitude toward Russia's avoiding a capitalist phase of development and Russia as a "spark" setting off revolution in Europe, see Weeks, pp. 117-18 and 150-51.

22. From Tkachev's letter to Engels, in 1874, in Tkachev, III, pp. 88-89.

23. For a discussion of the Leninist concept of spontaneity and consciousness, see Alfred Meyer, *Leninism* (New York, 1962), pp. 28-36, and Weeks, pp. 87, 106-07, and 124.

24. Tkachev, I, pp. 445-46.

25. Ibid., p. 446. Here Tkachev uses the term "intellectual minority" in application to *any* era or *any* type of society.

26. Tkachev, III, pp. 69-70, from his 1874 article, "Tasks of Revolutionary Propaganda in Russia."

27. Tkachev, III, p. 88.

28. From Tkachev's 1876 article in *Nabat* entitled "Our Illusions." Also: The peasant "loves traditional forms of his life and does not want to lay a finger on them," Tkachev, III, pp. 263-65.

29. Tkachev, I, p. 49.

30. Tkachev, III, p. 9.

31. Tkachev, VI, pp. 456-57, from an 1876 article written for *Delo*, entitled "Pedogogy—the Legitimate Daughter of Psychology."

32. Tkachev, III, p. 64.

33. Tkachev, I, p. 51.

34. Ibid., p. 48.

35. Ibid., p. 20.

36. Ibid., p. 70.

37. Tkachev, III, p. 84.

38. Tkachev, I, pp. 173-233, the text of Tkachev's "Catechism," which may have predated Sergei Nechayev's more famous one. Tkachev's appeared in *Delo*, Nos. 4-5, 1868, under the title "The People of the Future and the Heroes of the Petty Bourgeoisie."

39. Tkachev, III, p. 266, from "Rising Forces," published in *Delo*, Nos. 11-12, 1868.

40. Ibid., p. 266.

41. Ibid., p. 350. It would not be surprising, Tkachev confessed, if socialist ideals "met opposition from these same 'toiling masses' " (Tkachev, III, p. 371). This is an interesting anticipation of what actually took place when, under Lenin's rule, a "Worker's Opposition" formed within the ranks of the Communist Party.

42. V.D. Bonch-Bruyevich, *Izbranniya sochineniva v trekh tomakh* (Moscow, 1961), II, pp. 314-16.

43. See N.V. Volsky (Valentinov), *Encounters with Lenin (Vstrechi s Leninym)* (New York, 1953), pp. 113-19. This volume includes an interesting preface by M.N. Karpovich. This work is sometimes cited in Soviet attacks upon Western scholars, especially those who seek an early Jacobin-Blanquist influence bearing on Lenin in the 1880s before he took up Marxism.

44. S.I. Mitskevich, "Russkiye yakobintsy," *Proletarskaya Revolyutsiya*, Nos. 7-8 (1923), pp. 119-21.

45. *Proletarskaya Revolyutsiva*, Nos. 6-7 (18-19) (1923), p. 16.

46. Mitskevich, "On the Problem of the Roots of Bolshevism—An Answer to Comrade Baturin," *Katorga i Ssylka*, No. 3(16) (1925), pp. 92-101. This article was recently attacked (but without giving the reader any citation for Mitskevich's article of 1925) in Valk and Dyakin, *V.I. Lenin i russkaya*, p. 190.

47. Most of the text of Stalin's letter may be found in V. Varlomov, *Bakunin and the Russian Jacobins and Blanquists as Evaluated by Soviet Historiography*, ed. B.J. Nicolaxevsky (New York, 1955), pp. 26-27.

48. Valk and Dyakin, *V.I. Lenin i russkaya*.

49. Ibid., p. 190, note 58.

50. *Obshcheye Delo*, No. 83, 1886; quoted in M.K. Lemke, "K Biografii P.N. Tkacheva (po neizdannvm istochnikam)," *Byloye*, VIII, 1907, pp. 156-72. This interesting article includes pictures of Tkachev and his family, which were reproduced in Weeks, *The First Bolshevik*, between pages 66 and 67.

2

The Dictatorship of the Proletariat

DARRELL P. HAMMER

The dictatorship of the proletariat, Lenin once wrote, was one of the most important ideas in Marxism.[1] But looking back from the vantage point of the Lenin centenary, the importance of this concept seems to lie in the interpretation which Lenin gave it, an interpretation which is significantly different from Marx's own conception of the postrevolutionary state. For Marx, the important thing about the proletarian state was that the proletariat would rule. For Lenin, however, the distinguishing properties of the dictatorship of the proletariat were the functions which this new state would perform. Marx saw the proletarian state as the product of revolution; Lenin saw it as an instrument of the revolutionary movement, carrying forward and consolidating the transformation of society. It is true that Marx, in one of his very rare references to the dictatorship of the proletariat, described it as a "transition" to a "classless society."[2] But he clearly thought of it as a culmination of the class struggle. Lenin, in contrast to this, thought of the dictatorship of the proletariat as spanning a whole historical era.

Lenin's interpretation of the dictatorship of the proletariat has subsequently been reduced to an article of faith in the official ideology of the U.S.S.R.[3] Soviet doctrine teaches that after the proletariat has taken power there follows a period of "revolutionary transformation" between capitalism and communism, a period when the remnants of the old capitalist order are dismantled and the foundations of the new, communist society are being laid. The government of this transitional period is the dictatorship of the proletariat. This proletarian state is not merely an instrument for seizing and holding power (although that is its first objective). The purpose of the dictatorship is to create a new social order, and it is fated to depart from the stage of history when that job has been done. Thus, according to the doctrine, the proletarian state will eventually "wither away." The official Soviet view is that the dictatorship of the proletariat survived for more than forty years after the Bolshevik revolution. In 1961, by decree of the Twenty-Second Congress of the Communist Party, it was announced that the dictatorship had come to an end, and its place was to be taken by a new political structure which was called the "all-people's state" (*vsenarodnoe gosudarstvo*). According to the Party program adopted in 1961, "the dictatorship of the proletariat has accomplished its historical mission and from the point of view of the needs of internal development is no longer necessary in the

USSR. The state which arose as a state of the dictatorship of the proletariat has been transformed in the new and modern epoch into an all-people's state."[4]

All this, however, is doctrine rather than political theory. The doctrine is an important component of the official ideology of "Marxism-Leninism," but it is not an important part of classical Marxism. The historical origins of the doctrine have to be sought elsewhere. In fact, Marx never really explained what he meant by the "dictatorship of the proletariat," and Lenin did not fully develop his own ideas on this subject until after 1917, when the dictatorship was already in power. Moreover, a study of prerevolutionary history will reveal that the strategy and tactics of the first proletarian state were not entirely original with Lenin, but were, to a considerable degree, anticipated by Russian revolutionary thinkers of the nineteenth century, and in particular by the *narodnik* philosopher Peter L. Lavrov (1823-1900). Accordingly, this chapter will examine not only Lenin's views, but also earlier approaches to the problem of the revolution and the postrevolutionary order. The first, or *narodnik*, solution will be examined primarily from the viewpoint of Lavrov. The second approach, which is the orthodox Marxist solution as adapted to Russian conditions in the nineteenth century, is to be found in the writings of G.V. Plekhanov (1856-1918). We shall then try to trace the evolution of Lenin's ideas between the two crises of 1905 and 1917, and it will be seen that Lenin's mature views on the subject of the postrevolutionary state and its functions are strikingly similar to the thinking of Lavrov.

While the term "dictatorship of the proletariat" can be traced to Marx, it is not a part of his basic work on political theory. In the *Communist Manifesto*, Marx and Engels describe the "state" as simply the organized power of one class for oppressing another. From this definition it logically followed that with the disappearance of classes, the *need* for the state would disappear. Lenin accepted this idea, and it became the theme of *State and Revolution*, written in 1917. But the important and practical question, of course, is not *whether* the state will disappear, but *when*. Marx and Engels were not utopian anarchists, any more than Lenin was. They did not expect the state to disappear all at once. On the contrary, they made it clear in the *Communist Manifesto* that the aim of the proletariat must be to seize power. The postrevolutionary state thus would be "the proletariat organized as a ruling class." This brief statement, however, is all that the *Communist Manifesto* has to say about the political order after the revolution. Marx and Engels were then much more concerned with social and economic questions than with politics, and the *Manifesto* gives more attention to the abolition of property than to the ultimate abolition of the state. It was not until two years later, when he wrote *The Class Struggles in France*, that Marx referred for the first time to "the class dictatorship of the proletariat."[5]

But how important was the "dictatorship of the proletariat" in Marx's systematic thought? Having mentioned it once, in this rather offhand way, Marx never used the term again in any published writing.[6] Although the phrase is

Marx's, he never offered any detailed statement about the structure of the prole-tarian state.[7] There is no Marxian theory about the dictatorship of the pro-letariat.

Many years later Kautsky remarked that it was unfortunate that Marx had never explained what he meant by this term, and then proceeded to offer his own interpretation, which was bitterly attacked by Lenin.[8] Kautsky also drew fire, a few years later, from the Soviet theoretician V.V. Adoratskii. His analysis, which was written to mark the fiftieth anniversary of Marx's death, is apparently the most detailed discussion of the "dictatorship of the proletariat" to come from the pen of a Soviet scholar.[9] It is not a very enlightening exposition. Typi-cally, Adoratskii describes the dictatorship of the proletariat as the "decisive" question in Marxism, the "core" of Marx's theory, "basic and central in Marx's teaching about the proletarian revolution."[10] This is certainly the standard Soviet evaluation. But Adoratskii offers Lenin as his authority: Lenin organized the Soviet state as a dictatorship of the proletariat, and thereby "enriched" the Marxist theory.[11] Thus to deny the necessity for the dictatorship of the prole-tariat is "treason to Marxism."

The first *narodnik* writer to be concerned with the structure of the postrevo-lutionary state was Peter N. Tkachev (1844-1886).[12] Tkachev is best known as the leading Russian Jacobin, and indeed he was more preoccupied with the prob-lem of overthrowing the autocracy than with the details of the political structure which was to replace it. But Tkachev was certainly not an anarchist, and he never doubted that some such structure would have to be erected by the revolu-tionaries after the fall of the old regime. In a programmatic statement of 1875, Tkachev wrote that the aim of the revolution, quite simply, was to seize power: "in other words, the immediate and direct aim of the revolution, must be noth-ing else but to control the power of government, and to transform the present conservative state into a revolutionary state."[13] He thus believed that the destruction of tsarism would be only the beginning, and not the end of the revo-lution in Russia. After the seizure of power, the revolutionaries would carry out a radical transformation of Russian society, and to do this they needed the authority of the state.

Of course in the 1870s the great controversy among the revolutionaries was not about the state, but about the role of "propaganda" in the revolution—over whether it was worthwhile, for example, to go into the villages to carry the revo-lutionary idea to the "people." Tkachev never thought that it was, and he criti-cized Lavrov, among others, for having too much faith in the ability of propa-ganda to influence the masses before the revolution. Tkachev always believed that the best propaganda was revolutionary action and it is clear that he had more faith in force than in persuasion. Thus the major "propaganda" effort should follow, and not precede the revolution. Propaganda would be most effec-tive "when material force, when political power is in the hands of the revolution-ary party."[14]

Tkachev admitted frankly that the revolutionary party would be in a minority; this was the theme of *Revolution and the State*, a short book published in 1876. "The revolution must be accomplished by the more or less intelligent and revolutionary-minded minority."[15] Such a revolution would, of course, be a "revolution from above," and Tkachev did not try to conceal this fact. Having seized power, the revolutionary minority would continue to act "from above"— it would make use of the power of the state, and *"state power* is the highest type of organized power," to compel the majority to obey.[16] Tkachev was extremely skeptical about the revolutionary potential of the masses. The reason that the revolutionary minority needed political power was precisely because the majority was virtually inert (*kosnoe*), because the masses, at the critical moment, would not understand what the revolution was all about.

Lavrov disagreed with Tkachev on many essential points, including the efficacy of propaganda during the prerevolutionary period. He agreed with Tkachev that the revolution should be prepared by a "secret organization," but believed that the organization should concentrate on propaganda and agitation until it has sufficient popular strength to seize power.[17] Yet while Lavrov expected the revolution itself to be the result of a mass uprising, he too had no faith in the ability of the masses to govern themselves, at least in the immediate postrevolutionary period. Therefore the secret organization (which Lavrov variously calls the "party" and the "union of social revolutionaries") must establish itself as the government of the revolutionary state. Now Tkachev did, at one point, mention the "party" as existing after the seizure of power, but he never developed this idea. The concept of the *party* as a group of "critically thinking individuals" who would govern the workers' state—this is Lavrov's most important contribution to the development of revolutionary ideas in Russia.[18]

Lavrov's ideas about the postrevolutionary regime were developed most fully in *The Element of the State in the Future Society*, written in 1875.[19] In this book, Lavrov looked forward to a future society in which the element of political power would have disappeared, when all human needs could be met by the community without any need for "coercive authority." But the message of the book is that this happy condition would not be reached "on the day after the revolution." There would have to be a rather long transitional period between the overthrow of the old order and the complete development of the new society, and during this period the revolutionary party would have to keep political power (the "element of the state") in its own hands. Like Tkachev, Lavrov expected this to be government by minority, although he argued that all government is minority rule anyway, and the only question is, "Which minority is to have power?"[20] Of course, another question which must occur to any reader is, How long will this "day after the revolution" last? The answer to this question goes to the heart of Lavrov's theory about the revolutionary state.

The primary task of the revolutionary party, once in power, is the reeducation and rehabilitation of the masses. Lavrov expected that the great majority of the population would be indifferent and even hostile to the aims of the revolution. Most of the population, on the day after the revolution, would be ignorant and uneducated; those who were educated would carry into the new era the habits and attitudes that they had learned under the old order.[21] Consequently, a rather long period of time might pass—perhaps the lifetime of a whole generation—before the task of reeducation and rehabilitation was accomplished. During this transitional period Russia would be ruled by a temporary dictatorship. It would have to be a dictatorship because the revolutionary party needed unfettered political power in order to accomplish the task.

But, Lavrov continued, even with the arrival of a new generation born and educated in the new order, indoctrinated with the ideas of the revolutionary party, there might still be a need for the state. This need would arise out of the international situation in the postrevolutionary epoch. Lavrov expected that the revolution would come to Russia independently of events in the western world, and he called his revolutionary state "Workers' Russia." But after the establishment of the Russian proletarian dictatorship, the western states might well remain under capitalist rule. These western and imperialist states would, of course, be hostile to revolutionary Russia. Thus, workers' Russia might be under continuing threat from the outside, from "neighboring countries where the social revolution has not yet taken place."[22] Ideally, one of the first acts of the revolutionary government would be to disband the old, tsarist army. But realistically, the revolutionaries must prepare for the possibility of a "people's war" between Russia and the imperialist world.

There can be no peace between the new and the old orders. Wherever the social revolution may stop after the successes of the first moments, it must immediately, *for its own defense*, send messengers of the social revolution beyond its borders. It must immediately take offensive action by units sent further and further beyond the border, so that the territory of *workers' Russia* on which the new structure of workers' socialism will rise, will not be surrounded by an area in a state of agitation and unrest. It must see that as far as possible beyond the borders of the new society the still undefeated enemy will be preoccupied with apprehension and internal disorders.

Moreover, given the present situation in Germany and Austria, it is rather important that the victorious uprising in Russia, which organizes the territory of *workers' Russia*, finds support in the social-democratic unions of workers in these countries. If the social revolution has already taken place there, or if open conflict has at least broken out between the socialists and the regime, then the Russian socialists can consider themselves safe. But if Russia has to take up the struggle earlier, then the Russian socialists (i.e., the members of the Social Revolutionary Union), aware that the explosion is coming, must give serious thought to creating firm enough relations with their foreign comrades, that the German and Austrian social democrats will resolve to use all their strength for preventing their governments from moving troops across the Russian border. In the same way, on the day after the revolution, *workers' Russia* must, for her own defense, maintain the closest ties with those neighbors who share her ideas and might provide her with very powerful support in the struggle—if, of course, they have managed to bring their own enemies under control, but also in case they have not accomplished this, but merely prevent interference by their governments in the revolutionary movement in Russia.[23]

This external danger is another reason for the survival of the state, as an organized institution, after the revolution. Workers' Russia needs an army for defense, and an army cannot exist without a state to support it. But an army, as Lavrov very clearly recognized, represents a great danger to the revolution. Therefore he proposed certain precautions in dealing with the army—for example, the institution of "observers" who would be young and thoroughly reliable members of the party assigned to watch over military operations.

The revolutionary state would thus have a well-organized structure, and Lavrov had rather specific plans on this point. He said that the first responsibility of the state (except, perhaps, for military defense) is to provide for the economic needs of the population. For this purpose, immediately after the seizure of power the party is to organize a "committee of works and supply," which is to be responsible for organizing the economy. The committee, in turn, is to organize what Lavrov called an "executive council"; like the committee, the executive council will consist primarily of party members. There is also to be a larger body, the "national union," in which nonparty members may be invited to participate. Eventually the national union is to be an elected body—and nonparty members may be elected into it so long as they are "reliable." With the passage of time, the number of reliable people will increase until the overwhelming majority supports the revolution. The revolutionary party itself will gradually grow to be a majority of the population, and the political structure of workers' Russia—the revolutionary state—will slowly wither away.

Now the Marxist scenario for the Russian revolution, at least as drawn by Plekhanov, was quite different from this. The early Marxists were much more pessimistic about the prospect for revolution; their theory taught them that they must wait for history to run its natural course before the proletariat could come to power. The Russian Marxists of the ninteenth century could not accept Tkachev's estimate of the situation, in his famous open letter to Engels: "our people, for all their ignorance, are much closer to socialism than the peoples of Western Europe, although the latter are more advanced."[24] Tkachev's argument was that the Russian people were not yet oppressed by capitalism, *and need not be oppressed by capitalism in the future*. Once the autocracy was destroyed they could proceed directly to the building of socialism.

This is exactly what Plekhanov denied in *Socialism and the Political Struggle*. The basis of Plekhanov's political analysis was the theory of the "double yoke."[25] (In the program of the first organization of Russian Marxists,[a] Plekhanov wrote that their problems would be doubly complicated in Russia because

[a]The Liberation of Labor Group, organized in Geneva in 1883.

the working class was oppressed by the "double yoke" of emerging capitalism and dying feudalism.) Thus Plekhanov set, as the immediate aim of the Marxist party, the achievement of a "democratic constitution" which would guarantee civil liberties such as freedom of speech and universal suffrage. Once this was accomplished, that is, once the feudal yoke was thrown off and capitalism was in power, the stage would be set for the socialists to come forward with their program. From the theory of the double yoke thus follows the famous theory of the two revolutions, of a "bourgeois" revolution which would overthrow the tsarist autocracy, and the proletarian revolution which would lead to socialism. To confuse these two revolutions, Plekhanov once wrote, meant to postpone them both.[26]

Given this rather subtle analysis, the proper strategy for the socialists must be to cooperate, if possible, with the liberals in bringing about the first revolution. Then, with the establishment of constitutional government in Russia, the Marxists could come forward with their revolutionary and socialist program, and could work toward the second revolution. Of course the socialists must be careful not to be swallowed up by the liberals; they must remain loyal to their Marxist ideas. "For," Plekhanov said, "without a revolutionary theory there cannot be any revolutionary movement."[27] But the revolutionary theory taught Plekhanov that the time had not yet come for a socialist seizure of power. That would have to be preceded by a long period of preparation. "The revolution is only the final act in a long drama of revolutionary class struggle. . . ."[28] It seems quite clear that Plekhanov had some hope that the drama would be acted out under conditions of constitutional government. While he did not say so directly, it would have been consistent with his views to expect that the socialists might come to power by legal means. Nor was this inconsistent with orthodox Marxism. Engels himself was to write, in 1895, that "The Marxists had more to gain from legal methods than from illegality."[29]

The proletariat, once in power, would establish the "dictatorship of a class."[30] This was to be a dictatorship of a majority. A premature seizure of power would lead only to a dictatorship of revolutionary *raznochintsy*. Now to achieve a true class dictatorship required that the proletariat be sufficiently mature and well prepared for the task of ruling. That time had not yet come, and so Plekhanov was forced to admit that a socialist government in Russia was not an "early possibility."[31] In *Our Differences* Plekhanov asks the rhetorical question, "What would happen if the revolutionaries followed the advice of Tkachev and Lavrov?" And he answers his own question: the result would be a disgraceful fiasco.[32]

Thus there were fundamental and far-reaching differences between the Russian Marxists and the *narodniki*, both in their analysis of history and in their expectations about the future. If we take Lavrov as the principal theoretician of the *narodniki*, the differences can be summarized in the following way:

The Coming Revolution

Marx (as interpreted by Plekhanov)	*Lavrov*
Revolution is a product of industrial development. The success of the revolution depends, primarily, upon objective economic conditions.	The success of the revolution depends upon a variety of subjective factors, including the readiness of the revolutionaries to seize power.
The revolution will begin in the West.	The first workers' state will be in Russia.
The liberation of the working class will be accomplished by the working class itself.	The revolutionary leaders must expect the workers to be indifferent, and even hostile to the revolution.
The revolution must be preceded by a long period of preparation and efforts to raise the class consciousness of the workers.	The revolution must be followed by a long period of reeducation and rehabilitation of the masses.
The dictatorship of the proletariat will be a dictatorship of the majority over the minority.	The revolutionary dictatorship will be minority rule, operating through the party of social revolutionaries.

Lenin gave very little attention to these questions in the early part of his career. Like other Marxists, he probably believed that the revolution lay in a somewhat remote future and, at least until 1905, he was much more concerned about problems of party organization and tactics than about the structure of the proletarian state. In the most important work of this early period, *What Is to Be Done?* (1902), Lenin mentions the "dictatorship of the proletariat" only once, and then in a footnote: "the basic economic interests of the proletariat can be satisfied only by means of a political revolution that replaces the dictatorship of the bourgeoisie with the dictatorship of the proletariat."[33] This was good social-democratic doctrine, but hardly relevant to the situation in Russia, where the "dictatorship of the bourgeoisie" was not yet a reality.

In 1905, however, it appeared that the bourgeois revolution might actually be underway. From the point of view of the social-democratic leaders, a crucial question was the attitude which the workers' party should take toward a bourgeois government which might emerge from this revolution—toward what the social-democrats (including Lenin) soon were calling the "provisional revolutionary government." On this question Lenin quickly found himself isolated from virtually all the other leaders of the social democratic party, including Plekhanov.[34] But on one important and basic point Lenin was still in substantial agreement with Plekhanov, and that was the theory of the two revolutions. The revolution that was beginning in Russia, as both Plekhanov and Lenin agreed, was a bourgeois revolution which (if successful) would put the bourgeoisie in power. This revolution, Plekhanov wrote, would for the first time create conditions in which it would be possible to think seriously about a proletarian revolution.[35] Lenin, no less than Plekhanov, was ready to welcome the transformation of Russia into a parliamentary democracy on the western model. "Direct representation of the interests of the ruling class, in the form of a constitution, is necessary for a country which wants to be a European country and which is forced by circumstances, under the threat of political and economic defeat, to become European."[36] Lenin warned that the liberal movement against the autocracy was a bourgeois movement serving bourgeois interests. Nonetheless he regarded this "struggle for political freedom and a democratic republic within a bourgeois society" as a necessary first step in the ultimate direction of socialism. This, of course, was precisely what Plekhanov had said in *Socialism and the Political Struggle*.

Lenin was not content, however, just to sit back and rejoice in the coming victory of the bourgeoisie over tsarism. In January 1905 he was already writing about the "joint struggle of the proletariat and bourgeoisie against the autocracy";[37] and in March he considered the establishment of a revolutionary regime to be a real possibility. He was now concerned with the tactical question—not whether the social democrats should lead the revolution, but whether they should participate in a future "provisional revolutionary government." Lenin readily agreed that any government which emerged from the revolution of 1905 would not be a "dictatorship of the proletariat."[38] But he did not agree with the left-wing social democrats, like Parvus and Trotsky, who said that the party should not enter a government that it did not control. All the party's leaders agreed that the proletariat was still in a minority, that it could not hope to gain power except in coalition with other classes, and any revolutionary government must, necessarily, reflect the classes which supported it. Lenin insisted that the party should be ready to join the provisional government—and to make this tactic more acceptable he now decided to call the provisional government a "revolutionary dictatorship of the proletariat and the peasantry."[39]

The terminology now becomes somewhat confusing. Lenin made it quite clear that the "revolutionary dictatorship of the proletariat and the peasantry" was only another name for the "provisional revolutionary government." It was not, therefore, a socialist government. In fact Lenin foresaw that the socialists (read: Marxists) would be only a minority within this government. But he insisted that the party should not lose this opportunity to get its foot in the door. In April and May the Bolsheviks met at the Third Party Congress, in London, and on Lenin's recommendation they approved a resolution on participation in the revolutionary regime. However, the resolution spoke only of a "provisional revolutionary government."[40] It had little to say about the form of this participation, except that any Bolsheviks who entered the government would remain under strict party control.

It is part of the conventional wisdom about Lenin that by the time he wrote *What Is to Be Done?* he had virtually given up on the proletariat as a revolutionary force. It is certainly true that Lenin was much less optimistic than Marx had been about the revolutionary potential of the working class. But Lenin did continue to believe, for some years after he wrote *What Is to Be Done?* that the socialist revolution could not succeed until it had overwhelming proletarian support. On this point he was quite orthodox—at least until 1917. Like Plekhanov, Lenin expected that the period following the bourgeois revolution would be a period of preparation and propaganda, when the proletariat would grow in size, and power, and political consciousness. Now the establishment of a "revolutionary dictatorship of the proletariat and the peasantry" might hurry along this process. But like Plekhanov twenty-five years earlier, Lenin warned against a "premature" seizure of power by the proletariat alone. In 1905 he still thought that the "subjective" conditions for a socialist revolution were not yet developed. The masses—even the "democratically minded" masses—were not yet ready for socialism.[41] He describes the proletariat as scattered, uneducated, and ignorant—and therefore unready.[42] It still had not occurred to him that a socialist party might seize power and then, *after* the establishment of the dictatorship of the proletariat, use that power to develop the political consciousness of the working class.

Lenin's scenario is laid out in his best-known work of 1905, *Two Tactics of Social Democracy in the Democratic Revolution.*[43] It is also laid out, much more concisely, in a short note written in June, under the title, "A Picture of the Provisional Revolutionary Government."[44] Here he describes the moment when tsarism has been "beaten in St. Petersburg—beaten, but not destroyed" (*"razbito, no ne dobito, ne ubito, ne unichtozheno. . . ."*). The autocratic regime is replaced by the provisional revolutionary government, which appeals to the people with a program for the establishment of a republic and a complete agrarian reform. Social democrats join the government, subject to instructions from the party. The outcome may be all-out civil war, with the object of destroying tsarism, and establishing a republic with complete political freedom. The result will be a victory for the *minimum* program of the social democrats, but not yet a victory for socialism.

And such a victory certainly will be a dictatorship, i.e., it must inevitably be based on military force, on arming the masses, on an insurrection, and not on any institutions created in a "legal" or "peaceful" way. It has to be a dictatorship, because to bring about the changes which are urgently and absolutely necessary for the proletariat and peasantry will arouse desperate resistance by the landlords, the big bourgeoisie, and tsarism. It will be impossible to break down that resistance, and to repel attempts at counterrevolution, without dictatorship. But it goes without saying that it will be not a socialist, but a democratic dictatorship. It will not be able to touch the foundations of capitalism (without a series of intermediate stages of revolutionary development). At best it may be able to accomplish a basic redistribution of landed property to the advantage of the peasantry, establish consistent and complete democracy including the creation of a republic, root out all the Asiatic and oppressive features not only from the village but from industrial life, take the first steps toward improving the lot of the worker and raising his standard of living, and finally, *last but not least* [In English in the original—D.H.] —carry the flame of revolution into a socialist revolution. The democratic transformation will not go beyond the framework of bourgeois social and economic relationships. Nonetheless such a victory will be of immense importance for the future development of both Russia and the entire world.[45]

Thus the struggle with the autocracy ends in the establishment of the "democratic dictatorship." How long Lenin held on to this view is impossible to determine. By 1906 he was already attacking Kautsky for advocating a "democratic dictatorship of proletariat and peasantry," rather than a socialist dictatorship of the proletariat.[46] But Lenin, like Marx, still did not explain what he meant. He did promise, at the end of *Two Tactics of Social Democracy in the Democratic Revolution*, to write something about the dictatorship of the proletariat.[47] But in the twelve years between revolutions Lenin was busy with other problems, and he did not return to the question of the postrevolutionary state until 1917.

Lenin's classical work on the theory of the proletarian state is *State and Revolution*, written in 1917 but not published until the following year. In this book he described the "smashing" of the old state and the gradual "withering" of the new state which replaced it. But he still had little to say about the practical problems of governing Russia during the transitional period, or about the actual structure of the dictatorship of the proletariat.[48] *State and Revolution* is thus quite different from Tkachev's *Revolution and the State*.

A large part of *State and Revolution* is devoted to a discussion of the Paris Commune. Engels, it may be recalled, had once written that the commune had been a dictatorship of the proletariat.[49] In fact Lenin's preliminary notes for the book contain the following interesting comment: "Must find out, did Marx and Engels talk about the 'dictatorship of the proletariat' *before 1871*? Apparently not!"[50] The commune had been the organizational form of the proletarian revolution, a form to replace the old "bourgeois" state. But Lenin quoted Engels, with approval, as saying that "the commune was no longer a state in the true sense."[51] At best it had been a transitional state, which suppresses the old exploiting classes during the period of transition to communism—and under communism, the state will have withered away. Both Marx and Lavrov published short histories of the commune, and the differences in interpretation are quite instructive. Marx wrote, in *The Civil War in France*, that the commune had been essentially a "working class government" which held in its hands a "lever" for breaking the economic foundations of class rule. He does not criticize the commune for failing to use this lever. There is no suggestion, in Marx's analysis, that the proletariat was not prepared for the commune. On the contrary, he wrote that the workers set out "in the full consciousness of their historic mission."[52]

Lavrov, in contrast to this, was very critical of the commune.[53] He said that the failure of the commune was fundamentally a failure of leadership. The leaders were not ready for the revolution, and when it happened they failed to come forward with an organization and a program for action. In particular, they failed to make adequate preparations for the military defense of the city. There should have been a disciplined party, organized before the uprising and ready to take command of the situation. (It will never be possible, Lavrov warned, to organize a party while fighting in the streets.) Plans should have been worked out well in advance. The party should have been able to force through its own program against other proletarian leaders who might not yet comprehend the aims of the revolutionary government.[54] Only then could the proletarian party have overcome "the inevitable lack of political understanding in the masses, who always follow those who seem most sure of themselves in thought and action."[55] In particular Lavrov criticized the commune for putting political reform ahead of economic revolution. The commune should have destroyed the existing relations of property and wealth, and established the proletariat in economic, as well as political power. This economic revolution would have provided a basis for later political development, and such institutions as freedom of expression and representative government.

The first Russian edition of Marx's history of the commune contains an interesting introduction by Trotsky, which apparently was Trotsky's first statement of his own views on the "dictatorship of the proletariat" and the "permanent revolution."[56] The two concepts are inextricably linked. In fact Marx himself said so in his first (and only) published statement on the subject: "socialism is the *declaration of the permanence of the revolution*, the *class dictatorship* of the proletariat as the necessary transit point to the *abolition of class distinctions generally....*"[57]

The revolution, Trotsky said, is a struggle for power. The masses rise up in response to the most elementary and instinctive forces; they often have no clear idea of where they are going. The crucial question of the revolution is which party the masses will follow.[58] Trotsky was therefore opposed to any coalition of parties, which would only confuse the outcome. In particular he was opposed to Lenin's 1905 strategy of a "dictatorship of the proletariat and the peasantry."[59] The revolution must be a revolution *in Permanenz*, a "permanent revolution" which would lead directly to the dictatorship of the proletariat.

Trotsky disposed very quickly of the argument that history was not yet ready for the proletarian state. The timing of the revolution, he said, depends on economic factors such as the "level of production forces" less than on "subjective" factors, including the international situation. In words which remind us of Tkachev, Trotsky wrote that it might very well happen that the proletariat would come to power earlier in a backward country than in a country which had a highly developed capitalist system.[60] His evidence for this emphasis on "subjective" factors is the experience of the Paris Commune. "It goes without saying that the Paris Commune of 1871 was not a socialist commune; its regime was not even the developed regime of a socialist revolution. The 'Commune' was only a prologue. It established a dictatorship of the proletariat, the necessary prerequisite to the socialist revolution."[61]

By 1917 Lenin, too, was opposed to a "revolutionary democratic dictatorship of workers and peasants." The strategy of 1917 was the strategy of permanent revolution, which meant the immediate seizure of power and the establishment of a "dictatorship of the proletariat." But it was not until after the Bolsheviks were in power that Lenin tried to formulate what he meant by "dictatorship of the proletariat." The most important documents for an understanding of Lenin's views on this subject are *The Proletarian Revolution and the Renegade Kautsky* (1918), and *The Infantile Disease of Left-Wing Communism* (1920). In 1919, Lenin was again planning to write a treatise on the dictatorship of the proletariat, but it was never finished. He did, however, produce a number of short articles or notes on the subject in 1919 and 1920:

1. "On 'Democracy' and Dictatorship," *Pravda*, Jan. 3, 1919, XXXVII, 388-93.
2. "On the State," Lecture at the Sverdlov University, July 11, 1919, XXXIX, 64-84.
3. "On the Dictatorship of the Proletariat," outline of an unwritten article, September 1919, XXXIX, 259-68.
4. First draft and plan of a brochure on the dictatorship of the proletariat, September-October 1919, XXXIX, 453-61.
5. "Economics and Politics in the Epoch of the Dictatorship of the Proletariat," first part of an article in *Petrogradskaia Pravda*, Nov. 7, 1919 (the second part was never written) XXXIX, 271-82.
6. "The Elections to the Constituent Assembly and the Dictatorship of the Proletariat," *Kommunisticheskii internatsional*, December 1919, XL, 1-24.
7. "Notes of a Publicist," *Kommunisticheskii internatsional*, March 1920, XL, 129-39.
8. "On the History of the Question of Dictatorship," *Kommunisticheskii internatsional*, November 1920, XLI, 369-91.

The one threat which runs clearly through Lenin's writings of 1905, and also through his work of the postrevolutionary period, is the familiar assumption about the political backwardness of the working classes. The masses were not expected, at least in the short run, to comprehend the aims of the revolution. For this reason, Lenin wrote in 1920, communism would reach its goals only after a long period of time had elapsed.[62] To try to bring "full communism" to reality immediately after the seizure of power would be like trying to teach higher mathematics to a four-year-old. There is an interesting echo of Lavrovism in the following statement: "We can (and must) begin to build socialism not out of fantasy, or out of human material especially created by us, but with what has been left to us by capitalism. There is no denying that this will be 'difficult,' but no other approach to the problem is serious enough to warrant discussion."[63]

Lenin's general attitude toward the working class was the same in 1917 as it had been in 1905, and earlier. But in 1917 the conclusions which he drew were quite different. Earlier he had written that the dictatorship of the proletariat would not be possible until after the working class had reached a higher level of political consciousness, and for this Lenin had believed (as Plekhanov had believed) that a long period of preparation would be necessary. But after 1917 we find Lenin arguing that, precisely because of the backwardness of the masses, the dictatorship of the proletariat was not only possible but absolutely necessary— necessary in order to accomplish the task of reeducation of the people. Where once he had seen the masses as a constraint on how far the revolution could go, now he saw them as a great challenge to the revolutionary state.

Lenin's philosophical view of the state did not change after the revolution. This view was derived primarily from Engels' *Origin of the Family, Private Property, and the State*; it assumed that the state had its origin with the first division of society into classes, and in a genuinely classless society there would be no state. "The state is a machine for maintaining the dominance of one class over another."[64] *This was no less true of the dictatorship of the proletariat.* The proletarian state, too, was a weapon to be used in the class struggle. This is how Lenin summed up the strategy of the revolutionary government: "the proletariat must first overthrow the bourgeoisie and seize *for itself* the power of the state, and then use this power, that is, the dictatorship of the proletariat, as a class weapon for the purpose of winning the support of a majority of toilers."[65] Thus "on the day after" the revolution the proletariat must begin using its political strength, and *also economic means*, to win wider support among the nonproletarian masses. This emphasis, which Lenin often repeated, on meeting the *economic* needs of the masses reminds us of what Lavrov had written about the failures of the Paris Commune. Lenin was not immediately concerned about the establishment of political democracy. That lay in the future. And he was convinced that the masses in Russia were no more concerned about it than he was— or at least, they were far more concerned about satisfying their immediate economic needs.

This apparently is what Lenin had in mind when he called the dictatorship a "class weapon" to be used in winning the support of a majority. He never admitted explicitly that his regime was based on minority rule. At one point he referred to it as a "dictatorship of the great majority."[66] But he knew perfectly well that to accept the will of the majority, in the conditions of 1918 and 1919, would have toppled the regime. He certainly believed that he had the support of a majority of the "advanced" and "political consciousness" element in the popu-

lation. He said that the Soviet state was a "dictatorship of the revolutionary people"—but it was not a dictatorship of the people in general. This was the case
because the "people" (*narod*) included large numbers who were frightened,
morally disoriented, and driven down by custom and prejudice.[67]

Lenin's definition of dictatorship remained essentially what it had been before: "Unlimited power, power beyond the law, power based on force in the
most direct sense of the word—this is dictatorship."[68] He was still ready to
defend "unlimited power" with the argument that all government is dictatorship
anyway, and what matters is to replace one dictatorship by another. "The democratic republic, the constituent assembly, universal suffrage, etc., is a dictatorship of the bourgeoisie, and for the liberation of labor from the yoke of capital
there is no other way but the replacement of this dictatorship by the dictatorship of the proletariat."[69]

There is, however, one new element of fundamental importance which appears in the postrevolutionary writings, and that was the role of the party within
the dictatorship. Actually Lenin never connected up the party and the dictatorship until 1920. Of course no one who was familiar with Lenin's views on the
party, as developed in *What Is to Be Done?* and in later works, would be surprised at the dominating role of the party within the Soviet state. But in his
theoretical work, as distinguished from political practice, Lenin was very cautious. He never said, as Lavrov did, that after the revolution the party would
become *de facto* the government of the workers' state. Lenin was very sensitive
to the charge that his regime was really a dictatorship of the party, and he was
never as frank as Lavrov had been in describing how the party would control the
government. But he did write, in 1920, that while all power must go to the
soviets as representatives of the workers and peasants, "their vanguard, the party
of the revolutionary proletariat must *lead* the struggle—this is what the dictatorship of the proletariat is."[70] And at the height of the crisis of 1921 he admitted
to the Tenth Party Congress that "the dictatorship of the proletariat is impossible except through the communist party."[71]

The *narodniki* had all believed in a "special path" for Russia. That is, they
had believed that Russia was essentially different from western societies, and she
was destined to remain different in the future. The Russian Marxists, theoretically, rejected the idea of the "special path." But the dictatorship of the proletariat, as it worked out in practice, has been the logical culmination of this idea
about Russia's uniqueness. The "dictatorship of the proletariat"—or at least
Lenin's application of this term to Russian conditions—has become a wedge
which separated Soviet communism from western social democracy. It was a
formal political structure which cast into sharp relief the idea of a "special path"
for Russia. Perhaps it was inevitable that Russia should have gone this way. The
weight of *narodnik* ideas, as we have seen, undoubtedly would have propelled
the country toward revolutionary dictatorship rather than liberal democracy.
But it was certainly not inevitable that the dictatorship should have clothed it-

self in the banner of Marxism. For Marxism very clearly allowed for the possibility of a "peaceful transition to socialism" under conditions of parliamentary democracy. The early Russian Marxists believed in this possibility, and we should not forget that, to their contemporaries, they occupied the *right* wing of the revolutionary movement. And Engels, who was always alert to defend Marxism against the revisionists and reformers, wrote in 1895: "The irony of world history turns everything upside down. We, the 'revolutionists,' the 'overthrowers'—we are thriving far better on legal methods than on illegal methods and overthrow. The parties of Order, as they call themselves, are perishing under the legal conditions created by themselves.... And if *we* are not so crazy as to let ourselves be driven to street fighting in order to please them, then in the end there is nothing left for them but themselves to break through this fatal legality."[72] Unfortunately the social democrats never had this opportunity to thrive on legality. Lenin and his party took the path of dictatorship because there was no other way. But the dictatorship of the proletariat, far from being "enrichment" of Marxism, was an abandonment of the mainstream of the Marxist movement.

Notes

1. V.I. Lenin, *State and Revolution*, in *Polnoe sobranie sochinenii*, 5th ed., XXXIII, p. 24. (All references to Lenin's works are from this edition.)

2. Letter to J. Weydemeyer, March 5, 1852, in *Selected Correspondence* (Moscow, 1955), p. 83.

3. See, for example, *Politicheskii slovar'*, pod. red. Prof. B.N. Ponomareva, 2-e izd. (Moscow, 1958), s.v. "diktatura proletariata."

4. *XXII s'ezd Kommunisticheskoi partii sovetskogo soiuza* (Moscow, 1962), III, p. 302.

5. Karl Marx and Friedrich Engels, *Selected Works*, 2 vols. (Moscow, 1955), I, p. 223.

6. See E.H. Carr, *The Bolshevik Revolution* (New York, 1951), I, p. 235. The only other occasions on which Marx used the term were in the letter to Weydemeyer and in the *Critique of the Gotha Program*. The *Critique* was written in 1875 but not published until 1891, Marx-Engels, *Ausgewahlte Schriften in zwei Bänden* (Berlin, 1960), J. II, p. 29.

7. See also John Plamenatz, *German Marxism and Russian Communism* (London, 1954), p. 156.

8. Karl Kautsky, *The Dictatorship of the Proletariat* (Ann Arbor, Michigan, 1964), p. 43.

9. "Marks—vozhd' proletariata," in V.V. Adoratskii, *Izbrannye proizvedeniia* (Moscow, 1961), p. 148.

10. Ibid., pp. 149, 150, 153.

11. Ibid., p. 158.

12. This discussion of Tkachev relies in part on the work of Rolf H.W. Theen, "Petr Nikitich Tkachev: A Study in Revolutionary Theory" (Ph.D. dissertation, Indiana University, 1964).

13. P.N. Tkachev, *Izbrannye sochineniia* (Moscow, 1933), III, p. 224.

14. Ibid., pp. 55-87.

15. Tkachev, *Revoliutsiia i gosudarstvo*, III, p. 247.

16. Ibid., p. 253.

17. See P.L. Lavrov, *Filosofiia i sotsiologiia* (Moscow, 1965), II, p. 484.

18. See F.A. Walker, "P.L. Lavrov's Concept of the Party," *The Western Political Quarterly*, July 1966, p. 235.

19. *Gosudarstvennyi element v buduschchem obshchestve*, in *Sobranie sochinenii Petra Lavrovicha Lavrova*, vypusk VII (Petrograd, 1920).

20. Ibid., p. 106.

21. Ibid., p. 151.

22. Ibid.

23. Ibid., pp. 163-64.

24. Tkachev, "Otkrytoe pis'mo gospodinu Fridrikhu Engel'su," III, p. 90.

25. G.V. Plekhanov, *Sochineniia* 3-e izd. (Moscow, 1923), II, p. 359.

26. Ibid., p. 86.

27. Ibid., p. 71. These words, from *Socialism and the Political Struggle*, were to reappear in *What Is to Be Done?* and are usually attributed to Lenin.

28. Ibid., pp. 58-59.

29. *Selected Works* (1955), I, p. 136.

30. Plekhanov, II, p. 110.

31. Ibid., p. 111.

32. Ibid., p. 329.

33. Lenin, VI, p. 46.

34. See, for example, Plekhanov's articles "On Our Tactics in Relation to the Struggle of the Liberal Bourgeoisie with Tsarism," and "On the Question of the Seizure of Power," in *Sochineniia*, XIII, pp. 169-87, and 202-11.

35. Ibid., p. 170.

36. Lenin, IX, pp. 130-31.

37. Ibid., p. 190.

38. Lenin, X, p. 6.

39. Ibid., p. 30.

40. *Tretii s'ezd RSDRP, aprel'-mai 1905 goda* (Moscow, 1959), p. 451.

41. Lenin, II, p. 16.

42. Ibid., p. 45.

43. Ibid., pp. 1-131.

44. Lenin, X, pp. 359-61.

45. Lenin, XI, pp. 44-45.

46. Lenin, XIV, p. 186.

47. Lenin, XI, p. 76.

48. On the development of Lenin's ideas in this book, see R.V. Daniels, "The State and Revolution: A Case Study in the Genesis and Transformation of Communist Ideology," *The American Slavic and East European Review*, February 1953, p. 25.

49. In the Introduction (1891) to *The Civil War in France*, in *Selected Works* (1968), p. 262.

50. *Selected Works*, XXXIII, p. 158.

51. Ibid., p. 66.

52. Ibid., pp. 294-95.

53. Lavrov's views are contained in his book, *Parizhskaia kommuna 18 marta, 1871 goda*, written in 1879. This is the book which Trotsky recommends to Soviet readers in *Terrorism and Communism* (Ann Arbor, 1961), pp. 69ff. Quotations here are from the "fourth edition" (Leningrad and Moscow, 1925).

54. *Parizhskaia kommuna 18 marta, 1871 goda*, pp. 112-13.

55. Ibid.

56. Karl Marx, *Parizhskaia kommuna*, perevod L. Semeniuta s predisloviem N. Trotskogo (St. Petersburg, 1906). This is a translation of *The Civil War in France*. Trotsky's introduction is dated December 1905, and thus was written a few weeks before *Itogi i perspektivy*, which is the classical statement of the theory of permanent revolution. See I. Deutscher, *The Prophet Armed, Trotsky: 1879-1921* (New York, 1954), pp. 149ff.

57. *Selected Works* (1955), I, p. 223.

58. Trotsky, Introduction to Marx, *Parizhskaia kommuna*, p. ii.

59. Ibid., p. xviii.

60. Ibid., p. iii.

61. Ibid., p. v.

62. Lenin, XLI, p. 33.

63. Ibid.

64. Lenin, XXXIX, p. 67.

65. Lenin, XLI, p. 12.

66. Ibid., p. 381.

67. Ibid., p. 383.

68. Ibid., p. 380.

69. Lenin, XXXVII, p. 390.

70. Lenin, XL, p. 136.

71. Lenin, XLI, p. 42.

72. *Selected Works* (1955), I, p. 136.

3 Lenin, Bogdanov, and the Concept of Proletarian Culture

PETER SCHEIBERT

The attitude of Lenin toward the concept of proletarian culture has two aspects, one more fundamental and ideological, the other more tactical and political. In the first part of this chapter I want to emphasize the ideological implications which I consider to be important for the understanding of the present state of Communist theory in the Soviet Union.

In his *Critique of the Gotha Program* in 1875, Marx insisted that "in a higher phase of the communist society . . . the enslaving subordination of the individual under the division of labor and thus the contradiction of intellectual and manual work will disappear," and labor "will become the first necessity of life." "With the universal development of the individual . . . all sources of communal wealth will flow fuller than before." This sentence was quoted by Lenin in his notes to *State and Revolution* and used for his definition of "the highest form of communist society." The elimination of the division of labor remained the precondition to the otherwise undefined perspectives of the development of human society.

Both theoreticians were aware that no less important for the end of all repression is the annihilation of the state followed by its replacement by a more advanced form of social organization. For Marx, this form seemed to be achieved in the Paris Commune. But the question of *how* the state would be transformed into a Communist society remained open. "It could only be answered in theory," said Marx in his *Critique*. ". . . The Model of the Commune," with its so-called direct democracy, where all delegates could be recalled by the voters at any given time, was taken up by Lenin in his program in *State and Revolution*. He supposed that the conditions of a developed capitalist production had already created all technical conditions necessary to "reduce a good part of the functions of the old state machine . . . to simple operations such as registration and control of self-performing processes," that everyone who knew how to read and write would be able to perform these functions and receive the average worker's salary. Both aspects of a fully developed Communist society, optimal evolution of production and replacement of the traditional state apparatus, became more important with the rise of new conditions of production.

Under German war economics the capitalist economy had entered a new dimension, planning instead of anarchy. Bukharin called this system "state capitalism" in an essay which, due to Lenin's efforts, was not published in 1916.

43

In it he argued that the state, as the sole employer, would control all human processes and thus become a totalitarian structure. The state must therefore be destroyed immediately after the revolution. Lenin's *State and Revolution* was directed (in its first draft) against Bukharin's vision because he wanted to preserve the state as a means of suppression in the hands of the victorious proletariat during the period of transition.

The duration of the dictatorship of the proletariat seemed to depend to a large extent on technical and organizational conditions. The longer the dictatorship lasts, the greater the chance for the development of new methods of repression in the form of a new bureaucracy or state appartus. The vigor of the revolutionary movement, late in 1912, a surprise to Lenin and his comrades, seemed to open unexpected perspectives. The breakdown of the old economic system, that is, the rapid devaluation of the ruble and expropriation of the wealth of the old propertied classes, seemed to give a chance for redistribution by meeting, without the use of money, the demands of the people in consumer's cooperatives or communes. The introduction of the personal labor book and the payment of the workers with products of a plant seemed to be the decisive blow against the money economy. But it became immediately obvious that this new distribution order would work only under the condition that the state had sufficient consumers' goods at its disposal to satisfy the needs of all the members of the society.

With the transition to the New Economic Policy in March 1921, the establishment of communism was postponed for an indefinite period of time. The difference between town and countryside remained as before, so the prospect of a unified organization of distribution had to be abandoned. However, Stalin never lost sight of the ultimate goal of the perfect Communist society, as evidenced at the eve of the first Five Years' Plan. These few examples and facts give only the general background for ambitious projects for the change of man and the world in which he lives, i.e., the building up to the new proletarian culture.

II

In 1925, at the end of his book, *Literature and Revolution*, Trotsky predicted,

Communist life will . . . be built consciously, will be tested by thought, will be directed and corrected. Man who will learn how to move rivers and mountains, how to build places on the peaks of Mont Blanc and at the bottom of the Atlantic, will not only be able to add to his own life richness, brilliancy and intensity, but also a dynamic quality of the highest degree. . . . Man will at last begin to harmonize himself in earnest. . . . There can be no doubt that man's extreme anatomical and physiological harmony . . . gives the life instinct the form of a pinched, morbid and hysterical fear of death, which . . . feeds the stupid and humiliating fantasies about life after death. . . . Man will make it his purpose to master his own feelings . . . and thereby to raise himself to a new place, to create a high social biologic type, or if you please, a superman. . . . The forms of life will become dynamically dramatic. The average human type will rise to the heights of an Aristotle, a Goethe or a Marx. And above this ridge new peaks will rise.

The vision we just quoted did not prevent Trotsky from being condescending and abusive with the cosmist poets, who, within the movement of the proletarian culture, sketched a vivid poetic picture of the coming of the new cosmos. In 1920 a genial and desperate parody had already been written: *We* by Zamiatin. The age of War-Communism, an epoch of civil war, terror and hunger, had been the time of gigantic plans for the building of huge cities with fantastic glass skyscrapers, where people were to live together in free community and happy harmony.

But the N.E.P. brought with it not only the abolition of all autonomous cultural organizations and a rather abrupt end to visionary writing, but also brought to an end the debates on the future of man in a Communist society. But this City of Hope, this utopia to be achieved through science, cannot easily be put aside. Otherwise communism would be nothing but a system of bourgeois welfare on the basis of technical perfection.

The demand for the abolition of the division of labor cannot be considered only as a symbol, because self-estrangement of man cannot be otherwise overthrown. The problem of communism has always been essentially an anthropological one: man was to find a new relation to nature which is no more dangerous, but fully controlled, because at the end of his history, man has again become an integral part of the harmony of nature—a *Naturwesen*.

Marxism pretends to have unveiled man's history as a part of the history of nature. This had been indeed the position of integral materialism in the mid-nineteenth century, shared by the popular scientific writers of that time and preserved in the official ideology of the Soviet Union until our times. All new discoveries, from Einstein to cybernetics, have been taken over hesitantly, merely under a technical aspect, but never really incorporated into the official philosophy or epistemology, which therefore, instead of being constantly revised, seems to fade into nothingness in contemporary Soviet opinion.

Berdiaev spoke about "materialistic metaphysics" as the basis of this typical pattern of thought of the Russian radical intelligentsia. A fervent atheism proclaimed the fully emancipated man, i.e., a kind of collective superman first formulated by Chernyshevsky, a concept which lost none of its attraction right down to Trotsky. To a large extent, Chernyshevsky's *What Is to Be Done?* together with *Anti-Dühring* by Engels formed the image of the world in revolutionary Russia. Lenin himself was deeply impressed by Chernyshevsky's book, which he reread while in exile in Siberia. Here, too, in the dreams of the heroine, the world of the future was shown as a life of collective harmony, where man would finally become immortal. Death, the essence of nonprogress, would be overcome. If man should be nothing but an element of nature, and in no way be above or outside nature, it would be possible or probable that other human or superhuman beings could be discovered in other parts of the universe. On the other hand, if man were to become the master of nature through science and technology he would be able to conquer the universe. This idea had first been taken up by Nikolas Fedorov, who never published anything during his lifetime, but who was highly esteemed by Dostoevski, Tolstoi, and others. Though his main goal was a moral one, that of resurrection of our dead ancestors as a common cause of our time, and the occupation of the planets in order to have room for the myriads of the resurrected, his approach, too, was technical to a certain extent. The pioneer of Soviet space research, Tsiol'kovsky, was himself a follower of Fedorov. Here, too, overcoming death through a spirit of collectivity as a dominant concept.

III

The Russian revolutionary emigration in the fateful years after 1905 was more or less fully occupied with political struggles and factional intrigues, which served a shrewd technician like Lenin more than those theoreticians who pondered over the problems of a new man in a better world. But one of the most prominent Bolsheviks, who in 1907 for a time replaced Lenin as the head of the Bolshevik faction and controlled at this time the Party members in Russia, Alexander Malinovsky, better known as Bogdanov, developed a most original scientific *Weltanschauung*. That Bogdanov was an important party figure is shown by his serving on the three-man financial committee with Lenin and Krasin. This committee had in its control all the finances of the party, which, to a large extent, were the result of the ill-famed "expropriations." Nevertheless, Bogdanov was expelled from, or left, the Party in 1911; the exact details are not yet known.

In one of his early writings, Bogdanov gave a first account of his endeavors:

In a society of the highest developed type, with collectively organized labor, the individual ego will no longer be the center of a separate, individually psychic world, because of the abolition of personal internal contradictions and the elimination of sharp differences between people. As a result of the close reciprocal understanding of human beings, all attempts to set one's own psyche against the psyches of other men will disappear. The harmoniously organized collective experience will give harmony such an immense plentitude of life, that we, the people of an age of contradictions, are not able to imagine it in full.

Bogdanov developed his revised Marxism in a number of books and articles which were rather influential between 1906 and 1910 in Bolshevik circles, for example at the Party school at Capri. "Organization" was a key word for Bogdanov's research and his projects, and it did not lose its impact even after his disgrace. He tried to introduce the recent discoveries of physics and philosophy of science into Marxist or Materialist ideology, taking into consideration the phenomenological approach imposed by the progress of science. Unfortunately, today Bogdanov is best known through Lenin's pamphlet *Materialism and Empirio-criticism*, which, in fact, is nothing but a political diatribe without the slightest attempt at analysis or interpretation of Bogdanov's thought. Lenin stuck to the, at that time, already obsolete "realistic," i.e., unreflected, perception of the outside world. In so doing, he dogmatized the Engelsian standpoint and blocked thorough assimilation of modern science into the philosophic concepts of Soviet Marxism. In fact, Lenin's book was nothing less than an attempt at scholarship, but his sole goal was to discredit the only serious rival in the Party whom he had to face at that given time, 1909.

Bogdanov indeed had the courage to look at all doctrines, Marxism included, from an historical perspective:

History teaches that all systems of ideas, as revolutionary as they may have been during their rise and struggle for power, sooner or later became a brake, an obstacle to further development; they became a socially reactionary force. Only a theory which is able to explain these phenomena could avoid a fatal degeneration. Such a theory is Marxism, which has shown that each system of ideas is a result of a certain given social-economic formation. When this formation disappears, the vital importance of any system inevitably fades away. The enigma of the fate of ideologies is contained in the changes of the social-economic formations. . . . Marxism, as the ideology of the most progressive class, was forced to deny to all systems, its own included, an absolute relevance. Marxism claimed to develop itself according to the changing conditions of life of the proletariat. . . . But the old world, after a long and unsuccessful strife . . . created a vampire in the image of its foe and sent it forth to the struggle against life. The name of this delusion is absolute Marxism. This creature . . . transforms those who have been useful workers into enraged foes of the necessary evolution of proletarian thought. Our country has sacrificed to this delusion some of its best people: Plekhanov at an early date, now Lenin, besides other less important persons who were at least useful at a given time for the common goal. . . . Our class and we ourselves face a great mission, the creation of a new culture, for which everything past and present is nothing but raw material; harmonious collaboration of the collective will be the instruments of that culture.

These quotations explain Lenin's wrath and make understandable his dislike for what Bogdanov had to say. In fact, nobody in the Party concerned himself much with Lenin's private fights at that time. His book became prominent only after his death, during the struggles within the Party for a concept of the so-called Marxism-Leninism. This in fact was nothing other than Stalin's weapon for full personal and ideological control of the party. There was no "Leninism" prior to Stalin's "*Voprosy Leninizma*."

IV

What Bogdanov called "absolute Marxism," which had to be overcome in order to render the fighting proletariat its most efficient weapons, was in fact, what we call today vulgar Marxism, i.e., the thinking in the base-superstructure alternative, which is a revolutionary act aimed exclusively at the expropriation of the means of production without taking into account the perspectives of a revolutionary society. "Proletarian culture" did not mean workers' folklore, etc.—though the later movement tended in that direction—but implied a new definition of revolution as a "managerial revolution." Taking over meant a new management of plants and public administration by trained proletarians. Bogdanov felt that the failure of the revolution in 1905 was to a large degree caused by the low cultural standard of the uneducated, mostly illiterate Russian working class, which was able to start an upheaval, but did not know what to do afterwards. In addition, Bogdanov was under the influence of Makhaisky though as far as I know, he never quoted him. Makhaisky, predicted the rule of technical as well as other intelligentsia over the workers in a revolutionary society in which the intelligentsia would not share its know-how with the toiling masses and would therefore reintroduce capitalist exploitation under a new name. After the takeover, revolutionary intellectuals will be at the top and will develop all the qualities of a new managing class or bureaucracy—a dilemma which Marx, as I point out above, never faced and which Lenin tried to minimize in *State and Revolution*, only to become aware at the end of his life that this was destined to become the central problem of a socialist society. The relation between the proletariat and the leftist intelligentsia concerned all socialist or social democratic parties. But this problem was almost never discussed in the German Social-Democratic party because the difference in the levels of education was less vividly felt and because both strata met in legal party work and in Parliament. For a party which was represented by Bebel, among others, this problem seemed not to exist.

Organization was the key word for the coming age of technical civilization. Workers had to obey and comply with orders as long as they would not be taught to organize themselves. Bogdanov developed the idea that the origin of human thought, language included, came from the needs of early mankind to organize all common work and achievements through general agreement. All evolution of man came from the bare necessity of organizing collective efforts. This dynamic materialism seemed capable of overcoming not only the dualism between matter and intelligence, but also between nature and man—since nothing was perceptible, and thus real, which could not be named—i.e., organized.

The dualistic dilemmas, man and nature, cognition and reality, individual and society, dignity and death, cannot be overcome with the formula of "dialectics," which, in fact, has a psychological quality, but has never been proven in epistemology, neither by Hegel nor by Lenin nor by Adorno. I am afraid there is no true philosophy beyond Kant.

During the "Silver Age" of Russian literature, when all "progressive," i.e., fatally reactionary radical writers followed in the footsteps of Mikhailovsky or Plekhanov, and spoke about the decadence of bourgeois culture, Bogdanov's creed opened new perspectives: no more the magic circle of aestheticism, but the new proletarian approach to a *Weltanschauung*, that claimed to be technical and all-powerful, and yet could be taught to people who, in their youth, had not been overburdened with the relics of a decaying religious idealistic education. The fact that in our times political power means first of all disposition of the means of technical and economic management, has, as far as I can see, not been adequately understood by Marxist theory, because Marx himself was not able or willing to accept the impact of technology on the conditions, not only of bourgeois society, but of any society.

The moral aspect of Bogdanov's program was of primary importance: "*sobiranie cheloveka*," a new consensus of the working man in his collective. Revolution not only depended on the crisis of the contemporary economy, but at least as much on a certain ethical and cultural level among the proletarians. "The process of organization consists in the adaptation of one life process to another." As the models for an organized society are to be derived from modern industrial production, those closest to the processes, i.e., the workers, were more capable than members of other classes to realize this collectivist society. But the question remained open: how could a universal theory of organization, which implies all scientific progress attained in the past and which opens the perspective for a unified planned evolution of the world towards a new and ultimate reunion of collectivized man and nature, be at the same time within the reach of the average man, the average worker, studying at a future workers' university?

The process of a more of less spontaneous collectivization was found to be not only an intellectual one, i.e., taught in schools, and publicized in books, but concerned the individual as such, in order to break down the fences between man and man and the disparity of the psyche and the physical. Therein lies the importance of art.

Art organizes the social experience through living pictures, not only in the sphere of knowledge, but also in the sphere of feelings and desire. Therefore, art is the most powerful instrument of the organization of collective forces. In a class society art is the instrument of the class forces.

The spirit of proletarian class art is labor collectivism (*rabochii kollektivizm*) and expresses its feelings and its fighting creative will. The treasures of ancient art must not be adopted passively, otherwise they would educate the working class in the spirit of the culture of the old ruling classes and thus "submit them to their old form of life." "Art" means not only the fine arts, but all means of cultural manifestation in a spirit of collectivity.

V

The October revolution found the Bolsheviks in a situation which they had to face almost unprepared. Lenin knew how to deal with rival parties or groups, but the problems of administration and economy in the future society had never been fully discussed. The vague hints in *State and Revolution* made clear that power should be kept firmly in the Party's hand and not be shared with any-body—but that was above all. No plan existed for how to educate or what to teach people in a revolutionized country. Though Lenin himself had an attachment to Russian classical literature and to a certain extent to romantic music, he did not care much for contemporary culture, as such. His approach to "civilization" was pragmatic, and the word meant for him first of all, teaching the masses how to read and write.

Bogdanov stayed outside the Party and never asked for readmission under Lenin's leadership. But other Bolsheviks, though they had not been among Lenin's close followers, were accepted back in the party; for example, Lunacharsky. Some of them rose quickly to prominence, as the reservoir of outstanding intellectuals within the Party was limited. The "Proletarian organization for political enlightenment" was already founded in the summer of 1917, first in Petrograd. *Proletkult* found a powerful protector in Lunacharsky, the People's Commissar of Education. At the time of the October takeover general opinion prevailed that the new society was to be built by all progressive social forces, the powerful allies of the party. The autonomous growth of *Proletkult* outside Party control, but with public funds, corresponded to the quick development of other mass organizations, such as trade unions, cooperatives, etc. Because many of the leaders of the mass organizations were members of the Bolshevik party and, as during the struggle over Brest, strict party discipline was enforced, these organizations were put step by step under Party control. The logic of history during the first months or years of Bolshevik rule seemed to prove the truth of Lenin's concept of strict centralism as the only chance for survival.

Lunacharsky insisted on the autonomy of *Proletkult* and preferred in the first months of 1919 to slightly veil his own position when reporting to Lenin. He probably felt how useful any independent platform or lobby might be during fights in an indefinite future after Lenin's death. Among the ideologists of *Proletkult* there were quite a few ardent followers of Bogdanov who were aware of the importance of the task and who believed with Bogdanov that his organizational theory might be the guarantee for the evolution of autonomous proletarian culture and research. Since the French Revolution every age of upheaval was greeted with the hope for a new, all-embracing ideology and knowledge, altogether different from what had been taught and professed up to that point, i.e., a cultural revolution. But the great expectations did not materialize. Not only is man more likely to forget his collectivist idealism after a certain period of greyish everyday life, but the revolutionary contempt towards the cultural heritages of the past as well does not bear fruits.

The achievements of *Proletkult* in the different fields of art were interesting in their beginnings, but on the whole not too impressive. In lyrical poetry, machines and their beauty were praised in naive, but sincere and pathetic works.

Agitteatr, the political theater of and for the masses, which commemorated the revolution and incited the fight against the class enemies, proved to be important for future theater practice. But in the long run *Proletkult* proved unable to develop new forms of spontaneous self-education for the masses. Its activities in the smaller branches outside the capitals corresponded to such social events as before the war in the people's meeting halls. Though some eminent writers, for example, Bely and Esenin, took part in literary evenings where poems of work- ers were read and discussed, the intellectual movement of the revolutionary age had ties with *Proletkult* as such. Its orthodox followers defended the taste and prejudices of the artistically inexperienced masses and firmly took their stand against more complicated phenomena of contemporary art. This explains the continuous polemics against futurism in *Proletkult's* papers, while the futurists claimed that "revolutionary futurist art is the only collectivist one." The distrust of the true writer's intelligentsia and their tutors against everything not in line of a pathetic socialist realism caused an early exodus of most of the better *Pro- letkult* writers into a new group called Kuznica. So *Proletkult* died to a large extent a natural death; art cannot live when judged exclusively through its im- maculate class origin and orthodox class character.

VI

The first all-Russian Congress of *Proletkult* in September 1918 saw Bogdanov and Krupskaia as the main speakers. The line between proletarian and bourgeois education and science was drawn. Proletarian education would serve the organi- zation of working collective, astronomy had to become the science for preparing work in the universe. Technical experience, organizational intelligence and the courage for new syntheses were supposed to be closer to a proletarian mind than to any other. The workers were to study the necessary means of knowledge in "proletarian universities," the children were to be taught in "workers' schools" how to take part in the working process and how to organize it. Through organ- ized labor each member of the collective adheres voluntarily to the necessary discipline, as each worker's duties are fully understood and thus autonomously fulfilled. At this occasion Faust, who found the way to an active life at the end, was mentioned as one of the great heroes of proletarian poetry; his individual experience caused his false consciousness, but he was on the right path.

Lenin sent his best wishes to the congress, and seemed to expect the new organization to fulfill the duties of elementary mass education. But already, in March 1919, Lenin had become suspicious, when at a congress a resolution for fusion of *Proletkult* with the People's Commissariat was turned down. A few weeks later, Lenin again raised hell against "absurdities" which certain "de- fectors from the bourgeois intelligentsia" tried to impose upon the proletariat under "the disguise of true proletarian art." At the same time Lenin demanded, that "no parallel organizations should be created and that only one planned organization should exist." *Proletkult* proved more resistant to party intimidations than expected. In October 1920, Lenin sent Lunacharsky to another all-Russian *Proletkult* Congress, to ask for its immediate subordination under the People's Commissariat. Lunacharsky avoided a clash, so that a furious Lenin had to draft a resolution on *Proletkult* which he submitted the same day to the Central Committee. In the first draft of this resolution, Lenin demanded: "Not invention of a proletarian culture, but only a development of the best traditions and achievements of the existing culture from the viewpoint of Marxist ideology. 2. *Proletkult* should not be separated from the People's Commissariat, but shall become a part of it, or: party plus commissariat equals the total of *Proletkult*."

The final resolution of the Central Committee asserted that only under Kerensky's regime would an independent *Proletkult* have been acceptable. Now "petty bourgeois elements flocked into *Proletkult*, Futurists, Decadents, followers of an idealist philosophy, who were antagonistic to Marxism, or just good-for-nothings who talked the workers into bourgeois philosophical ideas (Machism); in art workers have been indoctrinated to appreciate perverse taste (Futurism)."

Late in the fall of 1920, during the debate over the trade unions and the workers' opposition, time had come for incorporating *Proletkult*. Lenin's first draft makes the political motives quite clear. During the revolution he had not cared much for Bogdanov and had not read his more recent books at the date of the reissue of *Materialism and Empirio-criticism*. Still he expected an independent factor to emerge somewhere underground. In the resolution we find some slander—*Proletkult* was deliberately identified with its archenemy, Futurism. But the main addressee was Bogdanov the "idealist philosopher." Bogdanov had retired from the executive committee of *Proletkult*. But his ideas did not disappear, and he succeeded as late as in 1924 in publishing a volume of his essays on proletarian culture. The story of the decay of *Proletkult* is of little interest. This attempt had had its day, but it was based on unreal, artificial assumptions. Besides, some parts of its initial theories about the importance of artistic design in industry, had in the meantime been taken up by the People's Commissariat. The "Proletarian Universities" were closed earlier under the pretext of the mobilization of all available proletarian manpower for the civil war, despite the protest of the students, but it was said that the Party's Communist universities served the purpose of proletarian and political education far better.

VII

The idea of a proletarian culture found in these years a rather original technical application. One of the most prominent "machine-poets" of *Proletkult*, A.K. Gastev, developed his concept of a most rational organization of labor, which owed much to Taylor but drew for its theoretical background heavily on Bogdanov. Organization of labor implied rationalization of the working process, though the idea meant more, i.e., liberation of the worker through self-determination. Indeed technical rationalization, at least at the time of Taylor, had some ambivalent implications, such as more intensive exploitation of the worker in an elaborate system of Machinery. Planning and planned economy were the means of implementing "organizational" principles into the building of socialism under difficult conditions. In a vast and underdeveloped country like Russia electricity seemed to be the best instrument for fast development of the national economy and, concurrently, development of a new social consciousness. Huge high tension supply networks should bring light and enlightenment even to the remotest places, expel superstition, and religion, and ease the peasant's hard labor. I quote from a contribution in one of *Proletkult's* papers of November 1919: "The highest mathematization (*matematizatsiia*) of economy will step by step liberate man from the yoke and depravation of a monotonous specialized manual work and thus prepare the abolition of the division of labor."

Gastev, a locksmith by training, opened in the fall of 1920 the Central Labor Institute (*Tsentral'nyi institut truda*), a more or less illegitimate child of Bogdanov's theory of organization (*organizatsionnaiia nauka*) which he had fully developed in these years. Gastev started with violent polemics against Bogdanov, while he traced the new type of proletarian in a scientifically industrialized industry (*nauenno postroennaia industriia*).

This type was characterized through a high degree of his mechanization of work, its normalization (*normalizovannost'*), through the objective character of his work, with no personal emotion, as well as through its precision . . . We not only face a mechanized individual worker, but also a mechanized system of work management (*trudovoe upravlenie*). No individual, no authority, but a type group (*"tip" gruppa*) manages other "types" . . . or a machine manages living people. . . . The mechanization (*massinirovanie*) of everyday thought (*mychlenie*), together with a high degree of objectivism, normalizes (*normaliziruet*) the psychology of the proletariat. . . . This tendency creates a strong tendency towards anonymity in proletarian psychology, which makes it possible to qualify a proletarian unity with A, B, C, . . . which tendency unconsciously makes individual thinking impossible and transforms it into the objective psychology of a class. It uncovers the new workers' collectivism, which makes itself felt not only in the relation of one human being to another, but in the relation of unified groups of people to unified groups of machines. . . . These phenomena of a mechanized collectivism are far from being personal. They are anonymous, so that the movements of these collective complexes come close to movements of matter. Apparently without any human face . . . with normalized steps, their faces without expression, without soul, without poetry and emotion, without cry or laughter, but with a manometer or taxometer.

Bogdanov tried to refute this vision of human machines, but he could not leave the magic circle created by his image of a collective *homo oeconomicus*. So he praised a "comrade-like collaboration" of the workers and distinguished between the creative engineer or manager, who develops new methods of production, and "the anonymous and spontaneous collective." The idea of the proletariat as the organizing force of the future machine age implied unified progressive will of the group or class; so the workers' collective turned out to become something like a superman. Gastev was no deserter from the ideology of proletarian culture. Full collectivization and organization of the human intelligence and will seemed in fact to give a chance for overcoming the division of labor and so gave a rather absurd answer to Marx' question in his *Critique*, which he had left open.

Gastev's institute busied itself during the twenties with the fight against inefficiency and unpunctuality in plants (*Liga vremeni*). Its experiments on the most rational way of swinging a hammer, etc., must have been quite a nuisance for the workers. Lenin pretended that Taylor's norm system would not be resented by the workers in a socialist society, but these standards, though it might not have been possible to avoid them, remain a serious argument against the slogan of spontaneous "comrade-like collectivism." Lenin said that the chance for realization of socialism depends on our achievements in combining Soviet power and Soviet organization with the most recent progress of capitalism.

VIII

In recent years, with the adaptation of cybernetics by Soviet scientific and political authorities, the question arose of whether this new science should be called cybernetics or, as before, theory of management (*nauka ob upravlenii*). This could have been the day of Bogdanov's at least partial resurrection. But Lenin's verdict has not lost its power. A Soviet authority in this field is Bogolepov, head of the section for theoretical problems of organization in the scientific council on the complex problems of cybernetics at the presidency of the Soviet Academy of Sciences. He quoted Bogdanov, who had been in some respects more farsighted than Wiener, as having predicted some of the foundation of this new science. Nevertheless, he said, Bogdanov was basically wrong: "organization is neither the essence of nature, nor an end in itself." The basis of all being is said to be formed through the self-movement of matter (*samodvizhenie materii*).

When applied to society, it is based on certain given social-economic laws, the character and the transformations which decide the whole complex of the history of humanity as well as the organization of its collectives in every stage of historical evolution. . . . The social activities of man are said to have an objective and a subjective aspect. The first concerns the impact of collective man on his objects of work. The subjective aspect consists in a socialist society in a methodical, god-oriented (*tselenapravlennoe*) creation of individual and material creative elements, which as to their effectivity, economy and safety, would be the best.

Bogdanov, during his lifetime, refrained from "materialist metaphysics," but spoke about highly formalized structures and their interrelations. At least to a layman's understanding, his approach is exactly the method of cybernetics, based on applied mathematics. Bogolepov proclaims a "Soviet theory of organization," as each phase of social evolution is said to have its specific momentum in the field of organization, all problems of organization should first of all be studied under the aspect of their adaptability to the social-economic system of socialism and communism. This seems to me a teleological superstructure, which does not affect the utility of Bogdanov's organizational theory (*organizatsionnaia nauka*). Its stringency has been doubted, but it can only be replaced by a better universal and formalized theory. Bogolepov's quest is for authorities, i.e., Lenin, and not for evidence; he is then a true follower of Lenin himself, who fought against Bogdanov with quotations from Engels, without references to experimental evidence, a step back to the pre-Galilean age. It is fairly certain that Soviet scholars in the field of cybernetics and related topics will not care much for Bogolepov's assumption or quest for a Soviet "*organizatsionnaia nauka*" or "Kibernetika." A Soviet scholar called the situation in contemporary Soviet theory of knowledge "polytheism," but still a biographical momentum, i.e., Lenin's fight with Bogdanov for the leadership in the party sixty years ago blocks free discussions on modern theories of knowledge, at least in public opinion, up to our own time. Intellectual history is said to have ended with Lenin. But if his authority would be questioned, the remnants of the moral basis for Party rule would fall asunder. So all of Lenin's verdicts have to be valid for an indefinite time.

IX

Speaking of man in a Communist society, two more aspects have already been touched upon that had been discussed again and again by the Russian intelligentsia since Chernyshevsky's time and were taken up by Bogdanov and some of his followers. The conquest of space and the immortality of man in a harmonized collective have since Fedorov, and quite independently, been treated by Bogdanov in his two utopian pieces of fiction, *The Red Star* (1908) and *Engineer Menni* (1913). In one of his early writings, Bogdanov had sketched "utopism" as the characteristic feature of a special type of psychic development: "strict consequence of thought and will, inflexible activity in the life struggle. This is the type of Jew, as sketched by Heine." In Russian history Bogdanov sees it in Avvakum and his "gigantic Power of an iron will." So "utopia" is not a void to be filled through arbitrary or undeterminate imagination, but a specific medium of perception, not a game, with some ironical intention.

The Red Star is Mars; an inhabitant of the Earth is given the chance to study the fully organized Martian society. Here production is socialized, because on a high stage of technically developed production, the specialization of the workers has through effective education been overcome. But the main feature of socialism is the fully effective organization of production: a central statistical mechanism registers and controls all production processes and distribution. Though everybody is fully free in the choice of his place of work, the necessary statistical balance is achieved for all available workers voluntarily, through continuous information about the production situation, rush to the plants to meet the deficits. In socialist society man is not free through "intelligence into necessity," i.e., obedience to a leadership, but freedom is real through statistical balance, i.e., full electronic control of production, which makes the change from one work to another necessary and voluntary. The people of Mars are continuously exchanging their blood and thus extending their lives almost indefinitely, so that death is in the end voluntary. Birth control is forbidden, because the energy of the society is decreasing with the diminution of the population; the problem of feeding the masses is solved through protein synthesis.

Engineer Menni describes the first attempts of the Martians to find the way from Martian capitalism to Martian socialism. In the last phase of capitalism the canals of Mars were built, which together with the adjoining woods can be seen from Earth. During the construction of the canals there were rumors of corruption and crime. The Martian proletariat was unable to check these irregularities because they did not have the specialized knowledge needed and so the son of the canal builder Menni demanded the remodeling of contemporary knowledge:

Each branch of contemporary science has its own language, a privilege for the initiated, a setback for the rest. Science has separated itself from life, it has ceased to know its destination, therefore all the fictitious problems in modern science and the detours in simple questions. . . . Science like it is today, does not fit for the working class, because it is difficult and defective. The working class seize it in order to transform it.

A group of Martian "cultural revolutionists" develop in collective work a "general theory of organization," i.e., just the problem which kept Bogdanov busy at the same time (1912).

The story of science fiction in Russia before and after the revolution has not yet been written. Its impact on public opinion and popular imagination was and, as I see, is still quite different from the West, i.e., a medium of perception. So there remains in a Leninist Russia always something latently Bogdanovian. In Soviet Russia a closer look reveals almost everything is different from what one expects. There exists not only an eminent religious subculture but also the tradition of cosmic and cosmologic speculation seems to persist up to today. Fedorov had his adherents, and with them the idea or the hope for an immortal superman. There have been Fedorovian programs even in the orthodox church in the twenties and thirties at least. Publicity as in the West kills esoteric thought, public opinion is shocked if something shows up which is not its line and a really serious challenge; Ezra Pound, for example, was treated worse by the West than Solzhenitsyn was by the East. It may be that intellectual life is best when working in secret in an age of repression. I think that Bogdanov's problems are for serious atheists some of the few that matter; so because of a Hegelian stratagem of reason (*List der Vernunft*) the unlucky "cultural revolutionary" is still alive.

References

Alexander Bogdanov, *Empiriomonizm* (1906), II-III.

——, *Filosofiia zhivogo opyta* (1913).

——, *Krasnaia zvezda* (Leningrad, 1928).

——, *Allgemeine Organisationslehre* (Berlin, 1926), I (German edition of *Vseobshchaia organizatsionnaia nauka*, 2nd ed., I).

——, *O proletarskoi kul'ture* (Leningrad, 1924).

D. Geyer, "Arbeiterbewegung und 'Kulturrevolution' in Russland 1917-1922," *Vierteljahreshefte für Zeitgeschichte* (1962), pp. 43-55.

D. Grille, *Lenins Rivale* (Köln, 1966). (The first biography of Bogdanov up to 1918, with an almost complete bibliography of Bogdanov's writings.)

Gudki, *Ezhenedel'nik Moskovskogo Proletkul'ta* (1919), Issues 1-6.

Iskusstvo v Proizvodsteve, *Sborniki Khudozhestvenno-proizvodstvennogo soveta otdela izobrazitel'nykh iskusstv Narkomprosa* (1921), I.

V.I. Lenin, *Sochineniia*, 5th ed.

Leninskii sbornik.

R. Lornez, U. Brügmann, G. Meyer, eds., *Proletarische Kulturrevolution in Sowjetrussland 1917-1921. Dokumente des Proletkult* (Munich, 1929).

V.L. L'vov· Rogachevskii, *Ocherki proletarskoi literatury* (Moscow-Leningrad, 1926).

Karl Marx, *Werke, Schriften, Briefe*, ed., H.J. Lieber.

A. Men'shutin, A. Siniavskii, *Poesiia pervych let revoliutsii 1917-1920* (Moscow, 1964).

Organizatsiia i upravlenie (Voprosy teorii i praktiki) (Moscow, 1968).

Proletarskaia kultura. Organ tsentra'nogo komiteta Vserossiiskogo Soveta Proletkul'ta (Moscow, 1918-1921), Issues 1-21/21.

P. Scheibert, "Die Besiegung des Todes. Ein theologisches Program aus der Sowjetunion." *Glaube-Geist-Geschichte, Festschrift Ernst Benz* (Leiden, 1967), pp. 431-447.

——, "Revolution und Utopie.—Die Gestalt der Zukunft in Denken der russischen revolutionären Intelligenz," *Epirrhosis, Festgabe für Carl Schmitt* (Berlin, 1968), pp. 633-650.

K.L. Seemann, "Der Versuch einer proletarischen Kulturrevolution in Russland 1917-1922," *Jahrbucher für Geschichte Osteuropas* (1962) IX, 179-222.

Sovetskoe iskusstvo za 15 let. Materaly i dokumentatsiia. (Moscow-Leningrad, 1923).

4

Between Fantasy and Reality: Lenin as a Philosopher and a Social Scientist

LEWIS S. FEUER

" 'We ought to dream!' I wrote these words and got scared," Lenin said in his famous factional pamphlet *What Is to Be Done?* published in 1902. He dreamed of a centralized revolutionary organization in which "Social-Democratic Zheliabovs" would emerge; then he would dare say, a socialist Archimedes moving the social universe with an organizational lever: " 'Give us an organization of revolutionists, and we shall overturn the whole of Russia!' "[1] But inevitably, he wondered whether "a Marxist has any right at all to dream." Was his dream a fantasy like that which had moved Zheliabov to assassinate a czar? Was he enthralled by an illusion that a few bold revolutionists could open the way to a remaking of society and humanity? Was his choice of Zheliabov as a hero-model one which indicated Lenin's own fear that in his dream he was losing his hold on reality? He pondered what the connection between dream and reality should be, and this problem never left him all his life. He wrote that he would conceal himself "behind the back of Pisarev: 'There are differences and differences,' wrote Pisarev concerning the question of the difference between dreams and reality. 'My dream may run ahead of the natural progress of events or may fly off at a tangent in a direction to which no natural progress of events will ever succeed. . . . Divergence between dreams and reality causes no harm if only the person dreaming believes seriously in his dream, . . . and if, generally speaking, he works conscientiously for the achievement of his fantasies. If there is some connection between dreams and life then all is well!' "[2]

More than a decade later, living in exile in Switzerland, with the world at war, his own movement shattered, Lenin was moved to think again: had fantasy penetrated his Marxist science? He immersed himself in the study of Hegelian texts and classical philosophy, seeking an answer to his life-problem. Then he confided boldly to his notebook that all human thought partakes of fantasy:

The approach of the (human) mind to be a particular thing, the taking of a copy (equal a concept) of it *is not* a simple, immediate act, a dead mirroring, but one which is complex, split into two, zig-zag-like, which *includes in it* the possibility of the flight of fantasy from life; more than that: the possibility of the *transformation* (moreover, an unnoticeable transformation, of which man is unaware) of the abstract concept, idea, into a *fantasy* (in letzter Instanz equal God). For even the simplest generalisation, in the most elementary general idea ('table' in general) *there is* a certain bit of fantasy. (Vice versa: it would be stupid to deny the role of fantasy, even in the strictest science: *cf.* Pisarev on useful dreaming, as an impulse *to* work, and on empty day-dreaming).[3]

This tension between fantasy and reality is probably the underlying theme of Lenin's work as a philosopher as well as his approach to social science. A man's philosophy and methodology are the outcome of his deepest strivings and anxieties. Lenin, as we shall see, in his lifetime alternated between two philosophies. At the outset, he endeavored to cling fast to reality; he was a simple materialist, ridiculing the dialectic of Hegel as virtual nonsense, and so hardheaded toward the sentimental "flabby" intellectuals that he reveled in the prospect of an authoritarian bureaucracy. When he brooded in solitary retreat during the First World War, however, he thrust reality away from him and allowed himself to yield to the solace of Utopian fantasy. Then he wrote that he was the only Marxist alive; he professed to find a master key to existence in the Hegelian triads; he saw the apocalyptic end of imperialism as a chapter in human history, and the virtual end of all bureaucracy within twenty-four hours after the triumph of the revolution. The materialist and social factualist became the metaphysician and Utopian. This oscillation between extremes remains embedded in Lenin's legacy to the intellectual life of the Soviet Union.

Lenin's first philosophical writing was part of his first book, published in 1894, entitled *What the "Friends of the People" Are and How They Fight the Social Democrats*. Like all his writing, it was polemical in character; Lenin was never impelled to study a subject for love of it; it was all part of a fight. In this case, Lenin was replying especially to the distinguished thinker of the elder generation, Nikolai Mikhailovsky, who had criticized the so-called dialectical method of Marx and Engels. What Lenin did was to reject dialectical materialism in favor of "scientific materialism." At the age of twenty-four, as a young revolutionary agitator, Lenin found the dialectic a lot of residual verbal nonsense. Anyone who reads the description of the dialectical method given by Marx in *Capital*, he wrote, "will see that the Hegelian triads are not even mentioned, and that it all amounts to regarding social evolution as the development of social-economic formations as a process of natural history." When Marx described what he meant by the dialectical method, asked Lenin, was there "even a single word, about triads, trichotomies, the unimpeachableness of the dialectical process, and suchlike nonsense, . . . ?" In effect, says Lenin, Marx's use of the word "dialectic" had become vestigial. "No other role remains for the triads than as a lid and a skin ('I coquetted with the modes of expression peculiar to Hegel,' Marx says in the Preface), in which only philistines could be interested." To coquette with phrases is scarcely the mark of a serious passion, even a philosophical one. Marx derived his prediction of the downfall of the capitalist order from a study of its facts and trends, not from triadic formulae, says Lenin, and what he coquettishly called the dialectical method was "nothing more nor less than the scientific method in sociology, . . . "[4]

This then was Lenin at the outset of his career, a self-confident scientific materialist, a believer in a complete "determinism, which establishes the necessity of human acts and rejects the absurd fable about free will,"[5] ridiculing the "subjective method" in sociology, rejecting any notion that psychological variables, intellectual, sexual, have any independent causal efficacy in history. The ensuing years brought a bitter party factionalism; the choice of comrades for Lenin was translated into a rejection of comrades. Peter Struve, Julius Martov, George Plekhanov; towards all of them Lenin had a strong emotional attachment, so emotional that he would be embarrassed by his own feelings. And toward all of them he disciplined himself in accordance with his avowal of the primacy of politics for a rupture of relations, disciplining himself to transmute love into hatred. It was as if Lenin had a compulsive need to turn this weakness of his into a hatred, to harden himself. When he broke with the father of Russian Marxism, George Plekhanov, whom he revered, he wrote a document which was poignant in the agony of its self-revelation:

We walked, bursting with indignation. . . . His (Plekhanov's) behavior was insulting to such a degree that one could not help suspecting him of harboring 'unclean' thoughts about ourselves. . . . He tramples us underfoot, etc. . . . My 'infatuation' with Plekhanov disappeared as if by magic, and I felt offended and embittered to the highest degree. Never, never in my life, have I regarded any other man with such sincere respect and veneration. I have never stood before any man with such 'humility' as I stood before him, and never before have I been so brutally 'spurned'. We were actually spurned. We were scared like little children when grown-ups threaten to leave them, and when we funked (shame!) we were unceremoniously brushed aside in the most incredible manner.[6]

Such mixed, heavy, confused feelings. It was a real drama; the complete abandonment of a thing which for years we had tended like a favorite child. . . . And all because we were formerly enamoured with Plekanov. . . .Young comrades 'court' an old comrade out of the great love they bear for him—and suddenly he injects into this love an atmosphere of intrigue! He compels us to feel not as younger brothers, but as fools to be led by the nose, pawns to be moved at will. . . . An enamoured youth receives from the object of his love a bitter lesson: To regard all persons 'without sentiment'; to keep a stone in one's sling. Many more thoughts of an equally bitter nature did we give utterance to that night. . . . Blinded by our love, we had actually behaved like *slaves*. To be a slave is humiliating, and the sense of shame we felt was magnified a hundredfold by the fact that 'he himself had forced us to realize how humiliating our position was.'[7]

Is it I, the fervent worshipper of Plekhanov, who am now filled with bitter thoughts about him? Is it I, with clenched teeth, and a devilish chill at the heart, hurling cold and bitter words at him in announcing what is almost our 'breaking off of relations'? Perhaps it is only an ugly dream?

Indeed, so profoundly moved was I that at times I thought I would burst into tears . . .[8] On the surface everything appeared as if nothing had happened; the apparatus must continue to work as it worked before. But we felt an internal twinge—instead of friendly relations, dry, business-like relations prevailed, we were always to be on guard, on the principle: *Si vis pacem, para bellum*.[9]

II

Statesmen—Balfour, Smuts, Clemenceau—have not infrequently written philosophical works, but invariably they have been written as postpolitical reflections on the meaning of things. Lenin is the only man in history who wrote an epistemological book as part of his tactical plan to defeat another faction within his party. The book has one thesis, that materialism, defined as the belief in the reality of the external physical world, is the only ideology to which a true revolutionist, scientist, or man of common sense can subscribe. Sometimes he confuses this meaning of materialism as physical realism with materialism in two other senses, one, the notion that "nature is the sole reality," that supernatural entities don't exist, and the other, an evolutionary sense, in which materialism means that physical entities preceded the existence of mental ones. The villains of Lenin's book are the philosophical idealists and their ilk, from Bishop Berkeley to the physicist Ernst Mach, who dare to affirm that we can meaningfully speak only of observable elements. The book has more invective per page than any work written in the history of philosophy, and indeed, if one were to ask what its philosophical method was, we might say: usually the method of invective. Nonetheless, Bertrand Russell wrote a comparatively benign estimate of it, in 1934, to be sure, at a time during the depression when he was more sympathetic to Bolshevism.

While I do not think that materialism can be *proved*, I think Lenin is right in saying that it is not *dis*proved by modern physics. Since his time, and largely as a reaction against his success, respectable physicists have moved further and further from materialism, and it is naturally supposed, by themselves and by the general public, that it is physics which has caused this movement. I agree with Lenin that no substantially new argument has emerged since the time of Berkeley, with one exception.[10]

This one exception Russell oddly enough found in the instrumentalist theory, which he attributed to Marx, that "truth" is a practical rather than a theoretical conception.

How shall we appraise Lenin's argument, and why was it that any departure from materialism struck him as a deviation and heresy, making its proponent a fit candidate for excommunication?

Lenin himself acknowledges: "by no proofs, or syllogisms, or definitions would it be possible to refute the solipsist."[11] Then what shall be done with the person who says with Fichte: "the world is my sensation" (or with Wittgenstein in our time: "I am my world")? "Any healthy person," writes Lenin, "who is not an inmate of an insane asylum, or in the school of idealist philosophers" holds to " 'naive realism'," a belief which "consists in this, that he believes reality, the environment and the things in it, to exist independently of his perception."[12] The mental health, the sanity of the party, seem to Lenin to be at stake with the philosophical issue of materialism, "a problem concerning the confidence of man in the evidence of his sense-organs." Materialism, he insists, is "the instinctive viewpoint held by humanity which accepts the existence of the outer world independently of the mind."[13] Those philosophies which purport to explicate a nonspatial, nontemporal existence are "products of a diseased mind." Nor will Lenin admit of any departure from the definition of truth as correspondence to fact. He is impatient with empiricists and pragmatists who speak of truth as an "organizing form of human experience," or who try to translate "the objective character of the physical world" as its "intersubjectively verified" status.[14] For, says Lenin, there are all sorts of ways for organizing human experience; every culture, as we would say, is a socially endorsed form for organizing human experience. And for the majority of mankind, Lenin observes, "house goblins and wood demons" are part of a "socially organized experience"; if so, then to say they exist is "truth," if all "truth" means is its employment to organize human experience.[15]

What perturbs Lenin is that every definition of truth, other than as simple correspondence to fact, somehow loosens man's hold on reality. Every other definition refuses to acknowledge that the person does really get to know something about the existent world; every other definition concedes that the world given to us in perception may still be a phantom, a stage-play, an illusion. Every other definition of truth, by its very departure from the criterion of correspondence, introduces into itself an "alienation" of man from reality, as the current phrase goes. As Lenin states it, the idealist philosopher takes sensation not as a connection with the external world "but as a screen, as a wall which separates the mind from the outer world."[16] The empiricists, Lenin protests, "do not sufficiently trust the evidence of our sense-organs." The Kantians likewise say, "that the thing exists in itself, but is unknowable." And the final test of the "absurdity" of a philosophy is that it leads one toward solipsism, toward the view that "the world is my sensation."[17]

Lenin expounds what philosophers call a "copy theory of knowledge"; "sensations," he writes, are "the true copy of the objective world." A sound scientific theory, he holds, is "a copy, as an approximate reflection of objective reality." Scientific truth is founded on "a reality which is copied, photographed, and reflected by our sensations."[18] Among revisionist Marxists today, especially the group of young Yugoslav philosophers associated with the magazine *Praxis*, Lenin's theory of sensation has been especially under attack. It is charged that Lenin's view that sensation provides a reflection of reality is the epistemological source of Stalinism. Lenin did, of course, insist that "human practice," which had eventuated in man's domination over nature, "is a result of an accurate objective 'reflection' within the mind of man."[19] Although the science of any given historical period is only a relative approximation to the truth, still, said Lenin, each approximation does incorporate more of that absolute truth: "but it is unconditionally true that this picture reflects an objectively existing model."

The revisionist Marxists, however, seem to me to have fallen into the Leninist fallacy in reverse; their argument that Lenin's theory of reflection is the foundation for Stalinism seems to me to be based on misconceptions concerning the relation of philosophy to politics. The *Praxis* philosophers argue that Stalinism was founded on the notion that the correct theory in social science was a "reflection" of the inevitable line of development; therefore, it would be sound practice to compel everybody to follow that line of development; the Communist party, as scientific Marxists, would enunciate the correct line. Instead, say the *Praxis* philosophers, there are alternative lines of possible development, and the decision as to which will be actualized rests on the involvement, the engagement, of human actors who make their own history. The "truth" is not a "reflection" of a preexistent or predetermined reality but rather something which is created in human decision which shapes, constructs, and reconstructs reality rather than "reflects" it.

We might undertake to reply to the revisionists on Lenin's behalf. We would say: the revisionists are not really discussing the definition of truth; they are arguing against sociological determinism. The revisionists are arguing that the basic laws of sociology do not have a determinist form but that rather they are characterized, as far as predictable outcomes of systems are concerned, by domains of indeterminacy; hence, the initial states of a given social system, together with the laws of social science, never provide one with both the necessary and sufficient conditions of the emergent social state; the unpredictable role of human involvement and choice among indeterminate alternatives must be taken into account.

Let us assume that this revisionist standpoint is true. Still, it will be clear that it in no way challenges Lenin's conception of truth as correspondence to fact, or sensation as reflection of external reality. For the objective truth will now be regarded as stated by laws which provide for indeterminate domains; a principle of sociological indeterminacy will be the objective truth rather than sociological determinism. In either case, we shall be accepting as our criterion for scientific decision the crucial status of sensations as "reflecting" the objective state of things. The sociological indeterminist defends his standpoint just as much as the determinist by appealing to perceptions as reports or reflections of external reality. He avers, for instance, that perceived acts of human intervention are necessary to social outcomes, but he accepts the veracity, at least provisionally, of his perceptions, or sensations. There have been many naive realists who were democrats; and I do not think their democratic politics were inconsistent with their reflectional epistemology. The Yugoslav revisionists, like Lenin, like Stalin, have drawn too close a relationship between philosophy and politics, even though in their case, their concern is with an underpinning for more liberal values; they remain ideologists.

III

What strikes the reader as strange is the vehemence which possesses Lenin when he discusses this issue of the reality of the external world. He avails himself of Russian literary resources to ridicule the empiricists—Valentinov is like Gogol's *Petrushka*, Chernov is like Voroshilov in Turgenev's *Smoke*, others call forth Gogol's Inspector-General, the philosopher Avenarius is like Turgenev's rascal.[20] For the great philosopher-physicist Ernst Mach, Lenin rises or stoops to the most demagogic invective: "The philosophy of Mach, the scientist, is to science what the kiss of Judas is to Christ. Mach betrays science into the hands of freedom...."[21] It would have been of no avail to point out that Mach was a stubborn anticlerical all his life. But Lenin seems himself as the Christ whom the empiricists are betraying. Nor would it have availed to observe that Mach had been, even before Lenin was born, a pioneer in the advocacy of socialistic reforms. Here was simply for Lenin a most menacing heresy, comparable to that of Judas Iscariot, subtly gnawing away at the heart of his doctrine.

The German Socialists, the French Socialists, the Italian Socialists, the American Socialists, scarcely attached any political importance to philosophical materialism. Jaurès, the great French leader, was drawn to Kantian ethical idealism, as were even such German leftists as Karl Liebknecht and Kurt Eisner. In America, the leftist organ *The International Socialist Review* was enthusiastic for the philosophy of Ernst Mach. And to Mach, the world owes the imperishable debt for the inspiration his philosophy gave to the young student in Zürich, Albert Einstein. For Einstein, partaking much of Machian ideas, especially under the stimulus of his student friend, Friedrich Adler, who was both a Marxist and a Machian, was guided to the critique of absolute space and time as unobservable entities. The theory of relativity was largely conceived under the influence of Machian emotions and a Machian frame of mind, trying to expel from one's physical theory whatever was not translatable into an observer's experiences. To Lenin, however, the philosophy of Ernst Mach signified a veritable threat to his sanity.

Indeed it is such highly personal psychological reasons rather than anything political or sociological which explain why Lenin attached so much importance to his materialism. Often enough, Lenin gave indications that he kept guard over an unstable personality, threatened by the fear of illusion, the fear of a commitment to an unreal world. Lenin's older sister told, for instance, how shaken Lenin was when he read Chekhov's short story *Ward No. 6:* " 'Volodya summed up its effect on him in these words: 'When I finished reading this story last night, I felt positively afraid. I just could not remain in my room but had to get up and go out. I had the feeling that I, too, was locked up in Ward No. 6.' That had happened late at night when we had all gone to our rooms and some were even asleep, and he had nobody to talk to. Those words lifted a veil from his state of mind. . . ."[22] This was in the winter of 1892 in Samara. Chekhov's story was being published in a periodical,[23] and Lenin was writing his first major work, *What the "Friends of the People" Are*; he was already a Marxist, and condescending towards the idealistic Narodniks of the older generation who were his neighbors. And in the midst of his materialistic philosophizing, the veil lifts, and he is filled with anxiety. Chekhov's story tells of an understanding reflective physician, who is in charge of a mental asylum; then through the intrigues of an assistant, he himself is declared insane. He finds himself then at the mercy of the brutal caretaker, Nikita, who beats him cruelly; the sane man has patronized the sadistic forces which misuse him, and declare him insane. He has lived in illusion; death ends his torment and insoluble problems. No wonder Lenin had the feeling that he too was locked in Ward No. 6, this strange prophetic dream was far more accurate than the Utopian declamation of *The State and Revolution*, for in the Soviet society the sane writers today find themselves thrust into insane asylums, a practice Stalin initiated and Nitika continued; thus the Soviet dialectic reached its new high stage, the rational transformed into the irrational.

Seeking to exorcise an inner anxiety of illusion, the fear that perhaps his Marxist learning was an exercise in fantasy, in myth, Lenin responded with an over-determination of his materialism. Leon Trotsky reports that when he first met Lenin, the latter was indeed drawn to Machian doctrines.[24] But now he exorcised the Machian and the solipsist within himself. He especially polemicized against Dr. A.A. Bogdanov, a disciple of Mach, who together with Lenin had for a few years led the Bolshevik party. But now Bogdanov was leading a faction opposed to Lenin. Bogdanov, a remarkably exploratory and clear-thinking mind, was also given to psychoanalyzing his contemporaries' philosophical divagations. He thus exerted his art on both the idealist Berdyaev, whom Lenin scorned, and on Lenin himself. Whenever Bogdanov would see Berdyaev, the latter tells, he "kept on asking all sorts of odd questions, such as, How did I feel in the morning? How did I sleep? What was my reaction to this or that? It eventually emerged that in his view my philosophical tendencies were evidence of an impending psychic disorder, and he, being by profession a psychiatrist, wanted to discover how far the process had gone."[25] Bogdanov similarly indicated many years later what he thought was the root-source of Lenin's materialism: " 'as a doctor, I concluded that Lenin occasionally suffered from a mental condition and displayed symptoms of abnormality.' "[26]

We might call the fear that one's avowed goals are an illusion the "revolutionary anxiety." Since he is putting himself against the established norms and values of society, the "revolutionary anxiety" arises in moments of doubt; the phrases, the clichés, the programs, the manifestoes, suddenly acquire a hollow ring. The safeguarding of his materialism was a kind of defence mechanism against the revolutionary anxiety. Otherwise Lenin could have reacted mildly against empiricist and solipsist views, regarding them as men of common sense do as rather paradoxical intellectual standpoints, but scarcely looking upon their exponents as Judases, or ideological plotters. Lenin is so eager to confute the scientific standpoint of Ernst Mach that he allows himself to embark upon a polemic against the principle of economy in scientific logic, the principle which advises us to choose the simplest hypothesis among those which conform to the facts. Lenin queries challengingly: wouldn't it then be more "economical" to accept the hypothesis that the atom is indivisible rather than that it is composed of "positive and negative electrons"?[27] Lenin's mistake is evident: he interprets the principle of economy as asserting that the world is simple; the principle does nothing of the sort: it tells you that, no matter how simple or complex the constitution of nature may be, you as a scientist will work with the simplest hypothesis which explains the facts. The hypothesis that the atom is indivisible was dropped not because it was simple but because it couldn't explain the experimental facts which such scientists as J.J. Thomson and Ernest Rutherford had adduced. Lenin's materialist defence mechanism, however, struck out wildly against whatever awakened his revolutionary anxiety. He struck out against the principle of relativity: "Another cause of 'idealistic physics' is the principle of *relativity*, the relativity of science, a principle which in a period of bankruptcy of old theories, imposes itself with special force upon physicists. . . ."[28] No wonder that when Einstein's friend, Friedrich Adler, read Lenin's book, he said all that Lenin had proved, apart from his patient capacity to write a big book, was that he knew nothing about the subject. Einstein himself, in later years, wrote limericks about the stupidities of dialectical materialism. But Lenin's anxiety and defence mechanism was transmitted into the psyches of generations of Soviet students.

Lenin, moreover, as a simple nineteenth-century Russian materialist misconceived the relation of philosophy to the sciences, indeed, we should rather say, the relation of *philosophies* to the sciences. For this relationship is not unlike that between the philosophies and the arts. As Lenin wrote Gorky in 1908: "an artist can draw much that is useful to him from any philosophy."[29] Similarly, different scientists have drawn inspiration in their work, models, analogues and motivations from the most diverse philosophies. In one mood, Einstein drew inspiration and guidance from Mach's empiricism; in another mood, he was doing work in the spirit of a follower of Boltzmann's atomism. Niels Bohr was somehow guided in his philosophy as a scientist, in his principle of complementarity, by a devotion to Kierkegaard and the pluralistic conciliation of his teacher Höffding. Heisenberg drew sustenance from Plato's *Timaeus*. Different philosophies are indications of different themes in the universe; none of them is controlling; and part of the life of science, the source of its vitality, is their unending alternation.

Many pages of Lenin's *Materialism and Empirio-Criticism* are strewn with invective against educators and professors. These reactionaries, he writes, aim "to implant in the high school students the spirit of idealism"; the opponent of materialism is a "police officer in a professorial chair"; "the bourgeois professors have a right to receive their salaries from reactionary governments," because they defend medieval, transcendental absurdities. "Not a single professor," he writes, even the most eminent physicists and chemists, "can be trusted even so far as a single word when it comes to philosophy. . . . [T]he professors of philosophy are scientific salesmen of theology."[30] Why was Lenin's materialism so polemically oriented against these academics? The answer suggests itself in the facts of Lenin's own evolution from religion to materialism. Lenin's father, Ilya Nikolayevich, as Krupskaya tells us, "even though he was a teacher of physics and a meteorologist, believed in God until the end of his life. The fact that his sons had abandoned religion caused him anxiety." When the father complained to a friend "that his children were bad church attenders," the friend suggested: "Give them the stick, don't spare it." "Upon hearing this Ilyich, burning with indignation, decided to break with religion; he rushed into the garden, took off the cross that he wore around his neck, and threw it away." All this happened when Lenin was fourteen or fifteen years old.[31]

From Lenin's standpoint, his father, the teacher of physics, the director of primary schools, the religious believer, was another police officer in the guise of an educator. The curious bitterness against academics seems to have been a recurring reenactment of Lenin's rebellion against his father's authority and religious devotion. Throughout his life he was tearing the cross from around his neck; his materialism always retained the polemical cast because it was for him less a scientific standpoint than the projection of a fixated emotion of generational rebellion.

Lenin's materialism always remained invested with emotions for overcoming feminine, or unmanly, weakness, for proving his toughness. The reactionary professors, he wrote, were succumbing to "the kisses" of the idealists and pragmatists, and were allowing themselves to be "nailed" to a pillory; these were "shameful things"; the professors in advanced capitalist countries were living in "concubinage"; the empiricists entwined all the idealistic weaknesses into a "Chinese braid," this symbol of femininity, which Feuerbach had once cut off. Mach's "elements" were a "fig-leaf" for his idealism; kisses, concubines, fig-leaves, and Chinese braids, such were the metaphors for the emotional determinants of Lenin's materialism.[32]

If Lenin indeed had followed his own suggestions that solipsism and idealism cannot be logically refuted but only psychologically analyzed, he would then have been led as well to examine the psychological basis of his own doctrine. But he could never engage in such self-scrutiny. His notion that philosophies have political consequences would have largely collapsed, for the basis of philosophies lies much more in temperament, as William James saw, than in political affiliation. But just as Lenin shrank from the subjectivist ingredient in sociology, he suppressed the suggestion of its relevance in philosophical decision. For what Lenin would have feared above all was self-knowledge of the unconscious determinants of his own materialistic dogmatism. Then the neurotic anxieties, fears, and cruelties which led to his materialistic over-affirmation would have come to view.

IV

Meanwhile, Lenin struggled with his neurosis. His nerves for years previously used to afflict him with physical inflammations and complete sleeplessness. The later years of emigration were especially hard; comrades became insane and committed suicide. "Another year or two of life in this atmosphere of squabbling and emigrant tragedy would have meant heading for a breakdown," wrote Lenin's wife.[33] Fortunately for his sanity, the years of reaction were followed by revolutionary upsurge. Years earlier, after a series of squabbles which had led to the suicide of a famous student leader, Lenin wrote to his sister: "You'd better not wish any comrades from the intellectuals on me. . . ." "The worst thing about exile is these 'exile episodes.' " He had shaped and fashioned his personality to stamp out affections. "Friendship is friendship and work is work," Lenin would say, "and on this account the necessity for war will not disappear," as he would obliterate a friendship from his life.[34] From the time of his adolescence he regarded Turgenev's short story *Andrei Kolosov* as the last word on love and sincerity. "He felt that Turgenev showed here, absolutely correctly and in a few lines, how to understand properly what is rather pompously called the 'sanctity' of love. He often told me that his views on this question were exactly the same as those expressed by Turgenev in *Andrei Kolosov*. 'These', he used to say, 'are not vulgar bourgeois views on the relations between men and women, but real, revolutionary ones.' "[35] The story deals with a rather cold, calculating young man who without any compunction breaks with a girl who no longer pleases him. Evidently what pleased Lenin in the story was the hero's refusal to allow considerations of personal loyalty to sway him. When he saw Tolstoi's *The Living Corpse*, the rest of the audience sympathized with the character of the deserted wife in the play; Lenin sympathized with the deserting husband, and wanted to see the play again.[36] Lenin tried to emulate such models, but the effort in his case involved terrific emotional strains. Krupskaya, his wife, was, according to Bernard Shaw, one of the two ugliest women in Europe.[37] Lenin evidently could not bring himself to leave her when he loved another woman.[38] But in more trivial matters he could more successfully fashion his character to ideological requirements. He found chess tremendously absorbing, but it impinged on the revolution; he gave it up. Skating, hunting, the study of Latin—all were eliminated from the revolutionist's life.[a] He feared that music might deprive him of his capacity to be ruthless.[39]

---

[a]Lenin, wrote Gorky admiringly in later years, possessed in the highest degree the best qualities of revolutionary intelligentsia, "self-discipline often amounting to self-torture and self-mutilation." He describes how Lenin, after listening to Beethoven's *Appasionata* sonata, said: "But I can't listen to music too often. It affects your nerves, makes you want to say stupid, nice things, and stroke the heads of people . . . And now you mustn't stroke any one's head—you might get your hand bitten off. You have to hit them on the head, without any mercy. . . ." Maxim Gorky, *Days with Lenin* (New York, 1932), pp. 48, 52.

Such was Lenin's project for self-formation, to repress whatever spontaneous impulses and affections seemed inconsistent with the revolutionist's calling. When so much aggression is directed against one's self, the unconscious protests; a perpetual frustration of impulse and emotion always brings in its train a feeling of unreality; life loses its savor, and consists of a rehearsal of assigned lines in a play rather than a spontaneous partaking of life. The vehement reiteration of his materialism as a party tenet was proportional to his own feelings of unreality; he had to assure himself philosophically of an existence which his self-punitive actions were negating into nonexistence.

During the years of the World War, according to his closest coworker at that time, Gregory Zinoviev, Lenin "seemed to have changed even in his appearance." Living in the poorest quarter of Zurich, "in the house of a shoemaker, in a sort of garret, his hatred of the bourgeoisie became sharp like a dagger." "Many, who knew him before," wrote Zinoviev, "were surprised at the change which had taken place in him since the war." The shock of the collapse of the Second International had taken its toll. "The honor of the proletariat demanded that a war against this war be fought to a finish," and the "imperialist bandits" forever destroyed.[40]

V

During the miserable years of exile, the temptation of the total absorption into dreams waxed stronger. Krupskaya tells: "During those very hard years of emigration, concerning which Ilyich always spoke with a feeling of sadness . . . , during those years he dreamed and dreamed," taking heart as a desperate person does from the chance good cheer of others more prosaically miserable, from a French charwoman singing: "Mais votre coeur—vous ne l'ayez jamais," or from a Parisian café singer, with whom one evening he dreamed together of world revolution, or during sleepless nights reading the poems of Verhaeren.[41] When Inessa Armand and her daughter would visit him, Krupskaya narrates, "Ilyich liked to indulge in day-dreaming in their presence."[42] The dream always beckoned to a dialectical logic in which there were qualitative leaps to a reality transfigured. But it was precisely this dialectical logic which could tempt one into a qualitative leap beyond reality to the unreal, to fantasies in which one lost one's last moorings with the physical and social worlds. During the distress and isolation of the World War years, Lenin was converted to *dialectical* materialism.

From the triads and trichotomies which he had ridiculed in 1892 as a young scientific Marxist, Lenin in sombre isolation derived instead now a curious consolation, like an old believer falling back on new readings of sacred texts. He even wrote an "aphorism" in which he exulted in his solitary devotion: "It is impossible completely to understand Marx's *Capital*, and especially its first chapter, without having thoroughly studied and understood the *whole* of Hegel's Logic. Consequently, half a century later none of the Marxists understood

Marx!!"[43] At last he was the ultimate sectarian, the only one in the world in half a century who had divined the master's message; the mantle was his. Marx had in his maturity playfully belittled his coquetterie with Hegelian phrases; for Lenin the coquetterie became a passionate obsession: "Hegel actually *proved* that logical forms and laws are not an empty shell, but the *reflection* of the objective world," he wrote, then perturbed by his own flight to fantasy, he qualified it to "a brilliant guess." He invented more dialectical aphorisms: "*Dialectics* is the teaching which shows how *Opposites* can be and how they happen to be (how they become) *identical.* . . ." It was a Freudian dream world in which negation ceases to exist, the fantasy projected into a "logic" all its own. Without the Hegelian dialectic, the conception of development would be "lifeless, pale and dry"; the dialectic would make it "living," full of "self-movement," with "leaps." The vocabulary of this Hegelian conversion had the peculiar accents of a man of declining virility finding in the Hegelian words a kind of metaphysical restorative. And then he found in the Hegelian idealism itself the ultimate justification of revolution; the subjective will would create its own world, would posit the revolution itself. What was the meaning of "practice in the theory of knowledge"? Lenin said: "Alias: Man's consciousness not only reflects the objective world, but creates it." He indeed now preferred Hegel's theology to Huxley's agnosticism: "this philosophical idealism, openly, 'seriously' leading to God is more honest than modern agnosticism with its hypocrisy and cowardice."[44] He called, in his loneliness, for a metaphysics to sustain his fantasy, to give assurance to his will to revolution. A few years before he had berated Gorky for venturing even to think of God as a class-name for human ethical strivings. "Is not God-building the worst form of self-castigation? Everyone engaged in building *God* . . . *castigates* himself in the worst possible way, because instead of occupying himself with 'deeds' he indulges in self-contemplation." The God-builder was then for Lenin a philosophical masochist of the worst kind. Now however, in 1916, it was the scientific agnostic, with his perpetual demand for evidence, who most aroused Lenin's ire.

VI

It was during the war years, when Lenin's immersion in Hegelian dialectic was deepest, that he wrote the two works of social science for which he is most famous, *Imperialism: The Highest Stage of Capitalism* and *The State and Revolution.* Here the power of fantasy was superimposed on the facts; the fantasy, which Lenin regarded as inherent in every generalization, took possession; dialectic indeed became the logic of projected fantasy. There were no longer realistic studies such as his youthful *The Development of Capitalism in Russia.* Instead, Lenin found himself borne not by scientific prediction but by dialectical prophecy.

Lenin's thesis was imperialism in its economic nature was "moribund capitalism." The "destructive characteristics of imperialism" he wrote "compel us to define it as parasitic or decaying capitalism"; it was capitalism at "its highest historical stage of development," on "the eve of the socialist revolution."[45] Now here was dialectical method at its highest. For imperialism, as historians have documented, has been a universal theme in the world's history. The Egyptians, Babylonians, Assyrians, Greeks, and Romans had their imperialism; feudal Europe had its imperialism in the Crusades; the Arabs had their Moslem imperialism; the nomadic Tartars had their imperial state, while the sea-faring Scandinavians went forth in their Viking imperialism. The French Revolution brought into being a revolutionary imperialism. Far from imperialism today being the last stage of capitalism, it seems today to be a second or third stage of socialism. The Czechs today complain of a Soviet military and economic exploitation, while Fidel Castro charged in 1966 that Communist China was exhibiting toward his country "the worst methods of piracy, oppression, and filibusterism" that had characterized "the imperialist states." He said it all came down to the "fundamental question for the peoples: whether in the world of tomorrow the powerful nations can assume the right to blackmail, extort, pressure, attack, and strangle small peoples. . . ."[46]

Lenin, of course, was well aware that imperialism had been a recurrent, cross-systemic phenomenon. He was determined, however, to look at reality dialectically, to see all that he hated perish with capitalist society, and to see humanity making a qualitative leap into a new society in which imperialism would vanish together with the state and bureaucracy. He therefore was under an emotional compulsion to define imperialism in such a way so that it would end with capitalism. Nothing is so certain as a tautology, and Lenin was removing the question of imperialism in postcapitalist and precapitalist societies from the empirical domain simply by linking it through a definition necessarily to capitalism. So Lenin wrote:

[I]mperialism existed before this latest stage of capitalism, and even before capitalism. Rome founded on slavery, pursued a colonial policy and achieved imperialism. But 'general' arguments about imperialism, which ignore, or put into the background the fundamental difference of social-economic systems, inevitably degenerate into absolutely empty banalities, or into grandiloquent expressions like 'Greater Rome and Greater Britain'.

Thus Lenin defends his definition of imperialism as specific to modern capitalism, his well-known definition of imperialism as involving the dominance of monopolies in production, the merger of bank capital with industrial capital, the export of capital, the formation of international monopolies, and the territorial division of the whole world among the greatest capitalist powers.

There are considerable doubts concerning the actuality of the specific traits which Lenin insisted were characteristic of imperialism. Foreign investment was in Britain and the United States primarily financed through a re-investment of profits, and involved a very small net outflow of capital. Tsarist Russia embarked on imperialist ventures though it had no surplus capital for export; the French colonies as a whole imported more in their trade than they exported; the average annual return on the invested capital in such major imperialist ventures as the Witwatersrand mines did not exceed 4.1 percent; British economy was not characterized by a merger between financial and industrial capital; critics in the colonies complained that imperialist countries didn't export enough capital to make for the development of industry.[47] But all such specific criticisms, however, are minor when compared to the major methodological distortion in Lenin's perspective on imperialism.

For Lenin argues that "general" arguments about imperialism must degenerate into banalities. By the same token, one might have argued that Newton's general arguments about the gravitational attraction of all masses, or Einstein's arguments concerning all frames of reference, all observers, were "banalities" or "tautologies." A Leninist would have held that the specific differences between the moon's motion and that of the planets were the only kinds of subjects that could be fruitfully studied. Indeed, the Aristotelian resistance to Galileo's logic of mechanics had precisely something of this character. Lenin, in other words, failed utterly to appreciate the significance of general laws of science. And the reason why he so failed is that the element of fantasy possessed him when he confronted basic social realities. His emotions wanted to decree the end of imperialism as the consequence of the end of capitalism; his imperious revolutionary will wanted to annihilate imperialism; therefore, by a verbal sleight-of-hand he stipulated that imperialism could exist only under modern capitalism. He projected a whole evolutionary sequence of historical stages into a choice in the use of words obedient to his emotions. When Yugoslav, Polish, Soviet, Chinese, and Cuban Marxists, therefore, have tried to speak about the imperialist activities of Communist countries, they have found themselves stammering because of their Leninist inhibitions. To talk plainly of a Soviet or Communist or Socialist imperialism violated the binding rules of their Leninist political grammar; they struggled vainly with all sorts of equivalents. But to speak of "great-power chauvinism" is even more grandiloquent than the expressions such as "Greater Rome" which Lenin disliked. The dialectical tenet with its qualitative leap into the end of imperialism was a fantasy which simply could not be translated into reality.

Lenin wrote his *Imperialism* in Zürich, Switzerland, in the spring of 1916. Then came the March Revolution of 1917. The time for transposing fantasy into reality had come, and he dared not miss it. All sorts of fantastic schemes rushed through his mind. His sister Marya writes: "But how to get back? One fantastic plan after another was conceived by Lenin, but they were all impracticable. He spent sleepless nights worrying how to get away from Switzerland. In desperation he decided to act the part of a deaf-mute who had a Swedish passport. . . ." He asked an intermediary "to find a Swede who looked like Lenin." The intermediary, Ganetsky, wrote: "When I read the letter, I realized how depressed Lenin was, but all the same I had to laugh at this grotesque plan."[48] Even Krupskaya acknowledges: "His nights were spent building the most improbable plans. We could fly over by plane. But such an idea could only be thought of in a waking dream. Put into words, its unreality became at once obvious."[49] Then a proposal of his former friend Martov that they secure passage through Germany brought Lenin back to Russia.

During the months of August and September, 1917, while in hiding, and awaiting with growing impatience the seizure of power by his party, Lenin wrote his celebrated pamphlet *The State and Revolution*. It is a Utopia written in the language of social science, a melange of impassioned, unrestrained projective dreams together with harsh insistence on the necessity for violence in revolution. He never completed the pamphlet, for the October events intervened: "It is more pleasant and useful to go through the 'experience of the revolution' than to write about it."[50] Again dialectical logic, with its schema of qualitative leap into the new world, with its negation of all that was repressive in the bourgeois society, provided Lenin with the formalism appropriate to his fantasy. Given the economic groundwork prepared by capitalism, universal literacy, the discipline of the workers, then, wrote Lenin, "it is perfectly possible, within twenty-four hours after the overthrow of the capitalists and bureaucrats, to replace them, in the control of production and distribution, in the business of *control* of labor and products, by the armed workers, by the whole people in arms." This was a prophecy which never fulfilled itself; the "twenty-four hours" have been dilated into more than a half-century, but the time-coefficient is always expanded with added clauses and auxiliary variables. Accounting and control, predicted Lenin, will have been so simplified by capitalism so that its techniques will be "within the reach of anybody who can read and write and knows the first four rules of arithmetic." Then, said Lenin, bureaucracy will begin to "wither away." The antagonism between mental and physical labor will vanish, and with it, the economic basis of the state. While denying that Bolsheviks are Utopians, indulging in "dreams" of how to eliminate all administration, still Lenin insists, "within twenty-four hours" after the revolution, the managerial functions will be taken over by average city dwellers and performed for workingmen's wages.[51]

Were Lenin's predictions ever founded on more than projective fantasy? Had he made any study of the procedures of accounting and management? Had he made any effort to learn the facts of industrial psychology, or to come to terms with the views of elites and the distribution of abilities enunciated by such sociologists as Michels and Pareto? The amazing thing is that Lenin, for all his training as a statistical sociologist, simply yielded to fantasy. If, as Lenin said in 1916, every generalization contains an element of fantasy, then we might say that some generalizations contain far more fantasy than others; we might even devise a "fantasy-fact" ratio for generalizations, and state the proportion of fantasy-projection in relation to verifiable fact in the construction of hypotheses. And Lenin would now have rated very high indeed in his "fantasy-fact ratio."

Curiously, in his early manhood, in 1902, Lenin had ridiculed those who raised an outcry against bureaucracy. In those days he thought that only flabby intellectuals wanted to dispense with bureaucracy. The average worker, Lenin insisted, realized that bureaucracy is a technological necessity. The proletarian who has gone through the school of the factory, wrote Lenin, who knows the function of "the factory as a means of organization" can teach the unstable, bourgeois intellectuals the necessity of bureaucracy. Those who railed "against people being transformed into 'wheels and cogs' " were raising a "tragi-comical outcry" against the workings of the division of labor. The distinction between orthodoxy and revisionism, wrote Lenin, is the counterpart of that between bureaucracy versus democracy. He chose bureaucracy; those who rejected it, he argued, suffered from some psychological ailment: "There is a close psychological connection between this hatred of discipline and that incessant nagging note of *injury* which is to be detected in all the writings of all opportunists today."[52] Whatever this psychological ailment, Lenin himself in 1917 wrote pages of fantasy which went far beyond the ones written by those whom he had derided in 1902. The dialectical fantasy had superseded the method of social science.

VII

Persons who dwell in a world of political fantasy are apt to be characterized by great cruelty. For the very component which impels one to reject reality and to reach for a surrogate world is one of some deep, underlying frustration; and frustration, if it expresses itself in fantasy, is also laden with aggression against whomever seems to counterpose himself against that fantasy. Indeed, the fantasy itself can provide the formula needed for justifying aggression and presenting one's cruelties as historically justified. Certainly, the greatest of Lenin's contemporaries, among those who knew him, felt this ingredient of cruelty in Lenin's personality. Bertrand Russell in 1920 found him "dictatorial," and "embodied theory," with a "rather grim" laugh, lacking in "psychological imagination," and despising many people. Lenin, he wrote retrospectively, was a "narrow-minded fanatic and cheap cynic." "When I met Lenin, I had much less impression of a great man than I had expected; my most vivid impressions were of bigotry and Mongolian cruelty. . . . His guffaw at the thought of those massacred made by blood run cold."[53] Maxim Gorky, who had known Lenin for many years, wrote from St. Petersburg in the midst of the revolution that Lenin "has no pity for the mass of the people . . . Lenin does not know the people . . . The working classes are to Lenin what minerals are to the metallurgist." Lenin, according to Gorky, was a Russian nobleman with his distinctive psychological traits, prepared to incite the working class to outrages against innocent people, and deeming himself as authorized "in performing with the Russian people a cruel experiment."[54] Leon Trotsky in 1903 said that Lenin was a "party dis-organizer," a would-be "dictator" whose conception of socialism was that of a "barracks regime."[55] The gifted and idealistic Rosa Luxemburg thought tthere was a "Tartar-Mongolian savagery" about Lenin and his followers. The Utopian fantasy and the materialist harshness were a curious joint product, the two polarities of a personality racked with aggressions, toward self, toward others.

Lenin's materialist doctrine was absorbed into the official Soviet ideology, and its absolutism became an official tenet. The famous *Short History of the Communist Party*, to which Stalin lent his name, enunciated as canonical text: "Marxist philosophical materialism holds that the world and its laws are fully knowable, ... and that there are no things in the world which are unknow-able. . . ."[57] This is a large philosophical commitment to demand of every Bol-shevik. A more reflective, or postideological philosopher would say: Consider the two contradictory propositions, first: there are no things in the world which are unknowable, and second: there are some things in the world which are un-knowable.

The postideological philosopher would say further: how could we possibly verify either of these two alternative contradictory propositions? For even if it happened that all things in the world taken distributively were knowable, we should still never be able to know whether we had sampled or enumerated all things; and if, on the other hand, there were something in the world which was unknowable, how would we possibly know it? When Lenin writes: "beyond the 'physical,' beyond the external world, with which everyone is familiar, there can be nothing,"[58] the agnostic responds: what manner of proof can there possibly be for such a proposition? It lies in the indeterminate domain.

In short, unless some emotion weights the scale, and inclines us to one alter-native or the other, the philosopher without ideology acknowledges that we have here a pair of indeterminate alternatives, and that under such circumstances, an agnostic standpoint is justified. Lenin, on the other hand, endeavoring to contain his own propensity to fantasy, does so by overdetermining the indeterminate; he proclaims a materialism which is hard, dogmatic, and mandatory. That is why the new generation of dissidents in the Soviet Union, looking for a liberation from the thought-ways and emotional patterns of institutionalized harshness, of socialized sadism, have begun to turn toward philosophical idealism.

As the centenary of Lenin's birth is observed, the estimate of his life and work will be largely influenced by the pronouncement of the Central Committee of the Soviet Communist Party: "Lenin was the first thinker of the century who saw the achievements of natural science in his time as the beginning of an im-mense scientific revolution, who was able to disclose and to generalize in philo-sophical terms the revolutionary meaning of the fundamental discoveries made by the great explorers of nature."[59] This is precisely the kind of statement which places fetters on the minds of the Soviet people, their students, their scientists. For Lenin more than any other thinker in this century contributed to the retardation of scientific inquiry. In the name of his narrow-minded materialism he rejected both Einstein's principle of relativity and Freud's psychoanalysis. His writings on imperialism and the state have deprived Soviet students of the intellectual tools which they need for analyzing their own society. In the measure in which his name is exalted as the first scientist of the century, in that proportion the society which he founded shows that its thinking still remains infantile, enthralled by ideology rather than guided by science. The Russian intellectual liberation is only now beginning.

Notes

1. V.I. Lenin, *What Is to Be Done?* (New York, 1931), pp. 158, 119.

2. Ibid., pp. 158-59.

3. V.I. Lenin, "Philosophical Notebooks," *Collected Works*, trans. Clemens Dutt, 4th ed. (Moscow, 1961), v. 38, pp. 372-73.

4. V.I. Lenin, *What the "Friends of the People" Are and How They Fight the Social-Democrats* (Moscow, 1950), p. 54 ff.

5. Ibid., pp. 47-48.

6. V.I. Lenin, "How The *Spark* Was Nearly Extinguished," *Collected Works*, *The Iskra Period 1900-1902*, Book I, trans. J. Finsberg (New York, 1929), v. 4, p. 29.

7. Ibid., pp. 30-31.

8. Ibid., p. 32.

9. Ibid., p. 36. The intensity of Lenin's revolt against Plekhanov was such that it led Lenin evidently to misperceive Plekhanov's role in Marxist philosophy. It was well known, for instance, that Plekhanov had introduced the philosophical phrase "dialectical materialism." Lenin, however, wrote: "Marx often termed his viewpoint dialectical materialism." I have never seen this phrase in Marx's writings. G. Plekhanov (N. Beltov), *The Development of the Monist View of History*, trans. Andrew Rothstein (Moscow, 1956), pp. 276, n. 1; Samuel H. Baron, *Plekhanov: The Father of Russian Marxism* (Stanford, 1963), p. 287; V.I. Lenin, *Materialism and Empirio-Criticism*, trans. David Kvitko (New York, 1927), p. 208.

10. Bertrand Russell, *Freedom and Organization: 1814-1914* (London, 1934), pp. 223-24.

11. Lenin, *Materialism and Empirio-Criticism*, p. 226.

12. Ibid., pp. 47, 43.

13. Ibid., pp. 102, 36.

14. Ibid., pp. 152, 96.

15. Ibid., p. 97.

16. Ibid., pp. 101, 31.

17. Ibid., pp. 84, 69.

18. Ibid., pp. 225, 101, 102.

19. Ibid., p. 156.

20. Ibid., pp. 40, 70, 64, 304.

21. Ibid., p. 302.

22. A.I. Ulyanova-Yelizarovka, "Reminiscences of Ilyich," *Reminiscences of Lenin by his Relatives* (Moscow, 1956), p. 43.

23. Ernest J. Simmons, *Chekhov: A Biography* (Boston, 1962), pp. 300-301.

24. Leon Trotsky, *My Life: An Attempt at an Autobiography* (New York, 1930), p. 144.

25. Nicholas Berdyaev, *Dream and Reality: An Essay in Autobiography*, trans. Katharine Lampert (New York, 1962), p. 131.

26. Nikolay Valentinov [N.V. Volsky], *Encounters with Lenin*, trans. Paul Rosta and Brian Pearce (London, 1968), p. 236. Bogdanov, as Gorky recalled, "was an extremely attractive person, of a very mild character"; he used to anger Lenin by beating him at chess. He died, in 1928, it is said, as a result of experiments performed on himself in blood transfusion. Was it perhaps an act of suicide? For Bogdanov, with his theory of the role of intellectuals, might very well have found himself shortly afterwards a co-defendant in the trial of the Industrial Party; *cf.*, Maxim Gorky, *Days with Lenin*, p. 26; S.V. Utechin, "Philosophy and Society: Alexander Bogdanov," *Revisionism: Essays in the History of Marxist Ideas*, ed. Leopold Labedz (London, 1962), pp. 117-25. Lenin in 1920 in his preface to the second edition of his *Materialism and Empirio-Criticism* was still pursuing Bogdanov for "introducing bourgeois and reactionary views" in the guise of " 'proletarian culture.' " One might note that by contrast Nikolai Bukharin rendered a favorable judgment of Bogdanov's work: *cf.* Nikolai Bukharin, *Historical Materialism: A System of Sociology* (New York, 1925).

27. Ibid., p. 138.

28. Ibid., p. 264.

29. *The Letters of Lenin*, p. 265.

30. *Materialism and Empirio-Criticism*, pp. 264, 182, 145, 296-97.

31. N.K. Krupskaya, *On Education: Selected Speeches and Articles*, trans. G.P. Ivanov-Mumjiev (Moscow, 1957), p. 37. The current Soviet writing on Lenin's relations with his family and father suppress this incident, and depict Lenin's father as imparting to him "spontaneous-materialistic positions"; *cf. The Ulyanov Family*, ed. I. Baranov (Moscow, 1968), p. 114.

32. *Materialism and Empirio-Criticism*, pp. 298, 299, 239, 195, 116, 50.

33. Krupskaya, *Reminiscences of Lenin*, pp. 214, 76, 32.

34. *The Letters of Lenin*, p. 91; Krupskaya, *Reminiscences of Lenin*, pp. 7, 99.

35. Cited in Valentinov, *Encounters with Lenin*, p. 56; Krupskaya, *Reminiscences of Lenin*, p. 190.

36. Krupskaya, *Reminiscences of Lenin*, p. 311.

37. Bernard Shaw, *The Rationalization of Russia*, ed. Harry M. Geduld (Bloomington), p. 30.

38. Bertram D. Wolfe, "Lenin and Inessa Armand," *Slavic Review*, v. 17 (1963), p. 111.

39. Krupskaya, *Reminiscences of Lenin*, pp. 41-42; Relatives, *Reminiscences of Lenin*, p. 166 ff.

40. Gregory Zinoviev, *Lenin*, trans. John G. Wright (London, 1966), p. 38.

41. Relatives, *Reminiscences of Lenin*, pp. 203-204.

42. Krupskaya, *Reminiscences of Lenin*, p. 539.

43. Lenin, *Philosophical Notebooks*, p. 180.

44. Ibid., pp. 360, 212, 303.

45. V.I. Lenin, *Imperialism: The Highest Stage of Capitalism* (New York), pp. 126, 124, 7.

46. *The New York Times*, February 7, 1966.

47. Herbert Feis, *Europe: The World's Banker, 1870-1914* (New Haven, 1930); Cleona Lewis, *America's Stake in International Investments* (Washington, D.C., 1938), p. 285; Randall Henshaw, "Foreign Investment and American Employment," *American Economic Review*, v. 36 (1942), 663; Melvin Knight, *Morocco as a French Economic Venture*, p. 189; Frankel, *Capital Investment in Africa*, p. 91.

48. Relatives, *Reminiscences of Lenin*, p. 158.

49. Krupskaya, *Reminiscences of Lenin*, p. 337.

50. V.I. Lenin, *State and Revolution* (New York, 1935), p. 101.

51. Ibid., pp. 83, 84, 43, 79. Marxist theorists have always been naive about the nature of the administration of industry. Engels wrote in 1851 that "with six clerks I could organize an infinitely more simple, comprehensive and practical branch of administration." Karl Marx and Friedrich Engels, *Correspondence 1846-1895*, trans. Dona Storr (New York, 1935), p. 43.

52. V.I. Lenin, *One Step Forward, Two Steps Back* (Moscow, 1947), pp. 106, 94, 91, 90.

53. Bertrand Russell, *Bolshevism: Practice and Theory* (New York, 1920), pp. 35-44; Bertrand Russell, *Unpopular Essays* (New York, 1950), p. 171.

54. Maxim Gorky, *Untimely Thoughts*, trans. Herman Ermolaev (New York, 1968), pp. 85-88; *Modern Industrial Movements*, ed. Daniel Bloomfield (New York, 1920), pp. 289-99.   55. M.J. Olgin,

55. M.J. Olgin, *Trotskyism: Counter-Revolution in Disguise* (New York, 1935), pp. 67-69.

56. J.P. Nettl, *Rosa Luxemburg* (London, 1966), v. 2, pp. 579, 592-95.

57. Central Committee of the C.P.S.U., *History of the Communist Party of the Soviet Union, Short Course* (New York, 1939), p. 113.

58. Lenin, *Materialism and Empirio-Criticism*, p. 298.

59. "Central Committee's Theses on the Lenin Centennial," *The Current Digest of the Soviet Press*, v. 22, no. 2, February 11, 1970, p. 5.

**Part II
Lenin,
Law and Legality**

5

Lenin's Contribution to Law: The Case of Protection and Preservation of the Natural Environment

ZIGURDS L. ZILE

The Soviets doggedly trace the genealogy of their law to Lenin. The fundamental legal institutions, the salient concepts and principles, whole areas of legal regulation, and even (though less consistently) individual statutes and decrees are being linked to his name. This routine has had a certain conditioning effect. Lenin's leading role in laying the legal groundwork for the Soviet economic order, organizing the essential agencies of public order and expounding principles of socialist legality has become widely accepted even outside the Soviet Union. Such an acceptance is, in some cases, grounded in fact; in other cases, it may well denote resignation in face of the persistence with which quotations from the *Sochineniia* and flat assertions are imposed upon the reader of Soviet materials. The ritual of posthumous glorification has an especially great potential for distorting the historical accuracy of the more esoteric legal topics. Matters remote from the great political controversies are seldom closely scrutinized and, consequently, opportunities for cross-verification are diminished.

In this chapter I have chosen a relatively untrodden path. I propose to take a look at the alleged pedigree of one of the lesser components of Soviet law. More specifically, I will examine Lenin's contribution to the law of protection and preservation of the natural environment—a subject, although timely, not ordinarily regarded as Lenin's forte.[a]

Until the late 1950s, when deterioration of the natural environment became a matter of national concern, Soviet literature only tenuously connected Lenin's name with environmental protection and preservation. In fact, the 1935 subject index to the second and third editions of the *Sochineniia* referred neither to "Conservation" nor to such broader, related topics as "Forest Management and Forest Industry" or "Fish Management and Fish Industry." A small but unique monograph published as late as 1947 is quite subdued regarding Soviet conservation accomplishments and only makes a few cursory references to Lenin and Stalin, without in any way intimating that either had played a significant role in protecting and preserving nature.[1] The article on "Protection of Nature" (1955) in *The Great Soviet Encyclopedia* does not mention Lenin at all.[2] Since the late 1950s, by contrast, scarcely a book or article has omitted tribute to the contributions of Vladimir Ilyich. Yet, the fact that the reverent authors, for the most

---

[a]"Conservation law" is the more traditional, more commonly used term. "*Pravovaia okhrana prirody* (legal protection of nature)" is the rough Russian equivalent.

part, work the same mine—a brief 1958 note on the early Soviet legislation—suggests that the evidentiary deposit is not vast.[3]

The most recent Soviet book on nature protection that I have come across lists four "Leninist principles in the area of nature protection"[4] and asserts that "[t]he foundation to state protection of nature in our country was only laid after the October Revolution," and that "[i]n this a prominent role was played by V.I. Lenin."[5] I propose to take this statement as a working hypothesis and test it against what I have been able to discover about Lenin's contribution in this regard.

An individual in a position of political power can contribute to law mainly in three ways: by defining the ends of law, by devising specific laws as a means to an end, or by sustaining the process whereby laws are employed in pursuit of desired ends. Accordingly, to assess Lenin's contribution, we should, first, identify the genesis and substance of his thoughts on, and attitudes toward, protection and preservation of the natural environment as a proper end of law; secondly, review the originality and technical adequacy of the relevant laws attributed to him; and, thirdly, evaluate his talent and determination to make the enacted laws work in practice.

Lenin's Thoughts and Attitudes

Lenin's utterances about the natural environment are few. Man's relation to nature comes up in his writings mainly in connection with the so-called "grain question," the question of the ability of individual countries, or for that matter the world as a whole, to feed a growing number of people. Lenin rejected the theories of diminishing returns and falling productivity of soil and refused to sink into Malthusian gloom.[6] He scoffed at those "enthusiastic over birth control."[7] Looking at Russia, he found "sufficient territory and natural wealth . . . to supply each and all, if not with abundant, at least with adequate means of life."[8] On other occasions, he spoke of Russia's natural wealth as "immense" and "incredible."[9] As he saw it, the dire prognoses of the "hired scholars of the bourgeoisie" were but an expedient "to justify capitalism"[10] with all its mistakes, limitations and contradictions. "Development of the natural resources by methods of modern technology . . . [would] provide the basis for unprecedented progress of the productive forces."[11] Therefore, it was "necessary everywhere to introduce more machinery, to move toward the application of machine technology as widely as possible."[12] "Ah," Lenin exclaimed, "if we only had the means to set up all these technical experts in ideal working conditions! In twenty years Russia would be the most advanced country in the world."[13] He was certain that socialist relations of production would take waste out of this progress. Thus, forests would be saved by substitution of coal for firewood; coal, in turn, would be replaced by total electrification. Losses would be eliminated from the process itself by "the rational *distribution* of industry . . . from the standpoint of proximity to raw materials,"[14] a generally responsible attitude toward socialist property, compliance with technical rules,[15] and utilization of the by-products of one industry by another. On April 2, 1921, Lenin wrote in a letter to Serebrovskii: "Has the oil question been correctly posed in Baku from the point of view of coordinating the various aspects of the national economy . . . Shall we pump water (with oil) without using it for irrigation that would yield gigantic harvests of hay, rice and cotton? . . . Can oil industry be developed without developing agriculture around Baku?"[16] In short, the day was dawning when "no sinister force . . . [would] resist the alliance of the representatives of the sciences, of the proletariat and of technology."[17]

If there is any common theme running through these thoughts, it is that of rather crude economic utilitarianism. Indeed, one might say that Lenin's long-range solution to the "grain question" is consistent with a notion that man lives by bread alone. It implies that, if one only digs, dams, drains, plants, breeds, and irrigates, he can satisfy humanity's needs. It tempts one to calculate the value of a river in kilowatts of energy it can generate, and a wetland, in tons of grain it can grow after drainage. This view also justifies classification of animal and plant life into useful and useless. It can doom the wolf as nothing but trouble and elevate the carp and lamprey for their high protein yield.

Of course, this is, at least in part, a question of values. If mere physical survival of man (even in combination with some physical comforts) is the ultimate value, nature can perhaps be approached in materialistic terms. Lenin's thoughts should disturb those whose conception of the "highest quality of living" includes both material sustenance and spiritual enrichment for man on earth, now and in the future, and who see the natural environment as a source of both of these values.[18]

But even if Lenin's implicit view regarding the function of the natural environment were accepted, one could still have misgivings about nature's ability to perform, with man attempting to run the show. Lenin did not give adequate recognition to the limitations inherent in scientific and technological development. Science can only be planned and pushed to a degree. Scientific truths are always subject to revision. The means employed in dealing with concrete problems are essentially imperfect. The side effects of the imperfections are not entirely predictable. The imperfections and, consequently, the attendant uncertainties of scientific and technological efforts are likely to multiply when the means are scarce and the time is short. Therefore, every large-scale human intervention in nature's processes is hazardous, however well-intentioned and currently scientific.

Considering the state of the art of his day, Lenin's thoughts cannot, in any meaningful way, be considered a contribution. They were neither original nor carefully developed. Ecology has become a household word only recently, but its roots extend well into the past. The infant conservation movement of the mid-nineteenth century was already ecologically aware.

Engels' *Dialectics of Nature* has pointed passages Lenin might have wanted to reflect on. "Let us not . . . flatter ourselves overmuch on account of our human conquest over nature. For each such conquest takes its revenge on us. Each of them, it is true, has in the first place the consequences on which we counted, but in the second and third places, it has quite different, unforeseen effects which only too often cancel out the first."[19] Yet, Engels' book, as a whole, was not a plea for maximum abstinence on the part of man. On the contrary, it extolled manipulation of the natural environment by man because he was deemed to have the ability to know and correctly apply nature's laws. Marx agreed and also wrote with approval of consciously controlled transformation of nature and of man's duty to leave nature in a better state to the succeeding generations.[20,21] It was this aspect of the classical Marxist thought that Lenin embraced.

The first relevant Russian organizations and publications appeared toward the end of the nineteenth century. In 1872, a special commission of the Imperial Government reported that the destruction of forests by imprudent logging was producing changes toward a colder, drier climate, the silting of rivers and the desiccation of water sources, and urged protective legislation.[22] The Russian conservation movement made its greatest strides forward between the turn of the century and the First World War. Conservation groups and literature proliferated; foreign experiences were related to Russian conditions and action plans formulated. In 1912, on the initiative of Academician Borodin, a Permanent Commission on Protection of Nature was established within the Russian Geographical Society to propagandize, and work for, protection of individual resources, significant natural areas and complex environmental relationships. From 1913-1914, the first exhibition on nature conservation was held in Kharkov.[23] Many natural resources measures came before the State Duma, some of which were enacted into law while others remained in committees at the time of the Revolution.

The legislative precedents of the Duma, as well as the earlier imperial enactments, are of considerable importance to us, because it is precisely Lenin's legislative activity that is said to have made the greatest contribution to Soviet law on protection and preservation of the natural environment.

Lenin's Laws in Books and in Action

The Soviet decree "On Land,"[24] together with the appended "Instruction Concerning the Peasantry," abolished private ownership of land forever and converted all private holdings into public domain.[25] Moreover, "[a]ll subsurface of the earth, ore, oil, coal, salt and so forth, as well as forests and waters, of general state significance," were put "to the exclusive use of the state."[26] By virtue of this act, the Soviet state took upon itself the powers of direct use of the country's natural resources and the responsibilities for protecting the same from misuse. It became both the police and the policed. The state as a *razumnyi khoziain* had now to learn to contain the *khishchnik* in itself; it had to learn to match the zeal of its production campaigns with solicitude for the natural environment being drastically reshaped by exploitation.[b]

The Example of Forests

The tensions between the conflicting objectives and dual functions of the Soviet state originally emerged with regard to forests. Lenin had, on more than one occasion, decried the destruction of Russia's forests, especially, the denudation of vast regions during the industrial expansion of the late nineteenth century.[27] To prevent further damage after the Revolution, there was an immediate need for an organization to manage the forest reserves. The prerevolutionary forest service had some utility for this purpose. It had acquired considerable experience in managing state holdings, since more than 70 percent of the forests of the Russian Empire had been state owned, that is, had belonged either to the crown or the tsar's family.[28] However, the forest service was falling apart after the Revolution. It was undermined by the rising presumption against the validity of laws and legal relations antedating the Soviet power and by both traditional and deliberately fanned local hostility against the former representatives of the tsarist bureaucracy. One of the first tasks of the regime was to retard or stop this disintegration. As early as December 19 (6), 1917, People's Commissar of Agriculture, Kolegaev, addressed a communication to all land committees and local soviets asking them not to disband the forestry councils set up by the Provisional Government to manage state forests.[29] A month later, all forests were turned over to the provincial land committees with a mandate to establish forestry sections to supervise the exploitation of forests and their protection, improvement and renewal.[30] But administration was not by any means completely decentralized. Financing, for one, continued to come from the center.[31] And, on April 5, 1918, another directive over Lenin's signature went out to the soviets reaffirming the need for, and irreplaceability of, the forest specialists. Mass dismissals, the directive contended, were hurting the national interest at a time when reforestation had to be begun in war-denuded areas, and forests properly registered and their use subjected to regulation.[32]

The Decree of May 30 (17), 1918, known as "The Basic Law on Forests,"[33] attempted to replace the ad hoc measures by a single comprehensive regulation. Signed by Sverdlov, chairman of the All-Russian Central Executive Committee, and Lenin, in his capacity as chairman of the Council of People's Commissars, the decree dealt with the basic issues raised by the nationalization of forests: the position of citizens vis à vis the nationalized property, the relations between the central government and the local authorities, and the balance between use, on

---

[b]The two Russian terms mean "reasonable master" and "spoiler," respectively.

the one hand, and protection and preservation, on the other. This decree has been referred to in Soviet literature as "*Leninskii zakon* (Lenin's law)" and as concerned with "protection and renewal of forests."[34] However, a Soviet compilation of the pertinent archival materials does not in any way indicate Lenin's active participation in drafting the law.[35] Lenin's papers usually include copies of draft laws on which he worked. These copies either are entirely in his handwriting or contain handwritten corrections or notations of substance. The copy of "The Basic Law on Forests" bears no such markings.[c] The law appears to be a technical statute rather carefully worked out by a committee of five members (not including Lenin) of the All-Russian Central Executive Committee and a subsequent committee of the Council of People's Commissars composed of Stuchka, Larin, and Professor Faleev.[36]

The law itself, as mentioned earlier, was not exclusively or mainly a measure of environmental protection and preservation, but it did contain several important general provisions on the subject. Forests were to be managed "(a) in the interests of the general welfare and (b) on the basis of planned reforestation" (Article 77). Timber harvest was to be governed by the concept of sustained yield, that is to say, the harvest could not exceed the net growth (Article 78). In addition, harvesting was confined to forests designated for exploitation. The remaining forests were classified as protected (Articles 80-81). The purposes of the latter comprised: protection of soil, agriculture and populated places; preservation of the influence of forests on climate; protection of the sources, water levels and banks of rivers; the securing of sands and ravines; maintenance of sanitary, esthetic and cultural standards and values; and preservation of monuments of nature (Article 83). Except for the last two items, the enumeration followed the provisions of the Imperial Law of April 4, 1888, "On Forest Conservation,"[37] which used the concepts of protected (*zashchitnye*) and water-conservation forests (*vodookhrannye lesa*), concepts that dated back at least to Peter the Great.[38] In short, not only was Lenin's active participation in making Soviet forestry laws insubstantial; but the laws themselves were hardly original contributions. While it is still disputed whether the prerevolutionary forestry statutes, such as the Law of 1888, have had a noticeable beneficial effect on the country's forests, the successes of "The Basic Law on Forests" remain no less in doubt.

As the year 1918 wore on and the civil strife spread, important raw-material producing regions, such as the Donbas coal mining region, were either cut off from the territory under Red control or overland communication with them was greatly aggravated. The fuel shortage further slowed down the already declining economy and jeopardized the survival of the population in the coming winter besides. This explains why the decrees on forest matters following the Basic Law were almost invariably concerned with fuel. Procurement of fuel was

---

[c]The only notation by Lenin states that the draft was approved by the Council of People's Commissars on May 14, 1918. *Dekrety*, II, 312.

termed a task to be carried out immediately, on a mass scale and "without hindrance."[39] On August 27, 1918, a troika was created with "dictatorial powers" and responsibility to procure the largest quantity of fuel within the shortest time possible.[40] Four months later, the Chief Forestry Committee was established at the Supreme Council of People's Economy by a decree actually drafted and signed by Lenin to guide, regulate and administer the entire forest industry, and, specifically, to take "extraordinary measures" to supply the country with firewood and lumber. Forest management responsibilities were, in part, reallocated in derogation of the Basic Law on Forests.[41] Just prior to the last-named reorganization, a decree drafted by Lenin on behalf of the Council of Labor and Defense warned the Central Forest Section of the Commissariat of Agriculture (responsible, among other things, for the protection of forests) that "in the event of further red tape or one more complaint by the ... [troika], the entire membership of the Central Forest Section will be arrested and turned over to court."[42]

It became increasingly difficult to tell who was supposed to do what and control whom by what standards. Lenin conceded in a speech to a joint session of the All-Russian Central Executive Committee, the Moscow Soviet and the All-Russian Trade Union Congress, on January 17, 1919, that his government was accused of issuing decrees too hastily. "[B]ut what are we to do," he implored, "when we have to make haste because of the advance of imperialism, when we are compelled to make haste by the strongest scourge imaginable—the lack of bread and fuel."[43] Lenin's exhortations must have added to the confusion regarding priorities and impaired credibility of the rudimentary conservation law. In the fall of 1919, in a letter addressed to the party organizations, Lenin wrote:

The fuel question has moved to the forefront of all other questions. The fuel crisis must be overcome at all costs, otherwise one cannot resolve the problems of provisioning, war, or the general economy.

And it is possible to overcome the fuel crisis. Although we have lost the coal of Donetsk and are unable to speed up coal mining in the Urals and Siberia, we still have many forests; we can cut and bring in a sufficient quantity of firewood. . . .

[I]t is necessary to learn how to arouse enthusiasm among the working masses. It is necessary to strive for revolutionary mobilization of energy for the speediest preparation and delivery of the largest quantity of any kind of fuel—coal, oil, shale, peat and so forth, but above all firewood, firewood and once more firewood.[44]

Amidst this turmoil, on November 4, 1919, the beleaguered Central Forest Section of the People's Commissariat of Agriculture addressed a circular letter to all forest subsections of the provincial land sections. The letter pointed out the inadvisability of cutting certain forest expanses even under the prevailing circumstances. The Central Forest Section mainly had in mind "areas of future national parks and monuments of nature" as well as individual valuable species of trees.[45] It is not known to me whether this letter was the last bit of red tape that broke the "fuel tsars' " patience and perhaps put the whole Section on trial.

Although I have no direct proof of what actually went on in the forests, trees were probably cut in the most accessible and convenient locations, closest to population centers and routes of transportation.[d] Since railroads themselves were in a "critical fuel situation,"[46] log floating was accelerated on rivers.[47] It is not unrealistic to visualize trees being cut right along the waterways to simplify and speed up the operations. The essentials were in short supply, skilled manpower and means of transportation, in particular. For instance, loggers were exempted from military draft.[48] And if streetcars had to be commandeered to carry wood from Moscow's railroad yards,[49] there is no reason to suppose that it was any easier to get the logs from the harvest areas to the rivers or railroads. Protected forests and forests which should have been placed under protection probably suffered the most.

Further support to this interpretation is lent by a story told by Lenin's personal chauffeur. It seems that during one of his out-of-town jaunts in the critical summer of 1919, Lenin came upon workers of the Moscow "Bogatyr" plant and local residents cutting firewood with enthusiasm and revolutionary energy in the Sokolniki Forest. Deeply perturbed by such conduct, so the story goes, he immediately ordered the cutting to cease. This encounter allegedly led to a decree "On the Strictest Protection of the Suburban Forests within a 30-Verst Zone around Moscow"[50] and, later on, to the more comprehensive Decree of April 29, 1920, "On Protection of Green Areas (Gardens, Parks, Suburban Forests and Other Greenery)."[51] This decree is said to have been issued "on Lenin's direction," although it was not signed by him.[52]

Lenin signed three other laws affecting the use and preservation of forests in the early 1920s: "On Combatting Forest Fires,"[53] "On the Use of the Siberian Cedar,"[54] and on Crimean mountain forests.[55] The purpose of the first was self-evident. The second mainly dealt with the organization of the harvesting of cedar nuts. The third was addressed to the important problem of watershed protection. The fact that mountain forests either had not been declared protected by the forest authorities or had been cut in violation of an established protective regime (the decree refers to slopes cleared, without proper authorization, since 1917) further reinforces the suspicion that the implementation of the Basic Law on Forests left much to be desired. A recent study done under the auspices of the USSR Academy of Sciences observes that, "[u]nfortunately, realization of the measures provided for by this historic decree turned out to be difficult, and, therefore, these measures ceased to attract the attention they deserved. As a result, they were not until now subjected to adequate scientific treatment."[56] With regard to protection and preservation of forests, then, Lenin's contribution to making the enacted laws work in practice has been as unspectacular as his contribution to the formulation of the legal ends and means.

---

[d]That was the practice during the post-World War II crisis. V.N. Makarov, *Okrana prirody v SSSR* (Moscow, 1947), pp. 20-21.

The Example of Fish and Fisheries

Lenin's contribution to the law of protection and preservation of water resources concerns mainly fish and fisheries. The Chief Administration for Fishing
and Fish Industry (*Glavryba*) was set up within the People's Commissariat of
Provisioning on December 9, 1918.[57] Although the decree had an industrial
bias, it also charged the new agency with "the working out of appropriate measures for protection of water expanses in the interests of conserving the natural
fisheries; establishment of closed areas and seasons; general guidance in regulating fishing; and the practical realization of large-scale propagation of fish by the
state." *Glavryba* was reorganized on February 26, 1920, and its conservationist
duties redefined as "adoption, in general, of all measures called for by the interests of the country's fishing industry, measures to protect water expanses etc.,
and issuance, to these ends, of instructions, directives and binding decrees."[58]
Fifteen months later, Lenin signed still another decree on the same subject.[59]
This time *Glavryba* was reminded of its duty to issue "technical rules establishing closed areas, prohibited means of fishing and closed seasons, as well as organizing control over compliance with these rules through local agencies." *Glavryba*
was once more reorganized on September 23 of the same year.[60] It now
emerged as an agency distinctly concerned with production. Protection of fish
and fisheries as such had been dropped from the list of *Glavryba's* concerns.
Only references to artificial propagation and acclimatization of fish, "measures
furthering the development of fish and wildlife industries," and to "regulation of
such industries" remained. Finally, on September 25, 1922, the three immediately preceding laws were expressly repealed and their principal provisions more
of less restated in still another law.[61] In view of the inauguration of the New
Economic Policy, allocation of fisheries between the state sector and private
fishermen received considerable attention in this last-named decree.

Neither the periodic protestations of concern for the future of Russia's fisheries nor the repeatedly mentioned protective measures had any originality. The
challenge at the time was to produce regulations reflecting an appreciation of the
interrelationships between the condition of the individual fisheries, the economic situation of the local inhabitants, the long-range interests in protection
and preservation of fisheries and individual species of fish, and the present industrial demands. These factors had been extensively and thoughtfully weighed and
related in a Report of the Committee on Fishing of the State Duma of March 1,
1916. The Report also contained detailed Draft Fishing Regulations for the Empire.[62] I have not, however, found any such Soviet regulations from the period
investigated (with the exception of a very brief decree on the fisheries of the Arctic
Ocean and the White Sea)[63] or encountered any reference to their existence.

Fish and fisheries were to be the indirect beneficiaries of a decree "On the
Central Committee for Protection of Waters" issued by the Supreme Council of
People's Economy in February, 1919.[64] The new agency was empowered to
combat pollution of waters by industrial and municipal effluents. But, as usual,

no standards were set out and nothing was reported about the implementation of the decree.

If Soviet commentators are to be believed,[65] Lenin's principal contribution, apart from signing several of the foregoing decrees, was a letter to the Workers' and Peasants' Inspectorate. He had learned, Lenin wrote on December 5, 1922, that because of the wartime decline of fishing, sea-roach had reappeared in the Sea of Azov in commercial quantities. Sturgeon, too, was making a comeback. However, unrestricted, predatory fishing was threatening to wipe out the gains. Lenin continued:

By way of an example, it has been reported to me that even the agency of the Provisioning Committee on the Don [*Donprodkom*] responsible for the protection [of waters] has fostered predatory fishing in the protected zone; besides, there was a special tax—from 400 to 500 million rubles for each haul [*pritonenie*]—payable for the permission to fish in the protected waters.

The chief of the agency was dismissed from his post for predatory fishing on the Lower Don. This gentleman was only dismissed from his post. It is necessary to find out where he is and seriously follow up on the sufficiency of his punishment. . . .

A scare alone is not enough; prosecution and a purge would be proper for these outrages.[66]

While this letter can be read as an expression of concern for the fate of a segment of the natural environment, another interpretation is at least as plausible. The misconduct of the Don *was* outrageous. It evidenced rot in the sinews of the Soviet power which had to rely on the trustworthiness of its élite representatives in farflung territories. "Strict observance of . . . [Soviet] laws is necessary for the further growth and strengthening of the workers' and peasants' authority in Russia," declared one of the historic Soviet decrees.[67] Official corruption practiced in *Donprodkom* deserved to be fought as essentially subversive. On April 21, 1919, Lenin sent the following telegram to railway Cheka of Zhlobin: "Rabkin, the manager of a pharmacy, complains of confiscation of his bicycle by the railway Cheka. Follow up on this immediately and verify. If there are no special or military reasons [for the act indicated in your reply], you will be punished for the confiscation of the bicycle."[68] I am yet to see this telegram cited to illustrate Lenin's solicitude for bicycles, pharmacies or private property.

Without taking the Don incident as typical, one should recognize that managers and guardians of fisheries could conceivably have felt constrained to retreat from their conservation responsibilities under the mounting pressure to deliver large quantities of fish products to the state. The fuel crisis which placed heavy demands on Russia's forests was paralleled, in the context of fisheries, by the famine of the early 1920s. As the drought of 1921 dashed the hopes for an adequate harvest of crops, a search was on for other sources of food. The so-called "fishing [or fish procurement] campaign" of 1921 was mounted and conducted in response to the food crisis.[69] Again, while I have no direct evidence of what took place on Russia's fishing waters, one may infer that observance of protective regulations, if any there were, had low priority.

The Example of Wildlife and Hunting

On May 27, 1919, Lenin signed into law a draft decree "On Hunting Seasons and the Right to Hunting Weapons."[70] This act is said to show the concern of Lenin (who himself was a hunter, albeit neither a very outstanding nor a passionate one[71]) for industrially-hunted wildlife.[72] In fact, the initiative in this matter was apparently taken by zoologists of Moscow University.[73] It was an emergency measure to prevent the decimation or extinction of a few threatened wildlife species. It forbade the hunting of moose and wild goat, the gathering of eggs of wild birds, and the trading in freshly killed game. The People's Commissariat of Agriculture and the Scientific-Technical Section of the Supreme Council of People's Economy were asked to prepare a draft of permanent hunting regulations and lay them before the Council of People's Commissars not later than July 15, 1919, that is, half a month before the expiration of the temporary decree. The permanent decree, however, came out, over Lenin's signature, with a year's delay. Strictly speaking, then, the originally outlawed practices could have been legally resumed and carried on for a full, critical year. The 1920 decree mentioned "propagation and protection of game"[74] among the duties of the People's Commissariat of Agriculture, but did not contain specific rules on hunting. Apparently, the Commissariat was expected to, and later in fact did, issue the necessary regulations on closed seasons, protected species, etc. When, on August 24, 1922, another decree appealed for observance of hunting regulations, it presumably had such regulations in mind. Violations, the decree complained, were resulting in "predation on and destruction of wildlife."[75] One might add that destruction of wildlife was also proceeding with the sanction of law. Both the decree of 1920 and a decree of 1923, which superseded the former, expressly empowered the Commissariat to organize "detachments for extermination of predatory and harmful animals."[76]

Since I have been unable to locate the alluded to but unidentified hunting regulations, I could compare them with neither the prerevolutionary regulations in force nor those proposed for adoption about six years before the Revolution.[77] In any event, I have no reason to think that anything about them could enhance Lenin's otherwise negligible contribution.

The Example of Nature Preserves

The most conservation-minded feature of the hunting decree of March 1, 1923, was the provision enabling the People's Commissariat of Agriculture to "establish nature preserves, sanctuaries, game farms, laboratories, game parks, etc."[78] The idea of nature preserves and the like antedates Lenin and the Soviet power. But Lenin's name has recently been invoked in conjunction with conservation legislation of this type. And since other thin links have been considered between Lenin and the law, I shall also explore his relation to the legislation on nature preserves, if for no better reason, than for the sake of consistency.

On January 16, 1919, Lenin received a representative of the Astrakhan' Provincial Executive Committee, Pod"iapol'skii, to discuss conditions in the Lower Volga region. One of the matters concerned a proposal for a nature preserve in the delta worked out by Pod"iapol'skii and one Khlebnikov. After the presentation of the proposal, Lenin reportedly remarked that protection of nature was a matter of importance not only for the Astrakhan' province but for the entire Republic as well.[79] "At this time," a Soviet book comments, "the country was encircled by blockade and only few people talked of protection of nature and nature preserves. . . . One had to possess Lenin's genial foresight to regard this question important already at that time."[80] A decision to establish the Astrakhan' Preserve was adopted later that year by the Provincial Executive Committee.[81] On May 14, 1920, on the intiative of Professor Artem'ev and the board of the People's Commissariat of Education, the Commissariat was authorized to designate, with the concurrence of the Mining Council of the Supreme Council of People's Economy, certain portions of the Ilmen' Mountains in the Southern Urals as a State Mineralogical Preserve to be used exclusively for scientific-technical purposes.[82] The use of the preserve for other purposes required permission of the Council of People's Commissars. The Baikal State Nature Preserves and Game Farms were created in 1921 to protect and propagate various artiodactylous and fur-bearing animals, in particular, the sable.[83] Exploitation of the natural wealth was completely forbidden in these areas. At about the same time, plans were made for the Caucasian nature preserve eventually established in 1924.[84,85] The decree "On Protection of Monuments of Nature, Gardens and Parks," signed by Lenin on September 16, 1921,[86] has also been labeled "Lenin's decree."[87] The very ordinary decree briefly defines natural monuments, nature preserves and national parks and makes the People's Commissariat of Education primarily responsible for organizing and managing them.[e] According to a recent Soviet book, "[w]ith the issuance of this decree, creation of nature preserves became one of the most important forms of nature protection in the USSR. It was followed by a whole line of decrees and directives regarding its execution as well as its implementation."[88] These decrees and directives, suffice it to say, were adopted either during Lenin's final illness or after his death.

[e]Conceptually, the decree did not go much beyond the bare-bones definition contained in the decree on Ilmen' preserve. SU RSFSR 1920, no. 38, text 181 (signed by Lenin).

The early Soviet activities, including legislation, regarding nature preserves and monuments of nature were, by and large, continuations of prerevolutionary efforts. The first Russian nature preserve had been proclaimed, with the help of the Petersburg Academy of Sciences, at Lagodekh, in what is now the Georgian SSR, in 1912. The first sizable state nature preserves, Barguzinsk and Saiansk, were proclaimed in 1915.[89] Kedrovaia Pad' followed in 1916.[90] Astrakhan' preserve was proposed by Professor Zhitkov shortly before the Revolution. Almost simultaneously, Academician Nasonov spoke out in favor of establishing a Caucasian preserve, in particular to protect the indigenous bison (*zubr*).[91] There was also a fair number of areas privately owned or held by the tsar's family under a protective regime. Soviet commentators are apt to point out that only under the Soviet rule do all nature preserves become state establishments. But whatever its potential advantages, state ownership has not been such an immediate, unmixed blessing. The fate of the Kuban' princely hunting grounds is a case in point. The hunting grounds were organized in 1888. They covered about 1,250,000 acres under quasi-military protection. For thirty years, until the Revolution, there was no hunting on the grounds. The wildlife situation in the entire region improved immensely. It seemed that the survival of the Caucasian bison was also ensured. However, the species was exterminated after the Caucasian state nature preserve had been established there in 1924 and maintained without sufficient security guard.[92]

The legislative output of Lenin's years prompts several observations. First, the laws of the period were far more concerned with use of the natural environment than its protection and preservation. Admittedly, this is a question of balance; perhaps the use aspects should always receive more attention. However, if law is genuinely dedicated to environmental protection and preservation, this objective should not be presented as subsidiary to use. Secondly, the provisions concerning protection and preservation were technically deficient. They either stopped at pious generalities or excessively relied on administrative implementation, without prescribing meaningful standards or guidelines. Thirdly, the protective provisions, in their substance, were at best restatements or continuations of established, nonrevolutionary concepts and principles. Finally, whatever there is does not evidence any substantial, creative involvement by Lenin personally.

Notwithstanding the few cases in which Lenin is given credit for demanding strict law enforcement, the enacted laws were not effectively translated into action. The values implicit in the protective provisions readily bowed to those values which legitimated ruthless exploitation of nature.

To avoid any possible misunderstanding, I want to state emphatically that my criticisms are not in the least intended to belittle the job that Lenin faced in the years after the Revolution. He did, indeed, have bigger things on his mind than protecting wildflowers. But this chapter is not about what might have been, but what in fact was. That is to say, it seeks to measure the extent of Lenin's actual contribution and not his potential for making a contribution under other, possibly more favorable circumstances. The decisions to cut forests deserving the strictest protection for ecological reasons, during the fuel crisis, or to maximize the catches of fish without regard to the future of particular fisheries or species, during the years of famine, may have been politically the only decisions possible. I agree that those years were no conservation years. But, then, Lenin was no conservationist either, for much the same reasons. One should also note that the ideas and laws on protection and preservation of the natural environment did not flourish after the initial years of extreme hardship. The ideas and laws which are today attributed to Lenin did not survive his death as an influential legacy when they were mostly needed. A Soviet apology sums up the experience in these words:

Having come face to face with instances of irrational and purely predatory attitudes toward natural resources, many people are inclined to attribute the whole business to the personal qualities of the perpetrators of this evil. One must confess that, not infrequently, such accusations are well-founded. But let us pose this question: Why, notwithstanding the obvious and enormous harm done to the country's resources by such action, despite societal indignation, and even notwithstanding the existence of a whole complex of decrees and laws directed against such phenomena, we have not until now seen any substantial progress in the struggle against them? It seems that the very scale and persistence of such phenomena does not permit us to "write them off" as the product of the volition of certain individuals. To all appearance, there are objective forces at work here as well, brought forth by the peculiar conditions of the world's first state that has undertaken to build a new society. Under these conditions it has not been possible to allocate, out of the scarce state funds, the means necessary to manage the economy in strict conformity with the requirements of rational utilization of the natural resources, notwithstanding the fact that this task had been formulated by V.I. Lenin during the initial stages of socialist development and consecrated in many decrees.[93]

Only after the accelerated industrialization had caused too many "black streams . . . [flow] down black slopes"[94] voices rose to lament the fate of the natural environment at the hands of the managers of socialist property and economic planners. Thus, further investigations may show that Khrushchev rather than Lenin was the Teddy Roosevelt of the Soviet Union.

Notes

1. V.N. Makarov, *Okrana prirody v SSSR* (Moscow, 1947), pp. 5, 7-8, 20, 42, 49, 56 (three out of the four references to Lenin concern the same topic).
2. *Bol'shaia sovetskaia entsiklopediia*, 2nd. ed. (Moscow, 1955), XXXI, 477.
3. Shaposhnikov and Borisov, "Pervye meropriiatiaa sovetskogo gosudarstva po okhrane priordy," *Okhrana prirody i zapovednoe delo v SSSR* (1958), No. 3, p. 93.

4. N.I. Kostilukevich, ed. *Okhrana priorody: Priorodnye resursy Belorussii i ikh ratsional'noe ispol'zovanie* (Minsk, 1969), p. 9.

5. Ibid., p. 8. See also E.N. Kolotinskaia, *Pravovaia okhrana prirody v SSSR* (Moscow, 1962), p. 9, and A.I. Fedorov, *Okhrana i ispol'zocanie prirodnykh resursov* (Alma-Ata, 1964), pp. 71-77.

6. V.I. Lenin, *Sobranie sochinenii*, 3rd ed. (Moscow, 1930), IV, 179-89; hereafter cited as *Ss*, 3rd. ed.

7. Ibid., 4th ed. (Moscow, 1950), V, 139; hereafter cited as *Ss*, 4th ed.

8. Idem, XXVII, 134.

9. Lenin, *Ss*, 3rd ed., XXV, 512; XXVI, 18-19; XXVII, 135.

10. Lenin, *Ss*, 4th ed., XVIII, 338.

11. Lenin, *Ss*, 3rd ed., XXII, 453.

12. Lenin, *Ss*, 4th ed., XXXI, 478.

13. Institut Marksizma-Leninizma pri Tsk KPSS, *Vladimir Il'ich Lenin: Biografiia* (Moscow, 1963), 561.

14. Lenin, *Ss*, 4th ed., XXVII, 288.

15. Ibid., pp. 285-87.

16. *Leninskii snornik (Moscow, 1932), XX, 157-59.*

17. V.I.Lenin, *Polnoe sobranie sochinenii*, 5th ed. (Moscow, 1963), XL, 189. On Lenin's faith in science and technology see also E.B. Genkina, *Lenin—Predsedatel' Sovnarkoma i STO: Iz istorii gosudarstvennoi deiatel'nosti V.I. Lenina v 1921–1922 godakh* (Moscow, 1960), 114–143.

18. See, e.g. R.F. Dasmann, *Environmental Conservation* (New York, 1959). Contrast with Eric Hoffer, *The Temper of Our Time* (New York, 1969), pp. 93-94.

19. F. Engels, *Dialectics of Nature* (New York, 1940), pp. 291-92.

20. K. Marx and F. Engels, *Ausgewählte Briefe* (Berlin, 1953), pp. 233-35.

21. K.N. Blagosklonov, A.A. Inozemtsev, and V.N. Tikhomirov, *Okrana priody* (Moscow, 1967), p. 42 (quoting K. Marx, *Kapital* [Moscow, 1951], III, 789).

22. Ibid., p. 63.

23. Ibid., pp. 62-68; Makarov, p. 56.

24. Decree of November 9 (October 27), 1917. *Sobranie uzakonenii i rasporiazhenii Raboch-krest'ianskogo pravitel'stva RASFSR*, 1917-1918, no. 1, text 3; hereafter cited as SU RASFSR.

25. Decree arts. 1-2; Instruction art. 1.

26. Instruction art. 2.

27. Lenin, *Ss*, 4th ed., III, 460; XIXm 49.

28. G.N. Polianskia, *Pravo gosudarstvennoi sobstvennosti na lesa v SSSR* (Moscow, 1959), p. 63.

29. SU RSFSR 1917-1918, no. 6, text 93.

30. Decree of January 25 (12), 1918, SU RSFSR 1917-1918, no. 15, text 220 (not signed by Lenin).

31. See, e.g., Decree of February 2 (January 20), 1918, *Dekrety sovetskoi viasti* (Moscow, 1957), I, 562 (signed by Lenin); hereafter cited as *Dekrety*;

Decree of February 2, (1918, idem, p. 594 (signature undetermined); Decree of March 26, 1918, idem, II, 28 (signed by Lenin).

32. Idem, ii, 54.

33. SU RSFSR 1917-1918, no. 42, text 522 (the date is conventionally given as May 27 (14), 1918).

34. Blagoskolonov et al, p. 70.

35. Meant here is *Dekrety*, a useful six-volume series begun in 1957 but still incomplete after the publication of four volumes.

36. Ibid., pp. 312-13, 329. Professor N.I. Faleev, an authority on forests, was the author of *Lesnoe pravo* (Moscow, 1912). Polianskaia, pp. 78, 83.

37. *Svod zakonov Rossiiskoi imperii, tom vos'moi, chast 1, Ustav lesnoi,* izdanie 1905 goda, arts. p. 710-60.

38. Blagosklonov et al., p. 55.

39. Directive of June 18, 1918, *Dekrety*, II, 621 (signed by Lenin); Decree of August 2, 1918, idem, II, 133 (signed by Lenin); Decree of (ab.) November 28, 1918, idem, IB, 91 (signed by Lenin).

40. Decree of August 27, 1918, idem, III, 254 (not signed by Lenin).

41. Decree of December 27, 1918, idem, IV, 261.

42. Lenin, *Bolnoe sobranie sochinenii*, LIV, 408.

43. Lenin, *Ss*, 3rd ed., XXIII, 468.

44. Lenin, *Ss*, 4th ed., XXX, 119. On December 2, 1918, Lenin told the All-Russian Conference of the RKP (b) of the preoccupation of the Council of Ministers of Labor and Defense with the fuel problem and stressed the need for war-like measures to overcome the crisis. Lenin, *Ss*, 3rd ed., XXIII, 570.

45. Shaposhnikov et al., p. 95.

46. Decree of August 2, 1918, *Dekrety*, III, 133 (signed by Lenin).

47. *Cf.* Directive of June 18, 1918, idem, II, 621 (signed by Lenin); Directive of October 11, 1918, idem, III, 413 (not signed by Lenin).

48. Directive of December 4, 1918, idem, IV, 143 (signed by Lenin).

49. Decree of November 2, 1918, idem, III, 519 (signed by Lenin).

50. S.K. Gil', *Shest' let s V.I. Leninym: Vospominaniia lichnogo shofera Vladimira il'icha Lenina* (Leningrad, 1947), pp. 65-68.

51. SU RSFSR 1920, no. 32, text 157. See also Kostiukevich, p. 11.

52. Blagoskolonov et al., p. 71.

53. Decree of July 27, 1920, SU RSFSR 1920, no. 69, text 320. A telegram to all provincial executive committees written just weeks later, between August 10 and 13, 1920, urged the addressees to "make every effort necessary to prevent and fight forest fires." The telegram was signed by Lenin and bore a marginal note in his handwriting: "until a special new decree." Lenin, *Polnoe sobranie sochinenii*, LI, 256-57.

54. Decree of August 3, 1921, cited in Blagosklonov et al., p. 70.

55. Decree of November 28, 1921, SU RSFSR 1921, no. 77, text 650 (signed by Lenin). Shaposhnikov et al., p. 94, also speak of Lenin's concern for

the forests of Caucasian and Carpathian mountains and cite a decree of December 24, 1921, which, however, appears to be the same decree as that of November 28. The latter only concerns Crimea.

56. Vasil'ev, "Lesnye resursy i lesnoe khoziaistvo," in Akademiia nauk SSSR, *Prirodnye resursy Sovetskogo soiuza, ikh ispol'zovanie i vosproizvodstvo* (Moscow, 1953), pp. 137 and 159.

57. SU RSFSR 1918, no. 96, text 969 (not signed by Lenin).

58. SU RSFSR 1920, no. 12, text 78 (signed by Lenin).

59. Decree of May 31, 1921, SU RSFSR 1921, no. 50, text 265.

60. SU RSFSR 1921, no. 66, text 505 (signed by Lenin).

61. SU RSFSR 1922, no. 61, text 780 (not signed by Lenin).

62. State Duma, Commission on Matters of Fishing, Report on the Draft Fishing Code, March 1, 1916, *Prilozheniia k stenograficheskim otchetam Gosudarstvennoi dumy, IV sozyv, sessiia IV*, no. 88.

63. Decree of May 24, 1921, SU RSFSR 1921, no. 49, text 259 (signed by Lenin).

64. Decree from February, 1919, SU RSFSR 1919, no. 4, text 45 (not signed by Lenin).

65. See, e.g., B.Z. Slutskii, *Na strazhe rybnykh bogatstv* (Moscow, 1969), p. 16; Kolbasov, *Okhrana priorody po sovetskomu zakonodatel'stvu* (Moscow, 1961), pp. 6-7; Kostiukevich, pp. 10-11.

66. Lenin, *Polno sobranie sochinenii*, LIV, 317.

67. Decree of November 8, 1918, SU RSFSR 1918, no. 90, text 908 (not signed by Lenin).

68. V.I. Lenin, *O sotsialisticheskoi zakonnosti 1917-1922 gg.* (Moscow, 1958), p. 353.

69. Lenin, *Polno Sobranie sochinenii*, LII, 314; idem, LII, 3, 3, 246-47, 376; *Leninskii snornik*, XX, 228-300.

70. SU RSFSR 1919, no. 21, text 256. Makarov, e.g., refers to this decree merely as an enactment of the Council of Ministers, without mentioning Lenin. Makarov, p. 32.

71. Gil', pp. 53-57; Louis Fischer, *The Life of Lenin* (New York, 1965), pp. 18, 33, 380-83.

72. Kostiukevich, p. 10.

73. *Cf.* Blagoskolonov et al., p. 71.

74. Decree of July 20, 1920, SU RSFSR 1920, no. 66, text 297.

75. SU 1922, no. 54, text 687 (not signed by Lenin).

76. Decree of March 1, 1923, SU RSFSR 1923, no. 17, text 217 (not signed by Lenin).

77. See State Duma, Commission to Review the Draft Law on Hunting, Report on the Draft Law on Hunting, December 10, 1911, *Prilozheniia k stenograficheskim otchetam Gosudarstvennoi dumy, III sozyv, sessiia V*, no. 283.

78. *Supra* note 76. The earlier Decree of May 27, 1919, *supra* note 72, had

also referred to "*zapovednye mesta* (preserves *or* refuges)" in the context of restrictions on hunting.

79. Shaposhnikov et al., pp. 94-95 (identifies Pod"iapol'skii as "one of the well-known conservationists"); Kostiukevich, p. 11 (identifies Pod"iapol'skii as "chairman of Astrakhan' Provincial Executive Committee").

80. Blagosklonov et al., p. 72.

81. Shaposhnikov et al., p. 95.

82. SU RSFSR 1920, no. 38, text 181 (signed by Lenin).

83. Decree of January 31, 1921, discussed in Blagosklonov et al., *supra* note 23, p. 72 (signed by Lenin).

84. Kostiukevich, p. 12.

85. Blagosklonov et al., p. 423.

86. SU RSFSR 1921, no. 65, text 492.

87. Blagosklonov et al., p. 72.

88. Kostiukevich, p. 12.

89. Makarov, p. 42; Blagosklonov et al., p. 423. The date on Suputinsk is dually reported. See idem, p. 68 (year 1911) and p. 422 (year 1932). The latter source also puts Barguzinsk in 1926 (p. 422) and does not mention Saiansk at all (pp. 421-25).

90. Blagosklonov et al., p. 422.

91. Ibid., p. 67.

92. Ibid., p. 66; Makarov, p. 9.

93. Grin, "Problemy preobrazovaniia prirody i zadachi geografii," in Akademiia Nauk SSSR, *Priroda i obshchestvo* (Moscow, 1968), pp. 118, 124.

94. *Literaturnaia gazeta*, August 9, 1967, p. 10, transl. in *Current Digest of the Soviet Press* (1967), XIX, no. 33, p. 10.

6

Leninism: Rationale of Party Dictatorship

BERNARD A. RAMUNDO

Leninism continues to be relevant to government and law in the Soviet Union and may be expected to remain so for the life of the Soviet regime. The continuing relevance of Leninism stems from its practical utility as a source of doctrine and of respectability for governing society during the "building of communism." In effect, Leninism provides a useful theoretical rationale and credibility mechanism for Communist party rule of the Soviet Union. In endorsing the supremacy of Party rule, including the license, when necessary, to govern above and not within the law, Leninism institutionalizes a power system based upon Party dictatorship and conditional legality. The acceptability of this system is enhanced by showing continuity with the Marxist past and carefully nurturing a cult of Lenin and his ideas to provide flexible orthodoxy for Party policies in governing Soviet society.[1] Thus, Leninism is a facile governing tool because it states a manipulative theory of government and at the same time provides a sacred basis for enhancing the acceptability of manipulation. The purpose of this chapter is to describe Leninism as the theoretical and practical rationale of Party dictatorship and conditional legality.

Unlike Marx and Engels, who enjoyed the luxury of theory spinning without the prospect or responsibility of wielding power, Lenin had to translate theory into a practical power system. Marx and Engels provided a basis for such a system in their views on state and law. They considered state and law to be weapons in the class struggle which, in reflecting economic relationships within society, serve class interests. The existence of limiting, eternal laws, based upon abstract ethical principles such as nature, reason or justice was rejected.[2] In short, every state was deemed to operate as a class dictatorship. In Marx's and Engels' view, when the proletariat assumed power it too would use the machinery of state and law in a dictatorship against its class enemies.[3] Beyond this essential feature of the workers' state, the dictatorship of the proletariat, little was said concerning its detailed functioning as the model workers' state, the Paris Commune of 1871, was too short-lived to provide any meaningful experience. This silence was potentially troublesome for Lenin since an essential element in the theories of Marx and Engels was the concept of the withering away of the state, and strong anarchic elements existed which tended to discount the importance of the state once the proletariat seized power.[4]

Lenin drew upon Marx and Engels to forge flexible tools of Party power. He downplayed the theory of the withering away of the state and provided for the continuing existence of the dictatorship of the proletariat by proclaiming that the dictatorship would be necessary to effect the transition to communism.[5]

The essence of Marx's teaching on the state has been mastered only by those who understand that the dictatorship of a single class is necessary not only for every class society in general. . . but also for the entire historical period which separates capitalism from "classless society," from communism.[6]

Having provided continuity for the dictatorship, Lenin insulated it against the constraints of law and abstract ethics and morality.

Dictatorship is rule based directly upon force and unrestricted by any laws. The revolutionary dictatorship of the proletariat is rule won and maintained by the use of violence by the proletariat against the bourgeoisie, rule that is unrestricted by any laws.[7]

. . . We repudiate all morality taken apart from human society and classes. . . . We say that our morality is entirely subordinated to the interests of the class struggle of the proletariat. Our morality is derived from the interests of the class struggle of the proletariat.

. . .We say: morality is what serves to destroy the old exploiting society and to unite all the toilers around the proletariat, which is building up a new, communist society.[8]

The class character of state power was stressed: "For a Marxist there is no such thing as democracy in general—democracy exists only for the class."[9] Rights and democracy were not to be granted *in vacuo*; their grant had to be keyed to the needs of the proletariat. In an often quoted passage, Lenin rejected unlimited freedom of the press in favor of selectivity as to the extent of the freedom granted and the class beneficiary.[a] In effect, Lenin created a system of conditional rights and legality. Although he utilized ideology as a supporting rationale, he recognized that ideology could be burdensome to the wielding of power. He alleviated this burden by formulating the concept of "living Marxism," the essence of which is the avoidance of adherence to theoretical formulations of the past in the face of actual events, i.e., the adjustment of theory to reality.[10] Lenin completed his system of power by placing it at the disposal of the Communist party he led by proclaiming the Party's organizational and leadership role in effecting the transition to communism.[11] In this way, the dictatorship of the proletariat became the dictatorship of the Party.

[a]Lenin in a letter to Miasnikov commented upon the slogan of unlimited freedom of the press with the following questions: "What freedom of the press? For whom? For which class?" (V.M. Kuritsyn, "Bor'ba V.I. Lenina protiv Opportunizma," *Sovetskoe Gosudarstvo i Pravo* (Soviet State and Law) (hereinafter cited *SGIP*), no. 1 (1970), pp. 13-22.) (See also, Theses no. 6, p. 2.)

Thus Lenin drew upon the theories of Marx and Engels for legitimacy in fashioning a Party dictatorship uninhibited by law, morality or ideology in directing the "building of communism." His system of power had the trappings of orthodoxy and, at the same time, the practical flexiblity of revolutionary legality. Lenin's successors in power have felt the same need for apparent orthodoxy and flexible legality. It is not surprising, therefore, that the Leninist power system and technique of rationalization have been retained basically intact by these successors who have the added advantage of being able to invoke the ideological lore of Leninism for additional legitimacy.

The current line is that the Soviet Union has evolved from the dictatorship of the proletariat to the state of the entire people.[12] The directing role of the Communist party and its monopoly of power in governing society during the transition to communism remains unchanged. Thus, both the dictatorship of the proletariat and its successor, the state of the entire people, are party dictatorships. In recent legal literature both state forms are characterized as Marxist-Leninist socialist democracies in which the democracy accorded is subordinated to the interests of socialist and communist construction.[13] The emphasis on socialist democracy is an apparent aftermath of Czechoslovakia and the attempt there to introduce more objective democracy. "Democratic socialism," "pluralistic democracy," and other formulations which depart from the Soviet standard of limited democracy in favor of Party rule are rejected as the antithesis of socialist democracy, falling somewhere between Marxism-Leninism and imperialist ideology.[14] The formulations are specifically criticised for accepting, contrary to Marxism-Leninism, "bourgeois illusions about absolute personal freedom"[15] and the need for the Communist party to share power with other parties as a means of ensuring greater democracy.[16] In these polemical writings as well as the standard commentaries on state and law, party dictatorship and flexible legality are presented with the trappings of orthodoxy à la Lenin.

To provide the color of orthodoxy for Party rule, Soviet commentaries stress in combination the general relevance of Marx and Engels, Lenin's creative application of Marxism, and the charisma of Lenin and his wisdom. Lenin is portrayed as the founder of the Soviet state and socialist law who creatively expanded Marxism into a system of socialist statehood (government) and law.[17] "Marxist views on law and its role under socialism were worked out concretely in the works and practice of V.I. Lenin."[18] Lenin's pronouncements on the class essence of the socialist state and socialist law and their use to build the new society are buttressed by a showing that he actively and personally worked at the implementation of these pronouncements.[19] License for anything that cannot be subsumed under the basic principles of Marxist-Leninism is sought under the concept of creative or living Marxism which, Soviet commentaries carefully point out, Lenin formulated as the practical solution to the problem of applying ideology to real life.

He [Lenin] energetically fought attempts to convert the teachings of Marx and Engels into ossified, dead dogma. We do not at all look upon the theory of Marx as something final and inviolable,—he wrote—rather we are convinced that it is only the corner stone of that science which socialists must develop further if they do not wish to lag behind real events. Lenin viewed the creative development of Marxism as a necessary prerequisite for effective revolutionary theory, the key to the theoretical and practical solution to the problems confronting the working class. . .[20]

The characteristic of the Leninist ideas of law and legality . . . underscore the importance of Marxism-Leninism as living, creative teaching. Marxist-Leninist views on law are not dogmatic postulates; rather, they constitute a revolutionary theory which develops with the practice of revolutionary struggle and the demands of social development. As a consequence, with the development of conditions and of society, the profound meaning of the Leninist ideas on law in a socialist society are revealed with ever new facets.[21]

The manner in which living Marxism is utilized to explain new positions was demonstrated when the Soviet Union was declared to be a state of the entire people and no longer the dictatorship of the proletariat, the state vehicle apparently envisioned by Lenin for the transition to communism.[22] The mantle of legitimacy is assumed for the present leadership through continuity statements such as the following:

The basic principle established by Lenin for Soviet legislation and for the legislative activity of the Soviet state is even today the guiding light for the party and the entire nation of the USSR . . . for the further strengthening of the role of law in the building of socialism and communism.[23]

In the recent Theses of the Central Committee of the Communist Party of the Soviet Union, another credibility category, the experience and special art of the Party in applying Marxism-Leninism, seems to have been added:

Relying on the theory of Marxism-Leninism and the experience acquired through struggle, the CPSU works out policies, guides the masses and the economic, social, political and spiritual life of society. . .[24]

The Marxist-Leninist party of our epoch is . . . a party which is continuously mastering the complex art of applying the general principles of Marxism to concrete conditions. . .[25]

A recent Soviet commentary seeks additional credibility for the Party as a co-creator of Leninism: "The basic principles of socialist law and socialist legality were worked out by V.I. Lenin and the communist party in the course of the October revolution through the gathering of revolutionary experience, the practical work of building a state . . ."[26] Although the number of credibility categories has apparently increased, the technique remains the one worked out by Lenin, i.e., the invocation of orthodoxy in some form to gain support for the regime of Party dictatorship.

The Soviet Union remains the Party dictatorship created by Lenin. The need for the Party to direct the building of communism is a constant element in Soviet literature. "The most important principle of socialist democracy and of the entire political system of socialism, and the indispensable condition of progress along the socialist path is the directing role of the vanguard of the working class and of all toilers—the Communist Party."[27] There is, however, formal rejection of the concept of a dictatorship of the Party. The effort here is to stress the vanguard role of the Party lest it be considered to have objectives or purposes at variance with those of the working classes. "Actually the slogan 'dictatorship of the party' undermined the directing role of the Communist Party in the system of socialist democracy. The party as the vanguard of the working class only fulfills its directing role when it has the masses behind it, not when it draws away from them."[28] The substance of the matter is that the party is the locus of power, being the directing force in the building of communism. The importance attached to Party rule was demonstrated in the summer of 1968 when the Warsaw Treaty Organization states, less Rumania, occupied Czechoslovakia, where the Dubcek reform threatened "socialist democracy" and the primacy of the Communist party.[29]

The effectiveness of Party rule is reinforced by the concept of conditional or flexible legality which is a particularization of Lenin's basic approach that state power should be wielded in the class interest. "According to Lenin, the role of law like other social-political phenomena (e.g., democracy) cannot be estimated in general, abstractly divorced from the social-economic and revolutionary processes occurring in society. The role and importance of law in socialist society directly depends on the stage of revolution and in particular on the intensity and nature of class strife."[30] The absence of the constraint of law on the exercise of power has been a continuing feature of the party dictatorship as has been the preoccupation with legality. "Lenin said: 'He is a poor revolutionary who in a moment of intensive struggle is stopped by the inviolability of the law.' It is in this context that we should understand the well known Leninist principle that it is 'necessary to struggle in all ways for legality,' but never forgetting the limits of legality in revolution."[31] In the early days of the Bolshevik regime, the emphasis was on revolutionary legality, i.e., that legality necessary to further the cause of revolution. With the shift in emphasis from revolution to the task of building socialism and communism and the declaration that socialist law would operate throughout the transition to communism to effect that transition, revolutionary legality became socialist legality. "Socialist law . . . [is] the socially useful instrument for social development and for resolving the tasks of socialist revolution and of communist construction."[32] Just as revolutionary legality was a legality with a special purpose and bias, so too is socialist legality. Although there has been a shift in the specific purposes served by legality, the general purpose of serving the interests of the working class movement in building communism has remained throughout.[b]

Socialist legality, therefore, is class legality during the building of communism. It is that legality which is compatible with the needs of the working class movement as determined by the Communist party of the Soviet Union. Therefore, the modifier "socialist" is a rather candid indicator of a special type of legality.

The problem of legality, and that of the independent category "socialist legality," basically involves the practical realization and application of juridical norms. In this view of the matter, "socialist legality" is a category which expresses the unity of law and its practical application in a socialist society. This is how V.I. Lenin understood socialist legality. He spoke of socialist legality whenever there was a need to describe the practical application of legal precepts.[33]

The special legality is reflected in Soviet constitutional and legislative provisions which affirm the fundamental primacy, vis-à-vis legal institutions, of the task of Communist construction. This primacy is, in effect, a euphemism for the primacy of Party rule of the Soviet Union. For example, Article 125 of the Soviet Constitution states the conditional nature of freedom of speech, the press, assembly and street processions and demonstrations:

In conformity with the interests of the working people, and in order to strengthen the socialist system, the citizens of the U.S.S.R. are guaranteed by law:

(a) Freedom of speech;
(b) Freedom of the press;
(c) Freedom of assembly. . .
(d) Freedom of street processions and demonstrations.

The civil rights are ensured by placing at the disposal of the working people and their organizations printing presses, stocks of paper, public buildings, the streets, communication facilities and other material requisites for the exercise of these rights.[34]

Thus, these freedoms can only be enjoyed (a) in conformity with the interests of the working people and (b) in order to strengthen the socialist system. The Civil Code reflects similar conditionality: "Civil law rights are protected by law except where their enjoyment contradicts the purpose of these rights in a socialist society building communism."[35] These provisions are express statements of the overriding principle of socialist legality which conditions the operation of the Soviet legal system. The principle states a rationale for modification or de-

---

[b]Socialist legality actively promotes the advance of Soviet society towards communism. P.S. Romashkin, *Fundamentals of Soviet Law* (Moscow, n.d.), p. 24.

feasance of legal and other proclaimed rights under the color of the building of communism in the interest of party policies and decisions.

The Leninist concept of revolutionary legality and its current manifestation, socialist legality, negate the existence of inalienable or other rights which can be invoked against state power. Although the potential for instability and lack of predictability is thereby introduced into Soviet legal institutions and relationships, the principle of socialist legality does not mean that the Soviet legal system operates arbitrarily or *ad hoc*. Stability and predictability, important elements in the ordering of any society, are also important in a society building communism and, therefore, features of socialist legality. Moreover, the current need is not for relatively unstable revolutionary legality; but rather for stability to permit necessary internal development. Soviet writers note that under the Leninist concept of law there can be more or less legality depending on the course of socialist development and that societal conditions in the present state of the entire people permit the enjoyment of greater legality, i.e., more stability and more predictability.[36] The stability and predictability which are now a part of socialist legality do not, however, inhibit arbitrary state action when deemed critical to the building of communism.[c] A graphic example of this occurred which culminated in a statutory prohibition against retroactive application of increased penalties, a secret decree was enacted to permit application of the capital punishment, then recently authorized for serious cases of foreign currency speculation, to a notorious case of speculation where the acts and the trial occurred at a time when the penalty provided was limited to imprisonment.[37] Party resoluteness in waging a campaign against this type of activity transcended the general interest in legality. Other examples of convenient legality can be adduced to demonstrate the primacy accorded to the needs of Party rule.[d] That primacy is accorded party needs should not lead to the conclusion that socialist legality is sham legality in all or most cases. Socialist legality operates at its biased and purposeful worst in areas of special Party concern. More frequently it operates quite respectably because the basic regime interest in stability is not outweighed by special needs. One's view of socialist legality can be distorted if it is not recognized that the special areas, under present regime needs, are rather exceptional.

[c]Cf. "The result is that Soviet Government has no concern for the stability of the laws, and consequently no concern with the legality (socialist or not) of the regime." (K. Grzybowski, American Bar Association, *A Contrast Between the Legal Systems in the United States and in the Soviet Union* [Baltimore, 1968], p. 285). The Soviets have to be concerned with some level of stability and legality because stability and legality are part of the problem of government. The Soviets are not concerned with objective as distinguished from pro-regime stability and legality.

[d]"The Soviet Government felt free to violate the principle that criminal punishment may be imposed by courts only, and revived quasi-administrative penalties in the legislation on parasites, and in the comradely courts. It still uses the arm of terror by organizing campaigns against certain types of crimes singled out for suppression during a given period (recent examples are hooliganism, economic crimes, and parasites)." (Ibid., p. 285.)

In effect, the concept of "socialist legality" provides an institutionalized point of entry for Party policy even when at variance with the formal requirements of Soviet law. The compeling character of the concept, as did its predecessor, revolutionary legality, effectively precludes the existence of an independent judiciary notwithstanding the pronouncement of Article 112 of the Soviet Constitution that "judges are independent and subject only to the law."[38]

The dynamics of power of Party dictatorship in the Soviet Union remain essentially the same as Lenin conceived them. Although revolutionary legality has given way to socialist legality, the technique remains the invocation of a higher value, "the building of communism," in the cause of which unlimited power is wielded. To buttress this theoretical basis of power, the Marxist and Leninist past are constantly invoked to show that there is orthodoxy and continuity in the Party's discharge of its papal-like function in determining what is necessary for the building of communism.

The contribution of Lenin goes beyond the theory of unconditional Party power. He demonstrated the technique of harnessing ideology to the governmental effort and formulated the concept of "living Marxism" to exploit the ideological past. In addition to structuring a system of power with the trappings of orthodoxy, Lenin enriched the fund of usable ideology with his own works which, reflecting the practical considerations involved in assuming and wielding power, have more relevance than Marxism for those who have succeeded him in governing the Soviet Union.

Notes

1. In 1970, the year of the 100th Anniversary of the birth of Lenin, a special effort was made to relate current policies and practices to his ideas. (See, for example, generally "K 100-Letiiu so Dnia Rozhdeniia Vladimira Il'icha Lenina, Tezisy Tsentral'novo Komiteta Kommunisticheskoi Partii Sovetskovo Soiuza," hereafter cited as "Theses"; *Pravda*, December 23, 1969, pp. 1-4, "Lenin's name and cause will live forever" (p. 4); and the special centennial issue of *Soviet Life*, April 1970; and, specifically, M. Kh. Kalashnik, "The Historical Experience of the CPSU in the Implementation of Lenin's Ideas on the Defense of the Socialist Homeland," *Voprosy Istorii KPSS* (Questions Concerning the History of the CPSU) (November 1969), pp. 34-48, as excerpted in translation in Department of Commerce Joint Publications Research Service, *Translations on USSR Political and Sociological Affairs*, no. 49 (January 21, 1970), pp. 1-11; and A. Arnoldov, "Lenin and Cultural Progress," *Moscow News*, no. 7 (February 22-March 1, 1969), pp. 8-9.

2. See *Manifesto of the Communist Party* in *Selected Works of Karl Marx and Frederich Engels* (Moscow, 1949-50), I, 14-61 at 47. Engels' rejection of the

concept of eternal justice reflects the class interest orientation attributed to state and law: ". . . and always this justice is but the ideologized, glorified expression of the existing economic relations, at times from their conservative, and other times from their revolutionary angle. The justice of the Greeks and Romans held slavery to be just; the justice of the bourgeoisie of 1789 demanded the abolition of feudalism on the ground that it was unjust. . . . The conception of eternal justice, therefore, varies not only with time and place, but also with the persons concerned. . . " (Ibid., p. 565).

3. Ibid., pp. 439-40.

4. Ibid., pp. 470-78.

5. V.I. Lenin, *Marx, Engels, Marxism* 4th English Edition, (Moscow, 1951), pp. 378, 391, 395-96, and 398-99.

6. *Lenin on Proletarian Revolution and Proletarian Dictatorship* (Peking, 1960), p. 80.

7. Ibid., p. 81.

8. Lenin, *Marx, Engels, Marxism*, pp. 535-38.

9. Ibid., pp. 443. See also "Bourgeois and Proletarian Democracy" (excerpt from Lenin's "The Proletarian Revolution and the Renegade Kautsky"), *Soviet Life* (October, 1969), pp. 32-33.

10. Lenin, *Marx, Engels, Marxism*, pp. 385-86.

11. Ibid., p. 125.

12. See my "The Soviet State of the Entire People—Non-Marxist 'Living Marxism'," *The George Washington Law Review*, v. 32, no. 2 (1963), pp. 315-27.

13. V.M. Chkhikvadze, "Leninskie Idei Demokratii i Sovremennost'," *SGIP*, no. 1 (1969), pp. 5-18, at 7-9.

14. Ibid., pp. 6 and 14-17. See also I. Chkhikvishvili, "Socialism and Freedom," trans. from *Izvestia*, September 12, 1968, in *The Current Digest of the Soviet Press*, v. 20, no. 37, pp. 14-15.

15. Ibid., p. 13.

16. Ibid., p. 15, "Direction by the communist parties is the main condition and strongest guarantee of socialist democracy, its development, strengthening and flowering."

17. A.V. Mitskevich, "Rol' V.I. Lenina v Sozdanii Sovetskovo Prava," *SGIP*, no. 3 (1969), pp. 51-60, at 51. See also D.L. Zlatopol'skii, "V.I. Lenin—Sozdatel' Teorii Sotsialisticheskovo Narodnovo Predstavitel'stva," *SGIP*, no. 8 (1969), pp. 40-48; and "Theses," p. 1.

18. S.S. Alekseev, "V.I. Lenin O Prave v Sotsialisticheskom Obshchestve," *SGIP*, no. 9 (1969), pp. 3-11.

19. Mitskevich, pp. 52-58.

20. Theses, p. 1.

21. Alekseev, p. 4.

22. See Ramundo, "The Soviet State of the Entire People."

23. Mitskevich, p. 60.

24. Theses no. 7, p. 2.

25. Ibid., no. 17, p. 3.

26. Alekseev, p. 4.

27. Kuritsyn, p. 19; see also p. 21 and Theses no. 7, p. 2.

28. Ibid., p. 20.

29. See "Rech' Tovarishcha L.l. Brezhneva," *Pravda*, November 13, 1968, pp. 1-2, and Chkhikvadze, pp. 6 and 14-17. "The entire experience of political struggle convincingly demonstrates that the development, improvement, and application of socialist democracy is inextricably tied to the recognition and strengthening of the directing role of the Communist Party in marching towards the new society. That is why the CPSU . . . highly values the determined struggle which the fraternal communist parties are waging against any attempts to weaken the directing role of the communist parties, . . ." A.I. Denisov, "Kommunizm i Demokratiia," *SGIP*, no. 12 (1969), pp. 3-13, at 9.

30. Alekseev, p. 10.

31. Ibid., p. 5.

32. Ibid.

33. Alekseev, p. 5.

34. A. Denisov and M. Kirichenko, *Soviet State Law* (Moscow, 1960), Appendixes, p. 405. See also Amos J. Peaslee, *Constitutions of Nations*, rev. 3rd ed., III—Europe, part 2 (The Hague, 1968), p. 1005.

35. *Grazhdanskii Kodeks, RSFSR* (Moscow, 1964) Article 5, p. 8.

36. Alekseev, pp. 11-12.

37. K. Grzybowski, American Bar Association, *A Contrast Between the Legal Systems in the United States and in the Soviet Union* (Baltimore, 1968), pp. 138-41. See also Dietrich A. Loeber, "Legal Rules 'For Internal Use Only'," *International and Comparative Law Quarterly* (Jan., 1970), pp. 70-98.

38. Denisov and Kirishenko, p. 402.

7 Lenin and Parliament

ALFRED LEVIN

"The Duma is a police game, but there is no hint of a constitution in it."[1] This was Lenin's relatively early reaction to the institution of a legislative Duma and it remained essentially unchanged to November 1917. Our study focuses on the years 1905 to 1907, the years of conception, forced birth, and early development of the Imperial Duma. For these were the years of Lenin's most intensive examination of that institution and parliamentarism. Like all other Russian "public figures" he had to gauge this basic, new twist in the Russian political tradition. For Lenin this meant an analysis in terms of the progress of the revolutionary movement toward a proletarian victory and the dictatorship of the proletariat. He had to prove that the new, "popular representation," granted from above, and not his projected dictatorship, was undemocratic. His task was complicated by the need to prove this to the "petit bourgeois" wing of his own party and to all the other "democratic" elements seeking the subversion and elimination of the imperial regime.

For Lenin the Duma was bourgeois even in its Bulygin garb; a phenomenon in the capitalist superstructure. Hence he concentrated his attention and fire on that political element which he determined was the moving bourgeois force of the representative idea, the Kadet party. And his basic strictures on and considerations concerning the Russian parliament, and, to a degree, toward parliament in general, were largely determined by his conception of the nature, strategy and program of that party.[2]

Generally, his assaults on the Kadets were on a reasoned, consistent, ideological level, but to nail his points he was capable of indulging in low comedy, which appears to reflect some interesting overtones of an aristocratic contempt for stereotyped middle class mores. The Kadets are variously represented, particularly in moments of Lenin's obviously rising gorge, as capable of all kinds and sorts of compromise and skulduggery. They are "bourgeois hagglers," "stockjobbers," "craven, petty double-dealing souls," "honest brokers," "monarchist-minded patriots of the money-bag," and "hucksters." His exaggerated conception of the nature of the conversations between the Kadets and Premier S. Ia. Witte evoked the comment that "the haggling is making good progress. The chafferers are bawling their rock bottom prices, calling it a deal. . . ." He argued the Kadets would use a provisional, revolutionary government as a bargaining gambit "just as a customer threatens a shopkeeper he will go to another shop. Lower your price, Mr. Witte, or we shall go into the provisional, revolutionary government. . . ." They would take a stand variously for republican democracy or limited monarchy "for a fee," "for a professional salary or a lawyer's fee." These attitudes, at the least, offer some kind of material for those who are fascinated by Lenin's consciousness of his aristocratic origins.[3]

A number of axioms stand immovable in V.I. Lenin's concept of the Kadets. He would brook no challenge to his conviction that they were bourgeois in the Marxist sense. Hence under the impact of "objective circumstances," they had to develop a spirit of compromise and all of the strategy and techniques that frame of mind implied. And from the nature of Lenin's own goals, strategy, tenor of expression and rigidity of purpose, it is evident that he was of such a temperament that he could not tolerate Kadet compromise, passivity, or conditioned judgments, as norms of political action. He would accept them only *in extremis.*[4] Saltykov-Shchedrin, he asserted, had long ago translated this "but" of the Russian liberals into intelligible language: "ears will never grow higher than the forehead, never!"[5]

Kadet compulsion to compromise, Lenin maintained, stemmed from their fear of revolution and their need to make arrangements with autocracy and to control mass action. When Durnovo allowed the provincial Zemstvo Congress to sit in Moscow in November of 1904, "the bourgeoisie had promised a discount in return for a discount,"[6] and consequently their requirements made them a positive and lethal danger to the revolutionary cause. They were reformers, not revolutionaries, who would eliminate the "different shades" in the liberation movement. They did not want a complete democratic revolution with the overthrow of tsarism and landownership, and hence they sought control of the peasantry and workers. The very knowledge of their dominant position in the existing economic system, led them to aspire to dominate the revolution, and they were indeed a highly influential element. As petite bourgeoisie their intellectuals could easily attract the peasantry, who were likewise petite bourgeoisie. If the party of the proletariat were attracted to their reformist program, not based on class considerations, they would certainly convert it into a blind tool of the liberal bourgeoisie. Their propensity for bargaining was a dubious game "which would only harm the development of the political consciousness, solidarity, and organization of the revolutionary classes."[7]

Lenin's categorical identification of the Kadets as bourgeoisie involved him in some complexities of definition which he resolved simply enough to his own satisfaction by separating them into "big" and "petit" bourgeois elements; the right-liberal monarchists representing the landowners and the big industrial-commercial bourgeoisie, and the left wing representing bourgeois democracy.[8] The former had interest and purposes common to the middle class but differed widely from the democrats in their impact on society and their attitudes toward the established structure. They were easy to identify as openly counterrevolutionary liberals who had not yet made a final deal with the bureaucracy to share power for their own selfish interests, to the disadvantage of the "democratic" strata. Most of them were gathered in the Octobrist, Law and Order, and Commercial-Industrial parties.[9] But the Kadets were their blood brothers:

An Octobrist is a Kadet who applies his bourgeois theories in business. A Kadet is an Octobrist who, when not busy robbing the workers and peasants, dreams of an ideal bourgeois society. The Octobrist still has to learn something of parliamentary etiquette and political hypocrisy coupled with flirting with democracy. The Kadet has still to learn something of the art of bourgeois business trickery— and then they will undoubtedly merge. . . .[10]

Lenin's chief logical difficulty in demarking his neat categories lay in the identification of outstanding Kadet intellectuals as representatives of big business bourgeoisie. He named *Osvobozhdenie* as their organ in the pre-October 1905 period and included P.N. Miliukov, P.B. Struve, Prince Sergei Trubetskoi, F.I. Rodichev, and M.I. Gertsenshtein, all future Kadet leaders, as representatives of big bourgeois interests. He believed that they so feared revolution that they would combine with autocracy to limit the political and economic privileges of the workers and peasants.[11]

Apart from this caricature of the leadership of liberalism in the western tradition seeking a solution of conflicting interests and elimination, or the fullest possible limitation, of exploitation by means of political compromise, some like Prince Trubetskoi and Rodichev were landowners, aristocrats, and the rest were certainly not guided in their basic considerations by the "cash nexus" of the "big bourgeoisie." Their intellectual solutions may not have been the most reliable, but they regarded them as the most attainable, and they were not consciously concerned with self-interest of an economic order. Here, in essence, lay Lenin's difficulty with the Kadets. He reduced a dangerous competing program to hostile class terms. If successful it would thwart the realization of the proletarian revolution; hence it was counterrevolutionary, and its chief intellectual proponents were identified with the leadership of the economic class enemy.

Lenin would attribute "democratic" qualities only to the left wing of the Kadet party. He meant, of course, those elements more sympathetic toward direct, revolutionary action. But here, too, he was not particularly lucid or consistent. He tagged them as the bourgeois intellectuals yet he indiscriminately conferred that title on both wings.[12] In fact, he grouped the "liberal professors, rectors, vice-rectors and the entire company of the Trubetskois, Manuilovs and their like" among "the finest representatives of liberalism and the Kadet party, the most enlightened, the best educated, the most disinterested, the least affected by the direct pressure of the money-bag."[13] Few western liberals would quarrel with this characterization of their Russian counterparts. Elsewhere, he identified the Kadet party as a whole, along with the Party of Democratic Reform, as "left liberal monarchists" who "are not definite class organizations."[14]

Insofar as Lenin was specific in classifying the "radical" liberals, he held that they were the most purposeful and militant elements of the League of Liberation and the Constitutional Democrats. They were the "zemstvo democratic intelligentsia." They represented the petite bourgeoisie and were best able to speak for them. They were entirely acceptable as allies in the struggle for the victory of the proletariat and peasantry. Yet he warned that while they veered leftward in reaction to the rapid oscillation of the right liberals between the monarchy and the popular cause, the leftists, too, were vacillators. He attributed this condition to causes that were more than somewhat contradictory. They arose variously from the very nature of the leftist liberals as bourgeoisie and because they were "not an independent economic class and therefore . . . not an independent political force." To Lenin this conjured up the danger that, as a "usurped force," they depended on the influence of the bourgeois intelligentsia over those classes which had not yet worked out a political ideology of their own and so submitted to that of the bourgeois intelligentsia.[15]

Considering that Lenin concentrated on the parliamentary idea only when the need to counter it arose, he developed his basic premises with remarkable rapidity. While his supporting arguments were hardly flawless, he elaborated and applied these premises consistently and persistently in connection with every possible aspect of the evolving parliamentary movement. He reacted rather sharply to the charge that his intensely polemic writings were abusive. He felt impelled to reiterate what should have been obvious to his antagonists; that the double-dealing with which he charged the Kadets was due to what he regarded as "objective factors," not personal qualities. They had to compromise in the end with any force to assure that the popular revolution would not triumph. As bourgeoisie in a capitalist society these "Petrunkeviches," "Cavaignacs," and "Thiers" would support a two-chambered parliament (of the "German" type), law and order, and moderation toward official repression.[16]

In a word, like all other classes, Lenin maintained that these hoity-toity professors and aristocrats were concerned with self-interest. The Duma was an admirable instrument for simultaneously mobilizing popular support and restraining the popular, revolutionary movement from which they had much to fear. They well knew that it was not an institution that could or would lead to a revolutionary movement. It was a harmless operation, a playing at parliament, a sham parliamentarism employed to put an end to revolutionary action. Witness their willingness to abandon the boycott of the Bulygin Duma and enter it. A fully empowered popular representative assembly would be anathema to them because it would, in fact, be a constituent assembly in which popular elements would predominate. The only constitution they favored would be one that would suppress revolution.[17]

Arguing from Marxist class-analytical assumptions, Lenin simply could not entertain the argument that the Kadets were primarily interested in defending their ideal instrument for realizing realistic compromise in a world of hard, real relationships of forces. Their interest in utilizing parliament, even in truncated form, to further develop its strength as opportunity afforded, and their ploys to offset governmental and revolutionary assault on the delicate seedling he readily interpreted, variously, as cunning, panic stricken vacillation, or treachery.

The Bolshevik leader was ever concerned with the capacity of the Kadets to attract potential revolutionary elements and he repeatedly represented them as a dying, potentially reactionary element, because they tied their fate to an illusory constitution in the face of inevitable revolution. Hence he argued that it would be suicidal to support the party of parliamentary compromise. That could only prevent the real force of bourgeois democracy from asserting itself.[18] His image of the ideal world of the liberal leadership was a well-ordered society purged of "feudal" survivals and protected from encroachment by an upper house of the German order, a bureaucracy, an army and stiff press laws.[19]

Lenin postulated that perhaps the greatest danger from the Kadets to the revolutionary cause was their "objective" need to make a deal with autocracy which had good reason to welcome them. As ardent supporters of the "theory of compromise" they saw the tsar as standing above popular will, yet taking it into account, and they envisioned themselves as intermediaries between the autocracy and the popular will; they functioned in their "wretched" position of a "cadger" and a "go-between."[20] But they were not by any standards altruistic. They simply wanted to ransom themselves from revolution and needed to make arrangements with the ruling elements to get the greatest possible power, at least half of it, for themselves and restrict the power of the revolutionary people. They wanted parliamentarism to assure the domination of capitalism against the domination of the monarchy and the bureaucracy. Hence they could countenance the preservation of the tsar's prerogatives and some bureaucratic privileges. And they wanted a standing army—all in the face of the threat of revolution. At the Zemstvo and Town Duma Congress in November 1905, the liberals had indicated that a constituent assembly was to be summoned by the tsar and he was to approve of any constitution it brought forth.[21]

Lenin had no doubt that an agreement between the liberals and the ruling spheres was feasible. The Kadets were bemusing themselves with the notion that they were dealing with the autocracy on even terms. But they did have some bargaining power. They could embarrass the government, if they could not paralyze it, with the financial prerogatives of the Duma. And they could always conjure up the threat of supporting and stimulating revolutionary action. In addition, there were pro-liberal officials like Sergei Witte who would negotiate with them for the division of power. Lenin believed that the government considered the Duma innocuous enough, and it relished the prospect of drawing liberals further away from the revolution. Moreover, as the revolutionary situation developed and circumstances became more intolerable for the liberals, they were likely to intensify their efforts to reach some compromise.[22]

Lenin saw no prospect of success for the Kadets in this system of compromise. Popular sovereignty, not to mention revolutionary self-government, were incompatible with autocracy and even limited monarchy. They could be won only by force and the popular forces were simply not strong enough—yet.[23] He could not, of course, be expected to believe that the Kadets were not primarily concerned with sharing power (with the scramble for ministerial chairs); that they hoped to make parliament the predominant factor in Russian political life with the growing pressure of the popular movement; that their attitude represented an acceptance of the realities, the *sootnoshnie syl*, of the moment, not hypocrisy.

As Lenin would have it, the Kadets would always find themselves in a false situation because they really believed that peaceful negotiation with tsarism for basic change was possible. But that belief was positively dangerous insofar as their "constitutional illusions" attracted the popular masses. Then they might pervert the revolutionary consciousness of the people in time of "civil war" by recommending participation in the Duma, by rejecting force to defend freedom and popular rights while the government held its ground by "savage tyranny."[24]

Lenin was particularly concerned about the attraction of the Kadet appeal after their solid victory in the first Duma elections because they might leave the impression that they enjoyed wide popular support and attract left wing intellectuals, up to, and including the Mensheviks. There was a tendency, he held, not to analyze their dual character as landlords and petite borgeoisie. In the latter capacity they could well weaken the revolutionary movement by appealing to the property instincts of the peasantry. They were willing to alienate some landlord land (Lenin referred to this by holding that they were opposed to the alienation of all landlord land). But their requirement that the peasant pay for the land he acquired from the landlords was calculated to transform the "upper section" of the peasantry into an element of law and order.[25]

But again, in the long view, Lenin was certain that the plight of the Kadets was hopeless. They were not revolutionary leaders in a revolutionary era. Their masters were the big bourgeoisie and they lacked the backing of a united and really revolutionary class. Their appeal was essentially negative, against autocracy, and on the basis of an illusory constitutional structure. Their leading position was transient and fleeting, and would collapse with the inevitable fall of constitutional illusions. Peter Struve might be entirely correct in predicting that "the peasant in the Duma will be a Kadet!" The peasants would be enchanted by "feudal-minded landlords dressed up in all sorts of 'Octobrist' costumes . . ." and they would be attracted by "beautifully colored labels"—but only until "the course of events shows them . . . that the real fight for freedom for the people has still to be fought *outside* the Duma."[26]

Lenin's conception of the nature of the Constitutional Democrats was always vivid. He appears to have been preoccupied much more with their intellectual and programmatic challenge than with the obvious enemy, the autocracy, which was all too self-revealing. And, as we have observed, it was within the parameters of his assault on the Kadets that he unfolded his concerns about, his attitudes toward, and his tactics for dealing with the Imperial Duma. Although he might regard the Duma as a secondary area of conflict, Lenin never underestimated its significance for public opinion and the necessity for putting it in the proper perspective of the revolutionary process. From the early months of 1905 he considered that "tactics toward the State Duma still heads all questions of the revolutionary struggle . . . ," and even at that time he had some qualifications about the arguments for a boycott. He characterized the Duma as a focus of popular attention until mid-June, 1907.[27] But for all of its importance in Russian public life he warned that a true proletarian party could never countenance the Duma because it was a threat and a hindrance, if not a permanent barrier, to the socialist revolution. Only a freely elected constituent assembly could be a genuine Duma. It had to be elected by the people, entirely dependent on it, and not liable to dismissal. Only then could it meet popular needs.[28]

A bourgeois Duma and particularly the tsarist Duma could be no more than a hoax, a sham parliament to deceive people everywhere and especially the revolutionary masses in Russia. In one of his relatively few generalizations on the parliamentary process, Lenin argued that

everyone knows that bourgeois politicians always come forward with all sorts of slogans, programmes, and platforms to deceive the people. Bourgeois politicians always, especially before elections, call themselves liberals, progressives, democrats, even radical socialists solely for the purpose of catching votes and deceiving the people. This is a universal phenomenon in all capitalist countries. . . .

Throughout the world the liberal bourgeoisie had always deceived the peasants fighting for land and liberty—in the manner of the Russian Kadets.[29] Lenin was never at pains to conceal his negative attitude toward multiparty systems, characteristic of bourgeois parliaments.

The Russian Duma, in particular, was obviously a sham and a travesty of popular representation. In somewhat hyperbolic terms he demonstrated to his own satisfaction that the law of December 11, 1905 debarred the bulk of the peasantry and workers, and hitting nearer the mark, he assailed the unequal ratio of class representation. The creation of an upper house could only make the Duma "an important advisory appendage of autocratic bureaucracy," a "fig leaf of autocracy," a police and landlord Duma to plot against the workers and peasants. Its purpose was to strengthen autocracy by creating a facade of legal opposition and to save "some remnants . . . of autocratic and serf-owning Russia." It could thereby deal with an assured reactionary majority (Lenin sometimes numbered the Octobrists among the Black Hundreds) and the treacherous liberals. It could even share its power with them, and appeal for financial aid at home and abroad. At home its system of martial law, punitive measures and repression could guarantee restraint of oppositional agitation and activity.[30]

In the Russian statist, autocratic tradition, the art of compromise was not likely to get a high priority. For an element with a revolutionary purpose it was likely to be downright abhorrent. The Kadets and their parliamentary purpose were not exactly in this tradition, and Lenin assailed the very idea of parliamentary compromise as a facet of the Kadet campaign of deception. He repeatedly identified the Duma as a Kadet institution; "a board of burghers" to whom compromise was the essence of public life.[31] Yet he was somewhat defensive in defining his own attitude toward concessions. "Marxism does not reject compromises. Marxism considers it necessary to use them, but that does not in the least prevent Marxism as a living and operating historical force, from fighting energetically against compromise."[32] He always saw in the Duma an instrument for reconciling the differences between the middle class and autocracy: between the "bosses and money-bags" and the "enemy."[33] He acknowledged that "under a parliamentary system it is often necessary to support a more liberal party against a less liberal one, but during a revolutionary struggle for a parliamentary system it is treachery to support liberal turncoats who are reconciling Trepov [reactionaries] with the revolution."[34]

For the Social-Democrats, parliament was useful to enlighten and organize the proletariat. For the bourgeois liberals and radicals it was the only legitimate and normal means for conducting public affairs. They repudiated the class character of parliamentarism; they tried to blind the workers to the class nature of parliament as an instrument of bourgeois oppression and to its limited historical importance for the revolution. In Russia, parliamentarianism represented an effort to end the revolution by coming to terms with the old regime.[35] There were many examples of bourgeois betrayers of the people's freedom in representative assemblies (e.g., the German liberals and the Bismarcks). And the Kadets, after reaching an agreement with the Social-Democrats would strike a bargain with autocracy to substitute a Kadet ministry for a constituent assembly. That is why they opposed the creation of committees in the Duma to investigate famine relief operations. They pleaded that the Duma had to stay within the limits of the law, but their purpose was to use it against the proletariat and the peasantry.[36]

Yet the obvious and mounting differences between the Kadet leadership in the Duma and the ruling circles had to be reconciled with the "theory of compromise." Hence liberal censure of the government for the Bielostok pogrom and their demand for the resignation of the administration which could not cope with revolution meant only that they would substitute their own strong government to put down disorder.[37] The Kadet denunciation of the official appeal on land reform in the last days of the first Duma was only a patent display of cowardice. The liberals called for patience while the Duma produced a measure by legal procedures instead of openly declaring that no land laws could be realized by peaceful, constitutional, legal means.[38] And their connection over the Vyborg Manifesto only revealed that the timid Kadets were divided over it, and would not consistently follow a line of revolutionary action. They were more interested in ministerial chairs. They would participate in a revolutionary crisis only if it degenerated into a parliamentary crisis, and by every Leninist definition this could mean only compromise.[39]

The Kadets got their comeuppance, of course. The government sized up their "cringing" weakness and urge for conciliation and hardly hesitated to dissolve two Dumas. If this regime faced continued, Kadet opposition it would counter them with an Octobrist-Black Hundred coalition—even though the liberals could find common interest with some Octobrists.[40]

The Bolsheviks were not alone in charging the Kadets with a drive to settle down in a tsarist cabinet, but for Lenin it well nigh summed up his case against them. Kadet participation in a cabinet would have to come out of a deal between the liberals and the government, directed at the proletariat and peasantry. It would corrupt the minds of the revolutionary elements, and would make the convocation of a constituent assembly more difficult.[41] A Kadet cabinet would not wrest power from the court "camerilla" but only emerge as a screen for it, and would permit the government to pose as a constitutional regime.[42]

Lenin's doctrinal objection to a liberal ministry, responsible to the Duma, rested on the certainty that it would substitute reform through the Duma for revolutionary action,[43] and a reform Duma was a worthless exercise in parliamentary maneuvering. Under Kadet leadership the bourgeois Duma simply could not meet popular demands. The Kadets insisted on holding to a legal position which only revealed their impotence in the face of a government which had its own rules. They could haggle diplomatically with neither the autocracy nor the peasantry on the land question since fundamental material interests were involved. The government would never accept compulsory alienation of landlord property, and the Kadets would be reduced to proclaiming demands without settling anything.[44] By their insistence on working within the law, the Kadets revealed their futility and duplicity. In the first Duma, for example, they got the *Trudoviki* to withdraw their bill for abolishing capital punishment and sent it back to a committee for more talk.[45] They did react properly to the Bielostok pogrom by sending a delegation to the spot. But the results were meager for they did not nail the proper culprits at the apex of the political structure.[46]

It was the capacity of autocracy to dissolve the Duma with impunity that revealed the true weakness of parliament and its ineffectiveness as an instrument for legislation in the face of official opposition. It proved conclusively that constitutionalism was illusory and that methods short of violent overthrow of the regime were bankrupt. As early as September 1906, Lenin was predicting that the regime would have no qualms about changing the election law illegally to get a more conservative Duma because it was fighting for its life and the privileges of the ruling class; and because it was emboldened by the absence of a revolutionary response to the dissolution of the first Duma.[47]

The irony of the situation, as Lenin saw it, lay in the circumstance that the Kadets imagined that the first Duma which they unquestionably controlled turned out, in fact, to be a revolutionary organ with the purpose of overthrowing the regime. The early Duma period was not constitutional, but a part of the revolutionary upsurge.[48]

From his analysis of the circumstances in which the bourgeois Duma operated, Lenin concluded that it was not only incapable of functioning as a popular representation, but that it could never lead a revolutionary struggle, and only indirectly could it develop a deeper revolutionary crisis.[49] Here he made his case for the revolutionary as against the parliamentary process. He insisted that the major issues in the life of a nation were settled ultimately by force. There was no point in evolving an ideal constitution and program if the government "placed bayonets on the agenda." That could be met only by a revolutionary dictatorship.[50]

All these laws on the election of popular representatives are not worth a brass farthing until the sovereignty of the people has actually been won and there is complete freedom of speech, the press, assembly and association, until citizens are armed and are able to safeguard the inviolability of person.[51]

These goals could be realized only by a genuine self-government (a provisional government calling up a constituent assembly) which only a decisively victorious uprising could establish. Only this kind of uprising could oust reactionary officials, force reactionaries to emigrate, set political prisoners free, and defeat the government's army with city militias.[52] In fact, "only an open revolutionary struggle which could consign all . . . liberal Dumas to the rubbish heap will be of decisive consequence."[53]

Lenin pointed to the October 1905 uprising to demonstrate how inadequate parliamentary institutions, in this case, the Bulygin Duma, could be swept away. The hand of the proletariat had forced the liberals and *osvobozhdenie* gentry and even Witte to talk of "reforms that would undermine all of the artful devices of the Bulygin farce."[54] And he justified the Moscow uprising of December 1905, if only for the proof it offered that a popular uprising would draw into the revolutionary melee many elements from urban strata heretofore indifferent.[55] "The thing is, that it is just the revolutionary periods which are distinguished by wider, richer, more deliberate, more methodical, more systematic, more courageous and more vivid making of history than periods of philistine, Kadet, reformist progress."[56]

One of Lenin's fundamental arguments against the Menshevik tendency to get involved in parliamentary matters fixed the focus on revolutionary action outside the Duma.

The lessons of the Kadet Duma must be absolutely binding for us, viz., the lessons that the Duma campaign is a subordinate and secondary form of struggle, and that, owing to objective conditions of the moment, direct revolutionary action by the broad mass of the people still remains the principle form of struggle.[57]

After some hesitancy in his propaganda against the attraction of the Bulygin Duma, Lenin hammered at the need to utilize the electoral laws, the election campaigns and the behavior of the Dumas for exclusively revolutionary, agitational purposes. After he yielded on the matter of participation in the Duma his focus was entirely on propaganda and against involvement in parliamentary activity as such.[58] The election campaigns were eminently suited to his purposes. The election laws in themselves provided excellent materials for propaganda on the nature of autocracy, its class basis, the irreconcilability of its interests with those of the people.[59] They offered occasion for meetings, demonstrations, political strikes, revolutionary slogans calling for insurrection, immediate organization of combat squads and contingents of a revolutionary army. They were to expose simultaneously the bourgeois theory of compromise and every treacherous and irresolute step of the bourgeois constitutionalists.[60] Lenin warned insistently against immersion in elections primarily to name party candidates at various stages. Rather he urged his Social-Democrats to busy themselves with such matters as entering and utilizing election campaign meetings, by force if necessary, to transform them into workers' agitational gatherings. Here they might unburden themselves of every kind of propaganda against the government, the bourgeoisie and their representative bodies. And here they might call for immediate revolutionary action to establish a constituent assembly.[61] The use of force to "crush" police and military resistance was highly significant for the insurrectionary effort, for if the government imposed martial law or used incidents to arrest Kadet candidates or proscribe meetings, that would only further stimulate open and wider revolutionary activity.[62]

The Duma sessions could offer the same kind of agitational material without involving the Social-Democrats in playing at parliament and deals with the Kadets. Lenin apparently hoped that campaign agitation might prevent the meeting of the "Bulygin" and "Witte" Dumas, but failing that, the revolutionary elements were to assure that the "Duma farce" would not be the end of the revolution but the "beginning of a complete democratic upheaval which will kindle the fire of proletarian revolution all over the world."[63]

Lenin further perceived that the Duma was an admirable testing ground for discerning the state of public opinion. He claimed that from its mood he could determine the moment when the "boiling point is reached"; when the revolutionary democrats got dissillusioned with the Kadets and the liberals were impelled to call a constituent assembly as revolutionary action mounted. The democratic bourgeoisie would certainly become disenchanted with the Kadets when they chattered aimlessly and without results, and sought to restrict barricade action in the face of official outrages. The Kadets would have their illusions, so dangerous to the revolution, but when the Duma clashed with the government a new revolutionary crisis would emerge rapidly and might be near at hand.[64]

When the Social-Democrats entered the second Duma in force, Lenin was most unhappy with the deportment of the Menshevik-dominated faction. His criticism revealed his conception of how the perfect revolutionist should behave in a bourgeois Duma. In the context of his major revolutionary purpose it is obvious that he would oppose any engagement "in political project-mongering, or in drafting stillborn 'bills'." Socialist deputies must appeal to the people, ruthlessly tell the whole truth, expose all the crimes committed by the government, and call on the population to wage a revolutionary struggle.[65]

He disapproved mightily of the Menshevik tendency to attribute an intrinsic legislative value to the Duma as a revolutionary weapon and to cooperate with all oppositional groups.[66] He maintained that the Menshevik majority in the Duma faction violated Marxist precepts and tactics. They became too engrossed with Duma activity and ignored the revolutionary movement outside. They had done nothing to secure connections with their proletarian constituency. They always tried to prove the legality of their proposals against Kadet charges of illegality. If the revolutionary faction were to operate only within the framework of tsarist law, it would only consecrate itself to powerless inaction.[67] If the Social-Democratic deputies continued to emphasize reform legislation they would, again, confuse the population and retard its revolutionary development. The peasantry had already placed naive hopes in the Duma and were encouraged by the liberals for their petty class aims. Labor would react against inconsequential legislation (for the upper house would bar any significant action) and they would regard the parliamentary struggle as harmful and an interference with the progress of the Socialist revolution.[68]

Lenin charged that the Social-Democratic deputies had been too willing to cooperate with the Kadets. He particularly opposed their presence at Kadet-inspired conferences of all oppositional factions and groups for both informational purposes and political strategy. These conferences were especially reprehensible when the Polish National-Democrats (*Endeki*) attended. This consorting with the enemies of labor and prime "pogromists" was insulting to the Polish workers and minorities in the Kingdom. At worst, Social-Democratic participation in these conferences would confuse the Populist deputies and it would therefore behoove the faction to risk even isolation so that everyone would know at least where they stood in relation to bourgeois factions and programs.[69]

In the fifth Party Congress, which the Bolsheviks dominated with their Polish and Baltic allies, Lenin's resolution, adopted by the Congress, demanded that Social-Democratic factions emphasize in all their activities and statements those points which were especially peculiar to Social-Democracy as the Socialist proletarian party, and which differentiated them from bourgeois democratic groups. In their dealings with bourgeois parties they were to distinguish clearly between true and nominal democratic elements. Therefore it would be necessary to contrast strictly revolutionary Social-Democratic views with the policy of agreements and compromise with the old regime as practiced by liberal monarchist parties. And the Social-Democratic deputies were to avoid superfluous intercourse with these sociopolitical groupings.[70] They were to emphasize the practical, propagandist, organizational, and agitational roles of the Duma and their bills were to serve precisely these ends, and not direct, legislative aims.[71]

Lenin's influence was likewise evident in the Social-Democratic platform for the third Duma. It differed little from previous considerations and strictures on the Duma as such. It pointed out, in the light of the Electoral Law of June 3, 1907, that if more truly revolutionary fighters were named as deputies, the conservatives would have narrower range from which to choose deputies who would be more compatible to them. All non-socialist parties were declared anathema, and familiar promises were made to counter the Kadets, expound socialist viewpoints and revolutionary aims and to offer only socialist demands including a constituent assembly to establish a democratic, representative body, popular election of officials, civil liberties and a standing army instead of universal military service.[72]

The revolution was the all in all; the Duma always posed the danger of diverting it, confusing revolutionary purposes. At best it could be a necessary evil—a forum for propaganda or a reflection of the "bestial" nature of the "Asiatic" regime or the morally corrupt, conniving liberals. And this in itself might serve revolutionary purposes. But it was essentially a second or third rate arena for revolutionary activity; for a drive for the dictatorship of the proletariat. Hence the Bolshevik leader cared not a fig for its preservation and, like the election meetings, he would use it legally or illegally as it suited the revolutionary need. *His* wager was on the proletarian upheaval.

Throughout the period when Lenin concerned himself intensively with problems posed by the Duma, his considerations were conditioned by a dogged expectation of an imminent revolutionary upsurge and victory. It was extraordinarily difficult for him to accept the recession of the first revolutionary wave of the twentieth century. He saw only a brief period of temporary quiet for an accumulation of revolutionary energy and an assimilation of experience before a great, new onslaught. The revolution was bound to continue with the incessant repression and a mounting financial crisis. He could easily visualize a repetition of the revolutionary process of 1905.[73] He was not impressed by the electoral victories of the constitutionalists. The revolutionary crisis was too deeply rooted to be affected by the Duma's composition. The Kadets might call for patience in the first Duma but the rising tide of revolution had already overtaken them. In May of 1906 he was certain that peaceful parliamentarism was giving way to the settlement of state affairs by force and the resumption of the October uprising.[74]

Lenin regarded the aftermath of the dissolution of the first Duma as a juncture when worker outbreaks would be merged with a peasant uprising and military revolt. The "backward" elements of the peasantry had stored great hopes in the Duma and would surely react against the cavalier action and attitude of the bureaucracy. He expected that a revolutionary uprising could be prepared by the end of the summer of 1906. When that failed to materialize, he argued that the popular movement and the regime had reached a standoff, but he continued to insist that an upheaval was near at hand because the government was reestablishing its position rapidly by unheard of repressive action. And following the Vyborg events he predicted trouble when calls went out for taxes and recruits.[75]

Ideologically and temperamentally (perhaps the two are closely interrelated) Lenin identified himself squarely with the activist tradition in the Russian revolutionary movement. He was disturbed by Plekhanov's argument (in support of participation in the Duma) in the spring of 1906, that everything that contributed to the education of the people was good; everything that hindered it was bad. In his rejoinder Lenin averred that he could not imagine anything more lifeless "than reducing the tactics of the proletariat in a period of political revolution to the task of politically educating the people."[76] Life had to be more exciting, active, and purposeful than that.

The oft-told tale of Lenin's major, and ultimately acknowledged error on the boycott of the first Duma needs no repeating here. It is significant for our study to note that his arguments for the boycott were essentially an extension of his demand for emphasis on revolutionary activity outside the Duma; his argument against Duma activity as a diversion from direct, revolutionary attack inspired by the Kadets and the autocracy. He was never certain of the real value of the boycott, or the possibility of controlling the consequences of its abandonment. He saw it as only a "tiny particle" of the larger question of whether the revolution ended in December 1905, or was mounting toward a new climax. Since he was firmly convinced of the latter in the post-December days, he necessarily opted for a boycott. To fight in a parliamentary way was to fight "within the limits that we will prescribe by agreement with the monarchy."[77]

But from the very inception of the parliamentary period he never committed himself completely to the slogan and tactic of boycott, for that remained a function of the nature of parliament.

When a legal basis for the existence of political parties (including the Russian Social-Democratic Labor Party) is created in fact . . . then we shall have to reconsider the whole question of the insurrection, for to us, insurrection is only one of the important means, but one that is not always obligatory, of clearing the way for the struggle for socialism.[78]

This was in September 1905, the "Bulygin" period. But in the same statement he reassured himself with the contention that "if an uprising is possible and necessary, that means there can be no legal center for a legal struggle for the aims of the uprising. . . ."[79] If an uprising was necessary and possible the government would oppose it with force and the policy of playing at parliament was chicanery and clowning.[80]

The main thrust of Lenin's argument for the boycott was the need to maintain an intense agitational drumfire at a time when the participation of the liberal bourgeoisie in the Duma meant a slackening of their agitation.[81] Thus his disputations on the boycott controversy ran the entire gamut of his case against the Kadets and the Duma. The grounds are quite familiar. The Duma was a caricature of representation and participation in it would give the masses a distorted idea of the progressive aims of the proletariat. It was inadvisable and impractical to combine preparations for revolution and elections under the Law of December 11, 1905. The mood of the proletariat was depressed enough without leaving the impression that the revolutionary period was over. Furthermore it was dangerous to encourage the normal urge of the peasantry to participate.[82] Participation would inevitably mean support of the Kadets and involvement of the workers in a joint responsibility with them for a Kadet Duma and a Kadet policy. And that meant toning down the revolution.[83] Lenin analyzed the Witte election law to demonstrate that its whole purpose was to assure a safe Duma; to give the landlords and the big capitalists a preponderance over the workers and peasants. That was the reason for excluding "three-quarters of the workers" from the suffrage and sifting the election process through three stages with a minimum of convenience and opportunity for agitation.[84]

Then he offered a few practical considerations. If the Party came out legally or agitated at election meetings it would provide the police with a ready-made list of people to be arrested. And there was no freedom for effective agitation. Newspapers were closed and meetings were prohibited. This was another argument for making use of election meetings rather than campaigning merely for legal election of candidates.[85] Finally, Lenin insisted that all major worker centers, militant bourgeois democrats, peasant organizations and the parties of the national minorities—all real and potential revolutionary elements—stood in open and firm opposition to participation in the Duma.[86] In fact, after his change of heart on the boycott, he maintained that these political conditions, and not a socialist commitment, kept the Social-Democratic Party out of the elections.[87]

Lenin's shift to a participationist stance arose ostensibly from the decision of the Stockholm Congress to reject the above-mentioned considerations and take part in the elections to the first Duma where they had not been held. In an unusual show of compliance with the decisions of a Menshevik-dominated body he asserted his complete acceptance of the decision. "During the elections there must be no criticism of participation in the elections." "There can be no two opinions among the Social-Democrats about this."[88] The mark of the "Unity" congress was evident.

In all probability, the results of the first elections, and especially the behavior of the Caucasians who formed a Social-Democratic Group in the first Duma made a believer of him. His first reactions were negative, but significant. He observed that the Social-Democratic deputies were not authorized by the Party to act as its representatives; they had been elected from peasant and urban petit bourgeois curiae by direct or indirect agreement with the Kadets; and their first steps were none too reassuring. They should have voted, even if they stood alone, on the address from the throne. And they should have assailed the Kadets for duplicity on the land bill and noted their powerlessness when the tsar refused to receive them.[89]

But the subsequent deportment of the group seems to have convinced Lenin of the practicability and even the need of taking advantage of the Duma forum for his revolutionary purposes. His arguments for a boycott had rested upon considerations that were practical enough. But they were determined by theoretical principles which were rigidly set on a revolutionary course. Moreover they flew in the face of a reality which saw the entire nation focusing on the first two Dumas. Now the circumstances of a real, live group calling Lenin's tune fascinated and then attracted him. He welcomed its appeal directly to the people, calling on the proletariat not to be provoked into premature, revolutionary action. He heaped praise on the signing of the oath of allegiance to the tsar (a truly sad necessity) in the name of the people; on Deputy Ramashvili's attacks on the Kadets, his strictures on the isolation of the Duma from the popular mood and his assault on the authorities for the Bielostok pogrom. In a direct call to end the boycott in August 1906, Lenin demanded that the Social-Democrats take into account the "new lessons" of the Kadet Duma which showed that agitation could be conducted in, and around it, in conjunction with the peasantry and against the Kadets.[90] He maintained that his switch was determined "by prudence and practical considerations prevailing."[91]

Henceforth, Lenin carried the argument against the boycott with characteristic aggressiveness and persistence. It had, of course, served its purpose, but it was no longer useful or applicable. The boycott of the Bulygin Duma was a struggle to prevent a whole system of institutions of a monarchist order from coming into existence. It aimed to destroy or shake the old regime to prevent it from creating a limited monarchy and to guarantee the revolutionary path of struggle for the people. The socialists had had to exert every effort to sweep away the Witte Duma, as well, to continue the fight for a constituent assembly, and sustain the revolutionary spirit and Social-Democratic consciousness of the workers. Lenin averred that these goals were realized. The government felt impelled to issue a special law against boycott activity. Lenin treading on rather shaky logical and historical grounds maintained that the boycott campaign had distracted the attention of the government from the composition of the Duma enabling the opposition to execute a flank attack and get to the enemy's rear, i.e., to enter the Duma by stealth.[92] He argued that in the revolutionary situation of 1905-1906, the boycott had a fair chance of attaining success but failed because the antirevolutionary and compromising behavior of the liberals compelled the proletariat to take up the struggle even on the basis of a Duma campaign. After trying everything on the direct path of a revolutionary struggle, practical politics forced the Social-Democrats to adjust themselves to the institutions of the society in which they lived. That adjustment, confessed Lenin, was made only with great hesitation and called forth no little ridicule from various quarters. But he was proud to have kept his colors flying "long after the Kadets had crawled on their bellies under laws of counterrevolution."[93]

In these sad circumstances, Lenin contended, the Party had to reckon with compromise or face defeat. The slogan of the boycott had outlived its usefulness. The people no longer needed a warning against constitutional illusions. They had experienced them fully. Boycott could no longer prevent the revolution from being turned into a constitutional, monarchist blind alley. That was an accomplished fact. The population had progressively lost interest in the Duma especially after June 3, 1907. At that juncture the revolutionary forces were in no position to overwhelm the enemy with a frontal attack. The Party had little choice but to take the "zig zag," constitutional, monarchist path to revolution. This did not by any means exclude revolutionary action; it was but a longer, indirect route to the far away goal.[94]

In the course of the second elections, Lenin had emerged as the chief Bolshevik protagonist of active participation in the Duma, and many of his considerations were painfully elaborated in the face of fierce opposition from his Bolshevik comrades in the third campaign—after the events of June 3, 1907. His resolutions narrowly squeaked by, largely with the help of the border organizations, at a conference in July 1907. His fellow Bolsheviks had no heart for going through the motions of an election which could, by law, yield only paltry results, and many vividly remembered his boycott arguments.[95]

Actually, Lenin was on the defensive from the moment that he executed his about face, in the spring of 1906. He sought to detail concretely the kind of parliamentary action that justified his position. He pointed to the "division" of the first Duma into Kadet-Octobrist and Social-Democrat-Trudovik wings. He regarded a draft of an S-D appeal to the people as "extremely valuable" even if it were read only in the Duma. A speech in the Duma would not stir up any revolution, and propaganda in connection with the Duma was not distinguished by any particular merit, "but the advantage that Social-Democracy can derive from the one and the other is not less, and sometimes even greater, than that derived from a printed speech or a speech delivered at some other gathering."[96] Sensing the deterioration of the Kadet position in the electorate, Lenin postulated that participation in elections would sweep aside the "deeply mistaken opinion that the Kadets are the chief, or at any rate, important representative of bourgeois democracy in general."[97] Most significant for himself, he still sensed signs of an upswing in revolutionary activity in the nation at large. And the boycott slogan was to support, develop, and expand this incipient movement. That was the basic argument "that determines the tendency toward boycott among Social-Democrats."[98]

Lenin was not entirely sure of himself on the issue of the boycott and, much like his image of the Kadets, he tended to vacillate, to jump at every scintilla of evidence for a need to end his zigging and zagging. His problem, again, lay in the realities of Russian political life which left him little alternative but to accept a gift from the autocracy and the Kadets. Had he not been so certain of the im- mediate triumph of the revolution and the revolutionary purposes of the "petit bourgeois democracy," he might well have dropped his Marxist text earlier and saved himself the anguish of de-indoctrinating his Bolshevik comrades. In es- sence, and in his own context, consciously or otherwise, he was following the Kadet course he abhorred so thoroughly. He was compromising with reality. The subtle (from his point of view, insidious) influence of parliamentary life was be- ginning to reach him.

Having committed himself to enter the election lists, Lenin resumed his em- phasis on the exclusively revolutionary purposes of the Duma and elections. He clashed at once with the Mensheviks over the old and basic question of revolu- tionary allies. He brought forth in array his old and basic arguments against con- sorting with the Kadets. As applied specifically to election campaigns he would seek out agreement with bourgeois "allies" to get Social-Democrats elected to parliament if they were not detrimental to the "more permanent and more pro- found aims" of the Party. To join a list to elect a Kadet would "undermine the general revolutionary significance of our campaign for the sake of gaining a seat for a liberal. We would be subordinating class policy to parliamentarism." The Social-Democrats would lose what was lasting and durable in elections; the devel- opment of class consciousness and solidarity of the socialist proletariat. "We would gain what is transient, relative and untrue—superiority of the Kadet over the Octobrist." The only truly revolutionary allies could be the peasantry.[99] Technical blocs, he observed, had a way of becoming ideological, and the events of 1905 had propelled the Kadets rightward. Yet the threat of Kadet hegemony over the petit bourgeois democracy, and even the worker, was just as great. Lenin's theoretical considerations precluded acceptance of the circumstances that after the strong Kadet showing in the first two elections, particularly in the cities, the Kadets were in a seller's market in arranging electoral blocs. He was not ready to admit that in a competition for votes, labor was in a weaker posi- tion than the liberal ideologists.[100] Indeed, in applying his old theme of Kadet treachery to elections, he was certain that the liberals wanted a bloc with the Social-Democrats because they were well aware of their weakness. They knew how to apply in Russia the " 'English' bourgeois method of fighting the prole- tariat, i.e., not by violence, but by bribery, flattery, dividing, and cajoling the moderates. . . ."[101]

For Lenin there was no substance to the Menshevik argument that defeat for a Kadet would mean a victory for a rightist. That was artfully inspired by the Kadets to scare votes their way. These hypocrites were always ready for a deal with the Black Hundreds.[102] Even worse, blocs with Kadets worked to elect types like N.N. Lvov.

Do you know, workers and peasants, what sort of man N.N. Lvov is? He is a landlord, one of the founders of the *Osvobozhdenie* League, *i.e.*, one of the founders of the Kadet Party. For seven years he served as a Marshal of the Nobility. In the Duma he belonged to the most right wing of the Kadets. In other words, he not only opposed the Social-Democratic Workers' deputies and the Trudoviks, but even found that the Kadet Party was too far to the left! Even the Kadet land bill was too liberal for him.[103]

If the Mensheviks were willing to countenance blocs with the Kadets that was because they were essentially bourgeois intellectuals with a compulsion to subordinate the peasantry to the landlords.[104]

Two interesting facets of Lenin's thinking emerged from his polemics on alliances for elections. He was particularly insistent that, because of its central and influential position, the St. Petersburg Social-Democratic organization remain lily-white; innocent of any charge that it was on familiar terms with the liberals in the political arena. A decade before the Bolshevik Revolution he had gauged clearly how events in the Capital might affect the country at large.

In this metropolis whose newspapers circulate all over Russia, where the headquarters of all the political parties are located, which leads the country ideologically and politically, it is a thousand times more important to give an example . . . of the policy worthy of the October [1905] fighters who wrested a little freedom from the authorities, a policy worthy of the proletariat.[105]

The second by-product of his strategy for election blocs moves us into the realm of his attitude toward alliances with the Populists. And here he was just as picky. He stood adamantly against entering an all-inclusive "left block." You had to know how each group stood in its relations with the monarchists and the liberals; whether they were true revolutionaries or not. For Lenin, a "bloc of all left parties" meant "*subordinating* those who are willing to fight (and are capable of carrying the masses with them at the decisive moment) to those who prefer to play the same despicable game of loyalty that the Kadets played in the first Duma. . . ."[106] "Social-Monarchists" like the Popular Socialists of the Pieshekhonov feather were already under Kadet influence and not fit company for the party of the revolutionary proletariat.

Lenin's designation of allies for his immediate goal (and through it for his ultimate purposes) was self-evident from its definition: "the revolutionary dictatorship of the proletariat and peasantry."[107] He had been consistent in this matter from his earliest considerations of revolutionary strategy. Roughly, this followed the Marxist concept of the bourgeois revolution preceding the proletarian. But in the circumstances of the decade before 1917 it meant specifically a simultaneous assault on both autocracy and the big, "non-democratic" bourgeoisie, the liberals.[108]

Lenin found himself in complete agreement with Kautsky that the Russian revolution was neither proletarian nor bourgeois. He defined "revolution," of course, in terms of his specific purposes. And he had always argued that the bourgeois liberals wanted political freedom exactly to assure that the peasantry and proletariat would not emerge completely victorious. Thus, "to interpret the category 'bourgeois revolution' in the sense of recognizing the leadership and guiding role of the bourgeoisie in the Russian revolution is to vulgarize Marxism. A bourgeois revolution *in spite* of the instability of the bourgeoisie, by paralyzing the instability of the bourgeoisie—that is how the Bolsheviks formulated the fundamental task of the Social-Democrats in the Revolution."[109] He assailed the Mensheviks for characterizing this strategy as Blanquist. Their fundamental mistake was to believe that only the bourgeoisie could be at the head of the bourgeois revolution and they were scared to death by the prospect of the peasantry and proletariat winning power.[110]

It was obvious to Lenin from the summer of 1905 that since the peasantry and proletariat were in a state of insurrection, both could cooperate in a provisional government that would be a democratic (nonsocialist) dictatorship of the petit bourgeois and the bourgeois intelligentsia. To protect the interests of the revolutionary elements, this provisional government need not wait for a constituent assembly to establish a minimum program—i.e., the conditions for the free expression of the people's will, a democratic republic.[111] It was true, he admitted, that the Kadets still (in 1906) dominated the Trudoviks in parliament, but a parting of their ways was inevitable. They were already disillusioned by Kadet opposition to their bills abolishing capital punishment and the creation of exclusively peasant land committees to settle the land question. The notion that liberal strength rested on the strength of bourgeois democracy was an illusion—like most liberal parliamentary concepts.[112]

Lenin was almost euphorious about the possibility of establishing immediate Social-Democratic hegemony over the peasantry in the early Duma period. An underground party steeled in battle with the Plehve and Stolypin regimes was surely capable of influencing the masses to a greater extent than any legal party which took a "strictly constitutional path." It also had a distinct advantage over the Social-Revolutionaries who hid behind the Trudovik screen.[113] Loyalty to the principles of democracy and the interests of the real working masses would certainly call for a bloc between the Trudoviks and the Social-Democrats, "even at the cost of some seats in the Duma."[114] When applied concretely to the business of winning votes, Lenin felt that there were precious few Social-Revolutionaries among the numerous "non-party" peasantry at the grass roots level. Here there was no need to continue "to advocate before the masses, directly or indirectly (or even by assumption) a non-party policy; neither is there the least danger of obscuring the strictly independent class policy of the proletariat."[115] Lenin was quick to assimilate the finer points of the parliamentary politician's craft, or perhaps this was but an emanation of the positivist, activist, revolutionary tradition?

But the bourgeois democracy and the peasantry could remain allies up to a point; when the proletariat was ready and had to control them. In some of his earliest discussions of the tactics of the proletariat in the bourgeois revolution—during the turbulent summer of 1905—Lenin asserted that the purpose of a provisional government was to set up a democratic republic and replace autocracy for "the immediate interests of the proletariat, and from the standpoint of the final aims of socialism."[116]

The success of the peasant insurrection, the victory of the democratic revolution will merely clear the way for a genuine decisive struggle for socialism, on the basis of a democratic republic. In this struggle the peasantry, as a landowning class, will play the same, treacherous, unstable part as is now being played by the bourgeoisie in the struggle for democracy. To forget this is to forget socialism, to deceive oneself and others regarding the real interests and tasks of the proletariat."[117]

For the representatives of the socialist proletariat "the forthcoming revolution is only one of the steps to the great goal of the socialist revolution. Bearing this in mind we shall never merge with petit-bourgeois parties or groups however sincere, revolutionary or strong they may be. . . ." And he predicted that their interests would diverge on the road to socialism.[118]

It was eminently important, in this context, to combat efforts of the non-Marxian parties to obscure the antithesis between the petite bourgeoisie and the proletariat. They had to watch every "ally" from the bourgeois democrats as they would a class enemy. They had to preserve complete independence to split the "non-party 'Trudoviks' into opportunists (P.S.'s) and revolutionaries (S.R.'s), to *counterpose* the latter to the former, etc."[119] The Russian, urban petite bourgeoisie was never a reliable support for revolutionary parties in the old type of bourgeois democracy.[120]

In the Duma it was absolutely necessary to differentiate between the mistakes of the Kadets and the Trudoviks for the errors of the latter went further than those of the former; "that the 'Trudovik' mistakes [specifically Lenin was referring to land equalization] will be of a practical importance at a higher stage of the revolution than are those of the Kadets. . . . The Kadets' illusions will be obstacles to the victory of the bourgeois revolution. The Trudovik's mistakes will be obstacles to the immediate victory of socialism. . . ."[121]

The goal was obviously the dictatorship of the proletariat and it would be just that. Referring to the failure of the S-D group in the first Duma to take a clear, unmistakable, S-D stand the leader of the Bolshevik wing put it bluntly: "if the Social-Democrats had a majority in the Duma, the Duma would not be a Duma, or else Social-Democrats would not be Social-Democrats."[122] As a revolutionary force they would resort to a dictatorship against those who "exhort, admonish, regret, condemn, whine, whimper." The vulgar bourgeois point of view failed to see the dictatorship of the proletariat as a class dictatorship. They saw in it only a dictatorship in the dictator's personal interest detrimental to all liberties and democracy. That was because they were accustomed to seeing in the political arena the "petty squabbling of the various bourgeois circles and coteries. . . ."[123]

The long shadow was ominous for the parliamentarians. Autocracy had to be overthrown along with the Kadets. And when the revolutionary bourgeoisie replaced them, they would revert to the same, treacherous, counterrevolutionary, hence oppressive role. The conclusion followed inexorably. The only just society could be the dictatorship of the proletariat. And it could brook no opposition; no nonproletarian parties. The use of force against the oppressors of the people "is very good. It is the supreme manifestation of the people's struggle for liberty."[124]

Notes

1. V.I. Lenin, *Collected Works* (Moscow, 1962), X, p. 124.

2. Ibid., IX, pp. 179-87.

3. Ibid., pp. 172-73, 176, 457; X, 68, 69; XI, 382, 394.

4. Ibid., X, pp. 214-15.

5. Ibid., XI, p. 461.

6. Alfred Levin, "The Fifth Social-Democratic Congress and the Duma," *Journal of Modern History*, XI (December, 1939), pp. 492-93; Lenin, *Collected Works*, IX, p. 254.

7. Levin, loc. cit.; Lenin, *Collected Works*, IX, pp. 254, 382; X, pp. 232, 491, 493; XI, p. 34.

8. Ibid., IX, p. 135; X, p. 158.

9. Ibid., p. 158.

10. Ibid., XI, pp. 229-30.

11. Ibid., IX, pp. 134-35, 216.

12. Ibid., pp. 135, 215; X, p. 428.

13. Ibid., p. 353.

14. Ibid., p. 158; XI, p. 380.

15. Ibid., IX, pp. 214-17, 353-54, 481; X, pp. 158-59; XI, p. 380.

16. Ibid., IX, pp. 214, 260, 400; X, pp. 215-16, 230.

17. Ibid., IX, pp. 214, 255-56, 360-61; X, pp. 217-18, 256; XI, p. 358.

18. Ibid., X, pp. 232-33, 235-36, 264; XI, p. 380.

19. Ibid., X, p. 456.

20. Ibid., IX, p. 196.

21. Ibid., pp. 21-22, 173-76; X, pp. 63-64, 258, 456, 474.

22. Ibid., IX, pp. 180-81, 196, 429; X, pp. 63-64, 214-15, 228-29.

23. Ibid., IX, pp. 220, 297-99.

24. Ibid., pp. 132, 186-87; X, p. 134.

25. Ibid., pp. 269-70, 437.

26. Ibid., pp. 220-21.

27. Ibid., IX, pp. 182, 212; XIII, p. 23.

28. Ibid., X, pp. 28-29; XI, p. 338.

29. Ibid., pp. 335, 399-400.

30. Ibid., IX, pp. 180, 214, 400, 460; X, pp. 124, 128-29, 132, 138, 262, 296, 385.

31. Ibid., IX, p. 393; X, p. 358; XI, p. 466.

32. Ibid., XIII, p. 23.

33. Ibid., IX, pp. 277, 381-83.

34. Ibid., pp. 381-83.

35. Ibid., XI, pp. 277-78.

36. Ibid., X, pp. 237, 251, 264, 427-28, 485; XI, pp. 44-46, 62-63, 277-78.

37. Ibid., pp. 83-84.

38. Ibid., pp. 97-99.

39. Ibid., pp. 163-64, 244.

40. Ibid., p. 303; XIII, pp. 126-28, 130.

41. Ibid., X, pp. 483, 500.

42. Ibid., XI, p. 30.

43. Ibid., p. 72.

44. Ibid., X, pp. 414, 416, 432-33.

45. Ibid., pp. 430-31.

46. Ibid., pp. 508-12.

47. Ibid., XI, pp. 111-14, 115-17, 210-11.

48. Ibid., pp. 115, 117.

49. Ibid., X, pp. 292, 481.

50. Ibid., IX, p. 132.

51. Ibid., pp. 195-96.

52. Ibid., pp. 220-22, 249-50, 461; X, pp. 392-93.

53. Ibid., IX, p. 384.

54. Ibid., pp. 392-93.

55. Ibid., X, p. 94.

56. Ibid., p. 253.

57. Ibid., XI, p. 148.

58. For Lenin's early attitude toward the Bulygin Duma see Ibid., IX, pp. 63-65. For continuity of attitudes see Ibid., X, pp. 103-4, 448; E. Iaroslavskii, *Istoriia V.K.P. (b)* (Moscow, 1926-1930), I, p. 200; Lenin, *Sobranie Sochinenii*, (Moscow, 1921-1925), XIII, p. 44.

59. Lenin, *Collected Works*, IX, p. 192.

60. Ibid., pp. 183, 197, 223.

61. Ibid., pp. 263-64, 266-67, 356-58.

62. Ibid., pp. 269-70; X, pp. 103-4.

63. Ibid., IX, pp. 260-61.

64. Ibid., X, pp. 237-38, 273.

65. Ibid., XI, p. 35.

66. Alfred Levin, "The Fifth Social-Democratic Congress and the Duma," *The Journal of Modern History*, XI (December, 1939), pp. 487-88.

67. Ibid., pp. 489-90. Lenin referred to the Social-Democratic bills to create committees to investigate famine and unemployment relief.

68. Ibid., pp. 487-89.

69. Ibid., pp. 493-95.

70. Ibid., pp. 498-99.

71. Ibid., p. 503.

72. *Riech*, July 29, 1907, p. 3, c. 21; *Slovo*, July 23, 1907, p. 3, c. 5; August 23, 1907, p. 3, c. 6; Lenin, *Sobranie Sochinenii*, XVIII, pp. 632-33.

73. Lenin, *Collected Works*, X, pp. 140-42, 150-51, 263, 273; XI, pp. 209, 345.

74. Ibid., X, pp. 222, 387.

75. Ibid., XI, pp. 120-22, 129, 135, 138-39, 185, 244.

76. Ibid., X, p. 480.

77. Ibid., X, pp. 98, 112-15, 135, 250, 272.

78. Ibid., IX, p. 274.

79. Ibid., X, p. 273.

80. Ibid., p. 274.

81. Ibid., IX, p. 181.

82. Ibid., X, pp. 132, 161-62.

83. Ibid., pp. 208-10, 236-37.

84. Ibid., pp. 128, 131-33.

85. Ibid., pp. 98, 105-6.

86. Ibid., pp. 127, 132, 133, 295.

87. Ibid., p. 295.

88. Ibid., pp. 390, 503; XI, p. 20.

89. Ibid., X, pp. 362, 403-5.

90. Ibid., pp. 434-35; XI, pp. 20, 24, 26, 32, 145.

91. Ibid., X, pp. 423-24.

92. Ibid., XI, pp. 78-79; XIII, pp. 19-20.

93. Ibid., XI, pp. 299, 303, 382-83, 405-6.

94. Ibid., XIII, pp. 22, 23, 32-33, 35, 40.

95. *Riech*, July 11, 1907, p. 3, c. 7; July 12, 1907, p. 2, c. 4; July 20, 1907, p. 3, c. 4-5; July 25, 1907, p. 1, c. 7; p. 2, c. 1; July 27, 1907, p. 3, c. 2; July 28, 1907, p. 3, c. 4; Aug. 11, 1907, p. 1, c. 6; Aug. 14, 1907, p. 3, c. 5. *Slovo*, July 15, 1907, p. 3, c. 1-2; July 17, 1907, p. 3, c. 4; July 19, 1907, p. 3, c. 4; July 20, 1907, p. 2, c. 3; July 27, 1907, p. 3, c. 5. For arguments for and against participation within the Bolshevik ranks see Lenin's "Protiv boikotii" and Iuri Kamenev's "Za boikotii" in *O boikotie tretei dumy* (Moscow, June 1907). Lenin's stand appears in *Collected Works*, XIII, pp. 17-49.

96. Ibid., XI, pp. 103-4; XIII, pp. 42-43.

97. Ibid., XI, p. 294.

98. Ibid., XIII, p. 44.

99. Ibid., XI, pp. 253-55, 285, 435, 462.

100. Ibid., pp. 303, 340, 379-82, 403-4, 472.

101. Ibid., pp. 281, 447.

102. Ibid., pp. 313, 346, 465.

103. Ibid., pp. 397-98.

104. Ibid., pp. 445-47; Lenin, *Sobranie Sochinenii*, VII, pp. 462-72; *Slovo*, July 21, 1907, p. 3, c. 4; Sept. 13, 1907, p. 4, c. 5; *Riech*, July 25, 1907, p. 3, c. 3-4; July 27, 1907, p. 3, c. 2; Sept. 12, 1907, p. 3. c.

105. Lenin, *Collected Works*, XI, p. 464.

106. Ibid., p. 463.

107. Ibid., IX, p. 177.

108. Ibid., XI, p. 280.

109. Ibid., pp. 372-73.

110. Ibid., X, pp. 379, 453-54.

111. Ibid., IX, pp. 29-31; X, p. 110.

112. Ibid., pp. 486-87; XI, pp. 379-80.

113. Ibid., pp. 287-89.

114. Ibid., pp. 291-92.

115. Ibid., p. 290. He listed the Social-Revolutionaries, the Peasant Union, and some of the semi-trade unions and semi-political organizations as revolutionary. Ibid., X, p. 158.

116. Ibid., IX, p. 25.

117. Ibid., p. 135.

118. Ibid., X, p. 69.

119. Ibid., pp. 158-59; XI, p. 280.

120. Ibid., p. 365.

121. Ibid., X, pp. 455, 459.

122. Ibid., p. 405.

123. Ibid., IX, pp. 130-31; X, p. 246.

124. Ibid., p. 248.

8

Lenin and the Problem of Self-Determination of Nations

MICHAEL S. PAP

At the outbreak of World War I there existed on the European Continent two vast multi-national empires—the Austro-Hungarian and Russian. In the Austro-Hungarian Empire the Austrians governed the Poles, the Ukrainians, the Czechs, and the Slovenes; while the Hungarians ruled over the Croatians, the Rumanians in Transylvania, the Carpatho-Ukrainians (Ruthenians) and the Slovaks. Several millions of Jews lived in all parts of the Empire. Except for the Rumanians and Jews, all the subject nationalities belonged to the Slavic group. The subject nationalities encountered some obstacles in the development of their cultures and identity by officials of the ruling nations.

In the Russian Empire, which for centuries was ruled by autocratic Russian tsars on the basis of declared principle, One Tsar—One Religion—One Nationality, the linguistic and cultural rights of the non-Russian nations were curtailed and in some cases prohibited.

The basic objective of the Russian autocratic tsars, especially since Peter the Great, was the desire to "liberate" neighboring countries, particularly Slavic nations, from foreign domination. During the eighteenth century alone, Russian government spent sixty-nine years, more than half a century, on imperialistic wars against Sweden, Turkey, Persia, Prussia and China. All these wars, except the Russian-Swedish, were fought outside the boundaries of the Russian Empire. The nineteenth century, like the eighteenth, was also mostly spent on foreign wars to subjugate countries beyond the boundary of the Empire. In the nineteenth century, sixty-seven years were devoted to foreign wars, and only thirty-two years were spent on peaceful internal life.

As a result of the Russian aggressions, the Russian Empire grew immensely at the expense of the victims to the point where the Russians became a minority people in their own empire.

Valdimir Ilyich Lenin's interest in the nationality problem in the Russian Empire was aroused in 1897 after the last tsar's population census was published. Young Lenin was rather surprised that in spite of the centuries-old tsarist Russification policy, based on the idea of Autocracy, Orthodoxy, and Russian Nationalism, the census produced the following unexpected results: the majority of subjugated peoples in the Russian Empire declared themselves to be non-Russians, 56.7 percent; while out of the population of almost 126 million only 43.3 percent considered themselves to be Russians.[1]

137

In his early work, *Who Are the Friends of the People?*, written in 1894, Lenin considered the nationality problem a temporary phenomenon which would disappear with the victory of socialism.[2]

Lenin was in favor of the enforced assimilation process through Russification in the Russian Empire. He insisted that the Marxian ideology, which he endorsed as a young student, demanded elimination of national diversity among various nations and the creation of a society based on internationalist principles. For this reason, he promoted the idea of creating a centralized Russian-controlled Marxist Party.

At the First Congress of the Russian Socialist Democratic Labor Party (RSDLP), which was attended by nine Marxist delegates in 1898, the Nationality Problem was not discussed. The Manifesto of the newly organized party included only one nebulous phrase: "the right of nations to self-determination in the state will be recognized."

At the Second Congress of RSDLP, which met in Brussels and then in London during the Summer of 1903, Lenin incorporated the idea of the right of nations to self-determination in the Russian Empire into the political program of the Bolsheviks, since he believed it would serve a dual purpose: first, it would show the Russian Marxists' concern for the oppressive conditions of the non-Russians and offer solution on the basis of equality; and, second, it would secure unity of nations on the basis of a voluntary union. The party platform, therefore, included the following principles on self-determination.

3. Broad local self-rule; regional self-rule for those localities which distinguish themselves by separate living conditions and the composition of the population.

7. Destruction of the existing social order; full equality for all citizens, regardless of sex, religion, race, and nationality.

8. The right of the peoples to receive education in their native tongues, secured by the establishment of schools necessary for that purpose at the expense of the government and of organs of self-rule; the right of every citizen to use his native tongue at gatherings; the introduction of native languages on a basis of equality with the state language in all local social and government institutions.

9. The right of all nations (*natsii*) in the state to self-determination.

As the leading specialist on the Nationality Question in both the tsarist and Soviet Russian Empire, Dr. Pipes, points out, these ideas in the program were inserted under the pressure of the Menshevik faction, over the objections of the more centralistically inclined Bolsheviks.[3]

The hypocritical nature of Lenin's policy on self-determination, however, was recognized at this Congress when the proposal of the Jewish Bund to reorganize the Russian Marxist party on the basis of the nationality principles was rejected by the delegates by a majority of two votes. It was obvious that the Russian Marxists did not desire to solve the Nationality Problem on the declared basis of the right of self-determination. The centralist tendencies of the Russian Marxists were clearly demonstrated by Lenin's angry refusal to accept the idea of decentralization of the Party and reorganization of the Russian Empire on the basis of Federal principles which would secure equality among the nations.

Lenin argued that the position on self-determination taken by the Russian Marxist party was not to mean the desire of the Party to dismember the Russian Empire.

After 1903, Lenin spent much of his time and energy in polemics with Mensheviks, particularly the Jewish Bund, who continued to insist that the rights of at least cultural autonomy for the Jews and other non-Russians must be secured in the future Russian Socialist State.

In his subsequent writings, particularly in *Iskra*, Lenin repeatedly stated that the struggle for the right of self-determination did not mean that the Marxist must support every demand based on this right. As the Party of the proletariat, Lenin insisted, the Social Democrats had a vital positive aim to fight not for the self-determination of the nations and ethnic groups, but only for the proletariat in every nationality. The Russian Marxists must aim at the closest unity of the proletarians of all nationalities, and only in particular cases can they support the demand for the establishment of a class state or the formation of a loose federate union.

The Russian Marxists under Lenin's leadership at this early stage of development of their political strategy used the slogan of the right of nations to self-determination only as a weapon to destroy tsarist autocracy. The Central Committee of the RSDLP(B), for example, rejected the application of the Ukrainian Social Democrats who wanted to become affiliated members with the RSDLP on the basis of the right to at least national autonomy. The Central Committee simply stated that the exception made to the Jewish Bund, which was promised national autonomy at the Second Congress of the RSDLP, did not mean that this right can or will be expanded to other Socialist parties.

The evidence shows that the RSDLP did not advance any positive new proposals to solve the Nationalities problem in the Russian Empire after the 1903 split. Only Mensheviks insisted on the right of nations to cultural-poltical autonomy.[4]

It is important to notice that the other Russian political parties, which emerged after the 1905 Revolution, among them the strongest Constitutional Democrats (Kadets), did not fare better. In January 1906, the Kadets pledged to restore the equality status for all "Russian citizens"—and pronounced that the Constitution of the Russian Empire will also guarantee all peoples inhabiting the Empire the right to free cultural self-determination. The Kadets, however, insisted that the Russian language must be the language of the central institutions, the Army and the Fleet, the population of every region must be assured of the opportunity to receive elementary and, insofar as it is possible, higher education in the native tongue. The Kadets were in favor of political autonomy and cultural self-determination only for Poland and Finland.[5]

The other non-Russian nations were to be satisfied with a declared rights safeguarded by future leaders of Democratic Government of the Russian Empire. As Pipes pointed out:

The Russian liberals did little to advance the solution of the nationality problem in the Dumas in which they played an important role. The Socialist Revolutionary Party did not fare better. It believed that the establishment of a democratic society will solve the problem. All that was needed was to overthrow Tsarism, and the problem would simply disappear. They advocated a democratic republic with widest possible application of the federal principle to the relations among the individual nationalities; the recognition of their unconditional right to self-determination; the introduction of the native language(s) in all local public and state institutions.[6]

Lenin, the leader of the Independent Russian Bolshevik party since 1912, returned to the problem of the right of nations to self-determination only in October 1913. He spent the two years (1913-1914) writing extensively about what he now termed an urgent priority because of the rise of nationalist feelings in the Russian Empire. The first solid research paper entitled "Critical Remarks on the National Question" was published in *Proletarskaya Pravda*, #12, on December 20, 1913 (January 1, 1914). In this article, Lenin sharply criticized the editorial writings in liberal Russian newspapers, especially *Russkoye Slovo*, issue #198 (1913) in which he argued that the hostility towards Russian language in Russia is based on the artificial—in Lenin's word, forced—implanting of that language on the non-Russian nations. Lenin takes a negative stand on the proposition that even the opponents to the Russification policy would have to admit that requirements of economic exchange will always compel the nationalities living in one state (as long as they wish to live together) to study the language of the majority.

Lenin takes an exception to the explanation written in the *Russkoye Slovo:* "Even those who oppose Russification would hardly be likely to deny that in a country as large as Russia there must be one single official language and that language can be only Russian."[7] He claims that this logic is turned inside out and argues that little Switzerland only gained from having not one single official language but three—German, French, and Italian. He then draws parallels with the Russian Empire and points out that in Switzerland 70 percent of the population are Germans; while in the Russian Empire, only 43 percent are Great Russians; in Switzerland, 22 percent are French while in the Russian Empire 17 percent are Ukrainian; in Switzerland, 7 percent are Italian while in the Russian Empire 6 percent are Poles and 4.5 percent are ByeloRussian.[8]

Lenin then comes to the conclusion:

Why should "big" Russian Empire, a much more varied and terribly backward country, inhibit her development by the retention of any kind of privilege for any one language; should not the contrary be true, liberal gentlemen? . . .

The liberals approach the language question in the same way as they approach all other political questions—like hypocritical hucksters—holding out one hand (openly) to democracy and the other (behind their backs) to the federalists and police.[9]

The national program of the working class democracy was to be based on the refusal of all privileges for any one nation or any one language; the solution of the problem of the political self-determination of nations was to be accomplished by a completely free democratic method; the promulgations of a law for the whole state by virtue of which any measure (rural, urban, community, and so on) introducing any privilege of any kind for one of the nations and mitigating against the equality of nations or the right of a national minority shall be declared illegal and ineffective, and any citizen of the state shall have the right to demand that such a measure be annulled as unconstitutional and that those who attempt to put it into effect shall be punished.[10]

The above statement of Lenin can be branded as nationalistic. However, Lenin hastened to explain that between declaration of a policy and implementation of such a policy there was a difference. This allowed his followers to quote the most suitable paragraphs in subsequent interpretations:

The working class democracy in opposition to the nationalist wrangling of the various bourgeois parties over questions of language, etc., demands the unconditional unity and complete amalgamation of workers of all nationalities in all working class organizations—trade unions, co-operative, consumers', education and all others—in contradiction to any kind of bourgeois nationalism.[11]

Lenin recognized the existence of national cultures; but at the same time, he insisted that international culture must be given the dominant position:

The question is whether it is permissible for a Marxist, directly or indirectly, to advance the slogan of national culture or whether he should oppose it by advocating in all languages the slogans of workers' internationalism while "adapting" himself to all local and national languages.[12]

Bitterly attacking the Jewish Bund for advocating the right to develop national culture and placing the Jewish Socialists in the camp of enemies of the proletariat, Lenin points out:

Bourgeois nationalism and proletarian internationalism are the two irreconcilably hostile slogans that correspond to the two great class camps throughout the capitalist world and express the two policies—the two-world outlook in the national question. In advocating the slogan of national culture and building up on it an entire plan and practical program of what they call cultural-national autonomy, the Bundists are in effect instruments of bourgeois nationalism among the workers.[13]

Lenin did not fail to stress that assimilation of the non-Russians, particularly Jews, in Europe is, from the Marxist standpoint, a positive trend. After all, "the best Jews, those who are celebrated in world history and have given the world a foremost leader of democracy and socialism, have never clamored against assimilation."[14]

Lenin's attitude toward Ukrainians was as negative as it was toward Jews:

Take Russia and the attitude of Great Russians towards the Ukrainians. Naturally, every democrat, not to mention Marxists, will strongly oppose the incredible humiliation of Ukrainians and demand complete equality for them. But it would be a downright betrayal of socialism and a silly policy even from the standpoint of the bourgeois "national aims" of the Ukrainians to weaken the ties and the alliance between the Ukrainian and Great Russian proletariat that now exist within the confines of a single state. . .

Given united action by the Great Russian and Ukrainian proletarians, a free Ukraine is possible. Without such unity, it is out of the question.[15]

And again:

The proletarian cause must come first, we say, because it not only protects the lasting and fundamental interests of labor and of humanity, but also those of democracy; and without democracy neither an autonomous nor an independent Ukraine is conceivable.[16]

Lenin gave the Russian Marxists rather axiomatic advice when he categorically stated that Marxists will never, under no circumstances, advocate either the federal principle or decentralization, because the great centralized state is a tremendous historical step forward from medieval disunity to the future socialist unity of the whole world and only via such a state can there be any road to socialism.[17]

The reaction to Lenin's approach to the question of national self-determination by the other Russian Political parties, particularly the Kadets, aggravated Lenin. He was disappointed that his thesis did not receive any attention. He quotes only one Russian newspaper *Novoye Vremya*, (Dec., 1913-August, 1914), the mouthpiece of great Russian nationalism, which commented: "What to Social Democrats (Bolsheviks) is an axiom of political wisdom (i.e., recognition of the right of nations to self-determination, to secession) is today beginning to cause disagreement even among the Kadets."[18]

Finally, at the outbreak of World War I in 1914, Lenin wrote another monograph, *The Russian Marxists' Program on the Right of Nations to Self-Determination*, based on the decisions at the Second Congress of the RSDLP. He also entered into polemics with the colorful Polish-Jewish Marxist Rosa Luxemburg, who wrote extensively on the national question and autonomy in which she repudiated Lenin's postulates and ridiculed Lenin for his inconsistencies.

Lenin angrily answered Rosa Luxemburg—whom he regarded as an enemy of Russian Marxism because she dared to question the wisdom of the Bolshevik leader with axiomatic answers to all problems:

It is Rosa Luxemburg herself who is continually lapsing into generalities about self-determination (to the extent even of philosophising amusingly on the question of how the will of the nation is to be ascertained) without anywhere clearly and precisely asking herself whether the gist of the matter lies in legal definitions or in the experience of the national movements throughout the world.[19]

Lenin took an exception to Rosa Luxemburg's argument about his concept of self-determination. He vigorously denied the Luxemburg assertion that:

Despite the elasticity of the principle of the right of nations to self-determination, which is a mere platitude, and obviously equally applicable, not only to the nations inhabiting Russia but also to the nations inhabiting Germany and Austria, Switzerland and Sweden, America and Australia, we do not find it in the program of any of the present day socialist parties.

Referring to the paragraph 9 of the Program of RSDLP in 1903, Rosa Luxemburg insisted that: "Paragraph 9 gives no practical lead on the day-by-day policy of the proletariat; no practical solution of national problems."[20] Careful examination of the arguments used by Rosa Luxemburg leads one to the conclusion that paragraph 9 was indeed meaningless and did not commit the Russian Marxists to support national aspirations.

The question might be raised what practical approach to the national problem did Lenin have in mind. It could have meant one of three things: support for all national aspirations; support of the right to secession of any nation; or just an attempt to save the Russian Empire from disintegration by accepting Marxian concept of internationalism.

Lenin often argued that in the early twentieth century the proletariat of the Russian Empire was faced with a two-fold, or rather a two-sided task: to combat nationalism of every kind; above all, Great Russian nationalism; to recognize not only equal rights for all nations in general, but also the equality of rights regarding policy; i.e., the right of nations to self-determination, and at the same time a successful struggle against all and every kind of nationalism among all nations in order to preserve the unity of the proletarian struggle and the proletarian organization, amalgamating these organizations into a close-knit international association despite bourgeois strivings for nation exclusiveness.

During 1914-16 Lenin was preoccupied with the nationality question in the Russian Empire and was eager to prove that the Russian Bolshevik solution of the nationality problem was far superior to the solutions offered by the Austrian socialists, Otto Bauer and Karl Renner, who advocated extra-territorial national-cultural autonomy.[21]

Acting as a great tactician, Lenin formulated his views in August 1915, in his *Right of Nations to Self-Determination.* The war and the uncertainty of its outcome obliged him not to alienate the non-Russian nations of the Empire. He wrote:

The socialists cannot reach their great aim without fighting against every form of national oppression. They must, therefore, unequivocally demand that the Social Democrats of the oppressing countries (of the so-called "great" nations) should recognize and defend the right of the oppressed nations to self-determination in the political sense of the word; i.e., the right to political separation.[22]

He justified his somewhat new approach to the solution of the problem of oppressed nationalities on the basis of Marx's slogan that "no people oppressing other people can be free."

With the downfall of tsarist Russian autocracy in March 1917, the gradual disintegration of the Russian Empire began. Bolshevik government, first under G. Lvov and then A. Kerensky, insisted on preservation of the unity and indivisibility of the Empire, rejecting at first even cultural-political autonomy to the non-Russian nations. Upon his return to St. Petersburg in April 1917, Lenin seized the opportunity to exploit the nationality question in this new situation and declared the Bolshevik party's "uncompromising" stand on the right of nations to self-determination, including the right to secession.

In his first major statement while on Russian soil, Lenin declared at the Bolshevik Party Conference on May 12, 1917, that his party was taking a neutral, independent position in regard to the separatist movements. "If Finland, if Poland, if Ukraine break away from Russia, it is nothing terrible. We are for fraternal union of all nations. If there is a Ukrainian Republic, there will be closer contact, greater confidence between the two." Lenin speculated that if the Ukrainians would witness the replacement of the Miliukov Republic by a Soviet Republic, they would not break away.[23]

The subsequent developments demonstrated, however, that Lenin's proclamation on self-determination was to be regarded only as a useful slogan needed for the insignificant Russian Bolshevik party to gain strength and power. While organizing all-out attack on the Provisional Government, Lenin and his close collaborator Stalin, the Russified Georgian, considered the issue of self-determination as one of the most important features of the forthcoming Revolution.

It was the genius of Lenin and his propagandists which succeeded in creating great illusions among the non-Russian nations who believed that the Bolshevik party was the only political Russian party which was willing, and indeed eager, to give them, finally, a free choice; complete independence or federation with Soviet Russia or voluntary unity with New Russia.

This skillful tactic influenced many non-Russian leaders who decided to maintain, in most cases, neutral positions when open conflict between the Provisional Government and the Bolsheviks became a reality. On November 15, 1917, shortly after the Bolshevik seizure of power in Petersburg, the Soviet government issued an official declaration of the Rights of the Peoples of Russia in which the Soviet government, under Lenin's leadership, pledged to uphold the following principles:

1. The equality and sovereignty of the peoples of Russia.
2. The right of the peoples of Russia to free self-determination even to the point of separation and the formation of an independent state.
3. The abolition of any and all national and national-religious privileges and disabilities.
4. The free development of national minorities and ethnographic groups inhabiting the territory of Russia. The Declaration was signed by V. Ulianov (Lenin) as Chairman of the Council of People's Commissars and Josef Dzhugashvili (Stalin) as People's Commissar of Nationality Affairs.[24]

Lenin still believed that a declared right of a free self-determination, including secession, would lead to a voluntary union with the new Russian Soviet Republic. When he realized, however, that sugarcoated promises of equality and fraternity did not produce the expected results, the non-Russian nations, Finland, Estonia, Latvia, Lithuania, ByeloRussia, Ukraine, Armenia, Azerbaidjan, Georgia, Cossackia, and even Turkestan, gradually proclaimed national independence and separation from Soviet Russia, Lenin gradually changed the Soviet policy on self-determination. From December 1917 on he argued that the establishment of independent states by the non-Russians would be tolerated only if those states would accept Soviet form of government; that is, the dictatorship of the Russian Bolshevik party with some native leadership in it. To prove Lenin's determination to destroy the national republics, the Soviet of People's Commissars sent its first ultimatum to the Ukrainian Central Rada (Council) in Kiev on December 17, 1917, signed by V. Lenin, as Chairman of People's Commissars, and L. Trotsky, Commissar for Foreign Affairs, in which the Rada, representing various political parties and actually the governing body of Ukraine, was accused of playing under the guise of nationalism a double game, a game which, as it was stated in the ultimatum, for some time expressed itself in the Rada's refusal to recognize the Soviets and the Soviet power in Ukraine. The ultimatum demanded from the Ukrainian National government immediate removal of the obstacles to Soviet expansion by stopping the disarming of Soviet regiments and

Red Guards in Ukraine. The Rada was warned that in case no satisfactory reply to the Soviet Russian demands was received within forty-eight hours, the Soviet of Peoples' Commissars would consider the Rada in a state of open warfare against the Soviet government in Russia and in the Ukraine.

On December 19, 1917, Rada bluntly rejected the Bolshevik ultimatum, strongly repudiating Lenin's dual standard on self-determination:

The declaration of the Sovnarkom, in which the independence of the Ukrainian People's Republic is recognized, lacks either sincerity or logic. It is not possible simultaneously to recognize the right of a people to self-determination including separation and at the same time to infringe roughly on that right by imposing on the people in question a certain type of government. . . . The General Secretariat categorically repudiates all attempts on the part of the People's Commissars to interfere in the political life of the Ukrainian People's Republic. The pretensions of the People's Commissars to guide the Ukrainian democracy are the less justifiable since the political organization which they wish to impose on the Ukraine has led to unenviable results in the territory which is under their own control. Great Russia is more and more becoming the prey of anarchy and economic and political disruption, while the most arbitrary rule and the abuse of all liberties gained by the revolution . . . reign supreme in your land. The General Secretariat does not wish to repeat that sad experiment in the Ukraine . . . The Ukrainian democracy . . . is quite satisfied with its government. The only elements which are not satisfied with the composition of the Rada are those of Great Russian extraction, viz., the Black Hundred, the Kadets, and the Bolsheviks . . . The General Secretariat will facilitate in every way their return to Great Russia where their sentiments will receive the desired satisfaction. It is with this in mind that the anarchistically inclined soldiers of Great Russian extraction were disarmed . . . and given a chance to return to their homeland . . . The General Secretariat is doing its best to avoid bloody methods of settling political questions. But if the People's Commissars of Great Russia . . . will force it to accept the challenge, the General Secretariat has no doubt that the Ukrainian soldiers, workers, and peasants will give an adequate reply to the People's Commissars.

Rada's reply was signed by V. Vynnychenko, President, and S. Petliura, Secretary of War.[25]

Still another classic example of Bolshevik duplicity on self-determination was demonstrated at the Brest-Litovsk peace negotiations in January-March 1918, when Soviet Commissar of Foreign Affairs Trotsky insisted on the right of Russian Soviet government to represent all nations of the former Russian tsarist empire. He was strongly rebuffed by a member of the Rada delegation, Liubinskii, who stated:

The noisy declarations of the Bolsheviks regarding the complete freedom of the people of Russia is but the vulgar stuff of demagogy. The Government of the Bolsheviks, which has broken up the Constituent Assembly and which rests on the bayonets of hired Red Guards, will never elect to apply in Russia the very just principle of self-determination, for they know only too well that not only the Republic of Ukraine but also the Don, the Caucasus, Siberia and other regions do not regard them as their government, and that even the Russian people themselves will ultimately deny their right; only because they are afraid of the development of a National Revolution do they declare here at the peace conference and within Russia, with a spirit of demagogy peculiar to themselves, the right of self-determination of the peoples. They themselves are struggling against the realization of this principle and are resorting not only to hired bands of Red Guards but also to meaner and even less legal methods.[26]

Soviet Russian aggression and subsequent occupation of Ukraine, Byelo-Russia, Armenia, Azerbaidjan, Georgia, and Turkestan was aided by hostile attitudes toward these non-Russian nations taken by the leaders of the Russian Anti-Bolshevik White Armies of Denikin, Kolchak, and Yudenich, as well as the Western policy of preserving the indivisibility of the Russian Empire. As Stalin proudly pointed out at the Twelfth Congress of the Russian Communist-Bolshevik Party in Moscow in April, 1923:

Do not forget, comrades, that if we were able to march against Kerensky with flying colors and overthrow the Provisional Government it was because, among other things, we were backed by the confidence of the oppressed peoples that were expecting liberation at the hands of the Russian proletarians. Do not forget such reserves as the oppressed peoples, who are silent, but who by their silence exert pressure and decide a great deal. This is often not felt, but these peoples are living, they exist, and they must not be forgotten. Do not forget that if we had not had in the rear of Kolchak, Denikin, Wrangel and Yudenich the so-called "aliens," if we had not had the formerly oppressed peoples, who disorganized the rear of those generals by their tacit sympathy for the Russian proletarians—comrades, this is a special factor in our development, this tacit sympathy, which nobody hears or sees, but which decides everything—if it had not been for this sympathy, we would not have knocked out a single one of these generals. While we were marching against them, disintegration began in their rear. Why? Because those generals depended on the Cossack colonizing elements, they held out to the oppressed peoples the prospect of further oppression, and the oppressed peoples were therefore pushed into our arms, while we unfurled the banner of the liberation of these oppressed peoples. That is what decided the fate of those generals; such is the sum-total of the factors which, although over-shadowed by our armies' victories, in the long run decided everything. That must not be forgotten.[27]

The Soviet Russian destruction of the National Republics was completed by the end of 1920. Instead of National States, four Soviet Republics came into existence: RSSFR, Ukrainian SSR, ByeloRussian SSR, and Transcaucasian SSFR. Formerly, they enjoyed relative sovereignty status; however, the Russian Bolsheviks, particularly Stalin, started a campaign for the amalgamation of these Republics into one Russian Soviet Socialist Federated Republic. They openly declared that the unity among these nations could be achieved only through the liquidation of the Soviet Republics.

Suddenly, Lenin returned to the question of self-determination and insisted on a "voluntary" union of the four Republics because of the strong denunciation of Lenin by the Western Socialists and non-Russian Bolsheviks who claimed that he changed only the name of autocracy. Instead of a white tsar, there emerged a red one, they claimed, with the tendency to maintain an indivisible Russian Empire.

With growing resistance in the non-Russian Republics to the Bolshevik policy and mindful of history which would identify his Bolshevik movement as aiming at preservation of the Russian Empire, he wrote in his note to the Politbureau on October 6, 1922: "I am declaring a war against Great Russian chauvinism; not for life, but for death. As soon as I get rid of the damn tooth, I will eat it with all my healthy teeth."[28] On the other hand, Stalin proposed the idea of autonomization, making the withdrawal of state sovereignty from the independent socialist republics and their reduction to only locally autonomous status.[29]

As a result of Lenin's insistence, and by this time he was the undisputed leader of the Soviet Union, a Union of Soviet Socialist Republics was formed on the basis of the treaty promulgated in December 1922. The right of secession, which was "guaranteed" for each and every republic, led to a bitter debate among the Bolsheviks; but Lenin won out with his argument that the omission of such a guarantee would lead to suspicion that the Russians will continue the policy of Russification and the non-Russians would have no adequate defense against it. Lenin prophesied:

It is quite natural in such circumstances that the "freedom to withdraw from the union" by which we justify ourselves will be a mere scrap of paper unable to defend the non-Russians from the onslaught of that really Russian man, the Great Russian, the chauvinist, in substance a rascal and a lover of violence, as the typical Russian bureaucrat is. There is no doubt that the infinitesimal percentage of Soviet and sovietized workers will drown in that set of chauvinistic Great Russian riff-raff like a fly in milk.[30]

In spite of this, Lenin's torment about the equality of the Republics, and the right to secession, the terms of the treaty gave the Central Soviet Government in Moscow practically unlimited power. The Russian Communist party secured its legal right to intervene in the internal affairs of the member states and to suppress the opposition against Moscow among the non-Russian Communists. The Russian Communist party was in a position to adopt any resolution, since the great majority of the Party members were Russians. At the Eleventh Congress, for example, when the question of amalgamation of the republics was raised and the resolution for centralization approved, the delegates consisted of 341 Russians, 77 Jews, 10 Tartars, 12 Armenians, 9 Georgians, 19 Latvians, 8 Kirghizs and 46 others.[31]

After consolidating the Bolshevik power in all republics through terror and fear, the Soviet Russian Empire emerged with the Russian predominance. The pretense of the Russian Bolsheviks of their respect for national self-determination disappeared completely when Moscow initiated shortly after Lenin's death in 1924 an all-out liquidation of all non-Russian elements suspected in national deviations. Instead of Internationalism, Russification policy was forcibly introduced and by 1930 the Soviet Union emerged as One Indivisible Russian Empire, with only one difference from tsarist times: namely, the non-Russian peoples were allowed to glorify the big Russian brother in their own native languages and customs. The pretended national self-determination policy was carried on by Stalin to tragic absurdity in the 1930s when he ordered the liquidation of many non-Russians, including Bolsheviks, who in 1917-21 helped the Russian Bolsheviks to gain power in their own native lands.

Stalin's policy of promoting the Leninist concept of self-determination until his death in March 1953, can be termed organized genocide costing the lives of more than thirty million peoples.[32] In his brilliant testimony *Progress, Coexistence and Intellectual Freedom*, the famous Russian academician Andrei D. Sakharov, known as the Father of the Soviet H-Bomb, compared Fascist Germany with Stalinist totalitarianism of the Soviet Union and came to the conclusion that there were many common features between them and also certain differences. Stalinism, according to Sakharov, exhibited a much more subtle kind of hypocrisy and demagogy, with reliance not on an openly cannibalistic program like Hitler's but on a progressive, scientific, and popular socialist ideology.[33]

The greatest demonstration of Bolshevik cynicism and mockery on self-determination was the promulgation of the Stalin's Constitution in 1936, paragraph 17 of which "secured" the right of the Soviet Republics to freely secede from the USSR.

The invasion of the Soviet Empire by the Nazi barbarians in 1941 demonstrated the non-Russian contempt for Bolshevik colonialists, when millions of Red Army soldiers surrendered to the Germans rather than defend Stalin's brutal regime. After the war, Stalin returned to the policy of terror and extermination. Only his death in March 1953 prevented another wholesale genocide.

Today the Nationality Question in the expanded Russian Empire is as explosive as it was in 1917. Some brave authors, Chornovil, Dzyuba, Sakharov, Grigorenko, Solzhenitsyn, Amalryk, and many others, insist that the real, not declared, right of the nations to self-determination must be restored in the Soviet Union. They are warning the present leaders in the Kremlin that the continuation of the colonial policy of the tsars in the non-Russian republics will lead to the downfall of the Soviet Empire. They are calling for a halt to the organized anti-Semitism and Russification. They demand the restoration of human rights and freedom of choice for all. They demand the restoration of the Leninist concept of equality as expressed during the existence of the Provisional Government and after the establishment of Soviet Republics. Dzyuba, for example, in his brilliant monograph on *Internationalism or Russification?* states:

What triumphed later as regards the nationalities policy: Lenin's "torments," the "calmness" of the Philistine circles, or its end-product—Stalinist-style "harshness"? Anyone who has the faintest recollection of recent history, knows. But even now, when the miracle-working "red-hot iron" has dropped from Stalin's weary hands, Lenin's "torments" have remained buried in oblivion. To them, we still have a long way to go. A spirit of conscious or unconscious disdain for the nationalities' cause and of incomprehension of the nationalities question prevails everywhere. In recent decades almost no attention has been paid to it, neither in the press, in literature, in history, nor in social or educational work. Only perhaps in the fields of literary scholarship and art might you still hear the last gasps of piteous scholastic talk about "national form" . . .

But under this external crust of indifference and neglect the internal process of Russification and assimilation has been flaring up all the more fiercely.

In 1961 Khrushchev declared: "we will not conserve . . . national distinctions" (N.S. Khrushchev, *On the Communist Programme*, Moscow—1961—p. 88). In practice this meant: the mincing-machine of Russification may continue turning at full speed, we will not interfere with it.[34]

The Kremlin leaders will have to prove that Marx was wrong when he said in 1867:

In the first place the policy of Russia is changeless, according to the admission of its official historian, the Muscovite Karamzin. Its methods, its tactics, its maneuvers may change, but the polar star of its policy—world domination—is a fixed star. In our times only a civilized government ruling over barbarian masses can hatch out such a plan and execute it. As the greatest Russian diplomat of modern times, Pozzo di Borgo, wrote to Alexander I at the time of the Congress of Vienna, Poland is the great instrument for the execution of Russian designs on the world, but it is also an invincible obstacle to them, until such time as the Poles, worn out by the accumulated betrayals of Europe, become a whip in the hand of the Muscovite.[35]

It is regrettable that today the importance of the Nationality Question in the Soviet Russian Empire is properly understood and exploited *only* by Peking.

Notes

1. H. Bochkowsky, *Ponevoleni Narody Tsarskoi Imperii*, (Vienna, 1916), pp. 13-15.
2. V.I. Lenin, *Sochineniia*, (3rd ed.). (Moscow, 1926-32). I, 73; hereafter cited as: Lenin, *Sochineniia.*
3. Richard Pipes, *The Formation of the Soviet Union* (Cambridge, Mass., 1964), pp. 32-33.

4. Bochkowsky, p. 39.

5. Pipes, p. 29.

6. Ibid., p. 31.

7. Lenin, *Sochineniia*, p. 134.

8. Ibid., p. 134.

9. Ibid., p. 135.

10. Ibid., p. 135.

11. Ibid., p. 136.

12. Ibid., p. 138.

13. Ibid., p. 139.

14. Ibid., p. 141.

15. Ibid., p. 142.

16. Ibid., p. 143.

17. Ibid., p. 154.

18. V.I. Lenin, *Collected Works*, 4th ed. (Moscow, 1964). v. 20, p. 419.

19. Ibid., p. 428.

20. Ibid., p. 438.

21. Otto Bauer, *Die nationalitaetenfrage und die Socialdemokratie.* Marx Studien (Vienna, 1924). II, 527-28.

22. Lenin, *Sochineniia*, 2nd ed., v. 18, pp. 473-74.

23. Ibid., v. 20, p. 295.

24. Robert V. Daniel, *A Documentary History of Communism* (New York, 1962), v. 1, pp. 125-26.

25. James Bunyan and H.H. Fisher, *The Bolshevik Revolution, 1917-18: Documents & Materials* (Stanford, California, 1934), pp. 439-41; for more details see Michael S. Pap, *Ukraine's Struggle for Sovereignty, 1917-1918* (New York, 1961), pp. 10-13.

26. John W. Wheeler-Bennett, *The Forgotten Peace: Brest-Litovsk; March, 1918* (New York, 1939), p. 210.

27. J. Stalin, *Works* (Moscow, 1953), v. 5, p. 251.

28. V.I. Lenin, *Pro Ukrainu (About Ukraine)* (Kiev, 1957), p. 670.

29. Ivan Dzyuba, *Internationalism or Russification?* (London, 1968), p. 30.

30. V.I. Lenin, *Letter to the Congress. The Question of Nationalities or of "Autonomization," December 30, 1922* (Moscow n.d.), p. 23.

31. *XI Siezd Rossiiskoii Communisticheskoii Partii (B) March 27-April 1922: Stenograficheskii otchet* Partizdat (Moscow), p. 31.

32. For detailed discussion of this problem, see: *Genocide in the USSR*, (New York, 1958).

33. A. Sakharov, *Progress, Coexistence & Intellectual Freedom* (New York, 1968), pp. 52-54.

34. Dzyuba, pp. 32-33.

35. Karl Marx and Friedrich Engels, *The Russian Menace to Europe* (Glencoe, Ill., 1952), p. 106.

**Part III
Lenin and Economics**

9

Lenin and the New Economic Policy

ALEC NOVE

The New Economic Policy, initiated in 1921, was a response to a number of circumstances and forces, understood by the politicians of the time in mutually inconsistent ways. In this chapter, I shall be arguing that Lenin's own views were to some extent internally inconsistent. Among the factors involved were: revolutionary emergency, ideological preconceptions, political tactics, and just harsh overriding necessity, all of which tended to interact. Thus, it is extraordinary how often the most cogent ideological reasons are found for doing what must be done. It would be wrong to present a clear but superficial picture.

War-Communism

N.E.P. replaced "war-communism." What did Lenin think war-communism was? To this question too there are several answers, and a brief look at the problems involved is essential if we are to understand how he saw N.E.P.

Lenin's picture of the transition to socialism was never fully or consistently worked out. He was, after all, primarily a politician. To seize power seemed, even as late as 1916, a rather distant prospect. His past works on the development of capitalism in Russia, on imperialism, on the present question, were doubtless both interesting and important, but they did not, and could not, come to grips with the question of what actually to do. Full communism was a vision indicated by Marx, and doubtless Lenin saw that same vision. But nowhere could such a state of affairs arise without a period of transition of unknown duration. Evidently such a period could be particularly long in a country such as Russia, predominantly peasant, industrially semideveloped, culturally backward, even if revolutionary governments in Western Europe were to come to her aid, even if times were normal.

But of course in 1917 times were anything but normal. The war exhausted Russia, and its necessities had created numerous organs of state control, of material allocation, of rationing. Even so controversial a decree as the state monopoly of trade in grain, at fixed prices, dates from well before the seizure of power by the Bolsheviks, as a consequence of wartime emergencies.

During the last months before October, Lenin did express some views about economic policy, and these have often been quoted. For example:

155

In addition to the chiefly "oppressive" apparatus—the standing army, the police and the bureaucracy—the modern state possesses an apparatus which has extremely close connections with the banks and syndicates, an apparatus which performs an enormous amount of accounting and registration work, if it may be expressed this way. This apparatus must not, and should not, be smashed. It must be wrested from the control of the capitalists; the capitalists and the wires they pull must be *cut off, lopped off, chopped away from* this apparatus; it must be subordinate to the proletarian Soviets; it must be expanded, made more comprehensive, and nation-wide. And this *can* be done by utilizing the achievements already made by large-scale capitalism (in the same way as the proletarian revolution can, in general, reach its goal only by utilizing these achievements).

Capitalism has created an accounting apparatus in the shape of the banks, syndicates, postal service, consumers' societies, and office employees' unions. *Without big banks socialism would be impossible.*

The big banks are the state apparatus which we *need* to bring about socialism, and which we *take* ready-made from capitalism; our task here is merely to *lop off* what *capitalistically mutilates* this excellent apparatus, to make it even *bigger*, even more democratic, even more comprehensive. Quantity will be transformed into quality. A single State Bank, the biggest of the big, with branches in every rural district, in every factory, will constitute as much as nine-tenths of the *socialist* apparatus. This will be country wide *bookkeeping*, country wide *accounting* of the production and distribution of goods, this will be, so to speak, something in the nature of the *skeleton* of socialist society.

We can *lay hold of* and *set in motion* this *state apparatus* (which is not fully a state apparatus under capitalism, but which will be so with us, under socialism) at one stroke, by a single decree, because the actual work of bookkeeping, control, registering, accounting and counting is performed by *employees*, the majority of whom themselves lead a proletarian or semi-proletarian existence.

By a single decree of the proletarian government these employees can and must be transferred to the status of state employees, in the same way as the watchdogs of capitalism, like Briand and other bourgeois ministers, by a single decree transfer railwaymen on strike to the status of state employees. We shall need many more state employees of this kind, and more *can* be obtained, because capitalism has simplified the work of accounting and control, has reduced it to a comparatively simple system of bookkeeping, which any literate person can do.[1]

This is followed by the oddly ambiguous statement: "The important thing will not be even the confiscation of the capitalists' property, but country wide, all embracing workers' control over the capitalists and their possible supporters. Confiscation alone leads nowhere, as it does not contain the element of organization, of accounting for proper distribution. Instead of confiscation, we could easily impose a *fair* tax. . . ."[2]

These ideas, naturally, had little to do with the realities of this or perhaps any other time. However, it must be noted that Lenin did not advocate total nationalization and expropriation. "The capitalists and the wires they pull" suggests that the wires of control be snapped or taken over, rather than the capitalists expropriated. Nor did he demand their total expropriation on the morrow of the seizure of power. In the spring of 1918 he was still talking of "state capitalism," of control over employers. VSNKh was issuing instructions forbidding local authorities to nationalize industries without their specific authorization. Aware of the appalling state of the economy, Lenin gave especial emphasis to the establishment of order out of chaos, to the restoration of production, causing intense chagrin among those comrades who wished to preserve the forms and methods of "workers' control." Thus, some Soviet authors assert that Lenin intended all along speedily to expropriate the private industrialists and producers,[3] but the balance of the evidence seems not to support this view.

However, Brest-Litovsk was followed by the slide into civil war, and with it went the slide into war-communism. I have described and documented this process elsewhere.[4] There are many factors involved, including the interaction between ideological enthusiasm and desperate necessity. Kritsman asserted, in describing this period, that "were it not for external factors, the expropriation of capital would not have taken place in June 1918."[5] Lenin at times put things rather differently, but he was not by any means always consistent in his view, which must be examined more closely.

In looking back, he several times returned to the theme of a would-be gradualism disrupted by events. Speaking to the second congress of political educators (*politprosvetov*) in October 1921, Lenin said of N.E.P. that it was a "new" policy by contrast to the one that preceded it, but that "in essentials it was older than the preceding economic policy. Why so? Because our previous policy was calculated—though in the then situation we did not really calculate, rather assessed—that the old Russian economy could be directly converted into state production and distribution on a Communist basis. Yet if we recall our own economic literature, if we recall what the Communists wrote before taking power . . . and in the first period after taking power, for instance at the beginning of 1918 . . . we then spoke much more cautiously and circumspectly than in the second half of 1918 and during all of 1919 and all of 1920."[6] Reminding his audience of his own, more gradualist, position, he said that he had hopes that Brest-Litovsk would be followed by "peaceful construction." He blamed the "mistake of trying directly to pass to communist production and distribution" on "the overwhelming military problems and the desperate situation in which the republic found itself."[7] Returning to the same theme at the Moscow provincial party conference in October 1921, in a speech devoted wholly to N.E.P. he said with even greater emphasis that, by the spring of 1918, "We had expropriated more than we could control and administer, and that we should pass from expropriation . . . to the tasks of accountancy and inspection (*kontrol'*)."

(This under condition in which a large private sector continued to exist in industry.) Earlier illusions about direct and immediate construction of socialism were already becoming modified. "Already then, in a number of respects, it was necessary to move backwards." He went on: "We assumed that the two systems, the systems of state production and distribution and of private commodity-production and distribution—would be in conflict with one another under conditions in which we would build up state production and distribution, capturing it step by step from the hostile system,"[8] and that this was already the building of a new system, though there was at first no conception as to the relationship of the state's economy to the market and to trade. He cited as an example the "nationalization of advertising," a fairly futile measure, but one indicating that they expected a large private sector to exist and to advertise. He then pointed out, as also did Trotsky on an earlier occasion,[9] that another vital factor was the behavior of the bourgeoisie, and said: "The state power, the proletariat, attempted to move towards new social relations with, so to speak, the maximum adaptation to the then existing conditions, as far as possible gradually and without extremes. The enemy, i.e., the bourgeois class, tried everything to push us into the most extreme and desperate struggle. Strategically, from the point of view of the enemy, was this correct? Certainly, since why should the bourgeoisie, without having tried out its forces in direct conflict, suddenly accept us and obey?"[10] And again, "the bourgeoisie could not . . . accept those partial concessions which Soviet power was giving it in the interests of a more gradual transition to the new order. 'No part of transition, to be part of a new order' that was how the bourgeoisie replied."[11] (It matters little in the present context whether this is a fair picture of the then situation.)

Relations with the peasants were, of course, a key element in war-communism as they were *the* key element in N.E.P. Here it is well to appreciate that neither Lenin, nor any sane man, ever imagined that such relations could be built on confiscations, other than in an emergency situation. It may be, indeed, that some Bolsheviks thought of *produkto-obmen* (products exchange, or barter, not *trade*) between a socialist industrial sector and a predominantly private petty-bourgeois peasantry. Lenin, as we shall see, aimed at this in the very first stages of N.E.P. But in 1918 the problem was that the towns were threatened with starvation, and the "class struggle in the villages," and compulsory deliveries, were means of getting food. As the civil war progressed and economic disruption deepened, it was increasingly found that there was nothing to pay the peasants with. No doubt ideological prejudice against trade and its association with "black-marketeering" played its role, but no one should imagine that Lenin was *ideologically* devoted to the principle of confiscation of surpluses, which was the essence of the hated *prodrazverstka*, for its own sake.

So in a sense Lenin took the view that war-communism was a response to desperate necessity. But he over and over again said that "we committed errors." To that extent the return of what (he alleged) had been the original policy was a return to the right path. A return to the right path is the right thing to do, and cannot be described either as a defeat or a retreat. But Lenin also and repeatedly spoke both of defeat and retreat. The Bolsheviks deliberately tried to march directly into socialism and they had failed; they had lost a battle. At this same Moscow Party conference of October 1921, he developed at length his parallel with Port Arthur, and the related concept of necessary or positive mistakes. This argument, advanced with N.E.P. in full swing, gives us an interesting insight into his mind at this time, and is worth dwelling on.

The capture (by the Japanese) of Port Arthur went through two completely different stages. The first consisted of violent attacks which were all unsuccessful and cost the famous Japanese general (Nogi) a great number of casualties. The second stage, when it proved necessary to undertake an extremely burdensome, complex and slow siege of the fortress . . . , led in due course to the solution of the problem of capturing the fortress. If we look at these facts, then naturally the question arises: in what sense should we judge the first method adopted by the Japanese general against Port Arthur as a mistake? And if it was a mistake, then under what conditions had the Japanese army, in order to solve its problems, to speak of it and be conscious of it?[12].

On the face of it, he went on, the evident and bloody failure of the initial attacks meant they were a mistake. Yet, given the information available to General Nogi, he could not know the best way to proceed; there were great advantages to be gained from a speedy capture of the fortress, and he was therefore right to try. The "mistake" was therefore "necessary and valuable," and without it the Japanese army would not have gained the experience which led to victory, though at a very much later date.[13]

This was Lenin's parallel with the assault on bourgeois commercial relations launched unsuccessfully in 1918-20. (In the discussion that followed, one man suggested that *they*, Bolsheviks, were besieged in Port Arthur!) This was Lenin's way of reconciling the propositions that they had committed many errors, had all (he did not ever exclude himself) suffered from illusions, about what was possible, yet in the given revolutionary-military emergency they were, so to speak, constructive or necessary mistakes. As General Nogi did after his futile early assaults, one must retire, dig in and plan a more systematic offensive, to be launched much more cautiously and thoroughly prepared.

Retreat how far? Lenin devoted much eloquence to this topic, since morale of retreating troops is apt to break, and at the date he was speaking (October 1921) the retreat was continuing. But more of that later on.

The Transition to N.E.P.

It is not part of the present chapter to trace the evolution of Lenin's actual policies in 1918-21. It is, however, important to note his obstinate commitment to the essential features of war-communism. He knew of course, and frequently said, that the peasants were against *prodrazverstka*. He knew all too well the strength of the will to trade, the vast black market, the *meshochniki*. Yet, along with the vast majority of his colleagues, he was committed to a fight against these things as manifestations of "petty-bourgeois *stikhiye*." While his own statements were not among the more extreme, at least he did not object when others announced the imminent abolition of money, the substitution of rations in kind for wages, the provision of various services (tramcars, housing, etc.) free of charge, as part of the construction of communism today. Of course, the economy was ruined, industry was either producing for war or at a standstill, half of the urban population had fled the hungry and cold cities. While the war continued, his attitude would perhaps be accounted for by the need to concentrate all resources for the fighting forces and the (widespread) association of wartime free trade with illegitimate black-marketeering. Voices were raised early in 1920 in favor of abandoning *prodrazverstka*, allowing some freedom of private trade. Trotsky saw arguments in favor of this course, which was, as is known, urged by the surviving Mensheviks too. But Lenin said, in April 1920: "peasants must give their surplus grain to the workers, because under present-day conditions the sale of these surpluses would be a crime."[14] Why a crime? In many speeches at this period, both Lenin and his party comrades repeatedly showed themselves to be emotionally committed to the bitter and cruel struggle against the very concept of freedom of trade. Food was desperately short, industrial consumers' goods equally so, fuel and raw materials seldom available, and transport was so disorganized that they in any case could seldom be moved. Any goods which could be sold would command (did, in the black market, command) very high barter-prices. The regime depended on what was left as a ration. It seemed to Lenin that, even with the civil war won, those other enemies *golod, kholod* and *razrukha* (hunger, cold and ruin) were to be fought by the same method of coercion and control. The restoration of industry required food, yet peasant producers were unwilling to provide food without payment in industrial goods. Thus the peasants must be persuaded, and if not persuaded then compelled, to give food to the state, the workers, the army on credit. "We admit," said Lenin, "that we are despots to the peasants." The task of breaking out of the vicious circle must be "by military methods, with absolute ruthlessness and by absolute suppression of all other interests." However, "when we restore our industry we will make every effort to satisfy the peasants' needs for urban manufactures."[15] But it is quite clear that in 1920 he was not yet thinking of N.E.P. Indeed, the most extreme economic decrees of the war-communism period were adopted in November-December 1920, after the end of hostilities with Poland, presumably with Lenin's approval. The two decrees were: the nationalization of small-scale industry (most of which had been nationalized already) and the so-called *Posevkomy*, or committees, which were to make peasants sow and harvest as ordered. As late as December 27, 1920 he could still insist on the harshest *prod-*

razverstka measures.[16] He may still, during this year, have harbored illusions about weaning the peasants from their traditional attitudes, persuading them to see virtues in the collective approach. In his more sober moments he must have known that this was a matter for the future, as when he imagined that an abundance of tractors would convince the peasants of the virtues of communism. Yet in his famous interview with H.G. Wells, Lenin left the following impression upon Wells:

'Even now' said Lenin, 'not all the agricultural production of Russia is peasant production. We have in places large-scale agriculture. The government is already running big estates with workers instead of peasants where conditions are favorable. That can spread, it can be extended first to one province, then another. The peasants of the other provinces, selfish and illiterate, will not know what is happening until their turn comes!' It may be difficult to defeat the Russian peasant en masse; but in detail there is no difficulty at all. At the mention of peasant, Lenin's head came nearer mine; his manner became confidential. As if after all the peasant *might* overhear.[17]

In relation to the peasants, or the abolition of money, or repressing free trade, or in harboring illusions about leaps into communism, it is therefore clear that Lenin stuck obstinately to the extreme views held by the vast majority of his party comrades right through 1920. When could he be said to have begun to change his mind? My own view is that the first signs of a new approach could be dimly discerned on December 27, 1920, for on the very day he was insisting on maintaining *prodrazverstka* he also proposed encouraging peasants to produce more by issuing bonuses in kind to those who did so. "We have twenty million separate households, which are individually run and cannot be run otherwise. Not to reward them for increasing productivity would be basically wrong," he exclaimed.[18] Yet he failed to convince his comrades, who wanted to make the bonuses available only to peasant associations. While of course Lenin had not yet reached the stage of advocating N.E.P., he at least showed himself more willing than a majority of his friends to provide peasants with incentives. By then he could be in no possible doubt that *prodrazverstka* itself was, literally, counterproductive.

It is widely believed that it was the Kronstadt rising which was decisive. This is not really so, since the proposal to abolish *prodrazverstka* was put forward before Kronstadt. However, it is certainly true that peasant resistance and risings of so-called "Kulaks" were leading to a situation so catastrophic that the survival of the regime came ever more clearly to depend on the relaxation of the rigors of war-communism. Members of the party leadership began to sense the inevitable. According to the notes of the fifth edition of Lenin's works, Obolensky presented a report to the central committee on February 8, 1921, and in the discussion the view was expressed that *prodrazverstka* be ended and replaced by a tax. Lenin, according to the same source, made a "preliminary draft" of a resolution on these lines for the use of a special commission which was set up on that day to look into this question.[19] Open discussion of this question began in *Pravda* on February 17, the plenum of the central committee agreed to "replace *prodrazverstka* by tax in kind" (*prodnalog*) on February 24. The Kronstadt rising broke out on February 28, before the Party congress had met to adopt the new policy.

Lenin admitted freely that he did not expect the retreat to be as far-reaching as it in fact became. Typical of his views at the time was a short amendment to the draft resolution, which he wrote on March 3, which included a sentence about ensuring that "products-exchange should not degenerate into speculation."[20] Later he explained what had been intended.

A whole number of decrees ... all propaganda and legal enactments in the spring of 1921 were related to the growth of products-exchange. In what did this concept consist? ... It was assumed that, in a more or less socialist manner, we would exchange (barter) on a nation-wide scale the products of state industry for the products of agriculture, and through this products-exchange restore large-scale industry.... What happened? What happened was, as you all know ... product-exchange collapsed: it collapsed in the sense that it became purchase-and-sale.... The retreat had to continue ... product-exchange was a failure, the private market proved stronger than us, and we had instead ordinary purchase and sale, trade.[21]

Therefore the measure which passed effortlessly through the Tenth Congress of the Party in March 1921 was very rapidly followed by a rather different policy, mostly spontaneously, though it was "legalized" by later decrees. Private trade, small-scale manufacture, foreign concessions, even projects for mixed companies with the participation of Russian private capital, the abandonment of free distribution, the turning of state trusts into commercial enterprises—all this followed. To quote Lenin again, "We are now (October, 1921) in such a situation that we must retreat further yet, not only towards state capitalism but to state regulation of trade and monetary circulation." Having gradually, under force of circumstances, appreciated the overwhelming necessity of accepting this policy, Lenin quickly became its most eloquent propagandist. He showed very little patience with those who had ideological doubts or quoted the Founding Fathers or party resolutions against him. Preobrazhensky, for example, suggested that state capitalism was a form of capitalism: no, thundered Lenin, rubbish, scholasticism, there is no precedent in Marxist literature for a proletarian state to use (*inter alia*) capitalist and bourgeois elements to build up productive forces. He also criticizes Bukharin on the same issue: state capitalism is "a capitalism which we are able to limit, the boundaries of which we are able to limit, the boundaries of which we are able to determine."[22]

He spoke on this whole subject with passion and eloquence to the Eleventh Party Congress (March 1922), when he was able to assert that "the retreat was over." By this he meant that no further institutional-legal charges favoring the capitalists and Nepmen would be made. In this speech we see the clearest evidence of how he then saw N.E.P.

Lenin and N.E.P.: Political Tactics and Aims

Undoubtedly Lenin was actuated by a sense of political self-preservation. "If we had not begun to build (N.E.P.) we would have been totally defeated." Economic relaxation *had* to come in the spring of 1921 (if not earlier), otherwise he and his comrades would have been swept away. Lenin freely admitted this. Politically, his aim was to cling to power, so as to be able to resume the advance towards communism (just how, and when, is a complex question, to which we will return). In this connection, it is worth citing his notes: "1794 versus 1921," he wrote, twice.[23] Robespierre had been swept away by the French bourgeoisie. He, Lenin, would avoid his fate by bowing to the most urgent economic demands of the peasants.

For the party this represented a retreat, albeit a necessary one. Retreats are painful. They need particularly severe discipline, or panic can set in. Hence, he insisted on the need to repress party factions such as the "workers' opposition." (It was obviously no accident that the Tenth Congress which adopted N.E.P. also banned factions.) At the Eleventh Congress Lenin also expressed quite ruthless thoughts about other parties. "When a Menshevik says 'you are now retreating, I was always for retreat, I agree with you, I am with you, let us retreat together,' then we say in reply: 'for public manifestations of menshevism our revolutionary courts will shoot you. . . .' "[24] And again: "(if they say) the revolution went too far; we always said what you now say; permit us yet again to repeat it.' To this we reply: 'Permit us to stand you up against the wall.' "[25]

Therefore the maximum political control and *political* police repression was to be accompanied by economic flexibility and free trade. The bourgeoisie was being allowed to spread its wings, up to a point.

Not that Lenin was playing down the element of class struggle. On the contrary, within N.E.P. he saw "a desperate life-and-death struggle between capitalism and communism."[26] But the forms of this struggle were to be primarily economic, within the general *political* limitations upon capitalism, made possible by the party monopoly of power. "We all know," he said, "how in 1918 we got the bourgeoisie to work for us." Now "we do it by other means."[27] The idea was that they should do so voluntarily, while acting in pursuit of their own interests. It would be a form of "building communism with non-communist hands." But no more retreat. We know, in principle, how to work with the capitalists and the bourgeoisie. Of course, he insisted over and over again, Communists are much better at making speeches and passing resolutions than at being business-like. "Learn to trade." Right now, he insisted, there is endless talk of the necessity of *Smychka*, of the link-alliance with the peasantry, but can the Communists satisfy peasant needs? The capitalist-Nepman may be a profiteer, but the peasants can see he delivers the goods. "As for you, your principles are communistic, your ideals are excellent, you look like saints capable of instant transfer to Paradise, but can you run a business?"[28] Again, "we must prove that the ruined, hungry small peasant can receive effective help from the communists. Either we will prove this, or he will send us to all the devils." He may be prepared to wait and see. But before long the peasant might say: "if you cannot run the economy, get out!"[29]

In what form, then, can an advance be planned? Whether he was using the "Port Arthur" parallel or referring to the ending of the retreat, Lenin naturally thought of ultimate victory, of a resumption of the advance. Many later arguments centered upon what kind of timetable, what kind of advance, was intended. N.E.P., he insisted, was intended "seriously and for a long time." This means *competition*.

It is necessary to prove in practice that you work no worse than the capitalists, [he told the Eleventh Congress]. The capitalists forge a link (*smychka*) commercially with the peasants so as to get rich. You must forge a link with the peasant economy to strengthen the economic power of our proletarian state. You have the advantage over the capitalists because power is in your hands, only you cannot utilize them properly. See things more soberly, throw off solemn communist robes, simply learn simple business, and then we will defeat the private capitalists.

If we defeat the capitalists and establish the *smychka* with the peasantry, then this will give us invincible strength. Then the building of socialism will not be the job of that drop in the ocean, the Communist party, but of all the toiling mass. Then the ordinary peasant will say that they help me, then he will follow us, and then what if our steps will be a hundred times slower, they will be a million times more solid and strong.[30]

Lenin appeared to be saying that victory will come from *within* N.E.P. and through N.E.P. as and when the needs of the predominantly peasant society will be met out of the socialist sector of the economy. Therefore to learn to trade, to produce efficiently, was the form in which the class struggle was taking place. The Nepmen will retreat under the impact of competition, under rules and limits made by the "proletarian" (i.e., Communist-controlled) state.

Lenin was concerned with the political danger to the Party and within the Party represented by such a course. He cited Ustryalov and the *smenovekhovtsy*. Is the Party's policy over N.E.P. a tactic, or is it evidence of the Party's evolution or degeneration? The Party might sink into a "bourgeois morass, waving little red flags the while." Lenin admitted that the danger of such a development was real and had to be guarded against. He never grappled, however, with the problem of how to guard against it in the long run. He spoke again of the Party's determination to keep put, of the need to be efficient and businesslike, not to be led by the nose by bourgeois specialists and traders.[a] But what if the spirit which he feared penetrated into the party? For just such an accusation would later be made regarding the Bukharin-Rykov line. What would Lenin have said? But more of this in a moment.

Lenin's View of the Peasants During N.E.P.

The key to everything was the relation of the Party and the socialized sector to the peasantry. Lenin saw this clearly, and from the spring of 1921 we hear no more about any rapid move of the peasants towards socialist forms and attitudes. Of course he saw the peasants in a differentiated way. Some are *kulaks*, some poor, most of them are in-between. But in 1922, in the aftermath of a terrible famine, he emphasized "the overwhelming importance of the recovery of agriculture and of an increase in its output." Therefore "at the present time in relation to the Kulaks and the better-off peasants the policy of the proletariat should be directed particularly to the limitation of their exploiting tendencies."[31] (The kulaks and the potential danger they represented were seldom mentioned by Lenin after N.E.P. began.) In the same notes Lenin criticized Preobrazhensky for referring to "directives in the form of decrees" in relation to peasants, though he did also write that the crude "committees-of-the-poor" (*Kombedorskie*) methods might have to be reviewed if there was another war.

Addressing the Fourth Congress of the Comintern in November 1922, Lenin could claim with some pride that "the peasants are pleased with their present situation," unlike their feelings in February 1921, when, as Lenin also admitted, "huge masses of the peasants" were against the regime.[32] He deplored the still very poor condition of heavy industry and referred to urgent steps which were needed to see it on its feet. But here, as elsewhere, he proceeded on the clear assumption that the needs and wishes of the peasant masses, for trade and for goods, were the basis of Soviet economic policy, of the *smychka*, of the stability of the state.

Being busy, and stricken with ill-health, he had little to say about the future development of the peasants, until the much-misquoted and misunderstood article, "On Cooperation," one of his very last works, written in January 1923, was published in Pravda on May 26 and 27 of that year.

Under N.E.P., he wrote, with private trade legal, cooperation is of great and vital importance. "We overdid things in adopting N.E.P., not because we gave too much room for the principle of free industry and trade, but because we did

---

[a]It is interesting that Bukharin, speaking on February 5, 1923, outlined with prescient clarity a different danger: that ex-workers would turn into a ruling caste (see his *Proletarskaia revoliutsiia i Kul'tura* (Petrograd, 1932), pp. 42-7.

not think of cooperation." Cooperatives should be encouraged, should be given credits on favorable terms. Peasants should benefit from participation in cooperatives (Lenin had in view most of all consumer-cooperatives, since he referred repeatedly to "shops"). The whole population should become so "civilized" that they all participate in cooperatives and learn to count and calculate. That is "all" that is needed to move on to socialism, and Lenin put "all" in inverted commas, because of the low level of culture and mass ignorance. "To achieve through N.E.P. the participation of the whole people in cooperatives will require a whole historical epoch. We might with luck go through this epoch in ten or twenty years." It is necessary to be a "literate trader" (*gramotnym torgashom*). At present most Russians "trade in the Asian manner," but they must learn to trade as Europeans.[33]

Cooperatives then, are a means of ensuring the participation of the people in retail distribution, and so can be seen as a way of limiting private trade. State control over most of industry and state ownership of land would ensure that soviet cooperatives would be unlike those which exist in capitalist countries. Peasants should become increasingly involved in cooperation. But of course, Lenin insisted, this requires a "cultural revolution," a real change in peasant awareness and education; this is "necessary to become a fully socialist country," but it is also "immeasurably difficult."[34]

Years later, these arguments were alleged to be the "Leninist" basis of collectivization. This is plainly nonsense. Lenin was mainly concerned with consumer-cooperation anyhow, and even here, in the context of a long-term cultural revolution, as in some other of his later works, he shows himself acutely conscious of abysmal Russian inefficiency and ignorance, not least among his own comrades. Insofar as peasant producers' cooperation is concerned, he said nothing definite, and seems to have not gone further than some very moderate thinkers. The notes of the fifth edition of his works show him to have asked to read, *inter alia*, Chazanov and Tugan-Baranovsky. The latter, in a work published early in 1918, also spoke of slow and gradual cooperation, extending from joint marketing and purchasing very cautiously to the common ownership of scarce equipment and possibly beyond, one day, later.[35] There is nothing in Lenin's "On Cooperation" which suggests any more drastic solution than this.

His 1922-23 policy was clearly one of gradualism.

Bukharin and Lenin

Is it then right to agree with Bukharin's policy of the middle twenties as being in line with the latter-day Lenin?

A good case can be made for this by comparing Bukharin's declaration of, say, 1925-26 with Lenin's views of 1922-23. In my view this can best be seen by examining his *Put'k sotsializmu i raboche-krestyanski soyuz*.

Bukharin soon dismisses his own ultra-left past. "*Prodrazverstka* and the ban on (private) trade were quite unsuitable for the time when it was necessary to go over to rebuilding productive forces. . . ."[36] Now there is a union of workers and peasants under the leadership of the working class and of its "conscious vanguard." But the peasants are burdened with taxes, and charged high prices for urban goods. There is taking place "a struggle for an economic and business *smychka* with the peasantry. . . . This struggle is waged by our state industry and state trade against private capital, private traders . . . who try to make *their smychka* with the peasantry. . . ." It is essential to show "that the state economy is better able to satisfy the needs of the peasants than the private trader, capitalist or middleman." If these people gain economic influence over the peasants, this would be politically dangerous.[37] Of course, the peasants want higher food prices, the workers want lower food prices. But their unity will hold nonetheless, with the growing size and efficiency of large-scale socialist industry, which will oust the privateer gradually. While agriculture must expand, "we must increasingly achieve a state of affairs in which all industry will be linked together by a single plan . . . However, such a planned industry is unthinkable by itself: our industry produces to a great extent for the *peasant market*" (emphasis his).[38] If the peasant economy is to grow (went on Bukharin) it must become more organized. "It is self-evident that we cannot think that we can, or even should, persuade the peasants suddenly all to unify their land-holdings. Old habits . . . have such deep roots that to break them suddenly is just not possible. Yet none the less . . . the peasants will move in the direction of unification (*obyedineniye*)." How? Through cooperation.[39] Of course, the peasants are not a homogeneous class, there are kulaks, they must be limited, the poorer peasants must be supported. The poorest peasants might find it paid them to form *kolkhozy*, though even for them this would represent a sharp break with old habits of thought. Of course, the kulaks would form cooperatives too, and strive to gain influence over other peasants through the cooperatives. But all of them, including the kulak ones, will operate within an economy dominated by the state, and in some degree would "grow into the system" (*vrastat' v sistemu*), e.g., by having to keep their savings in the State bank. The cooperatives will initially be for marketing and joint purchases, perhaps also credit. They will extend, and thereby further strengthen socialism. Within the village and the cooperatives there will be a species of class war. But no longer will it take the form of "requisitioning the kulak's goods to give to the poor"; rather the middle peasant will become better off, using more productive methods, and will "overtake the kulaks."[40] No more must we have "administrative pressure and repeated confiscations and requisitions," some of which continued even after 1921. Against the village moneylender and petty trader we need not "direct coercion" but credit cooperatives and efficient retail distribution.

Bukharin insisted on the dependence of socialist industry on peasant demand, and therefore on the need to increase effective monetary demand among peasants. "Accumulation in one industry will increase the faster if accumulation in our peasant economy increases fast."[41] If industry overcharges, and so impoverishes the peasants, it will harm itself by becoming "deprived of its market in the villages."[42] He ended by asserting that, far from eliminating market relations, as was once thought, "we will reach socialism through market relations." Large-scale industry, in the hands of the state, will squeeze out the small men "through competition in the market." "N.E.P. is not a betrayal of the proletarian line, it is the only correct proletarian policy."[43]

What can we say in comparing all this with Lenin? Clearly, the two lines have much in common. Bukharin spelt out the "market" logic of Lenin's Eleventh Congress speech. Both saw logic in peasant cooperation, but both could see that it was to be a slow process, given objective difficulties and peasant opinion and habits. But Lenin did pay at least lip-service to the special urgency of restoring and developing heavy industry too. Above all, Lenin was a *Realpolitiker* to his finger tips. He was very well able to persuade his comrades that whatever was needed at the given moment corresponded to eternal verities, or at least was "correct" in some fundamental way. Convinced of the rightness of the logic of N.E.P., he lambasted his verbose and slogan-mongering colleagues, and strove to convince them that N.E.P. and its logic were in the highest interests of the Revolution. But suppose in 1927 he saw that an administrative solution could be made to work? He was not averse to resolving social contradictions by shooting, as his record abundantly shows. I will return to this point in the conclusion.

Lenin and Socialist Economics

A Soviet economist, in private conversation, once said the following: "Lenin did intend to resume the offensive on the bourgeoisie, to drive them out. But he did not want the Stalin type of command economy and expected socialist trusts and enterprises to operate autonomously by reference to a socialist market. He learned from the failure of centralization in 1918-1920." Several Soviet reformers have recently been quoting the Lenin of 1922 in support of their proposals to introduce elements of a market economy in the USSR of today. Are they right?

It is hard to say. Lenin presumably believed in the ultimate establishment of full communism. But he did believe in the relative longevity of N.E.P., and had no patience at all with the grandiose all-inclusive plans. Thus in the middle of 1921 we find him reacting as follows in a letter to Krzhizhanovski: "We are hungry, ruined, beggars. A complete, overall total plan for us now is a bureaucratic utopia."[44] Quite clearly there was no real way of organizing centralized planning in 1922 or 1923, and Lenin was far more concerned to urge the comrades to "learn to trade." He was still for electrification, of course, but he no longer spoke of the GOELRO plan, which so occupied him in 1920. In this same year he approved a measure which abolished all money taxes, but by mid-1921 he was a convinced partisan both of the restoration of taxes and of sound finance. We find him writing repeatedly to and about Sokol'nikov, urging the stabilization of the currency and even "the free circulation of gold." And indeed there was adopted by the government on April 4, 1922, a decree "on the circulation of gold, silver, platinum, precious stones and foreign currency," and not too long after that the new Soviet *chervonets* acquired international respectability and dealings in gold and *valuta* were a common occurrence in Moscow.[45] Only at one point did Lenin remain obstinate: he rejected any easing of the state monopoly of foreign trade.

Yes, Lenin in 1922 was a partisan of the market economy, of efficiency, of competition. But this is not to say that he would have remained so, that his GOELRO enthusiasm had vanished for all time. The situation required the most rapid restoration of the productive forces of Russia, with the help of the bourgeoisie; the market-and-money mechanism was needed to compel the fantastically-inefficient state enterprises to cut out waste and to produce what above all the peasants wanted, since N.E.P. *was* the *smychka*. But Lenin would surely resume his advocacy of the priority of heavy industry (which he theoretically established in the nineties), of electrification and of nation-wide planning, as, and when, this seemed practicable. In what form the economy would function in this new period was still unknown.

Conclusion

As the official Soviet histories assert, N.E.P. was indispensable, necessary, right, though we need not agree with them in accepting that the need for N.E.P. was seen by Lenin at just the right time. He was far better able than his colleagues to see the logic of N.E.P. as well as its necessity. Most Communists were incapable of dealing with practical affairs, they must learn to do business from men of business, they must prove to the peasants their ability to supply their needs. So the proper conclusions must be drawn. Hold on to political power, hold on to the economic "commanding heights," and in due course the socialist offensive will be resumed. At first he was hopeful of a revolution in Germany or some other advanced country coming to the aid of backward Russia. By the end of his days he must have known that this was, for a long time, a vain hope, but also that Soviet Russia had survived its crisis and would continue to exist.

But where would they go from there? In the debate which was to follow Lenin's name was invoked by all sides, and this debate, and the real issues involved, have yet to be seriously, and honestly described, in works published in the Soviet Union. The "Bukharin" argument has already been put. It was indeed in line with many things Lenin said and wrote in 1922. But experience would show that the socialist advance faced many obstacles. Large-scale state industry and state trade grew, sure enough, but the private sector grew also, until administrative measures inconsistent with N.E.P. were taken against it after 1926. If genuine competition proved the viability of the "privateer," would Lenin have had no recourse to police methods to ensure the advance of the state sector? He was fearful enough of the kulaks before 1921. Might he not have hearkened to the warnings of Preobrazhensky about the kulak danger, warnings discounted by Bukharin? What about the scale of accumulation, the urgency of heavy-industrial investment, the problem of agricultural marketings? Trotsky, who had supported N.E.P., was by 1925-26 attacking the Stalin-Bukharin leadership for dilatoriness in launching plans for industrial development. Lenin was removed by his disease from the political arena at a time when he was advocating policies wholly within the context and the bounds of N.E.P. But who knows, who can ever know, whether that other Lenin who advocated and practiced economic-social coercion might not have come back, faced with the problems which faced Stalin at the end of the twenties. I am not arguing that he would have carried out Stalinist policies, only that his writings and attitudes in his last two years of political life cannot be sufficient proof as to what he would in fact have done.

Notes

1. V.I. Lenin, *Sochineniia*, 5th ed. (Moscow, 1955-65), v. 27, pp. 105-7; here and hereafter, unless otherwise stated, my own translation from the Russian edition.

2. Ibid., p. 107.

3. See notably A. Venediktov, *Organizatsiya gosunderstvennoi promyshlennosti v SSSR* (Leningrad, 1967).

4. *An Economic History of the USSR*, pp. 52ff.

5. *Veshnik kommunisticheskoi Akademii*, no. 19 (1924), p. 26. For other similar views, see my *Economic History*, pp. 79-80.

6. V.I. Lenin, *Sochineniia*, v. 44, p. 156.

7. Ibid., p. 157.

8. Ibid., pp. 198-99.

9. *The Defence of Terrorism* (London), pp. 94-95.

10. Lenin, v. 44, p. 203.

11. Ibid.

12. Ibid., pp. 194-97.

13. Ibid.

14. V.I. Lenin, *Collected Works*, 5th ed. (Moscow, 1960-70), p. 121. Hereafter cited as Lenin (English).

15. Lenin, v. 40, p. 329; v. 30 (English), p. 332.

16. Lenin, v. 42, p. 193.

17. H.G. Wells, *Russia in the Shadows* (London, 1921), p. 137.

18. Lenin, *Sochineniia*, v. 42, p. 185.

19. Ibid., v. 43, p. 433 (editorial notes).

20. Ibid., p. 365.

21. Ibid., v. 44, p. 208.

22. Ibid., v. 45, pp. 84-85, 117.

23. Ibid., v. 43, pp. 385-87.

24. Ibid., v. 45, p. 89.

25. Ibid., p. 90.

26. Ibid., p. 95.

27. Ibid., p. 97.

28. Ibid., p. 79.

29. Ibid., pp. 77, 98.

30. Ibid., p. 92.

31. Ibid., pp. 44-45.

32. Ibid., p. 285.

33. Ibid., pp. 371-72.

34. Ibid., pp. 37, 76.

35. See A. Nove, "M.I. Tugan-Baranovsky," in *History of Political Economy* (Durham, N.C., 1970).

36. N. Bukharin, *Put'k sotsializmu i raboche-krestyanski soyuz*, 3rd ed. (Moscow, 1926), p. 11.

37. Ibid., pp. 25-26.

38. Ibid., p. 30.

39. Ibid.

40. Ibid., pp. 46ff.

41. Ibid., p. 41.

42. Ibid., p. 44.

43. Ibid., pp. 64-66.

44. Lenin, *Sochineniia*, v. 52, p. 76.

45. Ibid., v. 54, pp. 90, 139, 606, et passim.

10 Lenin, Peasants, and the Agrarian Reform

Roy D. Laird

If the greatness of a man is measured by his impact on the course of human events and not by a value judgment of the philosophy he furthered, Vladimir Ilyich Ulyanov—Lenin—must be regarded as the greatest figure thus far in the twentieth century. At this writing not even the combined impact of Winston Churchill, Mahatma Ghandi, and Martin Luther King has had an influence upon the course of human affairs equal to Lenin's. Without him there could not have been a Bolshevik Revolution in the fall of 1917. Moreover, there would not be the several Communist states of Europe and Asia, plus Communist Cuba, quarreling over which system is most correctly Leninist. Agrarian revolutions would be staged in the developing nations of Asia, Africa, and Latin America, but they hardly would be characterized as "wars of national liberation" by many Communist and non-Communist observers alike.

As noted elsewhere, Marxism (to be distinguished from socialist political philosophy as such) as a philosophical guide to political revolution should have died at the turn of the century, because the 1848 prophecy of the coming of utopian communism to the developed, proletarianized states of Western Europe was further than ever from reality.[1] Lenin successfully turned his peculiar Marxian lenses to seeking answers for what had gone wrong. Why had the 1905 revolution in Russia not gone further? Why had the (assertedly) growing class-consciousness of the Western European proletariat not produced Marxian revolutions?

Since for a Marxist, actually the Communist "science of society" can never be mistaken, Lenin's answer was that nothing had gone wrong; Marx's analysis remained correct. Revolution in the capitalist industrialized states was still inevitable. Indeed, it was just around the corner, but the last great wave of colonial imperialism at the end of the nineteenth century had given capitalism a temporary respite while bringing it to its highest, terminal stage. The 1905 revolution in Russia had stalled because doctrinaire socialists had not perceived the key role that must be played by the peasants in the unfolding revolution.

A present day Soviet academician stresses that Leninism is "a continuation of Marxism as an international doctrine."[2] Although this observation is correct, it neglects the essential changes Lenin imposed upon Marxism making it a meaningful international doctrine. As others have stressed, two essential contributions made by Lenin were: (1) the key role he assigned the Party in carrying forth

173

class-consciousness and in leading the revolution, and (2) the changed nature of the revolution, which he saw to be a result of imperialism's impact upon capitalism's role in world affairs. To these accepted revisions this writer would add a third major contribution. Although Lenin never abandoned the doctrinaire view that the industrial proletariat must lead the revolution (through the media of the Leninist party), the new role he assigned to the peasantry—his recognition that the peasant was essential to success in the Soviet experiment, between 1917 and his death in 1924—transformed the hope of communism from the exploited industrial workers to the rural poor. Lenin died in 1924 still believing that the industrial-based revolution in Western Europe was near at hand. Yet the changes he had made in the Marxist arguments, the success he achieved in 1917, and his arguments for the necessity of the New Economic Policy in 1921 all lead us to conclude that the Maoists have the better of the Leninist argument when they assert that what has evolved is a "war between the countryside and the villages."

Leninism, after all, is not just Marxian analysis; it is both a political philosophy and a highly flexible guide to action. As Krupskaya stressed, "to apply Marxist method to the analysis of new concrete situations . . . is the special substance of Leninism."[3] In sum, therefore, this writer's view is that Lenin's impact on the twentieth century stems from his recognition that a highly disciplined party was needed to carry forth the revolution in a world dominated by imperialistic actions wherein an increasingly dissatisfied peasantry in the developing nations (largely colonies or former colonies) would repeatedly mount agrarian revolutions. These revolutions, would in the end, rival the Industrial Revolution of the nineteenth century in changing the nature of man's world. Whereas Marx had perceived the enormous changes the Industrial Revolution was having on urban life in the industrial states, Lenin must be credited with seeing that the center of initiative in human affairs was shifting to that majority of mankind that resides in rural areas, extracting its livelihood from the soil. Semifeudal tsarist Russia fitted the pattern of Lenin's unfolding interpretations of the 1905 uprising.

From Emancipation (1861) to Revolution (1905)

Lenin's materialistic orientation magnified his conclusion (basically correct) that the peasants' political emancipation in 1861 had been of relatively little benefit to the former serfs. Saddled with impossible redemption payments for the pitifully small parcels of land they cultivated, the great mass of Russia's peasants were engulfed, without hope, in a poverty that was punctuated by periodic famine.

Prior to 1905, Lenin was not blind to the import of the peasants, but he saw them doomed as a class, in a process of change whereby "enormous numbers" were destined to be transformed into proletarians.[4] This change he thought he saw elsewhere, especially in Germany.[5] He later admitted that because of the narrow Marxian view that a socialist revolution would have to depend upon a class conscious proletariat, he had, in effect subscribed to the 1904 program of the Social-Democrats. In spite of the peasant emancipation of 1861 Russia remained semifeudal, and it was not until the lessons of 1905 were digested that Lenin recognized the importance of the mounting agrarian revolution to advancing Marxism in Russia.

Social Democrats were concerned with furthering the bourgeois revolution in Russia, transforming Russia out of its semifeudal state into full capitalism, since this was an essential first step in the evolution to communism. Lenin wrote that, "revolution in agriculture is inevitable," in 1901,[6] but the rural revolution he was predicting at that time was only technical and not political. As we shall subsequently stress, here is one realm in which he remained doctrinarily consistent, indeed dogmatic, since he believed that the Industrial Revolution was transforming the production forces in the countryside, just as thoroughly as it had transformed those in the cities. Indeed, he wrote that there is "nothing to prevent the abolition of the antitheses between town and country."[7] Until that happy day, however, production relationships in the countryside were such that bourgeois and petty bourgeois attitudes were inevitable in the minds of all but the poorest segment of rural society. Therefore, although he described the latter peasants as "semi-proletarian" as early as 1901,[8] his view of rural Russia was of a countryside destined for drastic change, including a mass disposition of peasants to the ranks of the urban proletariat.[9]

The New Workers' and Peasant Revolution

The most important change in Lenin's thoughts about the future course in Russia, after the lessons of 1905, lay in his recognition that a genuine agrarian revolution was mounting, one that paralleled the Marxian urban revolution to a degree that would allow Marxian socialists to take over the direction of affairs, even though predominantly peasant-agricultural Russia did not fit the Marxian conditions for rule. As early as 1901, he had asked the question whether a Russian revolution could succeed without "class struggle and political consciousness in the countryside," and his answer had been no.[10] Yet, his early vision centered upon a proletarianization of the peasantry. Now, although he still saw that process continuing, he focused on the essential role of a peasant-based agrarian revolution, a revolution that would serve the Marxian goals if it were properly harnessed and led by the proletariat. Here then lay the roots of his attitude towards the Stolypin reforms versus the mounting cry for nationalization of the land.

If 1905 had not impressed Lenin with the depth and scope of the peasant revolt, his tactic might well have been to support the Stolypin reforms. As it was, he asserted that the Stolypins were a "progressive landlord's program that advanced the capitalistic revolution."[11] Nevertheless, the advance of the agrarian revolt dictated that the Social Democrats must reject the reforms, because other forces were at work to transform the attitudes of the peasant masses at a much more rapid pace.[12] Stolypin's program would further the development of a reactionary rural bourgeoisie, whereas the mounting cry for nationalization of the land would accelerate the evolution of semiproletarian attitudes among the poorest peasants, in a cause with which the middle peasants would sympathize, and therefore, the majority of the population in the countryside could be counted upon to support a revolution in Russia.

Interestingly, from a doctrinal point of view, Lenin repeatedly stressed that the Marxists' alignment with the demand for nationalization of the land was not a direct move towards rural socialism. Socialism "means the abolition of commodity economy" whereas under the conditions prevailing in Tsarist Russia in 1903, land nationalization would be a capitalistic move.[13] Nationalization would allow the poorest peasants to join the small peasants in the cultivation of the land in a way that would free the largest amount of their capital for production development.[14] True, consenting to the peasants' call for nationalization probably would result in their later asking for "division." If socialist guidance could not see to carrying the revolution far enough, a later cry for restoration of the old system of land ownership could be expected.[15] However, Lenin believed that these risks had to be taken for at least two prime reasons. In the first place, nationalization was much more progressive than the Stolypin attack on the *mir*, and in the second, since nationalization was wanted by the peasant masses, the Social Democrats must support the demand in order to cement further the rural and urban revolutions.

The Needs of Production

Because Lenin believed nationalization would promote rural capitalism in Russia, he did not fail to cite evidence which he believed proved that production would be advanced. Assertedly, higher crop yields would result, because statistics revealed that such was the case where farming was carried out under capitalist relationships.[16] Lenin did read some of the more technical literature of the time, but here more than elsewhere one is left with the impression that his eye was looking only for material which supported the convictions he already held. Indeed, in the technical realm he seemed to be even more doctrinaire in his convictions than Marx. For example, if he ever shared Marx's passing question that the *mir* might embody a primitive rural socialism that could play a positive role in the transition to communism in Russia, this writer has not found the evidence. Certainly, by 1908, he was thoroughly convinced that the village commune must be destroyed, for it embodied "a medieval barrier dividing the peas-

177

ants."[17] Elsewhere, he argued that cooperatives enhanced production, but he saw them as a strictly capitalist institution, favoring the more well-to-do peasants.[18]

Lenin believed that the Industrial Revolution had provided agriculture with the base for changes in production methods, relationships and efficiency equal to the fundamental changes which had occurred in urban industry. True, he agreed with Kautsky that production efficiency in agriculture has special laws different from those of efficiency in industry.[19] Yet, from as early as 1900, he unqualifiedly equated the use of machines in farming with intensive cultivation.[20] Lenin argued that the necessary depopulation of the land would be accompanied by the fewer workers remaining in agriculture producing even more total output. Similarly, specialization in agriculture was presented as an unquestioned advance.[21] While he recognized there was nowhere in the world that all of these changes had occurred as yet, still he argued the "revolution in agriculture is inevitable,"[22] a fundamental change that surely would lead to the "abolition of the antithesis between town and country."[23]

Perhaps Lenin should be credited with great foresight in seeing as early as 1900 the future role of electricity as a source of production power.[24] However, Lenin's romance with electricity might have been at least equally furthered by his seeing positive and negative electricity as scientific verification of the universal application of the dialectic.[25] Since Lenin's day electricity has become very important in agriculture, but his view of its future really fitted more into his prophecy of political revolution than it did into a vision of production advances. He equated electricity with large scale production, which he saw as the essential base for agriculture industrialization, a change that had to come as part of the advance of Marxian Socialism.[26]

Collectivization, 1917-1924

Lenin was able both to persuade those colleagues who followed him into Bolshevism that the proletarian and peasant revolutions should be joined and to convince enough of the peasant leaders that Bolshevism was at least the lesser of evils (in terms of possible alternative governments), so that he and his followers could stage a successful urban coup in the fall of 1917, in tandem with the peasant rural revolt that had begun earlier in the year. Indeed, as we have stressed elsewhere, 1917 was the year of three revolutions in Russia: (1) the end of tsardom, (2) the peasants' successful taking of the land, and (3) the Bolshevik coup in the cities—which really marked only the beginning of that revolution.[27]

As promised, one of the initial acts of the new regime was to nationalize the land. More importantly, in practice, the peasants' take over of the land was not opposed. Thus, the continued joining of the two revolutions until 1921 was assured, in spite of the hated forced requisitions, because the peasants remained convinced that the reds were more apt to respect their land claims than would any possible white alternative.

The red victory over the whites, however, resulted in an even greater distortion of the economy than had occurred during World War I, and the revolt of the sailors of peasant origin at Kronstadt signaled to Lenin the imperative of the N.E.P. concessions to the peasantry. Not only had the joining of the two revolutions come to an end, but Lenin now realized, more than ever after 1905, that the mainstream of the Russian revolution had been peasant. Furthermore, although their representatives did not hold the seats of government, peasant power was the most important economic and political force in the USSR. If the commodity relationships the peasants insisted upon had not been returned to the countryside by the Bolshevik leaders, there was strong reason to believe the peasants would have insisted upon a new leadership that would fulfill such demands. Any significant advance of collectivization, therefore, be it in the form of agricultural *artels* or state farms, was out of the question.

Some 2000 communes and 4000 *artels* were said to exist in 1919. State farms had been created on former crown lands.[28] Yet, in spite of encouragement by the new government, less than one percent of the land and only three to four percent of the peasant families had gone into collective and government farms by 1927.[29]

Still Lenin believed that large-scale farming was essential to agricultural industrialization and that socialization was the only way to destroy small-scale farming.[30] In his earlier writings, Lenin had not been so dogmatic in asserting that large farms were superior to small ones; in 1900 he had argued merely that when all else is equal, large size is superior.[31] However, in 1902, he wrote that German studies purportedly demonstrating the superiority of small farms were fundamentally wrong, because they disguised the waste and underconsumption of the small peasant farmers.[32] Again, in 1908, he maintained that in spite of the asserted diligence practiced by the small private farmers, they could not match the advantages of large-scale farming, because "small-scale production implies dispersion of the technical means of farming and a squandering of labor as a result of dispersion."[33]

Lenin's view of the inevitable superiority of large farms was furthered by his commitment to the "gigantomania" of his tsarist predecessors. Thus he saw Russia as possessing a "gigantic amount of land . . . for colonization," vast areas for agricultural expansion both in "breadth and depth."[34] Collectivization was the key, and by 1918 he had convinced himself that such a transformation would result in at least a double or triple labor saving.[35]

After 1917, two major themes dominated Lenin's thinking about the future course of the countryside. First of all, he believed that collectivization was needed to bring socialism to the peasantry, and that the superior large-scale farms would solve once and for all the problems of production. Secondly, the lessons of war communism and the N.E.P. deeply convinced him that collectivization could be achieved only voluntarily and gradually. Some of the more zealous comrades argued that the peasants could and should be forced into the superior forms of production, and his answer was that such action would be stupid.[36]

Had Lenin lived beyond 1924, he might well have changed his mind and followed the Stalinist path of a forced "revolution from above." Yet such a reversal would have been of momentous proportions. Indeed, in 1919 he said, "we know we cannot establish a new socialist order now—God grant that it can be established in our country in our children's time, or perhaps in our grandchildren's time."[37] The communes and *artels* that had been established provided "a genuine nursery for communist ideas and views among the peasants,"[38] but decades at the least would be required to educate the peasantry to the advantages of the new life.

Agrarian Revolution

In spite of his having written that agriculture has special production needs, Lenin exhibited the myopia of "industrial fundamentalism"[39] that characterizes far too many urban oriented political leaders of the twentieth century. If he ever believed that the needs of agriculture are really different from those of industry, he not only neglected to continue his homework, but he forgot the first lesson and turned to preaching that machines, electricity, and scientifically trained agronomists would transform rural production. For him this became an "indisputable theoretical truth."[40] Therefore, Lenin's vision of the Russian, and the world's, countryside came to comprise a two stage revolution. First of all, he saw irresistible peasant demands carrying the Marxian revolution in backward underdeveloped countries. Secondly, after the reactionary, semifeudal systems were broken, industrialization would transform the peasant revolutionaries into a new social consciousness, and machines would provide man with an abundance of food. The second aspect of his agrarian doctrine is highly questionable. Indeed, evidence recently published by this author supports the conclusion that an industrial revolution in the world's countryside is largely a myth.[41] The first part of his revolutionary vision, however, seems to have carried profound truth.

Nowhere in Lenin's writings, as such, can one concretely document the view that he had shifted the Marxist doctrine from a worker-led revolution to a peasant-dominated revolt. To the contrary, he repeatedly emphasized the dominant role of the proletariat as the "ruling class" who must "lead the peasantry" to socialism.[42] Yet, in 1907, he was arguing that peasants' desire for the land was the key to future change in Russia.[43] Lenin's actions, in creating policies between 1917 and 1924 in response to peasant demands, speak louder than his doctrinaire formulations. More than this, subsequent revolutions in the name of Marxism-Leninism have been in predominantly peasant-agricultural settings. Further, "wars of national liberation," which look to the Leninist model, threaten in Asia, Africa, and Latin America. Therefore, while the Marxism born of the nineteenth century industrial revolution is dead, the Leninism born of the twentieth century agrarian revolution is very much alive.

Notes

1. Roy D. Laird, "The New Soviet Myth: Marx is Dead, Long Live Communism!" *Soviet Studies*, v. 18 (April, 1967), pp. 511-18.

2. P.N. Fedoseyev, "Great Threshold in the History of Mankind," *Izvestia*, April 3, 1967, p. 2.

3. N.K. Krupskaya, *Memories of Lenin*, trans. E. Varyney (New York, 1930), v. 1, p. 189.

4. V.I. Lenin, "The Workers' Party and the Peasantry," *Collected Works* (Moscow, 1963), v. 4, p. 422.

5. Ibid., "Capitalism in Agriculture," p. 138.

6. Ibid., "The Agrarian Question and the 'Critics of Marx,' " v. 5, p. 144.

7. Ibid., p. 154.

8. Ibid., p. 188.

9. Ibid., "Agrarian Question in Russia," v. 15, pp. 118ff.

10. Ibid., "The Workers Party and the Peasantry," v. 4, p. 427.

11. Ibid., "The Agrarian Program of Social-Democracy in the First Russian Revolution 1905-1907," v. 13, p. 243.

12. Ibid.

13. Ibid., "Agrarian Question in Russia," v. 15, p. 138.

14. Ibid., "The Agrarian Program of Social-Democracy in the First Russian Revolution 1905-1907," v. 13, p. 314.

15. Ibid., pp. 323ff.

16. Ibid., "Agrarian Question in Russia," v. 15, p. 144.

17. Ibid., p. 78.

18. Ibid., "The Agrarian Question and the 'Critics of Marx,' " v. 13, p. 178.

19. Ibid., "Capitalism in Agriculture," v. 4, p. 112.

20. Ibid., pp. 143ff.

21. Ibid., "The Agrarian Question and the 'Critics of Marx,' " v. 5, p. 158.

22. Ibid., p. 144.

23. Ibid.

24. Ibid., "Capitalism in Agriculture," v. 4, p. 114.

25. Ibid., "On the Question of Dialectics," v. 38, p. 359.

26. Ibid., "Third Congress of the Communist International: Thesis for a Report on the Tactics of the R.C.P.," v. 32, p. 459.

27. Roy D. and Betty A. Laird, *Soviet Communism and Agrarian Revolution* (Harmonsworth, England, 1970), p. 33.

28. Lenin, "Speech Delivered at the First Congress of Agricultural Communes and Agricultural Artels," v. 30, p. 175.

29. *The Kolkhozes in the Second Five-Year Plan*, Central Statistical Office (Moscow, 1939), p. 1, cited in Gregory Bienstock, Solomon M. Schwartz, and Aaron Yugov, *Management in Russian Industry and Agriculture* (New York and London, 1944), p. 130.

30. Ibid., "Speech at a Meeting of Delegates from Poor Peasant's Committees of Central Guberniias," v. 28, p. 175.

31. Ibid., "Capitalism in Agriculture," v. 4, p. 119.

32. Ibid., "The Agrarian Question and the 'Critics of Marx,' " v. 4, p. 119.

33. Ibid., "The Agrarian Question and the 'Critics of Marx,' " v. 22, pp. 181ff.

34. Ibid., "The Agrarian Program of Social Democracy in the First Russian Revolution 1905-1907," v. 13, pp. 245 and 423.

35. Ibid., "Speech to the First All-Russian Congress of Land Departments, Poor Peasant's Committees and Communes," v. 28, p. 343.

36. Ibid., "Speech Delivered at the First Congress of Agricultural Communes and Agricultural Artels," p. 198.

37. Ibid., p. 202.

38. Ibid., p. 204.

39. See T.W. Schultz, *Transforming Traditional Agriculture* (New Haven and London, 1964), p. 133, and Laird and Laird, p. 144.

40. Lenin, "Preliminary Draft Thesis on the Agrarian Question for the Second Congress of the Communist International," v. 31, pp. 161-62.

41. Laird and Laird, pp. 22-27.

42. Lenin, "Third Congress of the Communist International: Thesis for a Report on the Tactics of the R.C.P.," v. 32, p. 455.

43. Ibid., "The Agrarian Program of Social-Democracy in the First Russian Revolution 1905-1907," v. 13, pp. 239ff.

Lenin and Russian Economic Thought: The Problem of Central Planning

GREGORY GUROFF

The primary purpose of this chapter is to discuss Lenin's relationship to the development of Russian economic thought, especially as it concerns the problem of the industrialization of the country. A secondary purpose is to discuss Lenin's relationship to the origins of central economic planning in Russia. Planning should be understood in this context as a mechanism for organizing the economy, not in terms of substantive policy priorities, such as the Five Year Plans under Stalin.

The chapter itself is divided into three general sections. First, the development or perhaps more appropriately the lack of development of Lenin's economic thought up to the Revolutions of 1917. Next, some observations about the development of the Russian economy and Russian economic thought of the prerevolutionary period related to the problem of industrialization and planning. Finally, the postrevolutionary period during which the Bolsheviks moved slowly toward the articulation of basic policies. The nature of continuity in Russian economic thought and policy is important in understanding the origins of Soviet economic policy and thought, and thus crucial to an understanding of Lenin's contribution to this process. The problem is created by the fact that the development of Russian economic thought, especially in the period after the reign of Sergei Witte and the fundamental changes which occurred in economic institutions and the economy itself have been blithely ignored in our insatiable desire to write victors' history and examine in excruciating detail the machinations of the revolutionary parties.

The thrust of this chapter is that the development of Soviet economic policies, and more particularly the origins of central planning, are more clearly understandable as outgrowths and adaptations of Russian economic thought and Russian experience with the verities of the Russian economy, than as a product of Marxist-Leninist ideology or an imitation of foreign models, such as the German wartime economy. This is not to suggest that ideology and imitation have not played some role, but that they are clearly subordinate in their importance to the continuities which persisted.

The Development of Lenin's Economic Thought

Lenin was first and foremost a political creature and as such had little time for comment or analysis of specifically economic problems, thus, he had little to do

with the development of Russian economic thought in the prerevolutionary period. Furthermore, Lenin did not set forth his own economic views or any observations about the future organization of a socialist economy. He did, however,
reveal during this time a number of intellectual predispositions concerning the
Russian economy and its organization, which later marked him as leader of the
Soviet state. These predispositions can be gleaned from his writings which are
primarily concerned with political questions.

Lenin's public writings in many ways mirror the complex picture of the strivings and aspirations, the feuding and recriminations which marked the socialist
left. After the Revolution of 1905 failed to fulfill the hopes of the Social Democrats the Party was faced with a plethora of factional splits, ideological debates
and personality conflicts. Lenin engaged either actively or through comment in
all of these disputes. He entered these frays, if not with gusto, at least with un-
rivaled tenacity.[1]

The beginnings of economic resurgence in Russia in 1909, marked as it was
by the growing awareness and discussion of economic problems, was paralleled
in the Social-Democratic camp by the appearance of Lenin's cannonade against
the "deviations" of the Bogdanov-Lunacharskii group from the principles of
Marxist materialism. Lenin had long refrained from attacks on those within his
own group who had become involved with the philosophical ideas of Mach and
Avenarius. He often said that he would not stoop to debate with these obvious
renegades from Marxism. Nevertheless, with his patience sorely tried and his concern growing that the "god-builders" and their philosophical machinations were
a direct threat to the vitality and unity of the Bolshevik group, he finally wrote a
long, though poorly thought-out, reply and criticism, *Materialism and Empirio-
Criticism.*[2]

The work itself had little to do with economic theory or practice, and failed
to show Lenin at his best as a logician or polemicist. It was, however, indicative
of the type of activity which Lenin pursued throughout most of the prerevolutionary period. It is cited here primarily because it highlights the fact that at a
time when much of Russian society was becoming involved in discussions of economic activity, Lenin was turning more assiduously to political concerns. He was
constantly on the offensive against those who he sensed were either to his left or
right, in order to maintain the unity of the Bolshevik faction (irrespective of
overall unity of the socialist groups), to preserve for the Bolsheviks their chosen
role as the true friend of the workers while stripping this appellation from all
rival groups, and finally to preserve for the Bolsheviks the cloak of apostolic
succession from Marx and Engels. Lenin was thus in almost constant controversy
with all other political groups. The controversies themselves seldom involved
major ideological contentions, but were often petty and rarely had anything to
do with economic theory or practice.

As Alec Nove has pointed out, Lenin knew a great deal of economics and was
very adept at the use of statistical evidence. Nevertheless, after the completion

of his study, *The Development of Capitalism in Russia*, in 1899, he became increasingly involved in political activity and polemics and contributed little to the development of economic theory.[3] In addition, he had a disregard, verging on disdain, for the problems of what has come to be called micro-economics.[4] What, then, was Lenin concerned with in this period and of what relevance is it to a discussion of the development of Russian economic thought?

There are a number of continuous strands running through his works which give some indication of his economic views and predispositions. For instance, he battled unceasingly with the liberal parties, the Kadets and Octobrists, hoping to deny them the appellation "democratic," by arguing that they represented liberal elements within the bourgeoisie and thus could not by definition support democracy. They could, he wrote, support liberalism and constitutionalism, but their class allegiance made them in essence antidemocratic and counterrevolutionary.[5] In addition, Lenin viewed the predominant liberal parties as simply transitory representatives of the bourgeoisie. As the bourgeoisie grew both in economic and in political strength, a new party would emerge. Lenin for some reason saw the kernel of this future bourgeois party in the semilegal quasiparty of the Progressivists, although it seems clear that this group, despite finances and leadership provided by some Moscow industrialists such as Konovalov and P.P. Riabushinskii, was predominantly representative of the *dvorianstvo* [landed nobility].[6]

Lenin reserved his most vitriolic remarks, however, for colleagues within the social-democratic movement. The full-scale, scathing attack which Lenin directed at Bogdanov in 1909 was continued in a series of articles aimed at the whole "Vpered" group and was attended by endless snide and slighting remarks. The real focus of his assault, however, was on those to his right, the so-called "liquidators." Lenin argued they wished to destroy the illegal party apparatus and thus surrender its entire revolutionary program by becoming a parliamentary party. Lenin wrote that this was a complete misunderstanding of the present situation in Russia, that Russia was just entering the bourgeois stage and that the step of "liquidation" was in fact a complete sellout. Lenin first deliberately exaggerated, then viciously attacked, the positions taken by Martov, Dan, and others. He further argued that the "liquidators" were in collusion with bourgeois elements, were receiving aid from them, and represented only small, well-to-do working class elements. Adam Ulam cautions that Lenin's position should also be seen in the light of a tactic designed to secure support from several key elements, primarily Plekhanov, for it was during this period that Lenin felt most isolated.[7]

It is not surprising Lenin published so little on economics considering his continuous and time-consuming involvement in ideological controversies and political squabbles. Then too, he was constantly preoccupied with the procurement of funds for both his movement and himself, spending much of his time to arrange the securing of the Schmidt legacy from the legal heirs and later battling other social-democratic groups for the right to keep this money.[8] He also mapped and executed the plan to make the Bolsheviks a separate party yet making it appear that all the other social-democratic groups had deserted the true party. This effort, of course, culminated in the success of the rump congress in Prague in 1912.

Though Lenin's works for this period contain little that is directly addressed to theoretical or practical economic problems, much emerges indirectly or by implication which is relevant to the future course of action he was to take in the economic realm. For instance, at the base of his dispute with the "liquidators," aside from tactical considerations and personality conflicts, there was a difference in assessment of Russia's present position on the road to economic development. Here the question of Russia's uniqueness becomes crucial.

Lenin had contended in *The Development of Capitalism in Russia*, written in 1899, that although capitalism had been firmly and irrevocably established on Russian soil, it presented some unique aspects in that many forms of the old feudal order remained side by side with the new capitalistic forms.[9] After the Revolution of 1905 he was faced by those who hoped to make the Party more legal and who contended that this was possible because the bourgeois stage had already come. Lenin argued that this was not the case, that Russia had begun the transition from feudalism to capitalism but the end of the road had not yet been reached. He argued that although the bourgeoisie had gained and continued to gain greater economic power, they were still denied access to political power. Here he joined an ever-increasing chorus of the bourgeoisie who attacked the agrarian slant of the Duma, the State Council and the government bureaucracy. Under these conditions, Lenin argued, it was necessary to encourage capitalist advances which were much more rapid than those which had occurred under feudalism. He pointed out, however, that it would be a betrayal of the workers and an act of political suicide to forsake the underground movement and establish an exclusively legal party structure.[10]

The debate degenerated to trivial hairsplitting, but it had serious repercussions. The assessment of Russia's position along the Marxist scale of development was of crucial importance in determining immediate goals and tactics. Without ever doubting the eventuality of revolution, Lenin became quite pessimistic concerning its proximity and rightly so, considering the minute size of a following torn by interminable squabbles and feuds at the very time Russia was beginning to show signs of considerable economic vigor.

It is during this period that many of the ideas, sympathies and predispostions which later marked Lenin as leader of the Soviet state became evident. It is important to look first at Lenin, the man. Although he spent most of his adult life in exile he remained Russian. He never really became an international revolutionary figure, but remained a Russian émigré. Whereas many of his own despised class—the *intelligentsiia*—were as much at home in the salons of Paris and London as in St. Petersburg, Lenin could never assimilate. He was restless and unhappy in the major capitals of Western Europe: London and Paris remained for him "their cities, their buildings." He rarely learned the languages of the countries in which he lived.[11]

Although he would never have admitted it directly, he remained at heart a Russian nationalist—which is not at all in conflict with his vehement attacks on chauvinism. The question of national autonomy consumed much of his attention. He proclaimed sympathy with the oppressed national minorities of the Russian Empire, yet it seems clear that this was a tactical move—a true revolutionary, he argued, could not allow this potent weapon against the autocracy to go unused. Even in attacking the Empire for its oppressive policies Lenin conceded little to the national minorities, instead, he emphasized the importance of democratic centralism to the Party and the country in general. Lenin proclaimed that Marxists must support the existence of large and powerful states, for only they could foster rapid economic progress, and thus the advent of socialism. Those who supported petty states were in fact considered to be ignorant of the laws of history. It is clear in his attacks on the Bund and Mensheviks that national minorities could expect little from Lenin beyond the use of their own languages.[12]

Although he never addressed the problem directly, Lenin's works indicate that he viewed Russia as neither Asiatic nor European, seeing it as a colossus astride both continents with elements of both but possessing a number of unique characteristics. Even Karl Wittfogel admits that in the period after 1905 Lenin rarely discussed Russia's "semi-Asiatic" character.[13] Lenin continually refers to Russia as something apart. Russia in his view was becoming Europeanized but a confused pattern of development set her apart from the course previously experienced by the West. This attitude, perhaps a product of his own nationalism, allowed him the ideological flexibility to avoid an orthodox Marxist assessment of Russia's present and future.[14]

These attitudes as well as others Lenin shared with many Russians, not necessarily only revolutionaries. It is obvious that his ideological presuppositions and goals were not those of the Russian *intelligentsiia* taken as a whole, but many of his attitudes cut across political lines and reveal some striking similarities. His concern for economic development was shared by men such as Witte and a whole range of economists, industrialists, and bankers. His support of the great nation was close to that of many right-wing nationalists. His distrust of the enslaving nature of international capital interests echoed some of the fears of many Russians.[15] In the prewar period, for instance, Lenin devoted a series of articles to the machinations of the so-called international arms trust, claiming as did many Russian liberals that the trust was pushing Europe toward war simply to increase its own profits. In his attacks on the trust Lenin detailed the connections the leaders of arms companies had with both the military and political leaders of Western countries, yet he made virtually no mention of Russian capitalists in these charges. This is not to say that he exonerated Russian businessmen from the guilt of perpetuating the capitalist system.[16] In addition, Lenin shared with a wide spectrum of Russians a fascination with a grudging admiration for the United States. He was particularly drawn by the rapid economic development and the apparent freedom the workers enjoyed to organize and to protest their grievances.[17]

Lenin went beyond most in his fascination with scientific and technological innovations. He viewed the Taylor system as a device to exploit the workers, yet he was aware of its future use in a socialist society.[18] His interest, according to Krzhizhanovskii's testimony, did not wane after the revolution. He was fascinated by the uses of electricity and played with the idea of railroad engines run by perpetual motion machines and the possible uses of X-rays as ultimate weapons.[19]

These attitudes held by Lenin suggest a number of predispositions which would affect his policies in the future both politically and economically. His admiration of large and strong states and impressive undertakings, his latent nationalism and wariness of foreign things were to play a role in his policy decisions. Nevertheless, during this period Lenin had nothing original to contribute concerning economics and, in fact, little interesting comment to make. That he read the major Russian journals connected with economics is confirmed by the innumerable references in his works, but he rarely commented on their economic content.

For instance, in one of his articles, *Anketa*,[20] often cited as indicative of his economic views, it is clear that the greatest part of the article is devoted to political polemics, not to economics. The subject of the discussion is the survey (*anketa*) of producers' organizations, which was carried out by the St. Petersburg Imperial Technical Society. A book by A. Gushka on the survey is the principal target of Lenin's attack. Although he acknowledges the value of Gushka's collection of data, he argues that Gushka has misrepresented the nature of the organization,[21] and asserts that the organizations represent a stratum of the bourgeoisie concerned exclusively with questions of class interest. Gushka, he writes, misunderstands this and assigns these groups too broad a concern for the ills of society. Having disposed of Gushka, Lenin turns his attack on Ermanskii who had written a long review article of Gushka's book. Ermanskii, whom Lenin felt numbered himself among the Marxists, was criticized for not pointing out the difference in class outlook between himself and Gushka.[22] Unfortunately Lenin was not aware that the two men were in fact the same person.[23]

The same strands of political polemics run through all of Lenin's works which purport to deal with economic problems. He constantly alluded to the workers' poor position and this came to be the pivot of his attack on the "liquidators," claiming that the great majority of the poor workers supported the Bolsheviks and only well-to-do workers and the bourgeoisie supported the "liquidators."[24] Lenin was much concerned with the increasing concentration of capital, but rather than evaluate its economic significance, he simply used it to show the progress toward socialism.[25]

Though his works during this period foreshadow support of a strong state and reveal a continuing struggle to overturn the capitalistic one,[26] there is little to suggest the direction of future economic policies, with the exception of the previously mentioned intellectual predispositions, and little that is concerned with the contemporary economic situation.

What can be said here about Lenin's concerns for economic theory and analysis during the prerevolutionary period applies to most all of the future leaders of the Bolshevik party. Among this group there appears to have been almost no concern or discussion about the structure or the policies of the future socialist state. On the question of economic planning, Czeslaw Bobrowski concludes that:

From Marx to the October Revolution the problem of planning is absent from the preoccupations of the Marxist theoreticians and parties. Certain authors have attempted to find some sort of trace of the idea of planning in the Russian Social-Democratic party program of 1903. This derives from a linguistic misunderstanding, when it does not arise from an erroneous interpretation, this particular program only speaks about the rational organization of social production without further elaboration.[27]

During the war Lenin busied himself with the coordination of the activities of the Bolshevik faction and in a torrent against Russian and European socialists who had accepted the "defensist" position. He undertook the writing of his major ideological tract, *Imperialism, the Highest Stage of Capitalism*, which did not appear until 1917. Although Lenin ploughed through an enormous amount of statistical data while working on the book, the study emerged not as an analytical, but a didactic, work. Although Lenin drew heavily on John A. Hobson's classic study of imperialism, Hobson's work emerges as a more probing study.[28] As Louis Fischer observed:

Lenin did not conduct an inquiry in order to resolve a doubt. He wrote to demonstrate a firmly held article of faith: that capitalism was incorrigible and socialism "inevitable." The capitalist system would "never" improve the lot of the masses; that was not its business. Its business was to earn fatter profits in the colonies. But "inevitable" and "never" belong to prophecy, not to social science. . . . Lenin's theory of imperialism, however, was a wish—a wish that did not come true, the wish of a zealot, not the careful conclusion of a scientist.[29]

Lenin spent most of the war period in Zurich, which afforded an excellent vantage point for observation of the developments in the German wartime economy. He did not, however, seem to take advantage of his proximity. Although Lenin was later to urge that Russians use the German experience as a model, his works display only the most superficial acquaintance with the actual mechanisms which German wartime planners utilized to organize the economy.

When Lenin and the Bolsheviks seized political power, they had no comprehensive economic programs, but possessed a number of predispositions about the operation of the economy.[30] Above all, the Bolsheviks favored the industrialization of Russia and a redistribution of the nation's wealth, but failed to spell out the means by which this could be realized. Lenin had revealed his own naïveté about the workings of the national economy in *State and Revolution*, where he suggested that:

...Capitalist culture has *created* large-scale production, factories, railways, the postal service, telephones, etc., and *on this basis* the great majority of the functions of the old "state power" have become so simplified and can be reduced to such exceedingly simple operations of registration, filing, and checking that they can be easily performed by every literate person, can quite easily be performed for ordinary "workmen's wages,".....[31]

Lenin believed the capitalists had created the productive machinery and the only remaining task was to redistribute the wealth more equitably. However this simplistic analysis soon gave way to a more sober appreciation of the complexities of organizing the national economy. By April 1918, Lenin was to write:

The principal difficulty lies in the economic sphere, viz., the introduction of the strictest and universal accounting and control of the production and distribution of goods, raising the productivity of labour and *socialising* production in actual practice.... Without the guidance of specialists in the various fields of knowledge, technology, and experience, the transition to socialism will be impossible, because socialism calls for a conscious mass advance to greater productivity of labour compared with capitalism, and on the basis achieved by capitalism....[32]

Thus what appeared originally to Lenin to be simply a question of social justice and the reallocation of capitalistic wealth, became a problem of constructing a program for economic development—a project for which the Bolsheviks were totally unprepared. This problem had consumed the attention of numerous Russian proponents of industrialization in the century before the revolution, particularly in the decade preceding it. Thus Lenin was able to turn to some of these people for the expertise he needed to guide the new Soviet state. Lenin's willingness to seek assistance from non-Marxist specialists is explicable in terms of political expediency, and perhaps this attitude becomes more understandable in light of Leonard Schapiro's observations about Lenin, in a slightly different context: "The recognition by historians that Lenin must be regarded as more closely related to Russian tradition than to Marxism has made it possible to assess his true place within Russian 19th century political thought."[33]

The Development of Russian Economic Thought

Turning now to the second general section of this chapter it must be said that any attempt to describe the development of Russian economic thought related to the problem of industrialization and the conception of central economic planning, and the dearth of economic, political and institutional changes affecting this development, would require volumes.[34] Nonetheless, it is essential to investigate this development in order to understand Lenin's place in and contribution to Soviet economic policy.

During the nineteenth century a number of ardent but isolated voices were raised in support of the industrialization of Russia. Their main task seemed to be to convince their countrymen of the blessings of the industrial system and they expressed general agreement that industrialization could be best accomplished under the auspices of private enterprise. Yet, the absence of a sufficiently developed private economic sector gave their arguments an aura of unreality and in the final analysis almost all of them turned to the state for leadership in the process of industrialization, conceding their preference for private enterprise.

One of the first voices raised was that of Admiral Mordvinov, the long-time president of the Free Economic Society. Although he considered himself a follower of Adam Smith, his views closely paralleled, and may have been adapted from, those of Alexander Hamilton. In 1815, for instance, he wrote "Some Considerations on the Subject of Manufactures in Russia and on the Tariff," arguing for the need to protect domestic industries through the wise use of tariffs—this was a direct attack on a government which viewed tariffs strictly as a means of revenue. He hoped that private enterprise, supported by government benevolence, would be the prime mover in the process of industrialization. At the same time, he recognized the enormous importance of the state in the economy and went so far as to suggest that the state might construct factories and turn them over to private interests.[35] Mordvinov's views were supported by some, especially Kozodavlev, the Minister of the Interior, but they ran into stiff opposition from Yegor Kankrin, who was in firm control of economic policy, and who feared the coming of industrialization, because of the probable subsequent social dislocations.[36]

Another group of proponents of industrialization who favored private enterprise found themselves frustrated by the state's economic power. The Alexandrovskii Lyceum group of Bezobrazov, Lamanskii, Reutern, and Bunge saw the opportunity to encourage the private accumulation of capital when they and others were commissioned to restructure the banking system in the late 1850s. Although they all favored the establishment of a private and decentralized banking system, they felt compelled by the realities of the Russian economy to propose, albeit reluctantly, the formation of a State Bank.[37] Lamanskii became the bank's first director. Reutern and Bunge eventually became Ministers of Finance, yet were able to do little to encourage private enterprise. Reutern, for example, began the practice of floating consolidated foreign loans for Russian industry and evolved a system by which Russian industrialists could seek foreign loans only through the auspices of the state, thus tying the fortunes of industry even closer to the caprices of state policy.[38]

Ironically, it was Sergei Witte, who considered himself a follower of Friedrich List and did not appear to share the sympathies of other proponents of industrialization for private enterprise, who did more than any other person for the creation of a private economic sector.[39] Almost by inadvertance a self-supporting private sector was created as a spinoff from the economic progress made under Witte, thus bringing into existence a realistic alternative to the state in economic affairs. Despite severe economic setbacks caused by international depression at the beginning of the twentieth century and subsequent dislocations caused by war and revolution, the Witte system had created a solid basis for industrialization in Russia and by 1909 the country was beginning to show signs of renewed economic vigor.[40]

The economic debates changed significantly in scope and nature during the period of economic expansion after 1909. First, the desirability of industrialization was accepted by a growing segment of Russian society, which found its livelihood bound to the fortunes of continued industrial prosperity. No longer did spokesmen for industrialization have to prove the desirability of this process, but were now able to turn their attention to the more substantive problems of the organization and control of industrialization. Also, the debates which had been argued primarily in the academies and the government bureaucracy, took on a more public form, with increasing coverage of economic affairs being carried in the burgeoning press. This change reflected the fact that economic decision-making was now occurring outside of the confines of the state bureaucracy.

These changes in the economic debates were related to, and at the same time a part of, major changes taking place within Russian society as a whole.[41] A few observations about these changes might make the economic debates more understandable, especially since so little attention has been paid to them.

As Alexander Gerschenkron has pointed out:

...during those years [1905-1914] industrialization could no longer be the primary concern of the government. War and revolution had greatly strained budgetary capabilities.... But in Russia of the twentieth century, Count Witte's fall and the abandonment of his policies did not prevent a renewed outburst of industrial activity.[42]

He further stated:

...the economic progress born out of the policies of the nineties had been so great that in the years 1909-1914 a high rate of industrial growth could be maintained despite the greatly diminished scope of governmental participation in the economy.[43]

During this period industrial production grew at a rate of approximately 7.5 percent as compared with a high point of 9 percent in the late 1890s.[44]

More important was the fact that the private sector was developing its own resources and the changes in the economic debates mirrored only in part the growing strength of private enterprise. Banks were beginning to act, in Gerschenkron's terms, as a substitute for the failure of an underdeveloped domestic market to supply capital, thus taking over a function which only the government had fulfilled earlier. For example, total assets of state and private banks grew from 1,388 million rubles in 1900 to 2,039 million by 1909, and then jumped to 4,668 million by 1914.[45]

There was also an observable change in the pattern of foreign investments, heretofore always crucial to Russian economic development. With the exception of the depression period, 1900-1904, foreign investments in Russian industry exceeded domestically generated capital, but by the period 1909-1911, Richard Lorenz estimates that domestic capital made up nearly 75 percent of all invested.[46] At the same time, Russian security issues were sold increasingly at home, and between 1908-1912, nearly 75 percent of all Russian securities were purchased domestically.[47]

On the eve of the First World War, Russia was the fifth industrial power in the world in terms of aggregate output, yet in per capita terms she fell far down the list. Industrial output equalled only about half the value of agricultural production, an indication that Russian society had not become industrialized. The uneven development of industry and its striking concentration left large areas of Russia completely outside the process of industrialization. Yet the process was dynamic and revealed during the prewar years a serious impact on increasing numbers of the Russian population.[48]

There were, for instance, growing numbers of businessmen's organizations which resulted in a stronger capability to articulate the interests of organized industry. To be sure, the creation of these organizations was only a small part of the organizing zeal which captured all segments of Russian society in the wake of 1905. Businessmen's groups continued to suffer the traditional Russian disdain and suspicion of the merchant classes. Yet these organizations provided a forum for serious and practical discussion of Russia's economic problems. The most successful of these organizations was the Association of Industry and Trade, which served as a spokesman for large industry. Despite continual internecine quarrels, the Association provided the initiative and leadership for the establishment of the War-Industries Committees in 1915.[49]

The prewar years displayed significant changes within Russian society which aroused greater interest in the process of industrialization and made access to, and participation in, the debates concerning Russia's economic future much easier. Urban areas increasingly became centers of industry and managerial and technical personnel as well as workers concentrated in the larger cities, especially those of central Russia. More interesting is the astounding rise of urban literacy, which although little discussed is at extreme variance with the general picture of Russia as a country of abysmal illiteracy. An examination of literacy figures, when broken down by region and by age group, reveals a striking pattern. Urban literacy was usually more than double that of rural regions and the young were much more literate than the elderly. In Petersburg in 1910, for example, the level of literacy for men between 12 and 19 years of age was 94.4 percent, while for the same age group in Moscow the figure was 93.4 percent.[50] For all men over the age of six in the capital the rate was 86.3 percent in 1910.[51]

The cities which were the centers of economic as well as political life had by the outbreak of the First World War become almost entirely literate. In less than twenty years Russia had moved from last place among the major countries of Europe to first place in the world in numbers of book titles and editions published annually. In 1887 Russia published approximately 18 million books, by 1901 the figure rose to 58 million, it averaged between 130-150 million during 1905-1907, and doubled again by 1913.[52] The growth of periodicals and newspapers paralleled this expansion. For example, in Moscow, a city of under two million on the eve of war, *Russkoe Slovo*, a daily which had circulated 13,000 in 1900, had a circulation of between 700,000 and 800,000. The liberal *Russkie Vedomosti* circulated over 100,000 daily copies and there was a host of smaller papers. In the capital there were four newspapers with daily circulations in excess of 150,000.[53]

The growth of literacy and publications made public the issues which had long been the private domain of the government and learned societies. Further, it brought into contact individuals and groups who had long been physically and intellectually isolated from each other. The effect on economic debates was profound. Not only did the increase in published material provide the general reader and the specialist an abundance of new and recent material concerning economic theory and practice, it also gave an opportunity for groups and individuals to popularize their own projects and theories. Economic journals sprouted with an amazing rapidity and the major dailies devoted, at least by western standards, an inordinate amount of space to economic affairs.

Finally, changes within the economics profession itself profoundly affected the manner in which economists perceived the problems confronting the country. In 1902 the first economics faculty was established in Russia. Before that economics had been taught in the German pattern, as a function of the juridical faculty, which restricted its practical usefulness and emphasized its abstract or theoretical aspects.[54] In response to the increasing demand for trained technical personnel, Witte had urged the establishment of the St. Petersburg Polytechnical Institute at which the first economics faculty was founded.[55] This new faculty was designed to emphasize the relationship between economics and mathematical observation. New courses were established and first-rate students and faculty recruited. Reflecting the importance assigned to this new project by Witte, the Institute was given wider freedom in selecting its faculty, often taking on faculty such as Maxim Kovalevskii and Tugan-Baranovskii, both of whom had recently been removed from other positions on political grounds.[56] The faculty of the economics department at one time attracted such men as Tugan-Baranovskii,

Peter Struve, Chuprov, Posnikov, Ivaniukov, M.V. Bernatskii, V.E. Den, and M.I. Fridman.[57] It is not surprising that V.K. Dmitriev, a long-neglected figure whom Soviet scholars now claim as a forerunner of the work of W.W. Leontief, should have done his work at the Institute.[58]

Precisely at the time that industry began its expansion, the Institute and its counterparts in Russia began to turn out several hundred highly skilled economists and technicians. Many of the students of the Institute assumed prominent positions in the economics profession. E.S. Lure became a leading expert on syndicates and producers' organizations. Several were to appear later in the Soviet bureaucracy, most notably Stanislas Strumilin, A.M. Smirnov, L.N. Yurovskii, and Kogan-Bernshtein; however, only one former student, Molotov, appears to have risen to high political office.

These changes in the economy and its institutions were clearly reflected by the altered concerns in the economic debates on industrialization, both by increasing the practicality of the thrust of the debates as well as increasing the size of the audience and the number of participants in the debates. At the same time, Lenin and his associates seem to have been largely unaware of the nature of the changes affecting Russian society.

Three major economic issues came to dominate the debates among Russian proponents of industrialization. The first, the role of the state in the economy, was in many ways a continuation of debates carried on throughout the nineteenth century. A second concern was the emergence of syndicates and a high level of concentration of industrial enterprises. Finally, the capriciousness and unpredictability of Russian economic life evoked a growing demand for some form of national economic program. These issues taken together formed the basis for the discussion of the nature and direction of Russia's industrialization.[59]

All participants in the debate believed the government should act vigorously in promoting the industrialization of Russia, but the nature and extent of the state's involvement in the economy occasioned continuing discussion. A small minority appealed to the state to provide the entrepreneurial skills needed to industrialize the country. The predominant tendency, however, was to rely primarily on private enterprise, although there existed a marked willingness among most to favorably view the state as an active regulator of economic activity. There now appeared to be greater support for an active role of the state than had been the case in the previous century. This shift in attitude came, ironically, at a time when the state was actually playing a less important economic role and private enterprise was emerging as a major economic force for the first time. Practical objections to activities of the industrialists now created a hesitancy to give unqualified support to private enterprise—a hesitancy which had not been present in the previous century when private enterprise had been more a theoretical construct than a practical reality.

Nonetheless, most of the participants in these debates seemed to share a number of attitudes and perceptions about the industrialization process as it applied to Russia. Most seemed to understand some of the political and economic implications accompanying the process of industrialization. Economic development was equated with political power and the desire for industrialization thus contained elements of nationalism, a desire to see Russia as an independent great power. Although there was a fairly clear impression of the implications of economic development for Russia's international position, there seems to have been less awareness of the nature of domestic social and political changes which industrialization might entail.[60]

The existence of large-scale economic enterprises, the emergence and development of syndicates and other economic combinations were seen by most proponents of industrialization as natural and progressive, and, consequently they devoted most of their attention to the problem of who should control these enterprises, or how they might best be regulated. Combined with this attitude was a tendency to see prior development of heavy industry as a prerequisite for overall industrialization.

Russian industry had long been characterized by large plants and a good deal of concentration of economic power. In the early twentieth century, partly in response to the severity of the depression, syndicate-type agreements accentuated this phenomenon. Since Russia had little or no legislation concerning industrial combinations, the government's policy toward syndicates became arbitrary and was characterized by corruption and bribery. The government gave willing assistance to the formation of some syndicates, while attacking others. The alleged benefits accruing to, or restrictions imposed by, industrial combinations now became the focus of much bitter debate.[61]

Since much of the objection to syndicates was based on the allegation that they restricted output, the economic resurgence after 1909 mitigated much of this attack. Most accepted the growth of syndicates as a fact of economic life, and after 1909, there were few who argued that the syndicates ought to be annihilated. There was however a growing consensus that the state ought to play a major role in regulating the economic abuses of the syndicates. Even those, including many industrialists, who had earlier called for the unfettered development of syndicates began to recognize the inevitability and even the desirability of some government regulations.[62]

Great attention was thus devoted to a government commission established to draw up legislation governing economic combinations. But its failure to produce any results or to be representative of the society at large, created great hostility to the government. A widely held belief that the present political structure was an obstacle to economic development and that political changes would have to precede economic growth was generated.[63] This feeling was exacerbated by new government regulations on joint-stock ventures issued in the spring of 1914. These regulations were aimed primarily at restricting the role of Jews in industrial ventures and limiting the ability of corporate entities to own land. Heretofore the proponents of industrialization found few issues on which they could unite, but the government's action did more to bring them together than any action they could have undertaken on their own.[64]

The government's move, under great pressure, to rescind the regulations just before the outbreak of war in July 1914, did little to heal the breach between the government and the proponents of industrialization.[65] Hostility to the government and a new sense of common interest paved the way for increased cooperative activity which took place after the outbreak of war. Yet, the importance of the state as a factor in industrial development was conceded by even the most vigorous proponents of private entrepreneurship. Perhaps the most persistent appeal to the government was for the construction of a long-range state economic program. It was believed this would help to ensure greater rationality and predictability in the formulation of state economic policies and would help to create more stable economic conditions in the country.[66]

Enormous energy was devoted to demands on public agencies for long-term sectoral or all-encompassing programs, but all this activity produced surprisingly few results. The first efforts were directed exclusively at the state, but when it became apparent that the government was not inclined to move toward the realization of such a program many individuals and some organizations attempted to draft their own programs. For example, the major organization of businessmen, the Association of Industry and Trade, devoted a great deal of its energy to the elaboration of such a plan, even though the complexities of the task seemed overwhelming.[67]

There was the exceptional case of N.P. Petrov, who understood the enormous mechanism which would have to be created to administer a planned economy, but his views seem prophetic of another age. Almost inadvertently Petrov provided a glimpse of the future. Having presided over the work of the railroad commission he was well aware of the problems inherent in developing a long-range plan for even one sector of the economy. In a series of articles in the journal, *Novyi Ekonomist*, he attacked what he considered to be inaccurate perceptions concerning the development of the economy, both in Russia and abroad, as expressed by the Social-Democrats in their party platform.[68] He was most irritated by their resort to slogans and simplistic formulas and he attributed this to their economic naïveté. Petrov argued that the S-D's were content to call for "the regulation of the social-productive process," without ever indicating what they meant by this.[69] He set out to describe the necessary consequences of such a process, arguing that:

Systematic organization of the social-productive process, or it would be better to say the productivity of all mankind, can be achieved in no other way than the submission of all humanity in relationship to their productive labor to a certain unity of administration of the whole world. . . . In the obligations of this administration must be included a definition of the size of every type and mode of production not only for all localities, but also for the multitude of separate people. It must have the right to point out measures of regularization of productivity in cases of diversion, sometimes unavoidable under the influence of the elemental forces of nature. It ought to have the means to realize its indicated measures. Its organs must be spread everywhere; they ought to be in uninterrupted communication with each other and must penetrate into all places of manufacturing from large factories and plants to the rooms of the kustar. Everywhere they must follow after the fulfillment of the orders, which are defined for every producer, allowing neither retreat nor change by the producers in their own production, remembering that any kind of significant development or change without fail will destroy systematic production. Any digression from the adopted plan of the administration must be adjusted immediately and forcefully.[70]

Petrov seems to have clearly abhorred the possible development of such a system, but never further elaborated his views. More surprising perhaps is the lack of any comment on his articles in *Novyi Ekonomist* and the apparent absence of any response from the Social-Democratic camp. Lenin was at least a casual reader of the journal, for he commented on a number of articles which appeared in the journal.

The desire and the ability of the state to foster industrialization was being called into question, even by some who, in principle, supported state entrepreneurship. It was in this attitude that many moved farthest away from the traditions of the nineteenth century proponents of industrialization.[71] More frequently the state was spoken of as an obstacle to continuing industrial growth and her policies were met with open hostility. Increasingly the state was accused of formulating industrial policy for political rather than economic reasons.[72] By the outbreak of the First World War many proponents of industrialization were becoming convinced that only after major political changes had been effected could industrialization proceed at a desirable pace.[73]

These attitudes were reenforced by the government's activity after the outbreak of war. When the state failed to mobilize industry to support the war effort and actually pursued policies which gravely affected the ability of industry to supply the war machine, the Association of Industry and Trade seized the initiative by establishing the War Industries Committees.[74] These Committees drew into public life scores of the ablest industrialists, economists, and engineers, and provided a training ground for many who were later to staff the Soviet economic bureaucracy. For example, Strumilin, Leonid Krasin, Vladimir Groman, and Professor Grinevetskii all actively participated in the work of the Committees.

The Committees' major responsibility was in the area of coordinating the distribution of materials, not in supervising the production process. Many who worked in the Committees became aware of the need to understand the complex interrelationships among all branches of the economy, before any systematic control of the economy could be exercised. Committee staffs did in fact make some progress in making large-scale plans for the distribution of goods.[75]

The existence of the Committees was precarious as the government continued to treat all spontaneous efforts with suspicion. This hostility explains in part why many leaders of the War Industries Committees, such as Alexander Guchkov and Alexander Konovalov, greeted the fall of the autocracy without remorse and actively participated in the establishment of the Provisional Government.

The Post-Revolutionary Period

The third general area of this chapter revolves around Bolshevik policy after the Great October Revolution. It can be noted that there has been a continuing and still unresolved debate concerning the nature of Bolshevik policy in the first months after the Revolution, but it appears that Bolshevik economic policy in this period can best be described as one of improvisation.[76] Lenin was firmly committed to a policy of nationalization of both the land and the banks, but beyond this there seems to have been no firm idea of how to deal with industry. The policy of workers' control soon threatened to lead to anarchy and gave way to the more centralist policy of nationalization, however, even this policy was carried out erratically and without any clear planning.[77] Bolshevik economic policy evolved in relation to the exigencies of the civil war, the widespread destruction of industrial enterprises, the desertion of leading industrialists, and the scarcity of trained technical cadres.

As the Bolsheviks began to organize their economic bureaucracy, they quickly faced the problem of a shortage of trained personnel.[78] There were few highly trained engineers and economists among the Bolshevik ranks, most notably G. Krzhizhanovskii, S. Strumilin, P. Popov, and L. Krasin. Lenin correctly perceived that for the Soviet state to survive it would have to depend for some time on the expertise of the old bureaucracy.[79] Consequently, a determined policy to encourage non-Bolshevik technocrats to join Soviet economic organizations was established. This campaign was reasonably successful and many professional people soon began to work within the Soviet economic apparatus. Many leftist-leaning technicians who had served in the War Industries Committees suddenly found themselves in responsible positions.[80] The nationalization of industry, begun in the late spring of 1918, served to alienate the last remaining industrialists, but seemed to have affected the managerial cadres less severely.[81]

During the chaotic years of the Civil War little attention could be devoted to the problems of long-term economic programs, since there were enough difficulties just in attending to the exigencies of the current situation.[82] The questions of economic planning, which later dominated Soviet economic thought, were rarely discussed during this period. It was not until work began on the GOELRO project that the term "economic plan" began to appear regularly in Soviet economic discussions.[83] But even at this stage there was little agreement on what economic planning meant. For many it simply meant the amalgamation of a number of programs for various sectors of the economy, while for others it implied the development of a number of regional plans.[84] The idea of a single economic plan for the whole economy only slowly gained widespread acceptance.[85]

The origin of the ideas which underlay the development of GOELRO and thus Soviet planning are not yet fully explored. Few scholars trace the origins of planning to Marxism, but some do insist that the German wartime planning experience was both inspiration and guide for the development of Soviet economic planning.[86] Yet, there is much reason to believe that the roots of economic planning are more directly related to actual Russian experience.[87] As Alexander Gerschenkron has suggested:

Neither the great landmarks in the economic history of the Soviet Union over the past 35 years nor the specific institutional arrangements which are characteristic of the Soviet economy need be explained by recourse to Marxism. Rather, it is more plausible to explain both the formidable changes that have taken place and the *modus operandi* of the Soviet economy in part as a recurrence of a traditional pattern of Russian economic development; in part as stemming from the exigencies of a given situation and, most of all, as emanating from the mechanics of power politics—that is to say, essentially as necessitated by the desire of a dictatorial government to augment and to perpetuate its power position.[88]

There is some evidence to indicate a crucial link between prerevolutionary economic thought and Soviet practice was the work of the nearly obscure figure, V.I. Grinevetskii, Director of the Moscow Higher Technical Institute.[89]

Grinevetskii's work[90] was largely related to the study of the efficiency and working process of steam and internal combustion engines, which had specific application in two of Russia's infant industries—locomotive and diesel engine construction, and the construction of electrical energy stations.[91] With this background Grinevetskii became involved in the attempts of the War Industries Committees to mobilize the technical resources and manpower of the country for the war effort. He became president of the war-technical division of the united societal organizations and was deeply involved in the attempts to apply technical knowledge and processes to increase material output for the war.[92]

After the October Revolution, Grinevetskii remained for a time in Moscow. His technical experience during the war as well as personal observations caused him to record his own thoughts concerning the future of the Russian economy. He completed his work between January and June, 1918,[93] and then joined the stream of anti-Bolsheviks who fled toward the armed counterrevolutionary camps. His book was published in 1919 in Kharkov under the title, *Postwar Perspective of Russian Industry*.[94]

Grinevetskii died in Ekatrinodar in 1919, but his book had a major impact on postrevolutionary Soviet economic policymakers.[95] Leonid Krasin apparently recommended the book to Lenin's attention as early as 1919. Krasin was aware of Grinevetskii's earlier technical works and probably had had personal contact with him as they both participated in the same technical sections of the War Industries Committees. In addition, Krasin and Grinevetskii shared a fascination with the uses and potentiality of electrical power.[96] According to Nikolai Valentinov-Volskii, Lenin was intrigued by the book and read it quickly, filling it with personal notations. Despite objection to Grinevetskii's political positions, Lenin recognized the importance of the work and recommended it to a number of the key economic figures of the Soviet bureaucracy. He gave his copy first to Isuryupa and then to Rykov. Rykov lost the book and was reprimanded by Lenin "with almost foul words."[97] Valentinov contends that Lenin drew his inspiration for the GOELRO plan from Grinevetskii's book, for it was almost immediately after reading it that Lenin began to speak of the necessity for "a state plan of the whole national economy" at the base of which would be the electrification of the country—a problem to which Grinevetskii devotes a large amount of space.[98]

Grinevetskii's book became a handbook for those working in Soviet economic organizations, but the original edition had been published in such a small quantity that it was not sufficient. Thus in 1922 the decision was made, apparently at Lenin's direction, to reprint the book. The State Publishers decided that it would be awkward for them to reprint it in view of the anti-Communist tenor of the book, consequently the Publication Section of the Central Committee decided that *Tsentrosoiuz* should publish it, for at that time *Tsentrosoiuz* was considered a non-communized organization.[99]

In the introduction to the 1922 edition of Grinevetskii's book, Vl. Sarabianov wrote:

A single economic plan of the rebirth and the refoundation of the economy—this is not whimsy, not a fancy of the Soviet regime, this is an urgent need about which bourgeois economists have talked, about which the well-known Ballod of Germany and Professor Grinevetskii in Russia have written. . . . We have only one book, Professor Grinevetskii's, which deals with such a question in conformity with Russian actuality, if you do not count the work on electrification in GOELRO, in which the problem of a single economic plan did not undergo special investigation, appearing as its basis; the departure point for the constructions of GOELRO.[100]

Sarabianov commended the book for the author's unstinting realism in his presentation of the prewar and prerevolutionary economy. Grinevetskii's analysis, he pointed out, made possible a detailed investigation of the means of remedying the economy's shortcomings. Grinevetskii, Sarabianov wrote, was obviously an uncompromising supporter of the bourgeoisie and an opponent of the Bolsheviks, but this did not blind him to the needs of the Russian economy. What his opposition did do, however, was to make him underestimate the ability of socialism to solve these problems.[101]

Grinevetskii's analysis of the Russian economy, his plans for its reconstruction, and his impact on Soviet practices deserve greater attention than they have yet received, but this is not the place for a detailed examination of his views. A few observations might, however, be useful. Grinevetskii's work can be seen as the culmination of a tradition in Russian economic thought. His observations and experience made him understand the necessity of viewing the economy in its totality and investigating the interrelationships of all the sectors of the economy. He saw the Bolshevik regime as transitory and believed the reconstruction of the Russian economy would occur under a more democratic government. He accepted the necessity of continued foreign investment and rejected the idea of autochthonous development.[102] His policy priorities were much the same as those of the prerevolutionary proponents of industrialization, with some important exceptions. He emphasized the importance of completing an internal transportation network and the need to place priority on the development of heavy industry. He departed from earlier traditions in his view that future development was completely dependent on the expansion of fuel and power resources, and in his firm belief that the development of regional electrical power stations would underwrite future industrial prosperity.[103]

In his conclusions Grinevetskii listed the major tasks confronting the rebirth and development of Russian industry. Here he called for a battle against political and economic separatism and emphasized the necessity to bind Russians together as a "single economic organism."[104] He argued that it would not be sufficient to reconstruct Russian industry as it was under the old regime, but instead the reconstruction must proceed along new lines, undergirded by a single economic policy, conceived through the use of "systematic [*planomernyi*] preliminary accounting," and with a clear understanding of the interrelationship and interdependence of all aspects of the economy.[105]

For the Soviets, Grinevetskii's work presented serious ideological problems. There was little or no attack on the accuracy of his presentation of the past or present state of the Russian economy. In addition, his analysis of the problems confronting the revitalization of Russian industry generally became accepted by the Soviets as a fair one and the policy directives Grinevetskii suggested were not unacceptable, although the Soviet economy developed along more autarkic lines than Grinevetskii felt were possible. Yet, Grinevetskii was an anti-Bolshevik, an anti-socialist, who treated as complete naïveté the thought that Russia could lead the world socialist camp. Throughout the early post-war years Grinevetskii and his work were subjected to this ambiguous treatment of praise for his work and condemnation for his political views. In a later period there would be no room for this ambiguity.

Valentinov relates an interesting exchange with Trotsky which illustrates the existence of these dual feelings. Trotsky himself has often been depicted as the major proponent of centralized economic planning. In early 1925, when Trotsky's star was falling, he was appointed to *Vesenkha* in the position of president of the Main Concession Committee, head of the electrotechnical administration, and president of the Scientific-Technical Section.[106] In this latter capacity, Trotsky undertook his first official act, presiding over the dedication of the Heat-Engineering Institute named for Professors Grinevetskii and Kirsh.[107] Later, Valentinov had the opportunity to talk with Trotsky (October, 1925) and the subject of Grinevetskii came up when Valentinov cited Grinevetskii's figures during a discussion concerning the prewar condition of Russian industry. Trotsky is reported to have said:

Grinevetskii! First-class engineer-technician, first-class innovator, it is perfectly just that his name should be on the heat-engineering institute. But at the same time he is an insufferable, violent reactionary. Post-war perspectives consist for him in that nothing will survive from the October Revolution. Only the consequences of the absence by us of the blaze [plameni] of planning creations [plan-ogo tvorchestva], and without planning there is no socialism, from the narrowing of great planning tasks to the horizon of the cribdweller [shpargel'shchik] Grinevetskii became a kind of prophet, a teacher of planning.[108]

Valentinov remarks:

So, they called Professor Grinevetskii a "furious reactionary," this man who was a prophet, a forerunner, an inspirer of the concrete plans of economic and technological transformation of the country. His ideas, which underlay the plans of GOELRO, were expanded and deepened in the plans of OSVOK. In these and other cases the plans were worked out by non-party people. Therefore, when you have been a participant and a *survivant* of that epoch, when you know this history, which is unfamiliar to many historians of the Soviet Revolution—one can only shrug his shoulders when he reads or hears, that the cases of planning, which is becoming more widespread in this world, were laid by the creative thought of Soviet communism. This simply is not true.[109]

By the early 1920s the Soviets were becoming deeply involved in the development of the techniques of economic planning. The experience with the GOELRO program had revealed the complexity of the problems involved in attempts to coordinate the entire structure of the economy and exposed the inadequacy of the regime's expertise in the methodology of planning. Direction of GOELRO was subsumed under a new agency, Gosplan, which was created to direct the entire economy, although its authority was only gradually established.[110]

The economic bureaucracy which was to carry out the direction of the economy was still staffed predominantly by non-Communists. Lenin, for example, observed that "more than 200 specialists—almost all, without exception, opponents of Soviet power—worked with interest on [GOELRO], although they are not communists."[111] When Gosplan was set up in April 1921, only seven of the thirty-four man staff were members of the Communist Party.[112] This fact explains to some extent part of the continuing suspicion of the planning agencies within the party apparatus.

The idea of a single economic plan for the whole economy, administered by a single economic center, only slowly gained acceptance. There was still considerable debate whether or not plans should be drawn for each economic sector or for each geographic region and then simply amalgamated. In fact, much of the planning of the economy still proceeded by this process of amalgamation. But the commitment to the use of planning as a tool for economic development inspired a wide-ranging investigation of the techniques and methodology of planning.[113]

At first, most of those involved in the planning agencies, including the Communists, viewed economic planning in terms which were later to become known derisively as "geneticist." The later Stalinist use of economic planning as a system of coercion and quota-setting was virtually unknown during these early years.[114] By the mid-1920s, however, almost all Soviet economists came to accept central economic planning as integral to any policy of economic development, even though the methodology for handling the complexities of a planning apparatus were not yet clearly formulated.[115] The questions of the specific policy to be instituted still occasioned controversy and it was in this context that the "Great Industrialization Debate" occurred.[116]

Lenin's contribution to the development of Soviet economic policy appears then less in the realm of his original thought, than in his ability to adapt certain aspects of the Russian tradition to the service of the Soviet state. Although he had few concrete plans for economic policy, it seems clear that Lenin shared some of the intellectual predispositions of many Russian proponents of industrialization. Thus, his affirmation of their policies did not involve a complete reversal on his part. Lenin's flexibility and political acumen permitted him to appeal without hesitation to the expertise of the technocrats and to allow them to determine, within his limits, much of Russia's economic future.

As many others have observed, Lenin was primarily a political figure, and it was in political activity that his true genius lay. He was able to use all the tools at his disposal for furthering the Party's, and thus his own, power. In spite of much opposition from within the Party, Lenin did not shrink from drawing on the expertise of the non-Communist specialists when it appeared expedient to do so. It was Lenin's political skill which allowed the foundering Soviet state to survive, and ironically permitted the persistence of certain continuities of Russian economic policy and thought.

Notes

1. Adam Ulam, *The Bolsheviks* (New York, 1965), pp. 293-94.

2. Lenin, *Materializm i Empirio-Krititsizm, Polnoe sobranie sochinenii,* 5th ed. (Moscow, 1961), XVIII, 7-384 (hereafter cited as *PSS*).

3. Alec Nove, "Lenin as Economist," *Lenin: The Man, the Theorist, the*

Leader; A Reappraisal, eds. Leonard Schapiro and Peter Reddaway (New York, 1967), pp. 188, 190, 209-10 (hereafter cited as "Lenin as Economist"). On Lenin's use of statistics see: "Zarabotki rabochykh i pribyl kapitalistov," *PSS*, XXII, 24-25; and "Dorogovizna zhizni i 'tiazhelaia zhizn'," *PSS*, XXIII, 179-81.

4. Nove, "Lenin as Economist," p. 203.

5. Lenin, "Kadety i oktiabristy," *PSS*, XX, 212-16; "Itog," *PSS*, XX, 369-73; "Eshche odin pokhod na demokratiiu," *PSS*, XXII, 82-93; and "Kadety i krupnaia burzhuazii," *PSS*, XXII, 161-62.

6. See Lenin, "Natsionaly-liberaly," *PSS*, XXII, 244-46.

7. On the liquidators see Lenin, "Reformizm v russkoi sotsialdemokratii," *PSS*, XX, 305-18; "Priemi bor'by burzhuaznoi intelligentsii protiv rabochikh," *PSS*, XXV, 321-52; "Platform reformistov i platforma sotsial-demokratov," *PSS*, XXII, 167-75; "Sovremennaia Rossiia i rabochee dvizhenie: gazetnyi otchet," *PSS*, XXIII, 55-59; "Materialy k voprosu o bor'be vnutri s.-d. dumskoi fraktsii," *PSS*, XXIV, 93-110; "O natsional'noi programe Rsdrp," *PSS*, XXIV, 223-29; and "Ideinaia bor'ba v rabochem dvizhenii," *PSS*, XXV, 131-34, and also Ulam, p. 275.

8. On Schmidt money, see Bertram D. Wolfe, *Three Who Made a Revolution: A Biographical History*, rev. ed. (New York, 1964), pp. 379-81.

9. Lenin, *Razvitie kapitalisma v Rossiii, PSS*, III, 1-609, and Nove, "Lenin as Economist," p. 90.

10. For examples see Lenin, "Anketa ob organizatsiiakh krupnogo kapitala," *PSS*, XXI, 288-305, esp. 298ff.; "Dve utopii," *PSS*, XXII, 117-21 (although not published until 1924, it was written sometime prior to October 5, 1912); "Natsionaly-liberaly," *PSS*, XXII, 244-46; and "O natsional'nom programe Rsdrp," *PSS*, XXIV, 223-29, esp. p. 229.

11. Ulam, p. 280; Wolfe, pp. 379-81; and Louis Fischer, *The Life of Lenin* (New York, 1964), p. 70.

12. See Ulam, p. 292; *cf* Lenin, "Doklad mezhdunarodnomu Biuro," *PSS*, XXIV, 296-303 (although not published until 1924, presented January 31, 1914); "K voprosu o natsional'noi politike," *PSS*, XXV, 64-72 (written about April 1914, although first published in 1924); and "O prave natsii na samoopredelenie," *PSS*, XXV, 255-320.

13. See Karl A. Wittfogel, "The Marxist View of Russian Society and Revolution," *World Politics* (July, 1960), XII, 487-508, esp. 496-97.

14. Lenin, "Dve utopii," *PSS*, XXII, 117-21, esp. 120; "Platforma reformistov i platforma revoliutsionnykh sotsial-demokratov," *PSS*, XXII, 107-75, esp. 174-75, where Lenin complains of much that is "old Chinese" in both Tsarists and reformists; "Istoricheskie sudby ucheniia Karla Marksa," *PSS*, XXIII, 1-4, esp. 3; "Probuzhdenic azii," *PSS*, XXIII, 145-46; "Otstalia evropa i peredovaia azii," *PSS*, XXIII, 166-67; "O russkom upravlenii i o russkikh reformakh," *PSS*, XXIV, 20-21; and "Levonarodnichestvo i markizm," *PSS*, XXV, 235-37.

15. Lenin did not formulate his progressive views of imperialism until after the war broke out. See Lenin, "Kapitalizm i 'parlement'," *PSS*, XXI, 366-68.

16. Lenin, "Vooruzheniia i kapitalizm," *PSS*, XXIII, 175-76; "Kapitalisty i vooruzhenie," *PSS*, XXIII, 253-54; and "Burzhuaznye del'tsy—finansisty i politiki," *PSS*, XXIII, 258-59.

17. Lenin, "4000 rublei v god i 6-chasovoi den," *PSS*, XXIV, 271-73.

18. Lenin, "Systema Teilora—poraboshehenie cheloveka mashinoi," *PSS*, XXIV, 369-71.

19. G. Krzhizhanovskii, *Sobranie sochineniia* (Moscow, 1936), III, 87-89, cited in R.E.W. Davies, "Some Soviet Economic Controllers—I," *Soviet Studies* (January, 1960), XI, 299.

20. Lenin, "Anketa ob organizatsiiakh krupnogo kapitala," *PSS*, XXI, 288-305.

21. Ibid., p. 289.

22. Ibid., pp. 301ff.

23. For biographical information on Gushka-Ermanskii, see Lenin, *PSS*, XXV, 227-34.

24. Lenin, "Rabochii klass i rabochaia pechat'," *PSS*, XXV, 227-34.

25. Lenin, "O nekotorykh osobennostiakh istoricheskogo razvitiia marksizma," *PSS*, XXI, 84-89; "Kentsentratsiia proizvodstva v Rossii," *PSS*, XXII, 40-48; "Tri istochnika i sostavnykh chasti marksizma," *PSS*, XXIII, 40-48; and "Rost kapitalisticheskogo bogatstva," *PSS*, XXIII, 185-87.

26. See, e.g., Lenin, "K voprosu o natsional'noi politike," *PSS*, XXV, 64-72 (written about April 1914, although not published until 1924).

27. Czeslaw Bobrowski, *Formation du Système Sovietique de Planification* (Paris, 1956), p. 16.

A problem of translation exists for any discussion on prewar Russian economic attitudes toward planning. Nowhere in the economic literature for this period have I seen the term *planirovanie* (planning) or the adjective *planovoi*. However, the term *planomernost* and its adjectival form *planomernyi* appear often. This word really implies the sense of system, order or rationality rather than planning. It has often been mistranslated as "planning" by English-speaking scholars, but should be translated as "systematic" or "rational." Thus, *planomernaia politika* is systematic policy. Bobrowski suggests the following definition: 'Ce qui figure dans le texte [referring to the discussion of Marxist economic preoccupations] n'est ni le terme "plan" ni "planification" (en russe *planirovanie*), mais bien l'adjectif "*planomernyi*." Or, "*planomernyi*"—comme le "*plänmassig*" allemand—doit, selon le cas être traduit par "rationnel," "ordonne," "conforme au plan" mais jamais "planife." Dans le cas d'espèce il s'agit d' "organisation rationnelle" (*planomernaja organizacija*)' (p. 16). Friedrich von Hayek, in *Collectivist Economic Planning* (London, 1935), p. 32, suggests that the first use of the term "planned economy" (in German, *planwirtschaft*), in its contemporary sense, was in a memorandum prepared by the German Minister of

Economics, R. Wissel, and his assistant W. von Moellendorf, in 1919. The term was elaborated in a book by Wissel, *Die Planwirtschaft* (Hamburg, 1920).

28. Lenin, *Imperialism, the Highest Stage of Capitalism, Selected Works* (New York, 1939), V, 3-119; cf. J.A. Hobson, *Imperialism a Study* (London, 1954).

29. Fischer, p. 100; see also pp. 95-107.

30. The most detailed account of the development of early Bolshevik economic policy is found in: E.H. Carr, *A History of Soviet Russia: The Bolshevik Revolution, 1917-1923*, vol. II (New York, 1952). See also, Maurice Dobb, *Soviet Economic Development Since 1917* (New York, 1948), esp. pp. 82-149; Richard Lorenz, *Anfänge der Bolschewistischen Industriepolitik*, in *Abhandlungen des Bundesinstituts zur Enforschung des Marxismus-Leninismus: Institut für Sowjetologie*, Band XI (Koln, 1965); Bobrowski, *Formation du Système Sovietique*; Eugene Zaleski, *Planification de la croissance et fluctuations economiques en URSS*, vol. I, 1918-1932 (Paris, 1962); and F. Pollock, *Die planwirtschaftlichen Versuche in der Sowjetunion 1917-1927* (Leipzig, 1929).

31. Lenin, *State and Revolution*, as quoted in Robert V. Daniels, ed., *A Documentary History of Communism* (New York, 1962), I, 100-101.

32. Lenin, "The Immediate Tasks of the Soviet Government: The International Position of the Russian Soviet Republic and the Fundamental Tasks of the Socialist Revolution," (April, 1918), as quoted in Daniels, *A Documentary History of Communism*, I, 147.

33. Leonard Schapiro, "Learning from the Russians," *Encounter*, XXXIII (October, 1969), 69.

34. For a more detailed discussion of some of these problems, see Gregory Guroff, "The State and Industrialization in Russian Economic Thought, 1909-1914," (Unpublished Ph.D. dissertation, Princeton University, 1970).

35. On Mordvinov's views, see Helma Repezuk, "Nicholas Mordvinov (1754-1845): Russia's Would-Be Reformer" (Unpublished Ph.D. dissertation, Columbia University, 1962); H. Mordvinov, *Nekotorye soobrazheniia po predmetu manufaktur v Rossii i o tarife* (St. Petersburg, 1815), which is also contained in *Arkhiv grafov Mordvinovykh*, vol. V (St. Petersburg, 1902); and William L. Blackwell, *The Beginnings of Russian Industrialization, 1800-1860* (Princeton, 1968), esp. pp. 130-38.

36. For an excellent treatment of Kandrin's economic views, see Walter M. Pintner, *Russian Economic Policy Under Nicholas I* (Ithaca, N.Y., 1967).

37. V.P. Bezobrazov, *Otchet o deistviiakh kommissii vysochai uchrezhdennoi dlia ustroistva zenskikh bankov* (St. Petersburg, 1861), esp. pp. 12ff.; Bezobrazov, *Pozenlennyi kredit i ego sovremennaia organizatsiia v Evrope* (St. Petersburg, 1860), esp. pp. 196ff.; *Trudy kommissii vysochaishei uchrezndennoi dlia ustroistva zemskikh bankov*, 4 vols. (St. Petersburg, 1860), esp. vol. I. Also see N.K. Karataev, "Bvoriansko-liberalnaia ekonomicheskaia mysl', . . . V.P. Bezobrazov," *Istoriia Russkoi Ekonomicheskoi Mysli* (Moscow, 1959), II, Part I; hereafter cited as *IREM*.

38. For Reutern's career see A.E. Yanovskii, "Graf Mikhail Khristoforovich Reutern,"*Brokgauz-Efron*, LII (St. Petersburg, 1899), pp. 511-12.

39. On Witte's own views see S. Iu. Witte, *Konspokt lektsii o narodneu i gosudarstvennom khoziastve* (St. Petersburg, 1912), esp. pp. 415-568, and *Po nevedu natsionaliziia. Natsional'naia okonomiia i Fridrikh List* (St. Petersburg, 1912). The best treatment of Witte's policy is contained in T.H. Von Laue, *Sergei Witte and the Industrialization of Russia* (New York, 1963).

40. For economic developments in Russia from 1900 to 1914, see Roger Portal, "The Industrialization of Russia," *The Cambridge Economic History of Europe*, edited by H.J. Habakkuk and M. Postan (Cambridge, 1965), VI, Part 2, 801-872; Margaret Miller, *The Economic Development of Russia, 1905-1914* (London, 1926); Peter Lyashchenko, *History of the National Economy to the Revolution of 1917*, trans. L.M. Norman (New York, 1949); and Alexander Gerschenkron, "Russia: Patterns and Problems, 1861-1958," *Economic Backwardness in Historical Perspective* (New York, 1962), pp. 119-51.

41. George Yaney, "Social Stability in Pre-revolutionary Russia: A Critical Note," *American Slavic and East European Review*, XXIV (September, 1965), 521-27, esp. 522-23. Also see Leopold Haimson, "The Problem of Social Stability in Urban Russia, 1905-1917," Part 1, *ASEER*, XXIII (December, 1964), 619-42; Part 2, *ASEER*, XXIV (March, 1965), 1-22, and "Reply," *ASEER*, XXIV (March, 1965), 47-56; Arthur Mendel, "Peasant and Worker on the Eve of the First World War," *ASEER*, XXIV (March, 1965), 23-33; and Theodore H. Von Laue, "The Chances for Liberal Constitutionalism," *ASEER*, XXIV (March, 1965), 34-46. The problem of social stability in Russia between 1905-1917 has recently been the subject of an extended discussion among several American scholars. Although the emphasis of the discussion was on the disruptive nature of the dynamic movements in Russian society, George Yaney points to the creative aspects of this social change and argues that "in the midst of conflict the elements of a coherent social order were emerging." He also asserts persuasively that "the assumption that the writings of the pre-revolutionary intelligentsia describe their society as a whole is no longer tenable."

42. Alexander Gerschenkron, "Russia: Patterns and Problems," *Economic Backwardness*, p. 134.

43. Alexander Gerschenkron, "An Economic History of Russia," *Journal of Economic History*, XII (Spring, 1952), 157.

44. Alexander Gerschenkron, "The Rate of Growth in Industrial Production in Russia Since 1885," *Tasks of Economic History: Supplement to the Journal of Economic History* (1947), p. 149.

45. Miller, *The Economic Development of Russia*, p. 149. The figures are from *Vestnik Finansov*, no. 11 (1914), p. 515. Also see Lyashchenko, *History of the National Economy*, p. 703.

46. Richard Lorenz, *Anfänge der Bolschewistischen Industriepolitik* (Köln, 1965). The figures are taken from Wl. Sabrianow, *An der Schwelle des Zweiten Jahrzehnts* (Hamburg-Berlin, 1927), p. 25.

Year	Domestic Capital	Foreign Capital
	(In millions of rubles)	
1893-1896	104	145
1897-1900	112	451
1901-1904	209	182
1905-1908	339	371
1909-1911	913 (?)	284

47. Ministerstvo finansov, "Le marché financier russe 1908-1912" (St. Petersburg, 1913), Diagram no. 22, in Miller, *The Economic Development of Russia*, p. 164. Figures of comparable magnitudes for all private and government securities are given by Joseph M. Goldstein, "Banking Institutions and Foreign Capital in Russia," *Struggling Russia*, I, no. 15 (June 21, 1919), 212.

48. William L. Blackwell, *The Industrialization of Russia: An Historical Perspective* (New York, 1970), pp. 42-43.

49. For a detailed discussion of the development of businessmen's groups, and in particular The Association of Industry and Trade, see Ruth Amende Roosa, "The Association of Industry and Trade, 1906-1914: An Examination of the Economic Views of Organized Industrialists in the Pre-revolutionary Russia," (Unpublished Ph.D. dissertation, Columbia University, 1967).

50. I. Kh. Ozerov, *Chto delat?* (Moscow, 1913), pp. 199-200, 218; I.M. Bogdanov, *Gramotnost' i obrazovanie v dorevoliusionnoi Rossii i v SSSR* (Moscow, 1964), esp. pp. 28ff.; A.G. Rashin, *Maselenie Rossii za 100 let (1811-1913gg.): Statisticheskie ocherki* (Moscow, 1956), esp. pp. 287ff.; and Rashin, *Formirovanie rabochego klassa Rossii: Istoriko-ekonomicheskie ocherki* (Moscow, 1958), pp. 580ff.

51. Bogdanov, *Gramotnost' i obrazovanie*, pp. 28-29.

52. N. Rubakin, "Knizhnyi potok," *Russkaia mysl'*, no. 3 (1903), p. 10; "Iz knigi i zhizni," *Russkie Vedomosti* (December 17, 1909); and *Istoriia Moskvy* (Moscow, 1955), V, 480 and 492.

53. M.S. Cherepakhov and E.M. Fingeit (eds.), *Russkaia periodicheskaia pechat (1895-October, 1917): Spravochnik* (Moscow, 1957), esp. pp. 17-18; Thomas Riha, "Ricch': A Portrait of a Russian Newspaper," *ASEER*, XXII, (December, 1963), 663-64; and *Istoriia Moskvy*, V, 490.

54. Joad F. Normano, *The Spirit of Russian Economics* (New York, 1945), pp. 71ff.; and M.M. Filonenko, "Graf S. Yu. Witte i S-Peterburhskii politekhnicheskii institut," *Yubileinyi sbornik*, ed. A.A. Stakhovich and E.A. Vechorin (Paris, 1952), p. 60. On the general tendency of Russian science to concentrate on pure or abstract fields as opposed to applied fields, see Loren R. Graham, *The Soviet Academy of Sciences and the Communist Party, 1927-1932* (Princeton, 1967), pp. 3-14.

55. S. Yu. Witte, *Vospominaniia, Tsarstvoyanie Mikolaia II* (Moscow, 1922), I, 209-211; Von Laue, *Sergei Witte*, p. 207; and speech by Peter Struve (originally made in 1927) included in *Yubileinyi sbornik*, pp. 12-13.

56. Witte, *Vospominaniia*, I, 209-211; Speech by V.B. Eliashevich, *Yubileinyi sbornik*, pp. 19ff.; and Von Laue, *Sergei Witte*, p. 207.

57. "Vospominaniia G.K. Fediaevskago: Ekonomista 1-go priema 1902 g.," *Yubileinyi sbornik*, pp. 82-94.

58. On the remarkable work of Dmitriev as well as his even more extraordinary reappearance from obscurity in Soviet literature, see: Alec Nove and Alfred Zauberman, "A Resurrected Russian Economist of 1900," *Soviet Studies*, XII (July, 1961), pp. 96-101; Alfred Zauberman, "A Few Remarks on a Discovery in Soviet Economics," *Bulletin of the Oxford University Institute of Statistics*, XXIV (November, 1962), pp. 437-45; Alfred Zauberman, *Aspects of Planometrics* (New Haven, 1967), Chapter 5: "Link-up with Russian Economic Thought of the Early 1900's," pp. 47-58; and M.C. Kaser, "The Nature of Soviet Planning; A Critique of Jasny's Appraisal," *Soviet Studies*, XIV (October, 1962), 109-131.

59. For a more detailed discussion of these debates see Guroff, "The State and Industrialization in Russian Economic Thought," pp. 96-242.

60. V.P. Litvinov-Falinskii, *Nashe ekonomicheskoe polozhenie i zadachi budushchago* (St. Petersburg, 1908), pp. 142ff; A. Manuilov, "Industrializm i russke-germanskii torgovlyi dogover," *Russkie Vedomosti*, no. 52 (March 3, 1912), p. 2; P.P. Riabushinskii's speech to the Eighth Congress of the Association of Industry and Trade, published in *Promyshlennost i Torgovlia*, no. 11 (155), (June 1, 1914), pp. 564ff., and commented on in "S'ezd prodstavitelei torgovli i promyshlennosti," *RV*, no. 101 (May 3, 1914), p. 4; L. Kafengauz, "Nasha promyshlennosti i voina," *RV*, no. 171 (July 26, 1914), p. 2; K.T. Plitsyn, "Voprosy promyshlennago razvitiia Rossii," *IREM*, III, Part 1, 281; and Roosa, "The Association of Industry and Trade," pp. 173ff., 303.

61. On the growth of syndicates and the government's relation to them, see P.V. Kamenskii, *Znachenie torgovo-promyshlennykh trestov na zapade i u nas* (Moscow, 1909); Ya. I. Livshin, *Monopelii v ekonomike Rossii* (Moscow, 1961); E.S. Lur'e, *Organizataiia i organizatsii torgovo-promysalennykh interesov v Rossii* (St. Petersburg, 1913); and G. Tsyperovich, *Sindikaty i tresty v Rossii* (Moscow, 1919).

62. N.S. Zhukov, "Burzhuaznye teorii imperializma," *IREM*, III, Part 1, 325-45; "Russko-Germanskii dogover i promyshlennyia organizatsii," *Russkie Vedomosti*, no. 32 (February 8, 1914), p. 4; and for the views of Timirazev, former Minister of Trade and Industry and a leader of the Association of Industry and Trade, see "Gosudarstvennaia duma, zasedanic 13-ogo marta, dnevnoe zasedanic," *Russkie Vedomosti*, no. 60 (March 14, 1909), p. 3.

63. *Monopolii v metallurgicheskoi promyshlennosti Rossii, 1900-1917: Dokumenty i materialy* (Leningrad, 1963), pp. 117-588; L. Kafengauz, "Ditia nuzhdy," *Russkie Vedomosti*, no. 300 (December 30, 1911), p. 4; A. Trainin, "Pravitel'stvo i sindikaty," *RV*, no. 93 (April 23, 1913), p. 6; and "Editorial," *RV*, no. 105 (May 8, 1913), p. 1.

64. Roosa, "The Association of Industry and Trade," pp. 280-83.

65. V.V. Oreshkin, "Voprosy imperializma i sotsializma," *IREM*, III, Part 1, 122.

66. L. Yasnopol'skii, "Novaia rospis i clementy polozhitel'noi ekononichaskoi programmy," *Russkie Vedomosti*, no. 261 (November 13, 1909), p. 2, lamented that "we do not have up to now a concrete systematic plan of economic policy." N. Fridman, "Opyt finansovoi programmy," *RV*, no. 126 (June 4, 1909), pp. 1-2; K. Golovin, "Budto ne za chto priniat'sia," *Ekonomist Rossii*, no. 10 (1909), pp. 6-9; and Roosa, "The Association of Industry and Trade," pp. 263-309, esp. 270-88.

67. Roosa, "The Association of Industry and Trade," pp. 236-309.

68. N.P. Petrov, "Kritika sovremennago ekonomicheskago stroia," *Novyi Ekonomist*, nos. 1-2 (January 11, 1914), pp. 7-9; no. 4 (January 25, 1914), pp. 7-9; and nos. 8-9 (March 1, 1914), pp. 4-6.

69. A similar interpretation of the vagueness of the terms used in the social-democratic platform is expressed by Bobrowski, *Formation du Système Sovietique*, p. 16.

70. N.P. Petrov, "Kritika sovremennago ekonomicheskago stroia," *NE*, nos. 8-9 (March 1, 1914), pp. 5-6.

71. N.K. Karataev, "Teoriia 'Gosudarstvennego sotsializma'," *IREM*, II, Part 1, 151ff.; Kamenskii, *Znachenic torgove-promyshlennykh trestov*, pp. 1-10; I. Kh. Ozerov, "Yanzhul, Ivan Ivanovich," *Broksauz-Efron* (St. Petersburg, 1904), XXCII, 667-69; and I.I. Yanzhul, "Bismark i gosudarstvennyi sotsializm," *Vestnik Evropy*, no. 8 (1890), pp. 728-30.

72. *I. Kh.* Ozeroff, *Problèmes economiques et financiers de la Russie moderne* (Paris, 1916), p. 126; Roosa, "The Association of Industry and Trade," pp. 475ff.; and Editorial, *Russkie Vedomosti*, no. 100 (May 1, 1914), p. 1.

73. Karataev, "Teoriia 'Gosudarstvennogo sotsializma'," *IREM*, II, Part 1, 164; Roosa, "The Association of Industry and Trade," pp. 203-11; "Izo dnia v den," *Russkie Vedomosti*, no. 160 (July 12, 1913), p. 1; "Torgovo-promyshlennyi s'ezd," *RV*, no. 103 (May 6, 1914), pp. 2-3; *Promyshlennost i Torgovlia*, no. 11 (155) (June 1, 1914), pp. 564ff.; and P.P. Migulin, "Kogda zhe novyi poriadok?" *Novyi Ekonomist*, no. 26 (June 28, 1914), pp. 3-6.

74. "Russian Industries and the War," *The Russian Review*, I, 1 (February, 1916), 108-10. The best sources on the War-Industries Committees are: *Izvestiia Tsentral'nago Voenno-promyshlennago Komiteta*, nos. 1-300 (Petrograd, August 24, 1915-July 25, 1918); *Promyshlennost i Torgovlia*, 1915-1918; Semon G. Zagorsky, *State Control of Industry in Russia during the War* (New Haven, 1928), esp. pp. 82ff.; and L. Lesinskii, *Ekonomicheskaia politika Vremennogo pravitel'stva* (Leningrad, 1929).

75. Lozinskii, *Ekonomicheskaia politika Vromennogo pravitel'stva*, pp. 51ff.

76. The debate which has been carried on in Soviet literature concerns the

nature of Bolshevik policies before the official adoption of War-Communism. Several Soviet scholars have argued that Lenin's intention immediately following the Revolution was to introduce a program similar to the later NEP and that after some early attempts he was forced to move toward War-Communism because of the pressures of the Civil War. For an elaboration of this position see I.A. Gladkov, *Ocherki Sovetskoi ekonomiki: 1917-1920gg* (Moscow, 1956), pp. 136ff. For the most recent Soviet exchange on this topic see: E.B. Genkina, "K voprosu o leninskom obosnovanii novoi ekonomicheskoi politiki," *Voprosy istorii KPSS*, no. 1 (1967), pp. 58-70; V.I. Kuzmin, "Novaia ekonomicheskaia politika smychka sotsialisticheskoi promyshlennosti s melkokrestianskim khoziastvom," *ViKPSS;* " 'Voennogo kommunizma' k novoi ekonomicheskoi politike," *ViKPSS*, no. 3 (1967), pp. 66-72; R.M. Savitskaia, "V.I. Lenin i izpol'zovanie gosudarstvennogo kapitalizma v period mirnoi peredishki 1918 g.," *ViKPSS*, no. 3 (1967), pp. 57-66; and E.I. Beliantsev, "Nekotorye zamechanii k obsuzhdeniiu problem novoi ekonomicheskoi politiki," *ViKPSS*, no. 5 (1967), pp. 51-52.

77. Leonard Schapiro, *The Communist Party of the Soviet Union* (New York, 1960), pp. 190-91; V.P. Miliutin, *Sovremennoe ekonomicheskoe razvitie Rossii i diktatura proletariata* (Moscow, 1918), pp. 59ff.; I. Stepanov /Skvortsov/, *Ot rabochego kontrolla k rabochemu upravleniiu v promyshlennosti i zemledenii* (Moscow, 1918).

78. Carr, *The Bolshevik Revolution*, II, 185-90; M. Sobolev, "Ocherednye zadachi ekonomicheskoi politiki," *Ekonomicheskaia Zhizn*, no. 29 (February 8, 1919), p. 1; G. Lakin, "O gosudarstvennoi bukhgalterii," *EZ*, no. 68 (March 26, 1919), p. 1; F. Fokht, "Znachenie schetovodstva v voprosakh khoziastvennoi zhizni strany," *EZ*, no. 68 (March 29, 1919), p. 1. The Soviets were extremely concerned by the shortage of bookkeepers and clerical workers as is indicated by a series of articles.

79. Lenin, "The Immediate Tasks of the Soviet Government . . .," in Daniels, *A Documentary History of Communism*, I, 147-48.

80. Nikolai Valentinov-Volskii, "The Origins of NEP" (unpublished manuscript, Hoover Institution), pp. 63-70, 87ff.; M.C. Kaser, "The Nature of Soviet Planning: A Critique of Jasny's Appraisal," *Soviet Studies*, XIV (October, 1962), 109-31; and Rudolph Schlesinger, "A Note on the Context of Early Soviet Planning," *Soviet Studies*, XVI (July, 1964), 22-44. As late as April 1921, when Gosplan was established, only seven of the thirty-four technical and administrative personnel were Communists. See Z.K. Zvezdin, "Iz istorii deiatel'nosti Gosplana v 1921-1924gg.," *ViKPSS*, no. 3 (1967), pp. 45-56.

81. Miliutin, *Sovremennoe ekonomicheskoe razvitie Rossii*, pp. 58ff. See also Lorenz, *Anfänge der Bolschewistischen Industriepolitik*, and Carr, *The Bolshevik Revolution*, II, 81ff. and 185ff.

82. Carr, *The Bolshevik Revolution*, II, 176-99.

83. On GOELRO see V.S. Kulebakin, ed., *Trudy GOELRO: Dokumenty i materialy* (Moscow, 1960); I.A. Gladkov, ed., *K istorii plana elektrifikatsii Sovetskoi strany. Sbornik dokumentov i materialov. 1918-1920gg.* (Moscow, 1952); I.

Stepanov/Skvortsov/, *Elektrifikatsiia R.S.F.S.R. v sviazi s perekhodnoi fazoi microvogo khoziastva* (Moscow, 1922); and Professor K.A. Krug, *Programma rabot po elektrifikatsii Rossii* (Moscow, 1920).

84. On the concept of regionalism, see R.W. Davies, "The Decentralization of Industry: Some Notes on the Background," *Soviet Studies*, IX (April, 1958), 353-67; *Ekonomicheskoe raionirovanie Rossii: Materialy podkommissii po raionirovaniiu pri Gosplana* (Moscow, 1921); and G. Krzhizhanovskii, *Voprosy ekonomicheskogo raionirovaniia SSSR* (Moscow, 1957).

85. See for example: A Kaktyn, *Edinyi khoziastvennyi plan i ediny khoziastvennyi tsentr* (Moscow, 1920); Yu. Larin and L. Kritsman, *Ocherki khoziastvennoi zhizni i organizatsiia narodnogo khoziastva Sovetskoi Rossii, 1 noiabria 1917-1 iiulia 1920g.* (Moscow, 1920); Carr, *The Bolshevik Revolution*, II, 358-80; and S.N. Gusev, *Edinyi khoziastvennyi plan i edinyi khoziastvennyi apparat* (Moscow, 1920), esp. pp. 22-28.

86. Abram Bergson, *The Economics of Soviet Planning* (New Haven, 1964), esp. pp. 173ff., and E.H. Carr, "Some Random Reflections on Soviet Industrialization," *Socialism, Capitalism and Economic Growth: Essays Presented to Maurice Dobb*, ed. C.H. Feinstein (Cambridge, 1967), pp. 271-84, esp. p. 282.

87. See, for example, the works of Zaleskii, *Planification*, and Bobrowski, *Formation du Système Sovietique*, esp. "Le Communisme de guerre et les premiers essais de Planification," pp. 21ff.

88. Henry Rosovsky, ed. *Industrialization in Two Systems: Essays in Honor of Alexander Gerschenkron by a Group of his Students* (New York, 1966), p. 155.

89. Some scholars have mentioned Grinevetskii as the father of Soviet economic planning without any explanation or elaboration. See, e.g., Nicholas Timasheff, *The Great Retreat: The Growth and Decline of Communism in Russia* (New York, 1946), pp. 120-21, and S.V. Utechin, "The Bolsheviks and Their Allies after 1917: The Ideological Perspective," *Soviet Studies*, X (October, 1958), 127. Recently there has been an attempt by Leon Smolinski to rescue Grinevetskii from obscurity: "Grinevetskii and Soviet Industrialization," *Survey*, no. 67 (April, 1968), pp. 100-115, and "A Rejoinder," *Survey*, nos. 70-71 (Winter-Spring, 1969), pp. 172-77.

90. *Bolshaia Sovetskaia Entsiklopedia*, 1st ed., XIX, 391-93, and *BSE*, 2nd ed., XII, 618. Although the biographical details are approximately the same in the two editions, the second edition carries no mention of Grinevetskii's views on the economy. The article in the second edition summarizes the article in the first by S. Soloviev on Grinevetskii's life, but completely excludes the second article by L. Ziman on Grinevetskii's economic views.

91. *BSE*, 1st ed., XIX, 391-93, and *BSE*, 2nd ed., XII, 618.

92. *Russkie Vedomosti*, no. 155 (July 7, 1915), p. 4.

93. V.I. Grinevetskii, *Poslevoennye perspektivy russkoi promyshlennosti*, 1st ed., (Kharkov, 1919), "Ot avtora," p. 2.

94. *BSE*, 1st ed., vol.˙XIX, p. 392, and V. Sarabianov, "Predislovie," in Grinevetskii, *Poslevoennye perspektivy*, 2nd ed., (Moscow, 1922), p. ii.

95. An extremely laudatory obituary appeared in *Ekonomicheskaia Zhizn*, despite the fact that Grinevetskii had condemned the Bolshevik regime and fled from Moscow. See Mikh. Vindelbot, "Pamiati prof. V.I. Grinevetskogo," *EZ*, no. 99 (May 10, 1919), p. 1.

96. Lubov Krassin, *Leonid Krassin: His Life and Work* (London, n.d.), pp. 41-45.

97. See Nikolai Valentinov-Volskii, "The Origins of NEP," Part II, esp. p. 128. This memoir is a major source on the internal workings of the Soviet economic bureaucracy during the 1920s. The original Russian version is in the process of being published by the Hoover Institution under the supervision of Professor Bertram D. Wolfe. An English translation is currently being prepared by myself and Mr. Randell Magee.

98. Ibid., pp. 128-29.

99. Ibid., and Nicholas Timasheff, *The Great Retreat*, pp. 120-21.

100. Sarabianov, "Predislovie," in Grinevetskii, *Poslevoennye perspektivy*, 2nd ed., pp. ii-111. Karl Ballod, born in 1864 in Latvia, studied and taught economics in Germany and Latvia. In 1898, using the pseudonym "Atlanticus," he published his major work on the feasibility of a socialist economy arising in Germany. In 1906 the book was translated into Russian as *Gosudarstvo budushchago: proizvodstvo i protreblenie v sotsial'nom gosudarstve*, with an introduction by Karl Kautsky. The Russian edition was translated by A. Grodzinskii, and edited and introduced by M.V. Bernatskii, a member of the economics faculty of St. Petersburg Polytechnical Institute. A second edition appeared in 1920 published by *Tsentrosoiuz*. Ballod argued that "In any case, the whole social organism must depend on some sort of central power, which would guide and constantly regulate production by a uniform plan, corresponding to societal needs." (p. 156) Ballod also argued that if labor and supplies were used systematically, then income could be doubled or even tripled. This type of regular (*planomernaia*) economic work, he pointed out, can only occur under socialism. (p. ii, introduction by M.V. Bernatskii).

For biographical details see *BSE* (Moscow, 1926), IV, 540. There is no mention of Ballod in the second edition of the Encyclopedia. Valentinov writes in his memoirs:

"The first attempt to present statistically the socialist transformation of a country was done by Atlanticus [The German Professor Ballod] in his book, "Gosudarstvo budushchago," written in the latter half of the 1890s. Operating with figures and all sorts of calculations, he attempted to present the sort of quantity of change that would have to be undergone under socialism in all branches of the national economy of Germany from industry to transport. The book of Atlanticus, which is very dry, composed almost completely of figures, was greeted in the socialist world with respect. Before it, nor for 25 years after his book, no one studied such a category as 'perspective plans'." (Valentinov, "Origins of NEP," Part II, p. 105.)

101. Sarabianov, "Predislovie," in Grinevetskii, *Poslevoennye perspektivy*, 2nd ed., pp. ii-v.

102. Grinevetskii, *Poslevoennye perspektivy*, 2nd ed., pp. 1-2, 32-41, 54-68.

103. Ibid., pp. 23-33, 69-76, 99-102.

104. Ibid., p. 101.

105. Ibid., p. 100. This is given great emphasis in V. Sarabianov's introduction, p. ii.

106. Isaac Deutscher, *The Prophet Unarmed: Trotsky, 1921-1929*, II (New York, 1959), pp. 208ff., and Valentinov, "Origins of NEP," Part II, p. 160.

107. Valentinov, "Origins of NEP," Part II, p. 160.

108. Ibid., pp. 186-87.

109. Ibid., p. 130.

110. For the details of economic policy during this period see E.H. Carr, *The History of the Soviet Union: The Bolshevik Revolution, 1917-1923*, II, 296-316, 358-80, and *The Interregnum, 1923-1924*, IV, 11-160; and Dobb, *Soviet Economic Development*, pp. 125-207.

111. V.I. Lenin, "Doklad o taktike RKP 5 iiulia," *PSS*, (Moscow, 1964), XXXIV, 51.

112. Z.K. Zvezdin, "Iz istorii deiatel'nosti Gosplana v 1921-1924gg.," *ViKPSS*, no. 3 (1967), pp. 45-56.

113. The major sources for Soviet economic thought during this period are the daily, *Ekonomicheskaia Zhizn*; the journals, *Planovoe Khoziastvo* and *Vestnik Kommunisticheskogo akademii*; and *Trudy Tsentral'nogo Statisticheskogo Upravlenii*. An excellent selection of translated articles from this period are contained in Nicholas Spulber, *Foundations of Soviet Strategy for Economic Growth: Selected Soviet Essays, 1924-1930* (Bloomington, 1964). Also see F. Pollock, *Die planwirtschaftlichen Versuche in der Sowjetunion, 1917-1927* (Leipzig, 1929), and Zaleskii, *Planification*.

114. See for example V. Bazarov, *K metodologii perspektivnogo planirovaniia* (Moscow, 1924). Also see Bobrowski, *Formation du Système Sovietique de Planification*, and A. Kaufman, "The Origins of the Political Economy of Socialism," *Soviet Studies*, IV, (January, 1952), 243-72.

115. For example see R.W. Davies, "Aspects of Soviet Investment Policy in the 1920s," in Feinstein, ed., *Socialism, Capitalism and Economic Growth*, pp. 285-307.

116. For details of the debate, see Alexander Ehrlich, *The Soviet Industrialization Debate, 1924-1928* (Cambridge, 1960).

Part IV
Lenin,
Myth and Cult

12 Krupskaya: The Femine Subcult

ROBERT H. MCNEAL

A year before the centennial of Lenin's birth there was a kindred event, the centennial of Nadezhda Konstantinovna Krupskaya. To be sure, the celebration of this occasion did not come close to the scale, or redundancy, of her slightly younger husband's hundredth birthday. This is in keeping with the normal relationship of her relatively modest image to that of Lenin. There has never been any doubt that her glory is essentially reflected. It is, however, clear that the protracted, didactic veneration of Krupskaya is one of the institutions of Soviet culture, and one that has received scant attention in western scholarship. It is true that this cult has never been represented by some of the familiar artifacts of the male cults—probably a significant sign of male chauvinism. There are no cities named for Krupskaya, no institutional names excepting pedagogical ones, no monumental statuary, few public portraits, and no grave in the second-rank row behind Lenin, which includes the remains of even the mediocre Kalinin. On the other hand, it is probably true that no other Soviet political figure except Lenin has a larger body of published collected writings than Krupskaya, whose centennial celebration included the publication of a bibliography 528 pages long, listing 3943 separate items that she wrote, many of which appeared in numerous editions.[1] It also listed 1173 works about her, which is not in a class with the hagiographic literature about Lenin (or Stalin, formerly), but is probably ahead of any other Soviet political figure and certainly an indication of a special place in the Soviet pantheon.

Just what kind of place this has been has varied over the past half-century, and this chapter will attempt to sketch this development, with its fluctuations. The basis of Krupskaya's status is her valid claim to have been the first Leninist, and by implication the founder of the cult of Lenin. With her marriage to Lenin in 1898 she began a lifelong devotion to the promoting of his interests and image in the revolutionary movement. In the prerevolutionary years this task was performed discreetly but effectively as Lenin's secretary. In her continuous stream of Party letters, of which about 500 have been published, with more in Soviet archives, she established herself as Lenin's most effective advocate. With only moderate reference to his name or quotation from his writings she projected to the comrades, especially in the Russian underground, the profound conviction of his rightness, thus laying the basis for his and her own future claim to greatness.

During 1917 Krupskaya did little to further enhance her status, but she did

219

write a significant article entitled "Stranichka iz istorii Rossiiskoi Sotsial-Demokraticheskoi Rabochei Partii" ("A Page from the History of the Russian Social-Democratic Labor Party").[2] It was a short work, not especially prominent in its day, which is nevertheless remarkable for its anticipation of the next fifty years of Leninist historiography. At each step of the way from 1897 to 1917 Krupskaya portrayed Lenin's struggle against the deviators. While she herself does not appear in the narrative, it was a significant exercise in the creation of the Lenin image, and her right to this function.

After the October Revolution Krupskaya assumed the formal ceremonial role of wife of the head of state, in a properly socialist style. While never having to endure state banquets or other such traditional affairs, she was visible with Lenin on such occasions as May Day and military reviews. Most particularly she took a trip on the Volga and Kama rivers in 1919 as the main object of interest on an "agitation steamboat."[3] Stopping along the waterways for propaganda displays, she was repeatedly called from her stateroom (where she was supposed to be resting on doctor's orders) to appear before the masses. That Krupskaya, for all her well publicized modesty, accepted this role with some real satisfaction, is revealed in a letter from the steamer to her old friend Zinaida Krizhanovskaya. "I try to rest," she wrote, but "they send me a note from the transport workers: 'let her only say two words, and if she can't speak to us, let her only show herself.' Well, one has to go and speak."[4]

But possibly more important than this kind of ceremonial appearance or her real public service in the People's Commissariat of Education in these years was the unpublicized and unintended emergence of the idea that Krupskaya was an intercessor for those in dire straits, that she was Lenin's alter ego, but more yielding to supplication. Lenin himself seems to have accepted this idea. In a letter to Krupskaya while she was on the steamer, he wrote, "I read the letters asking for help that sometimes come for you and try to do what I can."[5] None of these appeals have been published, but a few surviving notes in Lenin's works convey the character of such cases. In one Krupskaya persuaded her husband to suggest to the Cheka that they release an aged professor of geology, whose daughter had appealed to Krupskaya, whom she had known in the 1890s. Although neither the professor nor his daughter had ever been close friends of Krupskaya, she was willing to convince her husband that the man had been "honorable."[6]

In another instance Lenin was induced by his wife to instruct the chairman of the Tambov *guberniia ispolkom* to arrange for the welfare of an old woman and her daughter who were in danger of starvation and apparently had appealed to Krupskaya, who had once been acquainted with them, slightly.[7] Even though the number of such cases may have been modest, the myth of Krupskaya the intercessor was born, more as folklore than as any intention of the authorities.

The death of Vladimir Ilyich posed new problems for both the authorities and Krupskaya concerning her public image. It is clear that she felt it her duty to assume the role of supreme custodian of the Lenin myth. There is a distinctly possessive character of her approach to the situation, which soon led her to comment adversely on the efforts of various writers, painters and actors to portray the departed hero of the revolution.[8] This was based partly on purely personal feelings rooted in twenty-five years of devotion to Lenin and at least partly on a realization of the political importance of controlling the image of Lenin. This was clearly a consideration at his funeral, which Krupskaya recognized for the major political event that it was, using the occasion to establish her claim as prime custodian of the myth. Eliena Krylenko, who passed by the coffin in the Dom Soiuzov, wrote to her husband, Max Eastman, "And his wife is standing there, looking at his face. She is standing there all the time. Nobody can replace her." The representatives of the Central Committee, on the other hand, were changed every ten minutes.[9] If this was somewhat exceptional conduct for the widow of the chief of state, it was even more notable that she delivered a eulogy at the funeral session of the Congress of Soviets.[10] While not imposing to read, we may believe the numerous Soviet memoirists who have recalled that, in the circumstances, it had the greatest emotional impact of all the eulogies. What is more significant is that we have good reason to think that Krupskaya had intended to use the occasion to deliver her own version of Lenin's testament, not the still-secret political advice that he had dictated a year before his death, but a ceremonial incantation that would establish her authority over the myth of Lenin. Only in 1960 did the party authorities publish, without explanation, the manuscript of an impressive litany entitled "Lenin," consisting of nine short statements of his achievements ("Lenin was the closest friend of the men and women workers, men and women peasants, the friend of all toilers.") and eight shorter statements of Lenin's departing behests ("Lenin bequeathed [the command] to gather more closely around the Communist Party.").[11] The resemblance of this document to Stalin's famous funeral speech is striking and strongly suggests that he and Krupskaya were in close competition for the role of high priest of the cult, and that he succeeded in winning for himself the right to deliver the only incantation of this sort at the time of the funeral.

Despite the rivalry of Stalin and others in the veneration and interpretation of Lenin's heritage, Krupskaya did assume a revered status as his widow. In the mid-twenties she was busy receiving formal delegations and addressing meetings, and as early as March 1924, she lectured on "How to Study Leninism," the first of her many efforts to establish her authority in this sensitive matter.[12] The following month her first memoir-article on Lenin appeared, beginning a stream of recollections, some of which were collected to form a small anthology entitled *Vospominaniia (Memoirs)* [sic] in 1926, which was reproduced with additions as the better known *Vospominaniia o Lenine (Memories of Lenin)* in 1930. While modest in tone, this famous work left no doubt concerning Krupskaya's intimate political comradeship with Lenin and in its many editions provided the most compelling argument for her own association with the cult of Lenin.

As long as she was politically associated with the opposition, however, her status was somewhat in doubt. At the Fourteenth Party Congress in 1925 her sister-in-law, Mariia, who was a Bukharin supporter, implicitly but plainly challenged Krupskaya's right to be the authoritative interpreter of Lenin's legacy.[13] According to the popular and plausible story, it was about a year later that Stalin threatened to appoint somebody else as Lenin's widow. A concurrent rumor campaign concerning Lenin's amorous life posed a very real threat in this direction. The decline in Trotsky's public stature clearly demonstrated the potential for demythologizing heroic figures of the era of Lenin, and around 1926 Krupskaya's future image was very much in doubt.

Her decision to abandon Trotsky and the united opposition in November 1926 averted this danger. From that time until the end of her life she was one of the most widely publicized and published figures in the Soviet Union. There was no lack of formal, ceremonial honors, including the Order of Lenin, election to the Supreme Soviet and its presidium, to the Central Committee of the Party, and to the Academy of Sciences. Her sixtieth birthday in 1929 and sixty-fifth in 1934 were celebrated with the fanfare of ceremonial meetings and speeches by various dignitaries (not including Stalin, however). Characteristically she refused to attend the first of these on grounds of modesty until the organizers of the affair mobilized the Young Pioneers to beg her to come. This she could not refuse, for by this time Krupskaya had become the universal maternal figure of Soviet Russia. "I was always very sad that I did not have children," she said, "but now I am not sad. Now I have many of them—Komsomols and Young Pioneers. All of them are Leninists, they want to be like Leninists."[14] She was often depicted meeting Young Pioneers and carried on a substantial correspondence with them, some of which was widely published as a popular book.[15]

With this image it was natural that Krupskaya should also be the patroness of Soviet women and two traditionally female occupations, school-teaching and librarianship, both of which were linked to her professional interests. In an era when traditional sexual and family mores were being restored in the Soviet Union, she was a suitable model. She had never been a radical advocate of female emancipation and regarded school teaching as a natural occupation for women because they have the natural vocation of childrearing. To be sure, she favored day care for children and the alleviation of chores of homemaking for working wives, but she was far from opposing the family and consistently represented Lenin as a paternal figure, with a fondness for other people's children.

As the mother of her people, it seems that Krupskaya continued to be regarded by many as a possible intercessor on behalf of those persecuted by the authorities, although Soviet publications treat this question with such discretion that almost no firm evidence is available. However, her personal secretary does recall that she received four or five hundred letters a day, often addressed simply to "Lenin's wife," or "Grandma Krupskaya" or "Moscow, the Court of the RSFSR, Chairman of personal affairs Krupskaya."[16] There was of course no such office, and Krupskaya never occupied any position in the judicial field, but it seems clear that the myth of Lenin's wife as intercessor was widely held among the common folk. This is also borne out by a supposedly popular poem quoted by her biographers:

We go to thee
With grief and tears.
Thou meetest us with tenderness.
We are warmed by thy tenderness.
We will not forget those kindly eyes.[17]

It is doubtful, however, that Krupskaya could do much for those who suffered in Stalin's era. Her principal biographers write: "It was unbearable pain [for her] to see how many honorable and devoted leaders of the party and people were shot. Krupskaya had been linked with some of them even in the period of the preparation of the revolution, and then in Soviet times."[18] This was not only a question of her physical helplessness before the authorities. It was also a question of her own status and the accommodation that she apparently made with Stalin when she left the opposition. I doubt that any formal agreement was ever undertaken, but it seems that both parties understood its terms. Stalin was content to see Krupskaya occupy a revered position as mother of her country and to share with her the role of chief propagator of the cult of Lenin, providing that she left to him the authority to determine the specific content of Leninism in current politics. In return for this status Krupskaya was expected to link the names of Lenin and Stalin in her writings, which she began doing in the early thirties, and to publicly praise the achievements of the state.[19] On one occasion this meant writing an article explicitly supporting the trial of her erstwhile friends Kamenev and Zinoviev.[20] The cult of Krupskaya was a great asset to Stalin in the thirties. As Lenin's most intimate comrade, who presumably could interpret his teachings better than anyone else (except perhaps Stalin), Krupskaya and her cult legitimized Stalin as "the Lenin of today."

As long as Krupskaya lived, both she and Stalin continued to accept this arrangement. Her seventieth birthday, falling on February 26, 1939, was intended to be a major affair, with tributes in print and speech at solemn meetings in her honor. While much of this did reach the press, the celebration was curtailed, because Krupskaya in fact lay dying in a sanatorium near Moscow. Even on her death bed she told the doctors that she was determined to attend the Eighteenth Party Congress, which no doubt would have given her a suitable reception. But she died on the 27th, and ceremonial reverences that had been intended for her birthday became her eulogies. The pomp and solemnity of this ritual was second only to Lenin's and Stalin's in Soviet history. Stalin led the procession of mourners, although he did not see fit to deliver a eulogy.

This may have been because he had already determined to diminish the cult of Lenin and nearly extinguish its femine subcult. We know from a Party decision of 1956 that as early as 1938 the Politburo had resolved to curtail publication about Lenin,[21] and it was reported at the Congress of Soviet historians in 1962 that just after her death the order went out, "Do not print another word about Krupskaya."[22] This order was fairly thoroughly carried out. Her memoirs of Lenin, so widely disseminated in the thirties, went out of print, as did most of her writings. From 1940 to 1954 only two modest anthologies of her works, on education and pioneers, were published, as compared with twenty-six anthologies, not counting diverse editions, in the previous decade. None of her writings about Lenin, including some that were in manuscript when she died, were published in the period 1940-1953, although a few short works that did little for her image, such as the essay on "How to Read a Book on Your Own" were reissued. While Krupskaya certainly did not become an unperson, her image no longer seemed useful to Stalin, and it was deliberately neglected.

The deflation of the cult of Stalin brought a corresponding Krupskaya revival. Khrushchev's secret speech of 1956 and documents that were published afterwards laid the groundwork for this change by revealing Krupskaya's quarrel with Stalin during Lenin's final illness. The memory of Krupskaya filled an important need in Khrushchev's alleged restoration of Leninism. The demythologizing of Stalin left a shortage of first-rank comrades for Lenin, whom the party wished to portray as the dominant leader, but not in complete isolation. The revival of the stature of Sverdlov and Dzerzhinsky could fill this gap for 1917 and the next few years, but Krupskaya was also needed as an exemplar of the devoted Leninist over the whole of Lenin's active revolutionary career. She was especially helpful to legitimize the de-Stalinization campaign because of her own resistance to Stalin in 1922-1923, while her continued loyalty to the Party until her death implied that a true Leninist, like Khrushchev himself, was excused from any obligation to martyrdom during the thirties. Her restored status as a symbol of the spirit of the Party fit perfectly the main historical interpretation of the Stalin years, that the essential purity of Lenin's Party continued through the reign of Stalin, regardless of the regrettable accidents of that period. True, the question of the true Leninist's relations with the cult of personality was too sensitive to be treated fully or frankly with respect to both the living Khrushchev and the deceased Krupskaya. New editions of her writings from the thirties carefully excised her numerous tributes to Stalin's leadership, creating the incorrect impression that she had been able to evade this aspect of the civic duty of that time. For example, a passage in which she originally said, "When Lenin died his cause was carried on by his former helper in all things, Comrade Stalin . . . ," was changed to read "When Lenin died the Party carried on his cause."[23]

The revival of Krupskaya's writings about Lenin was a natural part of the reinflation of his cult. An expanded version of her memoirs was issued in 1957 and subsequent editions; a children's version appeared annually in new printings for at least a decade beginning in the same year; and two other anthologies of her miscellaneous writings, entitled *O Lenine (On Lenin)* and *Lenin i Partiia*

(*Lenin and the Party*) were soon published. Of all the commentators on the hero, she clearly had resumed preeminence. Of all Lenin's comrades, she alone was honored by a separate room in the Central Lenin Museum in Moscow.

Her own subcult flourished appropriately. Vera Dridzo, her long-time personal secretary, emerged from deep obscurity to direct the substantial work of the Institute of Marxism-Leninism in this connection, including publication of archival material from the Krupskaya files. Of the many writings about Krupskaya that have appeared in scholarly and popular form, the two most prominent are probably the anthologies of memoirs, entitled *Vospominaniia o N.K. Krupskoi (Memoirs concerning N.K. Krupskaya)* (1966) and *Riadom s Leninym (Next to Lenin)* (1969). In the present survey it is impossible to indicate much about the content of such literature. A good deal of it is piously vacuous. Some of it is quite revealing concerning various aspects of Lenin's or Krupskaya's lives. In general it elevates Krupskaya as much as possible and totally ignores such inconvenient questions as the opposition in the twenties. Occasionally it challenges credulity. For example, Fofanova, in whose apartment Lenin lived when he first returned to Petrograd in the fall of 1917, has recently recollected that Krupskaya joined her husband in this clandestine residence. While this is not intrinsically impossible, it is remarkable that Nadezhda Konstantinovna never thought to mention this in her own memoirs, which rarely if ever fail to note her presence at crucial moments.[24]

The largest body of post-Stalin publications concerning Krupskaya come from the educators, many of whom seem to have retained a real admiration for her throughout the later Stalin years and welcomed the chance to revive her prestige, which reflects well on their profession. Their fundamental work was the publication in 1957-1963 of her *Pedagogicheskie sochineniia (Pedagogical Works)* in eleven volumes, a major editorial task which was apparently performed with some haste, for the Krupskaya bibliography of 1969 shows quite a few omissions. At the beginning of this major flood of publications by and about Krupskaya as the patroness of education, Khrushchev no doubt had a special interest in it, for he was attempting to execute educational reforms under the label of "polytechnicism," which had been Krupskaya's name for her version of Marxian pedagogy. To be sure, her ideas in this area were not identical with Khrushchev's or with those of leading Soviet educators, but much of her pedagogical theorizing is vague enough to justify quite a variety of programs, and it is her moral authority more than specifics that is important.

Today, on the centennial of Lenin's birth, the status of his wife in Soviet official and popular mythology seems secure. Her role as a propagator of the Lenin cult guarantees her immortality in the foreseeable future. Even a revival of Stalin's glory would not require much change in her status. Her maternal image serves well in the unending efforts to reach and mold the young, and in general helps to humanize the regime. Her devotion to pedagogical work and her generally harmless ideas in this area make her an appealing exemplar for the educators.

Finally, in a country that professes devotion to the equality of the sexes, yet is unable to produce female public figures of any consequence, Krupskaya is the one woman who can be presented as a great historic figure.

Notes

1. *Nadezhda Konstantinovna Krupskaya. Bibliografiia trudov i literatury o zhizni i deiatel'nosti* (Moscow, 1969).
2. *Soldatskaia Pravda*, May 13/28, 1917, also *O Lenine* (1960), pp. 13-18.
3. Her journal of the trip is in her *Pedagogicheskie Sochineniia*, XI, 729-40.
4. Ibid., p. 187.
5. Lenin, *Polnoe Sobranie Sochinenii*, LV, 374.
6. Ibid., LIII, 139.
7. Ibid., LI, 278.
8. "Otzyvy N.K. Krupskoi na vospominaniia i biograficheskie materialy o V.I. Lenine," *Istoricheskii Arkhiv*, no. 2, (1957), pp. 24-40; "Otzyvy N.K. Krupskoi na Khudozhestvenye proizvedeniia o V.I. Lenine," *Istoricheskii Arkhiv*, no. 4 (1958), pp. 67-84.
9. Max Eastman, *Love and Revolution* (1964), p. 339.
10. *Pravda*, Jan. 27, 1924, also *O Lenine* (1960), pp. 19-20.
11. *O Lenine* (1960), 11-12. The date given is merely "1924," and a published photocopy offers no additional clues on the date or purpose. My hypothesis is that Krupskaya intended to deliver this to the funeral session of the Congress of Soviets, but the Politburo learned of this and forbade her to assume the implicit authority to announce Lenin's testamentary wishes, which could have led to the revelation of his political testament concerning his successors. However, it is possible that she came to this quasi-liturgical form in imitation of Stalin after his famous eulogy, and then decided against publication, or was forbidden to publish. However, it seems to me unlikely that Krupskaya would have deliberately imitated Stalin, whose style she despised.
12. *O Lenine*, (1960), pp. 353-58.
13. V. Dridzo, *N.K. Krupskaya* (1958), p. 95.
14. *XIV S'ezd Vsesoiuznoi Kommunisticheskoi Partii (B) Stenograficheskii Otchet.* (1926), p. 299.
15. *Perepiska s pionerami* (1932), p. 1934.
16. Dridzo, pp. 90-91.
17. S.M. Levidova and S.A. Pavlotskaia, *N.K. Krupskaya* (1960), p. 275.
18. Levidova and Pavlotskaia, p. 280.
19. The explicit references to Stalin are numerous but generally short and ceremonial rather than substantive statements worth citing in detail. The spirit of the thing may be illustrated by the title that she gave to one routine preachment of 1937: "The Cause of Lenin-Stalin Will Triumph in the Whole World," *Krest'ianka*, no. 7 (1937).

20. *Pravda*, Sept. 4, 1936.

21. *Spravochnik partiinogo rabotnika* (1957), p. 364.

22. *Vsesoiuznoe soveshchanie istorikov* (1964), p. 260.

23. Cf. Krupskaya, *Izbrannye pedagogicheskie sochineniia* (1955), p. 708, and *Pedagogicheskie sochineniia* (1959), v. 606.

24. *Riadom s Leninym*, p. 104.

13 Lenin and Soviet Mythology

JACOB MILLER

I began work on this chapter by collecting the Leniniana in forty Soviet newspapers issued during the last week of March 1970, to see how the myth was shaping in the final run-up to the centenary on April 22nd. The harvest was fairly plentiful, at several items per issue, but in another sense more meager than I had expected. There seemed to be no conviction in any of it, however hard I tried to put myself in the shoes of the readers, the writers, and the organizers. There is no point in working on Soviet ideology without the utmost effort of sympathetic imagination to sit with its producers and consumers and share all their different backgrounds and current experiences, needs and responsibilities. In the first weekend of April, I was going through my notes, gloomily wondering whether the apparent emptiness of it all should be attributed entirely to the poverty of my sympathetic imagination, when news came of the removal from office of the four heads of Agit-Prop and the mass media. This cheered me up—perhaps without justification.

But the problem of apparent deadness remained. The *pafos*, or passion, as the Russians say, of the revolution and its more positive consequences is stored, in effect, in only two mythologies. One is that of traditional Russian nationalism, which is becoming increasingly extreme as the Marxist container becomes more empty. The other is built on the person of Lenin, and into this goes everything that is specifically of the revolution and the Soviet system, everything which is not appropriate to the older nationalist or chauvinist department. If the great centenary really was as broken-backed as the run-up seems to indicate, what are the implications for the Party, which has concentrated its Marxist legitimization increasingly in Lenin worship, and for the whole system?

I will return to this question in due course, but would first like to take a look at the nature of mythology, both in general and in its Soviet context, and the place of Lenin in Soviet mythology.

First, I define mythology as a reduction of truth to a form in which it can be held and handled. There could be a case for saying that objective truth, including scientific knowledge, especially at the frontiers of science, has a mythological element, in the sense that concepts are never adequate: the use of available concepts always implies some reduction. Fortunately, however, we are concerned here not with objective but with subjective truth, and in this we can be on firmer ground. There is subjective intuitive truth, such as emotional experience or

229

knowledge of another person's mood. We can leave that out also, because it is individual subjective truth, and not necessarily expressed in any way, whereas we are here concerned with social subjective truth, which has to be expressed because it is social. Let me give two examples of mythology as social subjective truth reduced to a form in which it can be held, handled and expressed.

The first was told by one of the founders of psychiatry, Jung, who was interested in primitive religion. He asked in an African village what myths, religious beliefs, etc., were current there, and was told by the villagers that they had none. He subsequently saw in the village a group of miniature huts, and asked about them. The villagers said that their ancestors lived there. But, said Jung, you told me you had no religious ideas or myths. Our ancestors, came the reply, are not myths, they are real and they do live in those huts.

My second example comes from Glasgow, three or four years after the Second World War, which brought great social changes to British industry in general and to the Clydeside shipbuilding industry in particular. An elderly man I met by chance and never saw again asked me whether I had heard about the young man who was given his cards (i.e., dismissed) in the local shipyard. I had not, so he told me what happened. Some retired foremen had been recalled to the shipyard. In prewar times a foreman never dismissed a man in words but just took off his bowler hat and dropped it. This is what one old foreman had done in the shipyard the other day. The young worker concerned, surprised, politely picked up the hat and handed it back to the foreman, who angrily told him what it meant. The young worker said he could take instructions only from the shop steward (the workers' representative on the job), and the latter tried to explain the new situation to the uncomprehending foreman. Fascinated by this juicy myth, I asked my informant whether any other incidents had occurred. Why yes, he said, exactly the same happened at another shipyard, but there the young worker kicked the bowler hat into the Clyde.

In the African case the relation of the community's present to its past is expressed not in historical or philosophical terms, or even in words, but in providing the huts and in rituals like supplying food. In the more sophisticated case, a most complex sociological and industrial development is expressed in narrative— the kind of stories that Clydeside people were telling each other in the pubs at that time. The fact that, objectively, the ancestors could not be living in those huts, while the incident of old foreman and young worker could have happened, is not a basic difference. Narrative myth will work and rework actual events and reorganize recollections for its purpose of accurate expression of subjective truth, just as it will invent completely when necessary for the same purpose. The condition to be satisfied is a story or history which accurately expresses a firmly held view, understanding or belief and which itself is circumstantially believed. Perhaps the Radio Erevan stories, and popular political jokes generally, could be regarded as a variant or analogy of political mythology: they fulfill a cognate *critical* function without the narrative being believed by anybody. However, for the purpose of this chapter there is no need to explore this general ground further or to propose any more definitions, except that a distinction is necessary between the managed elements of a mythology and the spontaneous elements.

If we say that mythology must be spontaneous, we exclude very much of the truth by which people live, and by which they can live because it is reduced by experts to a form in which they can hold and use it. The Old and New Testaments, by which a nation and a religion have lived, are among the better known examples of managed mythology; the material had to be written down and edited at various stages and selected for canonical inclusion. There is a very large element of managed myth in modern popular and school histories, though more in the totalitarian than the democratic countries. The question relevant to our present subject is the relationship of Soviet managed mythology to the need of Soviet citizens, in their capacity of human beings, for a truth by which to live. Apart from traditional religion, political jokes, and the higher literary levels of *samizdat*, what social nourishment for the soul exists in the USSR? More specifically, what part does Lenin play? Is the managed mythology of Lenin as irrelevant to subjective truth as it looks to the outsider? And in spontaneous, unmanaged mythology, does Lenin live in his little hut, helping somehow in social change?

My topic is of the kind that compels questions to be asked which cannot be answered. All I can do is to offer some more or less relevant personal observations and recollections.

I was in Russia on the centenary of Pushkin's death in 1937. Although I had been there for nearly a year, I was amazed at the time given to the Pushkin campaign, particularly on the radio and in the schools. But I was also surprised that it had so much real meaning for people. Perhaps this was because they loved Pushkin's poetry, which was so different from the actual nightmare of that year. I have looked up *Pravda* of the period and find that its Pushkiniana of 1937 carries distinctly more conviction than its Leniniana of 1970. Its five-week run-up (interrupted by the Radek trial) to the centenary on February 10, 1937, is basically dignified, informative, and pleasant. Reading these items now, incidentally, makes an impression quite different from my memory of an overwhelmingly incessant and reiterative Pushkin campaign: either memory errs or the press is only a pale reflection of the other arms of a campaign. The point I want to make here is that—comparing only one source, *Pravda*, in the two campaigns—Pushkin was alive in 1937 and Lenin is dead in 1970. If the managed mythology of Lenin is the flogging of a dead horse, that of Pushkin (insofar as *Pravda* departed from historical fact) served the celebration of him with a certain grace in its provision of information, drawings, pleasing critical essays, etc. The contrast between *Pravda*'s howls on the Radek trial during late January 1937 and the affectionate dignity of its Pushkin presentation is remarkable.

Even so, I would say that the political trials of that time were, as exercises in managed mythology, far more effective than the 1970 Lenin operation. But this comparison rests on possibly faulty memory of 1936-37 and an outsider's guesses on 1970, and may well be quite invalidated on various other grounds, in particular the context of extreme fear among intellectuals at that time, which gave belief a survival value, and the fact that many of my acquaintances were the relatively primitive "new men" of the time, whose own ideas, background and prospects genuinely fitted the trials' mythology. It is difficult to visualize any relevant section of Soviet society now, even the most unsophisticated, for whom an effective mythological function could be provided by such performances— except, possibly, the oldest among the present still active top 100,000, who are indeed the surviving New Men of the 1930s.

One of the themes in the Lenin centenary campaign was that of *khodoki*, emissaries of the people, coming to Lenin for advice, instruction, confidence. Yevtushenko published such a poem (*Khodoki k Leninu*) in 1964 but the centenary campaign produced more simple-minded examples. One such is a song published in the literary magazine *Pod'em*, January 1970, p. 173, which I translate roughly as:

> Collapsing to its knees, it seemed,
> Under the burden of its misery,
> Our country.
> But Lenin was in the world.
> He saw the way out of peril.
> Lenin the Wise.

> > Hungry, naked, barefoot,
> > From distant Volga and Oka,
> > From all the miles of all of Russia,
> > Came hurrying to him khodoki.

> And day and night to simple folk
> He gave himself utterly.
> And on Earth a miracle occurred—
> As in his prophecy.

> > Forever faithful to his will
> > We soared high up unto the Sun.
> > And after us the whole planet
> > Sends hurrying to him khodoki.

Anybody sufficiently interested and informed has to decide for himself whether the centenary managers effectively served some image of Lenin in people's minds and hearts by publishing material of this kind, or whether such material serves primarily the operation of the machine of management itself, in the sense that it exists and has to have a product. In view of the evidence for attention to modernization of political propaganda in the USSR during the 1960s the apparent ineptitude of the 1970 centenary campaign is unexpected.[1] The resistance even to slight modernization of propaganda content and method raises wider issues—as indeed does the resistance to slight modernization of the economic system. In both fields the gap between the needs of the country and the way in which the top people operate seems to be very great. In the field of propaganda, or more specifically mythology, there has been a reversal between the level of the rulers, who as a sociopolitical group have become less sophisticated, and that of the people, who have become more sophisticated. I find it difficult to imagine at a Party Congress in the early 1930s somebody reporting a conversation with Lenin held the night before, and the Congress acting on this, as happened in 1962. If we go further back, to the time of Lenin's death, his body was embalmed against the intentions of the leaders. Requests came from the provinces to postpone the funeral, and these turned into demands to embalm the body, demands so numerous and insistent that Moscow agreed. Perhaps in all this we have a hint of the Soviet malaise—the rulers (not the specialists or the practical administrators) have become more primitive and the ruled more sophisticated over the past fifty years.

I have attempted elsewhere to assess the factors in the Soviet ideological situation, comparing it to a theatre in which the entire audience sits on the stage.[2] I shall not cover the same ground here. Instead, I will try to answer the unanswerable questions posed above, about the managed and spontaneous aspects of the mythology of Lenin, by suggesting minimum conditions for their effectiveness, i.e., for them to constitute a genuine mythology.

1. Lenin's image must not lag behind the general development of the mental climate, the general educational and technical level of the country. This means that he must not now be presented as infallible. He was made infallible by Stalin in 1931 and this element of the managed mythology has since been strictly maintained (though it has been abandoned in respect of Stalin himself). Here perhaps we have a conflict between the needs of people for religion and the needs of people for mythology, in an advancing culture. One could easily demonstrate tendencies to make Lenin rather like Christ in some respects, but you cannot have the Son without the Father, and this indeed is one of the problems faced by the Lenin myth in Soviet ideology.

(I may add in parentheses that the problem need not be altogether insoluble: one could make a case—though a rather far-fetched one—for an emerging identity-relationship which is rather like the Trinity between Lenin the Son, Marx the Holy Ghost, and the Father as Marxism (in the sense of all-embracing, omnipotent and infallible Law, which the good obey and are saved while the bad disobey and are cast out), with at least two candidates for Satan as fallen angel (Trotsky and Mao). I make this suggestion seriously, in no spirit of disrespect for any person, religion or philosophical idea. But it is too late in the world's day to anthropomorphiże abstract relationships. The ideology department of the Central Committee, however much it might prefer a straight divinity, will not put more than its toe in this water, and it has neither the brains nor the respect for people and their needs that would enable it to do something more suitable for the modern mental climate. The founders of Christian theology were incomparably more open to pagan philosophies and people's needs.)

2. The managed mythology must serve and not bully the spontaneous mythology. If one accepts this condition for an effective mythology, there is no difficulty in developing the point. It obviously requires a relationship between rulers, specialists and ruled that is different from the relationship obtaining today in the USSR. It involves freedom of information and of expression, freedom for scholars to work and publish on Lenin and anything else worthy of research, and freedom for anybody to use the results in his own understanding of Lenin as a great man or of anything else. If a modern bible is to be written it can have authority as a foundation document only with the unconstrained participation of scholars—unless civilization is going to relapse, which could indeed make the Soviet managed mythology more effective.

Children are a special case in relation to points 1 and 2. They get Lenin—the babe in his crib, the boy with the world in his mind, the perfect man—from kindergarten onwards. But, like the community itself, children grow up.

3. Perhaps another condition is the passing of enough time for the managed and spontaneous mythologies to settle in together. After all, there was no Christian system half a century after Jesus. But things moved more quickly with Mohammed. And in the twentieth century, of course, incomparably faster. The time aspect leads us into such considerations as the relation between political power and mythology management, the rise of the mass media and the decline of philosophy, modern rates of growth in mass education, and so forth. Time seems to be, on balance, working against rather than for a settling-in process—unless, perhaps, the management can place Lenin and all he stands for firmly within Russian nationalism. Amalrik notes the tendency of the management to move over from a mythology of class enemies to one of national enemies—Chinese and Jewish. The anti-Zionist campaign, which on March 31 was moved up a notch to become reminiscent of the first public intimation of the Doctors' Plot, points in that direction. But racial xenophobia and pogroms could not make much use of Lenin. He was too firmly a man of the Russian enlightenment as well as a millenarian. The nationalist mythology is reaching a pitch that makes a collision with the Lenin mythology seem difficult to escape.

4. A further condition may be abandonment of the attempt to link Lenin with

everything. There appears to be no sphere of administration, the economy and public life generally, and no field of thought, which Lenin is not somehow made to preside over. The slovenliness of the connection in the great majority of centenary articles in the Soviet journals does not alter the fact of this impossible universalism. It reflects the universalism of Soviet Marxism, now anthropomorphized in Lenin. It rants about, urges on, meddles in and takes charge of everything—except the deeper needs of people—and so leaves the field, in the end, to traditional religion, which has the further advantage of not being continually disproved by discrepancies between itself and social reality. If the Ideology Department could limit Lenin a little, it would have more possibility of linking up his official image with what people may think of him. But the signs are all the other way.

One could go on suggesting conditions for a genuine Lenin mythology. I suspect that they would all point in the same simple direction, towards an increase of honesty and charity in public life and a lessening of that official hypocrisy and oafishness which is becoming more and more the hallmark of the Soviet state.

One turns with relief to the other side of the equation, the use that people spontaneously make of Lenin. This is of course anybody's guess, without benefit of reliable literary, journalistic or sociological reflection of what people feel, think or want. My own limited experience leads me to suspect that the *intelligenti* of Moscow and Leningrad have given up Marx and Lenin, while amongst the intellectuals (not to be confused with the *intelligenti*), including the immense number of graduates in the provincial towns, one easily finds people who are trying to go back to Marx and Lenin, or at least Lenin, and work things out again from there.

I wish somebody would make a systematic collection of Soviet political jokes, with the period when each was current, not for fun but for study. They are not mythology, because the events in a myth happened or are happening so far as the holders of the myth are concerned, but Soviet political jokes do have the subjective exactness of myth. I know only two involving Lenin: either my knowledge of these jokes is woefully deficient or they do keep clear of Lenin. One is quite up to Lenin's own standard in mordancy. It is about the Beryozka shops, those glimpses of a fabulous Western plenty into which the ordinary Soviet citizen without hard currency or a certificate cannot enter. Certificates are issued to certain categories of citizen, including those who work with foreigners and need to wear clothes of Western quality. A certificate is issued authorizing purchase without foreign currency of a pair of shoes, a suit, etc. This is called *sertifikatsia*. The joke is to tell what Lenin really said about the two conditions of Full Communism—Soviet power plus *sertifikatsia* of the entire country. Maybe this joke, which was current in 1968, reflects something positive about Lenin in people's minds, as well as something negative about his successors. The other Lenin joke happens to involve Pushkin. Prizes are announced for the best statues of Pushkin. The first prize is awarded for a statue of Lenin, the second prize for one of Lenin reading Pushkin, and the third for one of Pushkin reading Lenin.

A Scottish poet who read this chapter points out its omission of the myth-maker, the writer, who "may be telling 'a story' as if of the past but his function, it seems to me, is to open out a way to the future" by "some sort of ideal which has not happened yet." However one may define mythology, the omission of the free writers remains an omission. I do not know of any effort in *samizdat* literature to get to grips with Lenin and thereby redefine the quest behind the revolution, in order to serve the present and future. Solzhenitsyn's depiction of Stalin in *The First Circle* tries to help define what went wrong, as does—more directly—the study of Beria and his creature in Gouzenko's *Fall of a Titan*. The writers capable of providing new ideals are still monopolized by the problem of what went wrong. When we begin to meet Lenin on the same scale in *samizdat*, maybe a new stage will have been reached.

Notes

1. See, for example, David W. Benn, "New Thinking in Soviet Propaganda," *Soviet Studies*, 21 (July, 1969), 52-63.
2. In *Religion and the Soviet State: A Dilemma of Power*, Max Hayward and William C. Fletcher, ed. (New York, 1969).

14

The Lenin Cult and Its Uses

HARRY SCHWARTZ

My interest in the topic of the Lenin Cult was intensified some months ago when I read a Soviet newspaper article about the training of cosmonauts. According to this article, before Soviet cosmonauts rocket into space they are first taken to the Kremlin, where they visit Lenin's old office which has been maintained just as it was when he used it. In that "holy" shrine, the cosmonauts are apparently given time for reflection and thought as well as for vows that they will advance Lenin's cause by bringing new glory to the Soviet Union in space. I was struck then by the thought of how conventionally religious this whole ritual was, of how much it clashed in spirit with the official atheism of the Soviet Communist party. It all seemed so terribly ironic, especially, in view of Nikita Khrushchev's gibes early in the Soviet space program that Yuri Gagarin had gone into space and looked as hard as he could but had found neither God nor any angels. Yet here on earth these past two years the whole fantastic buildup toward the Lenin Centennial has been reminiscent more of the glorification of a miracle-working saint or of the deity than of honor for a mere mortal made of perishable skin, muscles, brain and blood. The Soviet poet who wrote shortly after Lenin's death that "Lenin lives and he is more alive than people that are living" believed then, no doubt, that he was merely exercising an artist's prerogative of exaggerating and intensifying an idea to express emotion. But that can hardly be used to justify the vast bureaucratic apparatus that has carried out these past two years' orgy of Lenin worship.

Of course this sort of personality cult for a departed leader is not entirely unique to the Soviet Union. There were modest overtones of the same sort of practice in the reverence my elementary school teachers many years ago showed toward George Washington. I was even required to memorize his farewell address and informed that his warnings against "entangling alliances" were still relevant. My impression, though, is that the Washington Cult—a pale shadow of its former self in my childhood—has weakened still further since. But there is still very much of a Lincoln Cult in some quarters, and the continuing flow of books about him, his life and his era shows no sign of early cessation. All of us have been witnesses to the creation of a Kennedy Cult whose raw materials have been a president and a senator, brothers, cut down by assassins as they reached their political primes. Some politicians in my home state are still trying to build brilliant careers on their relations with Kennedy, while Teddy's political career is by no means over.

237

But, of course, these American precedents are all rather insignificant compared to the worship of Stalin that was propagated during the decades he ruled the Soviet Union, or compared to the cult of Mao Tse-tung that is very much a reality in China today. And for completeness one should mention also the cult of Che Guevara among today's radical youth, so many of whom decorate their rooms with pictures of the fallen revolutionary and the words, "Che Lives!" Like the followers of Lenin, Guevara's admirers apparently cannot reconcile themselves to the fact that their hero is gone from their midst.

In a very real sense the Lenin Cult began no later than the day of his death in 1924. Certainly there was a barbaric splendor to the funeral that was given him, while the religious precedents for Stalin's remarkable speech—with its many vows to continue and be faithful to Lenin's cause—at that funeral are apparent enough. In the atmosphere thus created, the creation of the Lenin mausoleum in Red Square to house the fallen leader's embalmed body was a natural move. The idea was plainly to provide physical proof for future generations that there had been a Lenin and that he had been a wonder worker, a man of miracles. Stalin had been trained in the Russian Orthodox church and he understood the religious feelings of the Russian people. If Marxism required him to deprive that people of its Christian God, he would provide a Russian and Communist object of veneration instead.

Stalin's exploitation of the Lenin Cult was evident from the beginning of his rule in the mid-1920s. He presented himself as Lenin's faithful follower, as one whose primacy was justified by the fact that his fidelity to the master, his understanding of the master's teachings, and his insight into the master's intentions were greater than those qualities in other men. He presented the problem of ruling the Soviet Union as simply one of ascertaining how best to apply Lenin's policies and his ideas to different situations as they arose. Stalin sought initially to make Lenin Allah to his own role as Mohammed. As for Stalin's opponents, it was an important part of the campaigns to destroy them that they were presented as anti-Leninists, as deviationists who had opposed Lenin while he was alive and departed from the master's tenets even more after his death. It was implicit in this vast effort that any evidence showing Stalin's differences with Lenin—as in Lenin's famous last testament—had to be suppressed. If there were any doubts about the completely cynical use of the Lenin Cult by Stalin, they are removed by one fact: Stalin fastened his rule upon Russia by posing as Lenin's chosen successor, while knowing full well that one of Lenin's last great wishes was precisely that Stalin be removed from any major position of power over others. It is interesting to reflect that all the top Soviet leaders in the mid-1920s knew this, but—except for the exiled Trotsky—went along with the deception. It is not a very long distance apparently from revolutionary idealism to cynical manipulation of the masses.

Inevitably, the passage of time brought new problems which required Stalin to improvise new solutions, some of them very greatly at odds with Lenin's formulas. Stalin's shift from Leninist semi-egalitarianism to Stalinist encouragement of maximum differentiation of wages and incomes to provide incentives is one of many cases in point. This sort of thing quickly became known as "creative Marxism-Leninism," the code expression for deviations from Marxism and/or Leninism which were legitimatized by the fact that Stalin was now powerful enough to destroy anyone who said publicly that these new policies were either wrong or at odds with the old doctrine. When required, of course, Stalin's kept professors and scholars could always find a paragraph, a sentence or—in a pinch—even a phrase taken out of context in Lenin's writings to justify anything Stalin wanted to do. Moreover as time went by and Stalin's stature grew, that of Lenin's shrank relatively. The Stalinist rewriting of Soviet history over the decades constantly enhanced Stalin's role in past events at the expense of Lenin. It is interesting to speculate how far the process might have gone had Stalin lived and ruled until 1970. In such circumstances would Stalin have bothered to mark Lenin's one hundredth birthday, and if so would Lenin have gotten credit for anything more than "discovering" Stalin and preparing the way for Stalin's all wise, all beneficent, and all foreseeing reign? Only Stalin's death in 1953, it seems to me, may have saved the Lenin Cult.

With Stalin's demise, of course, his heirs were immediately faced with the problem of legitimatizing their claim to continued power. Stalin had provided the pattern for them to follow. So they dutifully turned the Lenin Mausoleum into the Lenin-Stalin Mausoleum, embalmed Stalin's body, interred it alongside Lenin's, and presented themselves to the world as the faithful continuers of the Lenin-Stalin tradition. But as the battle for primacy raged among Stalin's successors, the differences between Lenin and Stalin became one of the key issues. Khrushchev's justly famous 1956 speech exposing some of Stalin's crimes and revealing the anti-Stalin Lenin documents Stalin had suppressed was in part intended as a blow at the Molotov-Kaganovich faction. Khrushchev, in effect, used historic truth as a political weapon and resurrected the real Lenin. He went still further along this path in October 1961 at the Twenty-Second Communist Party Congress which ended with the decision to remove Stalin's embalmed body from the Red Square mausoleum so that Lenin would lie there in lonely splendor again. The religious quality of the proceedings is suggested by the fact that the decision to expel Stalin's body from the mausoleum was taken after an old party member's report of having "asked Ilyich for advice, and it was as if he stood before me alive and said: 'I do not like being next to Stalin who inflicted so much harm on the Party.' "[1]

Khrushchev, of course, sought to portray himself as being in the direct line of ideological succession from Lenin. But it must be said, to his credit, that he was prepared on occasion to repudiate explicitly past Leninist doctrines that he felt were outmoded. Thus in his 1956 report as First Secretary to the Twentieth Communist Party Congress, he replaced the Lenin-Stalin prediction of inevitable military conflict with capitalism, by the new view that war was not fatally inevitable. And when the Chinese in 1960 cited Lenin's views to attack Khrushchev's, the latter spoke out publicly in favor of adapting and changing classic positions to meet new needs. Thus he declared in Bucharest in June 1960: "We live in a time when we have neither Marx, nor Engels, nor Lenin with us. If we act like children who, studying the alphabet, compile words from letters, we shall not go very far. . . . One must be able not only to read, but also to understand correctly what one has read, and apply it in the specific circumstances of the time in which we live, taking into consideration the existing situation and the real balance of forces."[2] This, of course, was a very rational approach, exhibiting a spirit rather far removed from the quasi-religious idolatry that has at other times marked so much of the Soviet approach to Lenin.

But, of course, it is the present Soviet rulers—the Brezhnev-Kosygin-Podgorny group—that are responsible for the orgy of Lenin worship being carried out to mark the centennial of the birth of the founder of the Soviet regime. Anyone who has followed events in the Soviet Union these past two years knows that the glorification of Lenin has been on an enormous scale, exhibiting often a cloying sycophancy and simple minded reverence that must repel even many sympathetic observers. Many Soviet citizens are undoubtedly disgusted with the whole performance, and with its implied insult to the intelligence of the Soviet people. But the really interesting question is why the present leadership felt it necessary to go to these lengths.

One reason, of course, is that the present leaders are political pygmies who have neither Stalin's accomplishments nor Khrushchev's gifts for popular and demagogic appeals to the common man to buttress their claim to authority. Lacking personal charisma, understanding full well that they gained power by politically assassinating their mentor and benefactor, Khrushchev, Brezhnev and Company seek to elevate their own stature by focusing attention on Lenin. Implied in all the praise of Lenin is the idea that Brezhnev and Company are Lenin's successors, so if Lenin was a wonder working miracle man some of his magic must still remain with those who hold his power today.

The image of the Soviet man in the minds of those who planned this overblown celebration of Lenin's centennial must be a rather uncomplimentary one. The Soviet leaders, I suggest, appear to think of the bulk of their people as unsophisticated dolts. Their view is probably not too far from Andrei Amalrik's description of the Soviet people's mentality:

First, the still very low cultural level of the greater part of our people, more especially in the sphere of everyday culture. Second, the predominant role of mass myths vigorously disseminated by mass information media. And third, the extreme social disorientation of the bulk of our people. 'Proletarianization' of the countryside has engendered a 'strange class', neither peasants nor workers, with the twofold psychology of owners of their miniature homesteads and farmhands working on huge anonymous properties. What kind of consciousness this mass has about itself and what its desires are no one, I believe, knows. Furthermore, the colossal influx of the peasantry en masse from the villages into the towns has produced a new type of townsman also: a person who has broken away from his old environment, his old way of life and culture and who is finding it very difficult to acquire new modes of living, who feels himself very much out of place in them and is at one and the same time terrified and aggressive. He is also quite unable to understand to which level of society he belongs.[3]

But, of course, there are also millions of intelligent and sensitive people in the Soviet Union who have been revolted by the orgy of Lenin glorification. The Soviet newspaper *Komsomolskaya Pravda* was undoubtedly reflecting their views last February when it publicly attacked some of the grossest excesses of the Lenin Cult. But the examples it cited simply underline the flight from reason this campaign has encouraged. Thus it told of Moscow bakeries making chocolate medals portraying Lenin for use on cakes, of Moscow dance studios using the Lenin celebration and Lenin's image to spur interest in various types of ballroom dancing, and of one enthusiastic Leninist who proposed putting a portrait of Lenin on the facade of every building in the Soviet Union. *Komsomolskaya Pravda* could not have attacked even these excesses without official approval, so perhaps in the last stages of the centennial there were misgivings in very high Kremlin quarters. Possibly pointing in the same direction is the recent shakeup in the leadership of some key Soviet propaganda agencies, a shakeup some Moscow speculation has linked to Politburo dissatisfaction with the Lenin centennial excesses.

The annoyance of sophisticated Soviet citizens with the Lenin orgy calls our attention to the disadvantages of what is being done. Many members of the Soviet elite must realize that the huge resources devoted to the centennial could have been better devoted to their nation's real social and economic needs. Moreover there must be frank realization in some Soviet quarters that Lenin's ideas are obsolete because he lived before the technological revolution of our times, before the computer, before nuclear weapons, before intercontinental missiles and before man's entry into space. In an era when some people are arguing that the New Left is right, and that nobody over thirty really understands the nature of the world we live in, what are we to say about a man who would be reaching the century mark if he were still alive, and who, in any case, has been dead for forty-six years.

A second weakness or disadvantage of the Lenin Cult is the fact that it is an expression of Soviet—and even more narrowly, Russian—nationalism. The effort to have Lenin accepted as a universal god or law giver must inevitably fall flat because other nations have their own leaders whom they would rather honor. We can think of China's Mao Tse-tung, of Cuba's Fidel Castro, of North Korea's Kim Il-sung, of North Vietnam's Ho Chi-minh. And since we live in a world where racial consciousness is becoming ever stronger it is relevant to point out that Lenin was a white man. There are black nationalists in this country who have already publicly disparaged Marx, Engels, Lenin and even Stalin because they were "honkies" or white men.

The final difficulty of the Lenin Cult arises from the fact the Lenin heritage is a very ambiguous one, a multi-faceted one. Lenin, after all, wrote and was politically active from about 1890 to 1924, a period of roughly thirty-five years. His views evolved, changed and developed. He learned much over time and engaged in polemics in many different situations. He spent most of his adult life as a powerless revolutionary engaged in factional struggles that were really tempests in teapots, or so they seemed at the time. Then he became ruler of a great nation, and had many different and unexpected problems to solve. The result of course is that the heritage of Lenin as contained in his collected works, what he wrote, his injunctions, his advice, etc., is shot full of contradictions. As I said before, by hunting diligently enough, one can find a Lenin quotation to support almost any policy one would want to support on every issue. The result of that is that once Soviet leaders have elevated Lenin to an almost godlike status and support things by saying "as Comrade Lenin wrote in 1911," it encourages people who disagree with them to go searching as well. And they can find Leninist quotations to suit their needs! Thus the Lenin of the period of War-Communism was a very different man from the Lenin of the N.E.P. a few years later. If you want to compromise with the United States, as Khruschev did at the time of the Cuban Missile Crisis, in 1962, you can suddenly remember the Lenin of the Treaty of Brest-Litovsk who informed his colleagues that he was willing to accept whatever terms the Germans wanted to impose. If a Soviet leader wants to make a deal with the United States, he can recall the Lenin of 1919-21 who accepted American food aid and tried to hire Bernard Baruch, a capitalist if there ever was one, to run the Soviet economy. If you are an Uzbek or a Ukrainian who wants more independence from the Russians, you can find appropriate quotations in Lenin, etc. In a period when increasing numbers of Soviet citizens are able to, and willing and anxious to think independently, the Lenin heritage becomes a double-edged sword because much in Lenin can be quoted against the present Party line, whatever the Party line may be. And so in the long run, I should say, it is possible that the disadvantages of the Lenin Cult will be rather more important than the uses it has had up to now, making it a force for disintegrating rather than strengthening the Soviet Union and system.

Notes

1. *Pravda*, October 31, 1961. Speech of D.A. Lazurkina.
2. Quoted in Harry Schwartz, *Tsars, Mandarins and Commissars* (New York, 1964), p. 180.
3. *Survey*, Autumn, 1969, p. 63.

Part V
Lenin, Leninism and the
Present

15 Lenin's Letters as an Historical Source

JOHN L.H. KEEP

I

The correspondence of the great has always exercised a powerful fascination for the historian or the biographer. Ideally, it ought to reveal the hidden aspects of a man's psyche, his secret motivations and objectives; at the least it may cast light upon his personal relationships with others in a way that would not be apparent from more formal documents. In our age, the growth of modern technology and the public relations industry have, alas, all but killed this medium of communication. One may doubt whether any present-day statesman (with the exception, perhaps, of Charles de Gaulle) will bequeath to posterity correspondence which in the nineteenth century would have been deemed worthy of inclusion in one of those elegant tomes of *Letters and Papers* that graced library shelves. Least of all can the epistolary art prosper in an authoritarian society, for the qualities most in demand of the successful letter-writer—above all frankness and modesty—are not conspicuous in public life, which indeed may well be overshadowed by a false image of the Leader, deliberately built up as part of a system of ideological molding.

In this respect Lenin occupies a unique position among twentieth-century dictators. Not only was he personally less vain and less secretive than his successor, but his posthumous near-deification in the USSR has caused a tremendous effort to accumulate and preserve his literary legacy. Every scrap of paper to which he put his pen, no matter how trivial or ephemeral the subject, is of interest to the high priests of the Lenin Cult. The Central Party Archive in Moscow's Institute of Marxism-Leninism are said to have contained 29,800 items at the last count, in 1953.[1] The basis of the collection was laid in 1923 by a Central Committee appeal calling on all Soviet citizens to surrender to the Institute any Lenin documents in their possession. Trotsky has told us that they were promised photographic copies in exchange, but that this promise was not generally kept. Maybe this is one reason why, in the words of a recent Soviet historian, "the Lenin documents came in slowly, and often individuals surrendered them only after requests by the directors."[2] The history of the archive was a troubled one. In 1928-29 the Institute was merged with Istpart, and its "basic fund" grew so large that it was hard to use; then in 1939 Stalin, as part of his effort to rewrite Party history, ordered that the documents actually written by Lenin should be separated from the rest, thus arbitrarily breaking the relationship between them and making things still more difficult for any potential researcher with a disinterested concern for the truth.[3] These obstacles are now to some extent being cleared away. The full story of these pious laborers in the inner sanctum of Soviet historiography, could they tell it, would be an absorbing one.

Equally fascinating, so far as we can reconstruct it, is the tale of the efforts made over the years to publish such selections from Lenin's correspondence as would satisfy the shifting requirements of the Party line. These documents comprised most items in the so-called "Lenin Miscellanies" (*Leninskiye sborniki*) which appeared with decreasing frequency as Stalin got into his stride, until in 1945 the series seemed to have come to a halt. In 1959, three years after the Twentieth Party Congress had exposed some of Stalin's misdeeds, a new volume—the 36th—was issued. It contained a number of documents that hitherto had clearly been suppressed.

From time to time Lenin documents have also appeared in volumes of memoirs, central or local newspapers or journals, or various editions of Lenin's *Collected Works*. Publication has depended not simply upon a document's availability but also upon its "topicality," i.e., its relevance to the current concerns of the Soviet political elite. Each successive leader or group of leaders has striven to legitimize his authority in Leninist terms, to present his version of Lenin as the authentic one. This has often meant taking considerable liberties with the Bolshevik chief's writings. Thus, in the 1930s, Stalin would sometimes select for ostentatious publication in *Pravda* messages which passed between Lenin and his "closest comrade-in-arms" during the dark days of the civil war. The subject-matter of the *Leninskiye sborniki* was also adjusted to the spirit of the times. Volume 21, which appeared at the height of the collectivization drive, contained materials on the Party's peasant policy under "war-communism," and the last two volumes of the Stalin era, published during the Soviet-German war, dealt mainly with military questions. These selections did not, as is sometimes said, suppress all mention of Trotsky. Nevertheless certain documents which must have been in the archivists' possession at the time were omitted, without any public indication of the fact, while others were published in an abbreviated or distorted form. The most common ruse was to exclude the names of prominent Oppositionists from the text or from the instructions for dispatch, so that the very fact of their existence might vanish down the "memory hole" in the minds of all loyal Soviet citizens.

Stalin's assumption that the popular consciousness was infinitely malleable had the simplicity of genius, but it could not outlast his own mortal frame. In 1956 his successors, or some of them, loudly proclaimed their intention to restore "Leninist norms in Party life." Did this mean a total repudiation of Stalinist practices? Or were only those falsifications condemned which the new rulers found inexpedient?

It is now all too plain that the new fashion for veracity was a transient and fragile thing. Khrushchev's approach to politics was more sophisticated than Stalin's, yet in the first years of his rule, when under pressure, he resorted to the old Stalinist technique of selectively publishing Lenin documents which would afford the highest sanction for contentious current policies—for example, "peaceful coexistence" with the capitalist powers.[4] In general, however, it was the long-term rather than the short-term interests of the regime which have been given precedence. To put it differently, genuine scholarship in the fundamentals of the faith now has as much scope as is possible in an ideologically determined totalitarian polity.

We may now consider what this means in practice by taking a closer look at Lenin's correspondence as published in the fifth edition of his *Works* (hereinafter called the *Works*), concentrating on a limited period: the first three years after the October Revolution. This is to be found in volumes 50 and 51 of this edition, which appeared in 1964 and 1965—a time when Khrushchev was still in power or only just out of it, before the chill neo-Stalinist breezes had begun to blow in earnest. We have a total of 1455 items, nearly two hundred (194) of which are published here for the first time. The two basic questions which a historian must ask of this source, as of any other, are: (1) how reliable is it?, and (2) what value does it have for the student of Lenin and Leninism or of Russian history in the first years of Soviet power?

II

Let us take the question of reliability first. As a historical source the *Works* may be said to bear the hallmarks of their "iconological" function. On one hand, great care has been lavished on certain details in presentation: we are told in each case whether the item is printed from the original manuscript or from a copy, when it was written, and where it was first published. The chronological arrangement is also a great improvement on the thematic one favored in earlier editions of the *Works* and in the *Sborniki*. On the other hand, the documents are presented in isolation from their historical context. The object of the editors is not to encourage critical examination by dispassionate historians or biographers, but rather to provide an authoritative manual for the guidance of the faithful. Lenin has to be portrayed not as a creature of flesh and blood, bound to his fellow men by a complex network of personal and operational relationships, who like all mortals had his moments of doubt and whose actions were often contradictory, but as a lofty genius, serenely self-confident and consistent. To this end we are offered only the documents of which Lenin was the sole or joint author, but not those which he received, even where these would be highly relevant to an understanding of the problems that beset him and his attitude toward them. What we have is in effect an arbitrarily truncated body, a graven image that speaks but does not listen.

Only by dint of patient labor can we reconstruct the actual context in which a particular action was taken. Our task is not eased by helpful references to secondary sources, as might be expected in an academic enterprise of such magnitude.[5] Certainly the notes (printed at the rear) are far more informative than those in the fourth edition, which appeared in the late Stalin era; on the other hand, they fall far short of the standard attained in the second edition, compiled in the 1920s, although the scope of this edition was of course much slighter (a mere 105 letters for the whole Soviet period). In the notes to the fifth edition "incoming" messages are sometimes summarized or quoted in excerpt, with a reference (unnumbered) to the Central Party Archive. This is better than nothing, and whets one's appetite for access to this holy of holies, but is no substitute for a full collection that would enable one to see its subject in the round. The compilers of the apparatus (notes, biographical data, etc.) have clearly had to work under severe limitations. Thus the entry on Nadezhda Alliluyeva fails to mention the fact that she became Stalin's wife.[6] This can hardly be due to inadequate scholarship.

Politics are also to blame for certain "inaccuracies" (to use a polite euphemism) in the editorial matter accompanying the documents themselves. This, as already mentioned, normally includes a reference to the place of first publication, in one or two variant forms; either "first published in . . . " or "first published incompletely in. . . ." A check on some of these references in the first form shows that they should really be in the second, because the text as printed was in fact distorted, i.e., incomplete. A glaring example of this occurs in a telegram to Dzerzhinsky of August 1920. The annotation reads: "first published incompletely in 1938 in the journal *Bolshevik* no. 2. Published in full (facsimile) in 1951 in the book *F.E. Dzerzhinsky, 1877-1936*, Moscow." This latter volume does indeed contain what appears to be a facsimile of this message—but with the names of two of the addressees, Smilga and Radek, blotted out. The present edition enables one to reconstruct the original, but the editors presumably wished to conceal the fact that the document had twice been tampered with.[7]

Turning now to the reliability of the documents themselves, three main questions arise: have the distortions and falsifications of the Stalin era been made good?; do the documents published for the first time add much to our knowledge?; and can the collection now be regarded as complete? On the answers to these questions must depend our estimate of the editors' *bona fides*.

Fortunately we have an invaluable non-Soviet source to assist us here: volume I of *The Trotsky Papers*, edited by Professor Jan Meijer and published in the Netherlands in 1964, almost simultaneously with the *Works*. These papers cover the years 1917-1919 and include a number of Lenin documents as well as other Party papers of which Trotsky had copies made in the mid-1920s; these copies he then took abroad when he was expelled from the USSR. A comparison of the texts common to both volumes shows that we can answer the first question affirmatively: i.e., the proper names that were suppressed in earlier editions of the *Works* or the *Sborniki* have been restored. One example among dozens may suffice: Lenin's telegram to Lashevich of June 18, 1919, when first published in

Leninskii sbornik, omitted the words "from Smilga," which have here been reinserted.[8]

The second question we may also answer affirmatively. The documents published here for the first time include both runs of correspondence with particular individuals, notably Chicherin and Ioffe, which *may* previously have been suppressed, and individual items which *must* have been suppressed, because they form part of a series and the other items in it were published earlier. The former throw some new light on several questions relating to Soviet foreign policy. The latter are of considerable interest for the study of "high politics" during the civil war years, not least the nascent conflict between Trotsky and Stalin. We shall return later to this point, and shall indicate by asterisk in references to the *Works* those messages published for the first time since Stalin's death.

The third question could only be answered with complete assurance if one had free access to the archives. But there are good reasons for answering it in the negative, i.e., for suspecting that a significant number of Lenin documents remain unpublished.

In the first place, some items which appeared in the second and third editions of the *Works* have been excluded, without any explanation, from the present one. As there are only four instances of this, we may itemize and attempt to explain them here:

1. Two messages addressed to Stalin, of January 24, and April 3, 1919, about the Commissariat of State Control—a vexed issue on which the two leaders' views differed significantly—a point which the present editors evidently wish to conceal.[9]
2. One message addressed by Lenin to other members of the Council for Labor and Defense, dated April 1919, ordering emergency measures to cope with the "perfectly catastrophic situation on the railways." There are ample other references to this problem, and the omission of this letter may be due to editorial scruples about reproducing Lenin's unusually brutal, indeed cynical phrase: "let thousands more [workers] perish, but the country will nevertheless be saved."[10]
3. One message to Trotsky and others, dated May 18, 1919, dealing with the mobilization of Donets coal miners to check the White advance.[11] This was originally published with Kamenev as the addressee, but since this error was already corrected in the fourth edition, it is hard to see why the document should be omitted. It may simply be deemed of insufficient importance, in much the same way as a number of items published in the *Sborniki*, mainly of a very ephemeral nature,[a] have likewise been excluded from the *Works*—although some equally trivial ones have been included. More detailed study would be necessary to elucidate this matter further.

---

[a]One that is not (*TP*, No. 256) deals with the emergency measures undertaken to evacuate Petrograd in the face of Yudenich's advance.

But the main evidence for the incompleteness of the *Works* stems from a comparison with the *Trotsky Papers*. The latter contain 172 documents from Lenin's hand, of which fifty, or twenty-nine percent, are missing from the *Works*. (A further seventeen have been published in other Soviet sources.) Does this mean that the whole collection is about thirty percent short? An intriguing thought—but before we leap to conclusions we should remember that the years 1917-1919 may not be typical either of Lenin's correspondence habits or of the papers which Trotsky gathered together. Professor Meijer very plausibly suggests that Trotsky made his selection from the Soviet archives with the express purpose of accumulating material which would testify to his close relationship with the Bolshevik leader, a fact which his Stalinist enemies questioned.[b] If this is so, it would be natural to find an unusually high proportion of Lenin documents in Trotsky's collection from the civil war years, when the collaboration between the two men was at its peak, and when their relationship found expression on paper because Trotsky was usually absent from the capital. We shall have to await publication of the second volume of the *Trotsky Papers* before we can establish whether the new pattern in later years is very different from that of 1917-1919. All we can say for the present is that a significant (but uncertain) fraction of Lenin's correspondence, which we know to exist, is not to be found in the *Works*.[c]

Does this mean that it has been deliberately suppressed? The omission might be due to simple "technical" rather than political causes. The original documents may have been lost since the mid-1920s, when Trotsky took his copies (he did *not* take away any originals). There is some evidence to support this hypothesis. Meijer prints two messages from Lenin to Trotsky, sent on successive days in May 1919, only the second of which occurs in the *Works*.[12] Yet this shows Lenin taking a *more* charitable attitude towards Trotsky than the one which is omitted. The same apparently arbitrary juxtaposition of consecutive messages, this time addressed to Smilga, one printed and the other not, occurs in October 1919.[13] Unless we assume that the editors are playing a trick on bourgeois historians—a pleasing but extravagant notion!—we must conclude that they are here innocent of any political bias.

Does this mean that we can acquit them entirely? Far from it. Of the fifty Lenin documents exclusive to the *Trotsky Papers*, more than half (twenty-seven) are addressed to Trotsky himself; these often depict him in a positive light, or else add materially to our knowledge of important historical questions. There are

[b]This view is supported by the presence in the *Works* (*L*, no. 640) of a document *not* to be found in the Trotsky archives; a letter to the Central Committee of June 17, 1919 strongly critical of Trotsky.

[c]According to Iu. A. Akhapkin, of the Central Party Archive, about 14,000 Lenin documents remain unpublished, most of these being either brief resolutions on incoming reports, etc., or official documents which Lenin helped to compile. Akhapkin does not state that these categories account for all the unpublished items, p. 65.

too many of these messages, and they fall into too logical a pattern, for their omission from the *Works* to be due to pure chance.

Let us mention a few of these. On August 22, 1918 Lenin wrote to Trotsky that treason at the front makes it imperative for him to proceed at once to the Saratov area.[14] The editors must have known of this message, since Trotsky published it in his autobiography, which appeared in Berlin in 1930; yet they have chosen to ignore it. They have acted likewise with a letter sent to Trotsky on December 31, 1918, after the collapse of the Third Army, in which Lenin mentioned that "they" (presumably the *Revvoensovet* of the Eastern Front) wanted Trotsky to undertake an investigation into its causes. In this case Stalin went instead, and later he was to make much of the fact. Yet this document— significantly enough, without the materially relevant phrase *prosyat vas priekhat tude* ("they ask you to go there")—was published in 1960 in another Soviet work, P.G. Sofinov's study of the Cheka; Trotsky had published it in two of the works he wrote after leaving Russia.[15] Other documents exclusive to the *Trotsky Papers* illuminate the outbreak of the Stalin-Trotsky quarrel in May 1919, which led to the replacement of the Commander-in-Chief, Vatsetis,[16] or to the aftermath of this affair, when Trotsky tried to recover the ground he had lost.[17] There is also the matter of the famous "blank check" which Lenin gave Trotsky, endorsing in advance any orders he might give because "I am absolutely convinced in [their] correctness, expediency and necessity"; this likewise is omitted from the *Works*.

Now it might be thought that since most (though not all) of these documents were published by Trotsky abroad, Soviet editors would thereby be debarred automatically from infringing the taboo that surrounds them, for the existence of these writings has never been acknowledged in the USSR. However, even in Stalin's day it was found possible to print in a volume of the *Sborniki* a Lenin document which had first appeared in 1932 in Trotsky's *Stalin School of Falsification*,[18] although naturally enough without any indication of its prior publication. The present editors, however, have had to face a ticklish problem here, since they have made it their rule to give the data and place of first publication of each document printed. Their solution is to ignore Trotsky's work and to cite the *Sbornik* instead.[19] But what are they to do when they decide to publish a document that has *not* appeared previously in the USSR? Here they have simply dropped the customary annotation altogether, leaving a glaring blank upon the page.

There are four instances of this, all connected with disputes over strategy. The details are as follows:

1. Lenin to Trotsky, Serebryakov and Lashevich, September 6, 1919, informing them that the Politburo has overruled their representations and endorsed the strategic plans of the new Commander-in-Chief;
2. Lenin to Trotsky, October 17, 1919, informing him that the Council for

Labor and Defense has accepted his (Trotsky's) plan for the defense of Petrograd and instructing him to prepare to evacuate the city if necessary;

3. Lenin to Stalin, February 20, 1920, expressing fear that Denikin's shattered forces might nevertheless counterattack in the Donets;

4. Lenin to Trotsky, April 4, 1920, part of an exchange on Wrangel's intentions, in which Lenin accepts Trotsky's complaint that Stalin has bypassed the proper military channels in communicating directly with him (Lenin), and remarks: "there seems to be some caprice here."[20]

Do Soviet editors of Lenin's *Works* really still need to engage in such simple subterfuges? Now that so much of the correspondence with or about Trotsky has been (or shortly will be) published, could they not risk a more objective approach to the polemics of the Stalin era? One can scarcely imagine that the Communist party's aura of legitimacy would be seriously undermined by a frank recognition of the existency of Trotsky's writings and of his archive. The ideological barriers do not seem insurmountable. Perhaps this is a happy surprise kept in store for the present anniversary celebrations?

To sum up: the *Works* contain a selection, rather than a collection, of Lenin documents for the period in question, one which is less comprehensive or reliable than the editors would have us believe. Nevertheless it probably contains a fairly representative sample of the affairs which passed through Lenin's hands during his first years in power. In the absence of minutes of top Party and state organs, its value is very considerable. By reading Lenin's letters in conjunction with other sources, such as memoirs and official decrees, as well as the *Trotsky Papers*, we can gain an authentic glimpse from an unfamiliar angle of the inner workings of the Soviet dictatorship in its formative years.

III

Let us now try to prove this claim by examining, on the basis of this correspondence, the most important aspects of Lenin's activities during the civil war period. Three questions in particular lend themselves to analysis in this way: his efficacy as the Soviet State's "chief executive"; the role of coercion and terror in his conception of government; and his attitude to socioeconomic questions, above all to the peasant problem.

Two points may be made at the outset. Lenin's absorption in public affairs (perhaps his most salient characteristic) slackened as his health gave way under strains of office. This might be demonstrated diagrammatically, but it will suffice to state here that this diminution of interest is particularly noticeable in November-December 1919 and again in August-September 1920: it is on the latter occasion that he complains of feeling tired. When convalescing at Gorki, outside Moscow, he seems to have left the major decisions to others and to have busied himself mainly with relatively trivial matters. (On the other hand, after the attempt on his life in 1918 he recovered remarkably quickly.) Secondly, his interest in particular questions is often very spasmodic: he indulges in a kind of *shturmovshchina*, to use a later term. For example, in the spring and summer of 1918 he is much concerned with the supply problem, but it suddenly drops out of sight in September; his preoccupation with military matters is most intense in the spring and summer of 1919, but is relatively slight in 1920; the transport crisis bursts upon him unawares in December 1919; and his efforts to remedy individual grievances, while never wholly abandoned, reach a peak in November 1918 and after a break are suddenly resumed in August 1919.

Lenin's style of leadership was the product of his unusual ability to combine supreme self-assurance as a politician with great personal modesty. While taking it for granted that the life of the Soviet State would be shaped in conformity with his own ideals and prejudices, he was strangely reluctant to exercise the responsibilities that naturally fell to him as head of the Party and government. Characteristically, when in October 1918 he was asked to complete a question-naire, he entered his profession as "journalist."[21] The chief reason for this diffi-dence was ideological—an uncertainty as to the durability of the Soviet regime so long as the international socialist revolution remained in abeyance—a problem that need not be elaborated on here. The consequence was that for all Lenin's preeminence the early Soviet regime lacked a firm guiding center, and individuals and institutions were left fairly free to work out for themselves, by trial and error, their mutual relationships.

Lenin was not a man of faction—or more accurately, he ceased to be one after the October Revolution. That is to say, he remained utterly irreconcilable in his attitude to any group of persons deemed antagonistic to the Bolsheviks, but he did not identify with any particular group of persons within the Party or state. On the contrary, he endeavored to preserve a certain distance from all such groups, so reinforcing his natural paramountcy as the architect and symbol of the Revolution. He did not, like Stalin later, intrigue to divide his supporters and play them off against each other, but sought rather to rally them behind him in a solid front. He reacted strongly to any action likely to involve him in factional intrigue—*skloka*, as he called it. In July 1918 he received from Ioffe a dispatch which contained derogatory remarks about his immediate superior, Chicherin. Lenin rebuked Ioffe for placing him in an embarrassing position vis-à-vis the commissar for foreign affairs; he had no wish to become "an instrument of intrigue."[22] Similarly, two years later, when the Communists of Tula split into a majority of "hard-liners" and a minority of "liberals," and the former appealed to Lenin for his support, he replied that while he agreed with what they had told him, "if you wish to use my opinion against your 'opposition,' let them have both your letter to me and my reply. Then they will be [properly] informed and will be able to give me their version, and I shall not be informed partially."[23]

This tactful, common sense attitude towards his associates—one should scarcely exaggerate it into statesmanship—is exemplified by his handling of the celebrated antagonism between Trotsky and Stalin. His correspondence (in the *Works* and the *Trotsky Papers*) suggests that he strove to maintain a balance between the two rivals, whose complementary qualities he doubtless appreciated, but without complete success, for the shifts which took place in this triangular relationship came about spontaneously rather than on Lenin's own initiative.

In May 1919, when the conflict over military strategy and appointments burst into the open, he accepted most of the arguments put forward by the "military opposition" (with which Stalin was allied), but tried to soften the blow to Trotsky's prestige and self-esteem.[24] Only in June, after Trotsky had insinuated that Lenin and other members of the Central Committee had given way to panic, did he rebut the charge and turn it round against Trotsky and his military chiefs. He appears to have been somewhat appeased by Trotsky's offer to resign (July 5), but relations between the two men remained cool for about a month.[25] By mid-August Lenin was already expressing confidence that he could "work amicably" with Trotsky.[26] However, differences persisted over the employment of ex-officers in the Red Army, and when catastrophe threatened in the south in the late summer part of the blame naturally struck to Trotsky.[27] This gave an opening for Ordzhonikidze, an intimate of Stalin, to try to undermine Trotsky's position. Lenin's comments upon this message suggest that he was embarrassed and tried to temporize.[28] He was evidently relieved when Trotsky's successful defense of Petrograd made it possible to restore him to favor. During 1920 Lenin became disenchanted at the Stalinists' handling of the nationalities issue and also of certain strategic problems, but he did not withdraw his confidence from them.[29] Meanwhile Trotsky's standing remained high, especially during the Polish war, and it was only at the end of that year, as the "Party discussion" got underway, that his relationship with Lenin again deteriorated.[30]

One might add that despite continual friction Lenin also managed to maintain an effective working relationship with his sulky aide in Petrograd, Zinoviev.[31] There is little evidence in the correspondence on his relations with Kamenev or other leaders who stayed mainly in Moscow, and with whom he could communicate orally.

This political skill in handling individuals was, however, no substitute for a properly functioning network of institutions, and this the young Soviet State conspicuously lacked. The powers of the various administrative organs were ill-defined and conflicts of jurisdiction between them were endemic. From time to time Lenin tried to arbitrate between them, but he does not seem to have acted upon any clear principles. Moreover, his interventions frequently appear to have been disregarded and their effectiveness was thus doubtful; sometimes they actually seem to have made confusion more confounding.

His problems were aggravated by the fact that he deliberately maintained a large number of competing channels of communication, which got clogged. Through these channels he received large quantities of haphazard information of unequal value, which could not readily be checked against other independent sources, and was sometimes downright contradictory. Consequently he could seldom be quite certain that he was backing the right side in any controversy.

He was prone to intitiate more investigations into alleged shortcomings or abuses than could conveniently be followed up. These were sometimes triggered off quite casually. For instance, on three successive days in January 1920 he issued an order on fuel supply to a different organization, prompted respectively by a chance letter from a "specialist," an item in a newspaper, and an official report from the provinces.[32] This haphazardness was by no means untypical. Matters were taken up as and when they became urgent, with little regard for their relative importance. All this encouraged in Lenin and in others the illusion that he was exercising overall control, whereas, in fact, the most important decisions were being made elsewhere—or not at all. The attempt to direct everything from a single center, which flowed logically from the basic precepts of Bolshevism, was extremely naive, particularly in the chaotic condition of the civil war. Lenin had at his disposal only the most rudimentary secretarial organization, and his communications system was likewise primitive: he was forever complaining about his malfunctioning telephone.[33] Frequently he had to remind his correspondents that they should wire back how long telegraphed instructions had taken to reach them. How, therefore, could he intervene effectively in the jungle of the early Soviet administration?

Let us now look more closely at the effect of Lenin's intervention first upon the central and then upon the local government authorities.

There were, in practice, four main channels of authority in the civil administration at this time (the Red Army was arguably, more important than any of them). These were: the Communist Party, the Cheka (security police), and two of the commissariats, those for Supply and Transport. Each of these four agencies maintained a network of officials scattered throughout the country.

We shall discuss the Cheka and the Supply organization later in their appropriate context. So far as Party affairs are concerned, Lenin's correspondence for these years contains less material than one might at first expect. This reflects the fact that the Party was slow to assume in practice the "leading role" mapped out for it by Bolshevik doctrine. Not until November 1918 did Lenin make use of Party channels to bypass a bottleneck in the state apparatus,[34] and it was only in 1919, at the Eighth congress, that the Party's functions were formally laid down. Even so the proper relationship between Party and state authorities was far from clear even to a man as senior as Kalinin. In May 1919 he took a liberal view of his responsibilities to the Supply commissariat and was rebuked by Lenin for straying from the Party line: "Do not infringe the relationship between State and Party."[35] It was not until 1920 that Lenin spelled out for two of his correspondents' benefit what they should do to ensure that state organs complied with Party policy: they were to arm themselves with copies of the relevant decisions and complain directly to him, repeating the complaint as often as necessary. On the first occasion he added that "anyone who does not know this is naive," but on the second occasion he implied that he himself, had doubts about the efficacy of this procedure: "I shall sign [reminders and requests] in two minutes . . . and *sometimes* they will bring some practical benefit."[36]

As for the inner life of the Party, Lenin restricted himself to ordering the occasional investigation of suspected malpractices and ensuring that even the most junior organizations had the right to communicate directly with him, so that he might be fully informed of any lapses at intermediate levels in the hierarchy.[37]

What, one may ask, of the soviets, nominally the sovereign bodies in the "Soviet State"? These occupy an even more modest place in Lenin's correspondence for these years. The ambiguity of their role was made plain as early as November 1917, when he sends two messages to the soviet of Moscow (not then the capital): in one they are told that their action in replacing the provincial commissar (a post inherited from the previous regime, soon to become defunct) did not need the central government's approval, whereas in the other message Lenin did so confirm their action in dissolving the municipal Duma.[38] He concurred silently in the whittling away of the soviets' democratic rights. In April 1919 some villagers in Kursk province sought to exercise their constitutional prerogative of recalling their deputies and holding new elections. When Lenin heard of this, he asked the commissar for Internal Affairs as a matter of course to hold an inquiry, implying that this body's sanction for such a step was now required.[39]

Characteristically, there is no record in the correspondence of Lenin having intervened to define or regulate the provincial soviets' uneasy relationship with the ubiquitous supply commissars or other agents of the center. True, he did once take up the cudgels on behalf of the Moscow soviet against the Education commissariat, which wanted to close down the Maliy Theatre; but he may well have done so because this body had previously obstructed his will in similar matters, and in any case his intervention was unsuccessful.[40] On two occasions we find Lenin rebuking local soviets for contravening government policy, but the circumstances are extraordinary; a matter of the Allied landings at Archangel and Murmansk.[41] It is not so much a question of the soviets' power being deliberately curtailed as of their lapsing into impotence without the chief executive even registering the fact. And yet his ambitions to control them are limitless. He would apparently have welcomed the chance to enter into direct contact with each soviet in the land down to *volost* level—at least he once expressed such a wish in regard to all the *volost* soviets of Tula province[42]—which was clearly a fanciful notion. In the event he exchanged only a few messages with such local worthies.[43]

As the civil war progresses, so too does the size of the Soviet bureaucracy. It is hard even for Lenin to keep up with its ramifications. *Kto takoye Pravbum?* ("What on earth is 'Pravbum'?"), he once inquires querulously of Krasin. It turns out to be the Petrograd section of the Main Administration for the Paper Indus-try.[44] Later he asks Krasin for a copy of the table of accounts for the Transport commissariat, and on receiving it expostulated that it is "worse than the commis-sariat of State Control . . . a pile of official ranks, Chief So-and-so and Assistant So-and-so."[45] A month later he explodes again, this time to the central trade-union organization, which has delayed action on an order to send 10,000 metal-lurgical workers (no less) to repair railway rolling-stock. "I never doubted," he writes, "that there is still a great deal of bureaucracy in our commissariats, but I did not expect to find just as much of it in the trade unions. This is a tremen-dous scandal."[46]

But what *is* bureaucracy? In Lenin's eyes it seems like some monstrous para-sitic growth on an otherwise healthy body politic, and he has no idea how to cure it. In the instances just quoted he touches upon two of its characteristics: inflation of unproductive staff and obstruction of commands from the top. On other occasions he inveighs against officials' old-fashioned leisurely ways, partic-ularly their inability to submit regular reports in a brief, factual and businesslike form.[d] At other times he identifies the evil with corruption, and deplores the low moral standards of those in authority. In the countryside, he remarks to Zinoviev in April 1919, "there are few honest men . . . the need for honest men is desperate."[47] Even sharper is the judgment he passes of his officials, perhaps half in jest, in a letter to a leading Bolshevik agent in England: "one has to curse Russians twenty times and check them thirty times before they can do the simplest thing properly."[48]

What never seems to cross Lenin's mind is that these shortcomings are an in-separable concomitant of the centralization to which he is so strongly com-mitted in every field, and that he himself is by no means the least of offenders in this respect. In August 1918 he reprimands leading officials of the Supply com-missariat for indulging in "the devil knows what sort of bureaucratic red tape," in that they had failed to mobilize sufficient workers to help gather in the har-vest; yet in the same breath he lays down the exact proportion of trade-union-ists—twenty percent—who should be enrolled in each harvesting team, and is evi-dently quite oblivious of the contradiction.[49]

Equally harmful to efficient administration was his practice of meddling in petty matters of detail, however benevolent his intention may have been. A recent Western biographer remarks that he assumed the functions of an "All-Russian Complaints Bureau."[50] One might say that the role he aspired to lay somewhere between that of a public prosecutor and a chairman of a supreme administrative tribunal. His efforts to settle countless individual grievances took up time and energy which would have been better expended in deciding basic

---

[d]Not until January 1919 did he receive one which measured up to his expectations, as he remarked with pleasure to his secretary. The author, a minor functionary in Tula province, nevertheless failed to make much of a career in the world of Soviet officialdom. (*L*, No. 432.)

questions of state policy. They also demoralized ordinary Soviet functionaries, who never knew where they stood—as indeed was partly Lenin's intention. These men naturally tried to guard against his interventions from on high by bringing all vertical channels of communication under their control; meanwhile the stream of petitioners, encouraged by the success of the fortunate few, grew even larger. This phenomenon, by the way, had been a familiar feature of tsarist administrative practice before the "Great Reforms" of the 1860s. Old traditions die hard, and the village emissaries (*mirskiye khodoki*) who in former times had made their way to petition the divinely-appointed autocrat now stood patiently outside the doors of the Predsovnarkom.[51]

One cannot but be struck by the triviality of some of the petitions which Lenin feels it his duty to consider and, if possible, grant. As early as December 1917 he finds himself embroiled in the affairs of one particular steelworks in the Donets.[52] In March 1918 he asks why the clerks in the Moscow post office are required to work such long hours.[53] Then comes a string of complaints at the arbitrary requisitioning of property. In July 1918, as the war clouds gather in the east, Lenin writes to one Ivanov, in a village between Kazan and the Urals: "It is alleged that you have requisitioned some writing materials, including a table, belonging to the stationmaster. Return these objects at once. Telegraph your explanations...."[54] History, alas, does not record the fate of the stationmaster's table, nor that of the bicycle belonging to the pharmacist at Zhlobin, which calls forth two letters from the ever solicitous Vladimir Ilyich.[55] These are situations with comic possibilities worthy of a Chekhov. Yet there are others where it is a matter of life or death for the unfortunate petitioner, which bring us face to face with the grim realities of totalitarian dictatorship. It is to this aspect of Lenin's activities that we may now turn.

IV

Implicit in the foregoing is the self-evident point that a revolutionary state, as much as any other, needs sound laws, based upon popularly accepted notions of justice, if it is not to degenerate into an arbitrary tyranny. Yet Lenin's concept of "revolutionary legality" always remained valid, and was extended to justify any action, however reprehensible, deemed expedient by those in power. This development certainly had the leader's personal sanction, for as a trained jurist he was fully aware of the issues, yet deliberately chose to make as complete a breach as possible with "bourgeois" concepts of law. As he himself put it succinctly, "dictatorship is precisely the exercise of power unfettered by any law."

The correspondence not unexpectedly contains very little material on legal questions. In April 1918 Lenin called together senior members of the Justice commissariat, which until recently had been headed by a Left SR, and pressed them to step up their efforts "to make quicker and more merciless proceedings against the bourgeoisie, embezzlers, etc."[56] A few weeks later he made the same point in a letter to Kursky, the new Bolshevik commissar, and such a law was indeed passed.[57] But shortly thereafter, on the evidence before us, Lenin seems to have lost interest in such matters. The only practical step he took was to have a pamphlet printed, and distributed to officials in all commissariats, in which they were enjoined to observe "revolutionary legality."[58] Instead Lenin came to take the view that judicial cases were best handled by extralegal procedure, i.e., by the Cheka. Early in 1919, when the public prosecutor, Krylenko, opposed a Cheka move to have proceedings against a group of common criminals transferred to its jurisdiction, and the matter was referred to Lenin, he sided with Dzerzhinsky: "Krylenko," he observed dryly, "is fussing to no purpose."[59]

Dzerzhinsky, the Cheka chief, was one of the two persons (the other was Sverdlov) who had the right to enter Lenin's Kremlin apartment by a special door.[60] This close personal contact no doubt helps to explain why relatively few messages between the two men have been preserved. The possibility of using physical coercion on a massive scale against actual or potential enemies of the new order can never have been wholly absent from Lenin's mind, but in the first weeks of Soviet power he proceeded circumspectly, confining himself to threats of court proceedings against recalcitrant "bourgeois," and recommending that some of those arrested be sentenced to a limited term of forced labor in the coal mines.[61] By the following June, however, the situation had changed considerably, and he could insist on much harsher measures. It was now a question of threatening capital punishment or encouraging indiscriminate killings by the mob. After the assassination of Volodarsky he sent a notorious message to Zinoviev instructing him not to obstruct "mass terror" by Petrograd workers against (unspecified) "counter-revolutionaries"; this he considered "perfectly correct."[62] It is interesting to note that he was still cautious enough to advise restraint in dealing with foreigners who aided the enemy, since he feared that this might provoke reprisals; such persons were to be done away with only if they offered resistance, whereas Russians in the same category were to be shot out of hand.[63]

The "Red terror" began in earnest on August 9, 1918—not, as is often stated, after the attempt on Lenin's life on the thirtieth of that month, and seems to have been prompted less by the Allied intervention than by peasant risings. Three major innovations were now made: first, the shooting of innocent hostages received Lenin's sanction;[64] second, specific groups of the population were earmarked by him for the supreme penalty (including—rather curiously— "hundreds of prostitutes who made [our] soldiers drunk, ex-officers, etc." in Nizhniy Novgorod);[65] third, execution by hanging, as distinct from shooting, was recommended for the first time[66]—a measure calculated to produce a particularly horrifying effect upon morally sensitive and historically conscious Russians. On August 22 Lenin also advised his agent in Samara, his birthplace, that "vacillating elements" were to be shot out of hand, "without asking anyone or permitting idiotic red tape," whereas as recently as the ninth of that month he had ordered such people to be confined to a concentration camp.[67] By August

30 he was suggesting to Trotsky that even top-flight military commanders on the Red side, such as Vatsetis, should be shot if the military operations outside Kazan should be delayed or prove unsuccessful.[68] Fate then took a hand: on that very day the author of these bloodthirsty epistles himself fell victim of a terrorist's bullet.

It would be nice to think that the experience sobered him: certainly there is a gap of several months in the correspondence before the next outburst of ferocity. However this may be, by May 1919 Lenin is calling for "the most merciless repression, cost what it may" of rebellious Don cossacks or suspected White sympathizers in the Saratov area,[69] and for a further toughening of the hostage system: those taken are now to include officers' families, not just the officers themselves.[70] He has now forfeited his earlier respect for public opinion abroad, for he entertains the rather crazy notion that all foreigners living in Petrograd should be incarcerated in a concentration camp, to form a kind of pool of hostages.[71]

By this time a much larger proportion of his threats is directed "inwards," i.e., against people who could not by any reasonable criterion be considered opponents of the regime. Summary execution is recommended of anyone living in a frontline area who conceals the fact that he has a rifle, or of Red Army soldiers guilty of theft or acts of violence.[72] By 1920 he is naming even wider groups of potential victims: for example, civilian functionaries in the Moscow soviet who could not bring about an immediate improvement in the fuel supply, and Ukrainian peasants who were unable to meet their targets for deliveries of produce.[73] When Kamenev and others warn him that the Cheka's depredations in the Ukraine "had brought a mass of evil," he takes the line that this is simply due to the inferior quality of the personnel employed in the organization and orders a purge (chistka)[74]—incidently, the first occasion when this term appears in the correspondence.

This dismal catalogue shows plainly the truth of the old adage that "absolute power corrupts absolutely": the scope of the terror becomes steadily wider and its impact more arbitrary. Lenin remained creditably modest in his private life but behaved with increasing arrogance in the exercise of his police functions. In a fit of temper or pique he would order the punishment of men who caused him displeasure on some matter in which he happened to take a close personal interest. For example, as a journalist he was keen to maintain certain standards in the production of printed works. In October 1919 the State Publishing House brought out the minutes of the first Comintern congress, and Lenin discovered to his disgust that on page 99 of the pamphlet there were numerous misprints. He thundered to Vorovsky: "put those guilty in jail and make them paste correction slips into all copies."[75] A few months later, vacationing at Gorki, he noted that someone had felled an elm-tree in the park which he considered quite healthy. He put the blame on the manager of the sanatorium, a certain E. Ya. Veber, and sentenced him to one month's imprisonment. Nor was this just a passing whim which he regretted on reflection; one week later the order was confirmed.[76]

It is in this context that one should consider Lenin's interventions to secure the release of individuals arrested without due cause by the Cheka or other organs of authority, and whose fate was somehow brought to his attention—often by an old comrade, or by a female relative or acquaintance.[77] The importance of these actions appears to have been exaggerated by sympathetic biographers, although it is difficult to be certain, since such interventions were frequently effected by oral communication and have left no trace in the correspondence. This source yields evidence of no more than seventeen such incidents, nearly all of them concerning intellectuals. Of these pleas one was refused[78] and sixteen were granted. Of these, two yielded no result because of opposition by the Cheka;[79] in six cases the subsequent fate of the individual concerned is unknown;[80] and in the remaining eight cases the individuals were freed.[81] How representative this breakdown is remains uncertain.

The humanitarian role of Maxim Gorky in securing these favors is well known,[82] and here one need add merely that two cases in the last category were due to his persistence (Volny, Sapozhnikov). Gorky also won other material concessions for hard-pressed intellectuals,[83] and persuaded Lenin to countermand a terroristic order that had been issued by an irascible supply official.[84] In April 1920 Lenin gave Gorky a useful document instructing the Petrograd authorities to render him every assistance.[85] But he did not always deal with his old friend in a straightforward manner on this issue. In September 1919 he agreed to set up a commission to review the cases of arrested "bourgeois intellectuals of the Kadet type" and to free them where possible, but in informing Gorky of this he mentioned the names of only two of its three members; the third was none other than Dzerzhinsky. It was in this letter, one of the most revealing in the collection, that he attempted to rationalize the terror on the following grounds: first, it was essential for the regime's survival; second, the number of victims was far fewer than those resulting from the "imperialist war"; third, many intellectuals were not persecuted but were actively serving the new state; lastly, in any case such persons had a highly inflated view of their own importance, for in reality they were worth no more than a (four-letter word, suppressed for decency's sake in the original).[86]

Fortunately for the future of the Soviet State, he was not entirely consistent in maintaining this brutal position, but somewhat belatedly came to recognize the valuable role played by "specialists" of various kinds in the construction of the new order.

V

In the social and economic sphere, as in the political, Lenin's correspondence suggests that vital decisions were often delayed, or not taken at all, because basic ideological assumptions impeded clarity of thought and firmness of action. Yet in comparison with some of his colleagues the Party leader was an exemplar of rationality and common sense. As is well known, he long resisted the temptation to socialize industry wholesale; he also endeavored to check the excesses of anarchistic "workers' control" and to inculcate notions of labor discipline. Furthermore, he was prepared to tolerate a range of income differentials that many of his colleagues found shocking.

The left-wingers' citadel was Petrograd, where they enjoyed Zinoviev's protection. They regarded as potentially disastrous any relaxation of the centralized system of economic controls. Lenin was firmly committed to the maintenance of the state monopoly on internal trade—the fundamental principle of what later came to be called "war-communism"—but was anxious to utilize the resources of the cooperative movement in distributing rations, because he was confident that it could without much trouble be integrated into the general state economic administration. In November 1918 a government decision was reached to this effect but it met with opposition from the "Northern Commune," as the Petrograd Bolsheviks were pleased to call their organization. Lenin wrote to Zinoviev reassuring him that no harm would result from this step: "I ask you," he said mildly, "to give the cooperators a chance to work."[87] This plea had little effect. Cooperatives in Petrograd were forcibly closed down and their stocks requisitioned. These acts earned their tormentors a reprimand from Lenin.[88] Shortly afterwards a dispute broke out on this matter within the central Supply commissariat which called forth another intervention on his part in favor of the "liberals."[89] In May 1919 the Petrograd "supply commissar," the former Bolshevik Duma deputy Badayev, submitted his resignation in protest at the decision of his superiors in Moscow to allow a group of Ukrainian refugees resident in the former capital to retain in their possession some food supplies they had brought with them. Badayev argued that this would give them a privileged status vis-à-vis their less fortunate fellow citizens. Lenin amicably but firmly rejected his request, saying: "don't indulge in caprices. You're not a fine lady. . . . Get on with your work . . . and in future carry out all orders from the center."[90] The controversy was not stilled, but continued into the N.E.P. era, when it became a leitmotif of Soviet politics.[91]

The reverse side of the medal was that Lenin took a toughly realistic line towards the aspirations of the common people for some early alleviation of their hardships. So far as the industrial workers are concerned, ostensibly the backbone of the new order, it is remarkable how rarely they figure in Lenin's correspondence for these years. He had neither time nor inclination for exchanges of stereotyped messages with "the toiling masses," such as became a prominent feature of public life in the Stalin era.[92] The little he had to say on labor matters was concerned less with the workers' welfare than with industrial discipline, and in particular with the mobilization of workers for various military or semi-military tasks. Thus early in 1919 he ordered five thousand Petrograd employees to be resettled in Izhevsk Zavod, and in the following winter dispatched some workers from this isolated place in the approaches to the Urals—conceivably the same men—to the railway repair shops at Omsk, where subsequently sabotage was suspected.[93]

This was the moment when Trotsky and others had the unhappy idea of forming surplus Red Army soldiers into "labor armies" and employing them on civilian tasks. Lenin welcomed this scheme warmly and took steps to enforce it with a minimum of delay.[94] A few weeks later, however, he wrote to Trotsky: "I fear that we were in too much of a hurry over the labor armies, unless they can be used wholly to rush supplies to the Western Front."[95] These second thoughts implied only that the scheme was inexpedient, not that it was wrong in principle.

Towards the countless peasant millions Lenin's attitude was sterner still. They alone could provide the grain and other produce essential for the physical survival of the Red Army and the dwindling urban population. This basic task was given precedence over the implementation of general revolutionary strategy, which dictated that special care be taken to preserve the so-called *smychka*, or proletarian-peasant alliance. Industrial chaos, along with the effects of war and the Allied blockade, had put a virtual stop to normal market relationships, and massive coercion was seen as the only alternative. The shock troops in the battle for grain were armed gangs of desperate and hungry men from the cities, dignified by the name of "supply detachments." They were empowered to seize, for a nominal return, such produce as they considered surplus to the peasants' own requirements. From the countryman's point of view this system was an abomination, and it certainly acted as a strong disincentive for producing any "surplus" whatsoever.

The first reference to the supply detachments in Lenin's correspondence occurs as early as January 13, 1918.[96] They were still seen as an auxiliary weapon, the main emphasis being laid upon efforts to transport to the hungry cities what remained of the previous year's crop. But once the Brest-Litovsk treaty had deprived Soviet Russia of her Ukrainian bread-basket, the problem suddenly assumed catastrophic proportions. On May 10 Lenin urged Tsurupa, his Supply commissar, to send "twenty thousand men on a disciplined and merciless military campaign against the village bourgeoisie and speculators."[97] Ten days later he suggested that each provincial supply organization should have a leavening of up to fifty stalwart proletarians. When Tsurupa pointed out that this would make these bodies top-heavy, Lenin rather weakly replied that these men's function should be to agitate rather than to organize.[98] This remark showed how inadequately he had grasped the problem.

Not that he was entirely blind to the importance of giving the peasant producers some material incentives. Three weeks later he stated that "it is extremely important to make use of experienced honest practical men" (presumably merchants) to organize the collection of grain.[99] But he failed to appreciate that this idea was incompatible with wholesale coercion and lawlessness. Similarly, early in August 1918 he authorized Tsurupa to spend 30 million rubles on providing machinery and welfare facilities for the peasants, but in the same breath recommended that "a harvest drive upon Yelets province" be carried out by the starving populace of the surrounding countryside.[100] Another idea which he pressed strongly at this time was that the supply detachments should cleanse each area of its entire surplus before moving on to the next,[101] although there could scarcely have been a better way of alerting the potential victims as to what lay in store for them. It was only when some railwaymen protested at the depredations of these squads, and Transport commissar Nevsky boldly brought their protest to the government's notice, that Lenin gained an inkling of the true situation and ordered measures to be taken to restrain the wrongdoers.[102]

With the harvest, such as it was, gathered in and the Ukraine shortly afterwards opened up to Bolshevik reconquest, the supply crisis lost some of its urgency. During the winter of 1918-1919, and again in the following spring, Kamenev suggested that the state trading monopoly might be relaxed. On both occasions, however, he met stubborn resistance to the idea from his chief: it would mean, Lenin said, "a concession to the alien [class]," "a rotten compromise."[103] Kalinin, as we have seen, ran into trouble on the same score.[104] Lenin produced figures to show that the monthly rate of grain procurements by the state was rising rapidly[105]—and convinced himself that there was no need for any radical change of policy. The matter slipped from his attention until January 1920, when the Politburo examined a recent government decision to allow greater flexibility in determining the price of forage procured for State purposes. Lenin voted against the measure.[106]

Thereafter he is again silent until September 1920, when the peasants' plight is suddenly brought home to him in almost melodramatic circumstances. The tired and ailing leader goes hunting in the forests near Moscow. Passing through Bogdanovo, he is presented with a petition by the villagers, who complain that the local soviet, in order to meet its tax liabilities, has taken from the inhabitants, rich and poor alike, their entire crop, including the seed grain. To the local authority Lenin dispatches a letter that might have been penned by some eighteenth-century *grand seigneur*: "I can confirm the difficult supply position of the village of Bogdanovo, commonly known as Bogdanikha." Would they kindly investigate the matter and adjust its tax assessment?[107]

But were there not many thousands of Bogdanovos, scattered across the length and breadth of Russia, whose plight remained outside the dictator's ken? For them nothing was done until the strategic retreat of N.E.P., the inception of which in March 1921 owed much to multiplying signs of peasant unrest. The Party leader had been caught off balance by those "forces of spontaneity" he so distrusted, and which the Soviet State as yet found difficult to control.

VI

The material examined here also contains some interesting data on Lenin's handling of military and foreign policy matters, but perhaps enough has been said to demonstrate the value of this source. Whatever its inadequacies from an editorial standpoint, Lenin's correspondence affords the historian a unique means of penetrating the Bolshevik leader's mind and analyzing his approach to the myriad problems that beset him. It shows us that behind the facade of perfection presented to the world by the practitioners of the Lenin cult there was a fallible human being, a man of many parts, who was becoming increasingly frustrated at the imperfections of the new order. Within a few years he would also realize that the sickness went too deep to be cured by any remedy of which he knew.

Notes

1. Iu. A. Akhapkin, "Organizatsiia Leninskogo arkhiva," *Voprosy istorii*, 3 (1970), 60; cf. V.A. Lyubisheva, 'Vossozdaniye arkhiva Predsedatelya SNK V.I. Lenina', *Voprosy istorii*, 4 (1969), 47. This figure refers to 'Fond 2', established in 1939 (see below). In 1934 the archive comprised 26,687 documents by Lenin or addressed to him, and in late 1927 there were 34,493 items including 20,905 Lenin documents (p. 46).

2. Ibid., p. 41.

3. Ibid., pp. 48, 49.

4. *Kommunist*, no. 15 (1957), pp. 10-14.

5. There is one curious exception to this rule. The commentary on those documents in which Lenin expresses his interest in broadcasting refer to a work by A.M. Nikolayev, *Lenin i radio* (Moscow, 1960).

6. V.I. Lenin, *Polnoye sobraniye sochineniy*, 5th ed., 56 vols. (Moscow, 1958-66), *LI*, 481. Hereafter cited as "*LI*, p. 000."

7. *LI*, no. 472. Cf. nos. 363, 365, where it is claimed, falsely, that the document was first published in full in the 1956 edition of Lenin's *Voyennaya perepiska* (Moscow).

8. *Leninskii sbornik*, XXXIV (1942), 174; *L*, no. 644; J.M. Meijer, ed., *The Trotsky Papers, 1917-1919* (The Hague, 1964), I, no. 314. Hereafter cited as *TP*.

9. V.I. Lenin, *Sochineniya*, 3rd ed. (1930-31), XXIX, nos. 186, 190.

10. Ibid., no. 191.

11. Ibid., no. 269; *TP*, no. 225.

12. *TP*, nos. 21, 217, 14 and 15 May 1919; *L*, no. 569.

13. *TP*, nos. 377, 378, 4 and 5 Oct. 1919; *LI*, no. 89.

14. *TP*, no. 50.

15. *TP*, no. 128; I am following Meijer's excellent notes here.

16. Ibid., nos. 207, 229, 273, 275, 278, 282; the latter is in *LI*, no. 616, but with Stalin as the addressee.

17. Ibid., no. 330.

18. Lenin to Mezhlaud, Voroshilov and others, June 1, 1919; *Leninskiy sbornik* (1942), XXXIV, 158.

19. *L*, no. 605. It was not the case that only previous Soviet publication was deemed to count, for where a Lenin letter had been published in a source as impeccably bourgeois as the *Times Literary Supplement* this was stated: *L*, no. *34.

20. *LI*, nos. *75, *101, *241, *370.

21. *L*, no. 347, Oct. 1918.

22. *L*, no. *204, 1 July 1918.

23. *LI*, no. 559, 20 Oct. 1920.

24. *L*, no. 577. For earlier moves, see nos. 390, 418; *TP*, nos. 148, 174. Despite some uneasiness at the turn of the year, Lenin's relations with Trotsky seem to have been generally good until this point.

25. *L*, no. *640; for the repercussions, see *TP*, nos. 275, 278, 285.

26. *LI*, no. *55.

27. *LI*, nos. *82, 98.

28. *LI*, no. 115.

29. *LI*, nos. *309, *436, *441.

30. *LI*, nos. 113, 138, *237, *270, *367, *370, *525, *536, 562.

31. *L*, nos. 179, 228, 348, *378, 400; *LI*, nos. 47, 79, 406, *534.

32. *LI*, nos. 201, *203, 206, 14-16 Jan. 1920.

33. *LI*, nos. 231, 405, 549.

34. *L*, no. 368.

35. *L*, no. *566.

36. Our italics. To Chicherin for Karakhan, *LI*, *394, 24 June 1920; to R.E. Klasson, no. 582, 2 Nov. 1920.

37. *LI*, nos. 79, *249, 252, 571.

38. *L*, nos. 14, 11, 19, November 16, 1917.

39. *L*, no. 496.

40. *LI*, no. 210; cf. *L*, nos. *131, 329, 338; 51, no. 174, on the question of displaying propagandist statuary in the Moscow streets, a matter which Lenin took very seriously.

41. *L*, nos. 118, 197.

42. *L*, no. 320.

43. *L*, no. 497; *LI*, no. 235.

44. *L*, no. 488, 12 March 1919.

45. *LI*, no. 165. The Russian is more expressive: *t'ma i kucha chinov, pod-, nad-, ot-, dlya i proch.!!*

46. *LI*, no. 205, 16 Jan. 1920.

47. *L*, no. 544.

48. *LI*, no. *424, July 15, 1920.

49. *L*, no. 254.

50. A. Ulam, *Lenin and the Bolsheviks* (New York, 1966), p. 528.

51. Cf., for example, *LI*, no. 193, 5 Jan. 1920: a touching appeal by a *khodok* from a distant factory for increased rations so that the men might work harder "for our revolutionary Russia."

52. *L*, no. 33.

53. *L*, no. 99.

54. *L*, no. 237.

55. *L*, nos. 524, 580, April 21, and May 20, 1919.

56. *L*, no. 111, April 15, 1918.

57. *L*, no. 134.

58. *L*, no. 385, cf. *LI*, no. 167.

59. *L*, no. 449.

60. P. Malkov, *Zapiski komendanta moskovskogo kremlya* (Moscow, 1959), p. 148.

61. *L*, nos. 26, *30, 36.

62. *L*, no. 196, June 26, 1918; cf. no. 202.

63. *L*, no. 213, July 7.

64. *L*, nos. 255, 261.

65. *L*, nos. 257, 259, August 9.

66. *L*, no. 292, August 20, 1918.

67. *L*, no. 302, cf. no. 259. The word used is *kontsentratsionnyy lager*.

68. *TP*, no. 61; not printed in the *Works*.

69. *L*, no. 573; *LI*, no. 4.

70. *L*, no. 625.

71. *L*, no. 609.

72. *L*, no. 624; *LI*, no. *57; June 6, and August 20, 1919.

73. *LI*, nos. 383, 433; June 16, and July 1920.

74. *L*, no. 615, June 4, 1919.

75. *LI*, no. 118, October 24, 1919.

76. *LI*, no. 393, June 22, 1920.

77. *E.g.*, by Krupskaya, *LI*, no. 61, or Kollontay, *LI*, no. *148.

78. *L*, no. 335; cf. *L*, no. *94, a similar case of refusal of permission to visit political prisoners.

79. *L*, no. 460; *LI*, no. 211.

80. *L*, nos. 278, 358, 374, 382; *LI*, nos. *148, 261 (in the latter case the victim was not jailed but "molested by the mob").

81. Palinski (Perm), *L*, no. 223; Palchinsky (Petrograd), *L*, no. 379; Rizen-kampf (Samara), *L*, no. 381; Kurdinsky (Petrograd), *LI*, no. 61; Pervushin (Kazan), *LI*, no. 268; Volny (Oryol), *L*, no. 514; Shorin (Nizhniy Novgorod), *LI*, no. 244; Sapozhnikov (Petrograd), *LI*, no. 287.

82. B.D. Wolfe, *The Bridge and the Abyss: the Troubled Friendship of Maxim Gorky and V.I. Lenin* (New York-London, 1967), pp. 95-98.

83. *LI*, nos. 389, 466, 561.

84. *LI*, no. 233.

85. *LI*, no. 324.

86. *LI*, no. *80; cf. no. 84 to M.F. Andreyeva.

87. *LI*, no. *378, Nov. 30, 1918.

88. *LI*, no. 400, Dec. 25, 1918.

89. *LI*, no. *477, Feb. 27, 1919.

90. *L*, no. *552, May 4, 1919.

91. *LI*, nos. 47, 216, *534; Aug. 7, 1919, Jan. 26, 1920, Oct. 6, 1920.

92. There are only two of these, both relatively early, to the workers of Rybinsk and Vytsa respectively: *L*, nos. 112, 161, 15 April and 31 May 1918. When a Party official in western Siberia sent a formal message of greeting to the leadership, Lenin not only refused to accept but ordered proceedings to be taken against the offending functionary for wasting state funds (*LI*, no. 254, 27 Feb. 1920). He did, however, accept a rather similar communication from some miners in eastern Siberia: *LI*, no. 504, 15 Sept. 1920. A number of goodwill messages also reached him from the "lower depths" of Soviet society, to which he sometimes replied, but these are not considered "canonical writings" and are to be found in a volume entitled *Tovarishchu Leninu. Pisma Yrudyashchikhsya Leninu, 1917-1924*, 2nd ed. (Moscow, 1969).

93. *L*, no. 448, Jan. 31, 1919; *LI*, no. 219, Jan. 29, 1920.

94. *LI*, nos. 196, 227.

95. *LI*, no. 254, February 27, 1920.

96. *L*, no. 51.

97. *L*, no. 139.

98. *L*, no. 147, May 20, 1918.

99. *L*, no. 180, May 11, 1918; cf. no. 130, April 1918.

100. *L*, no. 249.

101. *L*, nos. 275, 294.

102. *L*, no. 203, July 1; for an example, cf. no. 248.

103. *L*, no. 384, 546, Dec. 10, 1918, Apr. 1919.

104. Cf. supra, n. 34.

105. *L*, no. *607; *LI*, no. *5.

106. *LI*, no. *94, Jan. 1920.

107. *LI*, no. 490, Sept. 6, 1920; cf. no. 562, Oct. 31, 1920.

16 Lenin and Meta-Strategy

STEFAN T. POSSONY

Arguments about historical continuity are interesting, but rarely conclusive. There is, however, *one* area of study where historical continuity has been quite impressive. I am speaking of strategy. In this field V.I. Lenin excelled and broke new ground—in fact, he was the principal creator of the strategic pattern that has prevailed since World War I.

Lenin was the originator of Communist strategy, not Marx or Engels. Engels was a good strategic thinker, but it is questionable whether he can be regarded as a forerunner of Lenin. There is little question that *in strategy* Stalin was Lenin's creative and successful disciple. Brezhnev, too, has continued Lenin's strategic tradition effectively—we are observing the phenomenon every day.

The Leninist strategy is only in part tied to communism as a specific ideology or political movement. With adjustments, it can be used by non-Communists as well, and it can be used *against* the Communists.

Naturally, the strategy which Lenin invented *as a pattern*, has been developed and enriched by his successors, and he did not by any means invent all of it. I once compared Lenin to Philip of Macedon and Stalin to Alexander the Great—this comparison, evidently, applies *only* to strategy. Both Philip and Lenin were conquerors in their own right and they prepared the ground for great subsequent conquests. As distinguished from Philip, Alexander, and Stalin, Lenin's performance was particularly impressive since, when he started, Lenin was a nobody without money, territory, military force, or power. Lenin did not personally command on the battlefield, in which point he differs from Philip and Alexander, and to some extent from Stalin, but he designed Communist grand strategy. Within a remarkably short time, he conquered a gigantic country and the conquest, so far, has remained firm.

Before I continue, I should point out that today we are still talking on the basis of partial knowledge. We know more than we used to know ten or fifteen years ago, but many of the operations which Lenin ran are still inadequately analyzed and most of the relevant papers and strategic plans have yet to be published. L.A. Fotieva disclosed in 1956 that 500 telegrams, memoranda on phone calls, and letters on military questions have been preserved.[1] This would mean either that much documentation has been destroyed or that Lenin's *operational* role has been exaggerated. In any event, I do not imply that all strategic operations conducted under Lenin's top command must be imputed to Lenin himself. He could not have performed without able assistants, and some of those contributed to the body of Lenin's strategic doctrine.

In a volume devoted to Lenin fifty years after the revolution, John Erickson discussed Lenin's role as a civil war leader.[2] Erickson explained that Lenin effectively traded space for time, coordinated theaters of war, organized the Red Army and its command structure, made an attempt at exporting the revolution, and conducted its strategy by assigning priority to politics.

Lenin's first major strategic decision was to conclude the peace of Brest-Litovsk. He abandoned his earlier theories about the value of a militia and broke with socialist tradition by building a regular conscript army under a centralized command. He ran strategy himself through the central committee and four civilian "super-commissars" (Kamenev, Stalin, Ordzhonikidze, and Trotsky) as well as military specialists. He reserved for himself the role of "strategic mediator, manager and coordinator," and till the end of 1919, "grand coordinator." Throughout his tenure, he rejected command by committee and insisted on unity of command, yet he always performed in close association with the military command. He also placed great emphasis on the "internal front," and through the Cheka established "iron discipline." "Never . . . did he lose sight of the importance of the rear and the deep rear." Lenin operated closely with Trotsky as the man who ran the Red Army, but "the relationship between Lenin and Chicherin in shaping and pursuing diplomatic-strategic aims, was equally important."

In 1920, after the Polish attack on Soviet Russia, he prepared for all-out "revolutionary war," which without risking the soviet base was to conquer Poland and Germany. The attempt failed because Lenin had incorrectly assessed the revolutionary potentialities of the target countries.

In addition to his operational work, Lenin acted as military administrator and managed the "war machine at large." He also was the "chief assessor of the significance of victory." This picture may be a bit overdrawn but Lenin clearly was the top man and at the very least was the person to approve all major decisions.

For Lenin, warfare was "a combination of military, economic, diplomatic and psychological activity." It was his emphasis on the importance of the rear, which "chiefly distinguished his own sense of strategic priorities, from those set out in more formal military terms by the military." Duly impressed by the need for reserves and the morale factor, "his chief concern was to establish a connection between war and revolution" and to work out a "revolutionary strategy." He discovered that "peace" has a "potency all its own" because it offers a chance to deploy "the weapons of psychological warfare."

Whether Lenin had anything to do with it or not, I do not know, but I want to underscore that the Soviets pioneered in psychological warfare when with the first imaginative use of radio, they fomented a mutiny against the French Black Sea Fleet and among French ground troops in the Ukraine. Without firing a shot, they forced France to discontinue its intervention. The operation had long-

lasting effects on the French military establishment and weakened F
1919 until the period of World War II.

Erickson's analysis is far superior to that given by Marshal V.D. Sok
editor of the second edition of *Military Strategy*. Sokolovsky added
marks which show that Lenin was quite adept at handling operational
must be remembered, however, that Soviet *military* writers stay away fr
tions of combined politico-military strategy and devote themselves to operational problems exclusively. Perhaps the remark is in order that Lenin was his
own intelligence advisor, especially in the field of political intelligence. Therefore, he merits being compared with some of the great captains of history. For
example, Lenin's conduct of the civil war shows many similarities with the strategy Frederick the Great employed in the Seven Years War. Certainly, commanders like Frederick the Great and Napoleon displayed genius on the battlefield. But Lenin fought from a base of chaos and within a chaotic theater. Was
this one of the secrets of his success?

The civil war coincided with military interventions by Britain, France, Japan,
and the United States. There has been a great deal of Communist mythology
about those *Entente* actions, which we cannot discuss here, but intervention
there was. There is no doubt but that the Lenin government was highly worried
about the danger that under certain circumstances the *Entente* powers might
decide to eliminate the Communist regime. Lenin had an explicitly stated strategy for dangers of this type, namely to embroil the "imperialist powers" with
one another. If we are to believe Soviet Colonel D. Grinishin, writing in 1957,
Lenin aimed at beating the various hostile armies singly.[3] Lenin judged that the
Entente leaders were committing one stupidity after the other. As a result of
Lenin's strategy, Grinishin asserted, the *Entente* did not mount one single combined campaign, and the Red Army took care of the various foreign and white
armies one by one. It would go much too far to ascribe the stupidities of the
Entente and the anti-Communist Russian leaders to Lenin's strategy alone, but
that Lenin was playing a complicated game of "splitting tactics" very skillfully is
fairly clear, as is the fact that Communist propaganda was achieving substantial
successes which manifested themselves in operational effects.

The French magazine *Est & Ouest* devoted a whole issue (no. 444-445, April
1-30, 1970) to the centenary of Lenin and printed an article by Claude Harmel,
"Trois erreurs stratégiques de Lénine." These mistakes, according to Harmel,
were the seizure of power in 1917, the creation of the Communist International,
and the colonial revolution.

Harmel argued that Lenin wanted to be the "strategist of the world
revolution." He did accomplish a revolution in Russia, but that event failed to
trigger the world revolution; if the United States had not entered the war, a victorious Germany would have stamped out Lenin's strategic base. The Communist International was a mistake because it was essentially designed to break
the socialist movement. In due course, this strategy led to the emergence of

Nazism (and to World War II, I may add). The fomenting of the colonial revolution was derived from the idea that if the capitalist world were deprived of the profits and super-profits which it draws from the colonial countries, capitalism would collapse. Lenin's idea that the fate of world capitalism would be decided in India and China turned out to be wrong, yet the attempt to stir up colonial revolutions induced the Communists to enter into alliances with nonproletarian and nonsocialist movements and to expend their energies in countries which neither had a large industry nor even a proletariat.

These criticisms are valid if we overemphasize some aspects of Lenin's doctrine and the particular estimates which Lenin used to institute those policies. They are far less valid if strategy is understood as a game to increase power within a constantly changing world. Lenin's expectations were not fulfilled—almost predictably so. But did the Communists lose or gain power? Why should the observer who does not believe in Lenin's eschatology anyway argue that Lenin's strategy failed because he did not reach utopia? He didn't. Did he then, through his mistakes, advance the cause of democracy? He didn't, either. Yet those criteria seem to me to be more proper yardsticks.

M. Harmel believes that after November 1917 further resistance against the Germans was possible and that Lenin should have continued the war because the Americans might not have arrived in time to ensure the defeat of Germany. Mr. Erickson argues by contrast that, on the whole, Lenin's decision not to continue the war and instead to conclude a peace treaty through which space was traded for time, was justified. But he acknowledges that the deliberately rapid demobilization of the Russian Army before the Red Army was created and before an agreement had been reached with the Central Powers was very questionable.

I happen to agree that prolonged resistance was feasible. I also think that it was necessary to continue fighting, *if* the revolution was to be carried into Germany. I explained these points at length in my Lenin biography. I don't think the argument about the U.S. Army arriving in time is persuasive because by December 1917 the Americans already were arriving and Lenin was able to take this factor into account.

Both Erickson and Harmel are arguing this case in the abstract: I have attempted to show that the Germans were blackmailing Lenin. Hence Lenin was not free to select an optimal strategy but was compelled to do Germany's bidding; or else the Germans would have stopped giving Lenin the support which was indispensable if he wanted to stay in power.[a]

The seizure of power in 1917 was not orthodox, I agree, but power was

[a]On February 4, 1919, Lenin provided an explanation of his own: it would be far more difficult to begin a revolution in France or Germany than in Russia, but once socialism was established in those countries, it would be far easier to maintain it than in Russia where cadres and resources are lacking. "Up to now the character of the German revolution is not too clear . . . Il faut attendre." But the peoples will eat more and more of the socialist tart. "L'inévitable s'accomplira." Predestination is always an excellent justification for inaction. (Ludovic Naudeau, *En prison sous la terreur russe* (Paris, 1920), pp. 192ff.

"lying in the streets." Would anybody else have resisted the temptation? In any event, the record shows that by September-October 1917 the Germans were pushing Lenin into action. Since, to a great extent, Lenin was in the hands of the Germans and at their mercy, at least of their political pressure, but at the same time had only Germany as a potential or real ally, regardless of whether this ally was defeated or victorious, he was not very anxious to push a Communist revolution precisely in that country. Strategic necessity demanded that he contribute his share to derailing the revolution. No strategist can be successful if he does not regard some of his forces as expendable.

The Communist International was not a very effective instrument. Granted. Yet the notion that the Communists should have cooperated with the social democrats is hardly persuasive if the fundamental divergencies of strategic objectives by the Communists and socialists are taken into consideration. Rosa Luxemburg opposed the founding of the Comintern partly because she did not want predominance by the Bolsheviks and partly because she distrusted Lenin. She was right for several reasons, which may be summarized by the words, "class democracy." But she was wrong from the point of view of conquest strategy. The argument is tenable only if we talk as theoretical Marxists about an abstraction called the "proletariat" but not if, as strategists, we are looking for an instrument of political warfare.

Similar arguments apply to the colonial revolution. During Lenin's time, this program centered on the Middle East and India and was an almost indispensable counter to British strategy.

The Comintern and the colonial revolution, which was one of the Comintern's major tasks, had many defects, but they were the instruments through which the Communist parties, together with their subsidiary and front organizations, were brought to life, and were kept alive in many countries; and through which these parties were linked up with one another and with Moscow. The Comintern and the colonial revolution, as they were conceived and run by Lenin, must be judged on the sole basis of whether this international network of Communist organizations was important *strategically*.

Lenin did not create those instruments to take care of acute situations in this or that country. Instead he was interested in fashioning a strategic force which would be permanently available and could be used in the same way as an army or navy. That force was created, and as the International Communist movement, it still remains an active force. This is the essential accomplishment, regardless of whether the Comintern was a pretty bad organization and often indulged in stupid policies.

Lenin's score card looks something like this:

revolution of 1905   Lenin becomes professional
revolutions of 1917
    February   point advantage

July	failure
October	win
civil war	win
foreign intervention	win
European revolution	no contest
Hungarian revolution	failure, possibly throw the match
German revolutions	
all Germany, 1918/1919	no contest or throw the match
Bavarian, 1918	no contest
all Germany, 1921	failure
all Germany, 1923[b]	failure
war with Poland, 1920	draw
extend war and revolution to	
Germany, 1920	fail
support to Turkey	win

This shows five failures and four wins plus one draw and several no contests, which outsiders believed to have been contests.

In sum, Lenin conquered a powerful base of operations extending from the Baltic and North Seas to the Pacific, he created strong military and political operational forces, he set up a unique instrument of political warfare, and he established the Rapollo alliance with Germany.

To evaluate Lenin's performance as a strategist, it is necessary to distinguish between distinct levels of strategy. We identify, first, operational strategy which includes, *inter alia*, the selection of centers of gravity and battlefields, the moves toward the battlefield,[c] the choice of offensive or defensive modes of operating, the role and type of surprise, and so on. We identify, second, resource strategy, e.g., the building of a base, the creation of military and political forces, technology, weapons production, etc. Lenin was a pretty good operational strategist, but not exceptional, let alone "revolutionary," and since he destroyed more resources than he created, he was pretty mediocre as a resource strategist; except that he conquered his base and built novel and potentially powerful political forces.

There is a third level of strategy, which I would like to call "meta-strategy" and which deals with commanding, from the top level, military and political forces *interdependently*. These political forces include diplomacy, but this is an auxiliary force. The essence of the combination is *subversion*.

Lenin was a superb meta-strategist, and it is in this field of meta-strategy where he made his truly revolutionary contributions.

---

[b]Lenin was by then incapacitated.

[c]According to Clausewitz such moves are strategic, whereas moves *on* the battlefield are tactical.

In his book, *Power Through Subversion*, Laurence W. Beilenson argues that subversion was Lenin's preferred tool of strategy, as it has been the preferred tool of Lenin's successors. Beilenson defines subversion as follows: "The use of means illicit in the nation subverted (1) intended to overthrow its government in all or part of its territory . . . or (2) intended to cause action or inaction by the subverted nation primarily to benefit another nation without internally overthrowing the government of the subverted nation." I would change this definition slightly by saying that subversion is the use of psychopolitical and other means, whether licit or illicit, intended to overthrow or else neutralize, paralyze, influence, activate, or provoke a foreign government. The word "provoke" is here used in the sense of "inciting to action including incitement to commence war." For example, President Polk provoked Mexico into attacking the United States and Serbia, with Russia's help, provoked Austria-Hungary in 1914.

Subversion may be a substitute for war but according to the Communist scheme it is, in most circumstances, a necessary adjunct to, or element of war. For example, subversion is required to weaken the opponents of the USSR and to incite them one against the other, while in most instances a combination of subversion *and* war is required to establish Communist control over a country hostile to the USSR. In this scheme, subversion is super-ordinated to war, whether offensive or defensive. This is so because the objective of the Communist forces is not so much to defeat their opponent on the battlefield, but to establish Communist rule over the hostile country.

Aside from ideological talk about the "class character" of a conflict, Lenin's concept of "revolutionary war" is precisely that war is just one, albeit sometimes the decisive, element in the total process of conflict. War may be indispensable to knock-out the opponent in the tenth or fifteenth round, but the knock-out occurs if and when, and because, prior subversion has weakened the powers of resistance.

According to Beilenson, "Lenin believed that defensive wars would be necessary, and he predicted a final war between the communist camp and the capitalist camp because the latter would attack." I agree that in a defensive war subversion may be subordinated to military operations, if only because the very occurrence of a war which the USSR must fight defensively indicates that its subversive operations did fail. The final act of the conflict may, indeed, be a large war resulting from a "capitalist attack." But if Lenin's strategy were successful, this attack would be delayed until the Communists possess clearcut superiority of strength, and the attack would be initiated through provocation at a time when the *Communist* strategists judge the optimal moment for the showdown has arrived.[4] Or else the war can be dispensed with in the final act because subversion has been overwhelmingly successful and the opponent of the USSR surrenders.

In Beilenson's interpretation, Lenin "had no objection to winning new communist-controlled nations by a soviet aggressive war if it could be waged without risking the soviet base. But in urging and practicing caution about waging offensive war that had more than a minimal risk to the soviet base Lenin departed from . . . all the extensive conquerors. Lenin thus changed the strategic relation of these two striking tools by exalting subversion over offensive war as the chief tool to win the world." I believe this reconstruction is correct in that the preservation of the Soviet operational base commands first priority in all Communist strategies and that the Communists do have a more cautious approach to "offensive war" than, let us say, Napoleon or Hitler. This caution is actually mandatory because the Communist dictatorship has never been sure it did achieve legitimacy.

Nevertheless, I suggest that not too much weight be given to the highly tenuous difference between "defensive" and "offensive." A strategic defensive can be fought through offensive tactics; an offensive strategy could be implemented through provocation and then appear to be defensive; and from the first the plan may be to conduct a "counter-offensive" operation which requires an initial enemy offensive. The offensive-defensive mix is heavily influenced by changing technology and force relationships in the dominant weapons. One basic rule of psychological strategy is to preserve the appearance of the defensive because, as Trotsky put it, " the offensive . . . develops better the more it looks like self-defense."

Furthermore, the frequent interpretation that "revolutionary war" is a sub-variant of "offensive war" is incorrect: such a war also could be defensive or counteroffensive. The distinction between offensive and defensive is largely one of tactics and in some instances of operational strategy, and it is not on the level of meta-strategy. Regardless of which concrete war the Communists are engaged in, whether on their own volition or not, it would be a "revolutionary war" and it would aim at revolutionizing the enemy country. This means that their *main* operational system would be subversion, while violent military operations against hostile military forces would be just one element of their strategy and would primarily aim at making subversion most effective. Whether the military events are decisive in the sense that they would have the greatest impact upon the opponent, is irrelevant: the essential point is that the military and nonmilitary operations are conducted interdependently. Thus, victory or defeat are crucial inputs into the final outcome.

The decisive event per se is a change of policy, government, or regime in one of the belligerent camps. Of course, the Communists aim at such a change in the countries which they are fighting and they want to prevent such a change within their own territories; which is the primary meaning they attach to "security of base."

Subversion has been practiced since time immemorial, but Lenin's new departure was that he instituted subversion as the chief tool of conquest. In so doing he departed from the ancient tradition of practicing subversion in a sporadic manner, which operation Beilenson calls "spiggot subversion." This type of subversion is practiced to accomplish a specific operational goal at a particular time and place and thereupon to return to "non-intervention."

Lenin's departure from this routine was that instead he instituted subversion on a permanent and global basis. He also interconnected the various types of subversive operations to accomplish mutual stimulation; he involved in the subversive undertaking not only Communists but also non-Communist and even anti-Communist political movements; he interlinked operations and he ran simultaneously subversive operations in several countries which could be mutually "contradictory" but which were supposed to supplement one another; and he even conducted subversion against a country like Germany with which he was allied.

In the meta-strategic sense, therefore, Lenin's accomplishment was extraordinary indeed: he conceived a new type of strategy, which his successors have been able to apply against naively misinterpreting and incomprehending opponents. Hence an unprecedented subversive capability has existed under Moscow's control ever since the initiation of Lenin's rule. More specifically, Lenin devised the new strategic concept, he fashioned the initial tools of implementation, and he conducted the initial "shake-down" operations.

This is his real achievement and it counts for little whether or not during Lenin's time the Comintern was a disorganized phoney (which it was), whether he tried or didn't try to spark a European or even global revolutionary combustion (this was a silly concept anyway), or whether the economic ideas which were used to justify the colonial revolution were correct or false (they were invalid).

Not the least accomplishment of Lenin's was that he managed to utilize subversion even before he controlled a subversive base: it was through subversion that he came to power.

I realize that such statements create the impression of "over-simplification." Lenin's strategic operations before and after the seizure of power were complex, confusing, and contradictory; there were wrong anticipations, failures, and accidents; and opportunities and situations, which he was able to utilize, had not been created by him. I am not trying in this context to retrace Lenin's strategy and his improvisations historically and to correlate his strategy with the underlying social processes. Leadership does not take place in vacuo but necessarily is addressed to circumstances. I am concerned with Lenin's leadership as such. And I certainly do not suggest that the full strategic concept was in Lenin's head back in 1895 or 1903.

I *am* arguing that, retrospectively, Lenin's strategy can be described as that of permanent and global subversion in dialectic relation with revolutionary war.

Lenin arrived at this concept through several steps. His *What is to be Done?* (1902) was the origin, if I may put it this way. Through this book he established that the Communist party was not to be an ideological club but a combat party or combat force composed of professional revolutionaries. Whether Lenin's book was original or not—it wasn't—matters little because he did build the organization in this image and he learned the tricks of exerting widespread, occasionally even "mass" impact through a small elite group. He also conceived of his Party as a dominant element in a worldwide organization whose purpose was not that of holding international discussion congresses as the Second International was wont to do, but that of articulating and executing international socialist strategy.

Lenin also developed a new approach to propaganda. By organizing his group around Party newspapers and their distribution, he created, before the revolution, an organization which was making propaganda and was using the effect of this propaganda to enlarge and strengthen his organization. Lenin distinguished between propaganda and agitation, but in his operations he combined propagation or dissemination with organization and routine intelligence collection. This particular complex was partly connected with infiltration within and without the "labor movement." However, infiltration into "bourgeois" organizations and into the police, as well as illicit operations such as expropriations, were run separately and, of course, secretly.

During the 1905 revolution, Lenin picked up the concept of phased conquest or step-by-step advance, notably in the form of the "minimal program" and of the bourgeois-democratic revolution. He learned to appreciate the national factor and its potential development into national strife, as well as the importance of "anti-militarism," which aims at neutralizing or winning over the armed forces. He also was concerned with defeatism, which in the form of revolutionary defeatism, aims at fashioning revolution out of a military defeat. All these concepts lend themselves to effective subversive exploitation, in fact, they are in the nature of guidelines for subversion. According to my interpretation, "illicit means" overlap with the concept of "subversion" but, depending on existing legislation, some subversive operations can be quite legal.

Lenin also operated on an international scale, on the one hand, by soliciting and obtaining support from foreign socialist and liberal groups, notably in Western Europe and Germany, and on the other hand, by entering during the Russo-Japanese war into relations with the general staff of Japan.

It is not my intent here to evaluate the importance or effects of these various operations. I just want to identify some of the types of operations Lenin was interested in and which included money-raising and weapons procurement. Lenin was by no means the commander of the 1905 revolution, actually, his role was rather minimal, but he did learn about the practicalities of subversion and he understood the interrelationships between war and revolution. He also learned the lesson that "sectarian" approaches, for example nonparticipation in democratic elections, are counterproductive.

During World War I, while he continuously preached the idea that the war should be transformed everywhere into a civil war, he understood that pan-defeatism and pan-revolutionarism cannot work. Hence he settled on the practical concept that the war must everywhere be exploited to establish Communist influence, but that the overthrow of the tsarist regime was the lesser evil, i.e., the first order of business. This was the very concept which induced German social democracy to support the imperial war effort, but Lenin was smart enough to cover up his connection with the Kaiser's socialists. He recognized that his revolution (or subversion) was not feasible without the potent support of an organized state and he did not scruple to elect Germany as the main base of subversion although, of course, he remained in Switzerland and the Bolsheviks were active in Russia.

Once the tsar was out of the way, not by any help the Germans or Lenin had given to his departure, a powerful soviet emerged in Petrograd. The Bolsheviks had little to do with this event, too, and Lenin had disliked the institution in 1905. But in 1917 he was the first to comprehend "dual power," which basically means that the state authority is being "split." It seems to me that this insight prevented, in a subtle way, that the Petrograd soviet and the other soviets that had proliferated throughout the country were transformed into legislatures; instead they became predominantly executive organs which insisted on competing with the Provisional Government. Without the concept of dual power, the chances are that the Provisional Government and the soviets ultimately would have merged into a single governmental authority involving some sort of separation of powers. In this case, the idea itself—or rather the identification of a "fact"—was the strategy.

Lenin also saw the necessity of pulling elements of the army over to his side, to neutralize vacillating elements of the armed forces, and to involve the military in insurgent undertakings. For his political operations, Lenin secured adequate logistics in terms of money and media. On the strength of his propaganda he organized forces, procured arms and payments, and used the political, paramilitary, and military *dispositif* to seize power at the moment when the government was paralyzed.

The Germans were subverting Russia for the purpose of gaining victory. In this operation, Lenin was a tool of the Germans, although the German subversion included Bolsheviks other than Lenin and extended to non-Bolshevik groups. Lenin, of course, had no intention of helping the Germans to reach their objective but exploited them to reach his own. This sort of thing is not particularly rare or remarkable. For example, in 1915 the French Government—through Marcel Cachin, subsequently boss of the French CP—bought Mussolini to propel Italy into the war, but Mussolini pursued his own objectives, just as did the Sheriff of Mecca who had been bought by the British. Nor does the usual subversive relationship last for more than one transaction. In 1908, Aehrenthal, Austro-Hungarian foreign minister, bought Isvolsky, Russian foreign minister, and made a deal about Bosnia-Hertsegovina. The affair went sour, and Isvolsky became Austria-Hungary's implacable enemy.

Now, Lenin was not bribed but his operations were supported. There was nothing remarkable in this, since most revolutions are helped along by foreign subversion. But it was remarkable that in the specific strategy of subverting tsarist Russia through Lenin, many of the particular moves had been suggested to the Germans by Alexander Helphand (Parvus) who was a personal enemy of Lenin. Parvus was a Russian socialist as well as a member of the German Social Democratic party. He had been learning the same lessons as Lenin and he had acquired a far greater freedom of maneuver. He also had the ability to deal effectively with the German Foreign Office and explain to them revolutionary strategy in terms they would understand.[d] Through intermediaries Lenin and Parvus were in contact with one another and Parvus was close to masterminding the operation until April 1917, when Lenin cut him off.

The complexity of this particular subversion is increased by the fact that Parvus did not himself aim at a victory of Imperial Germany but desired to overthrow the tsar and effect a social revolution in Russia. He envisaged that, partly through operations he himself was planning and preparing, socialism would then be carried from Russia into Germany. At one time, he also expected that Lenin would help him in this strategy of dual revolution. Lenin was disinclined, and the German Foreign Office got rid of Parvus.

In all this, Lenin learned to appreciate fully the significance of techniques like infiltration, neutralization, polarization, and deception. During 1918, when he was eliminating the organized resistance by the Social Revolutionaries, and when he also deemed it necessary to extricate himself from German clutches, and to defend himself against subversion practiced by France and Britain, he learned about provocation.

In terms of classical strategy, Lenin supplemented the preferred operation of striking at the opponent's flanks by striking at his rear, and doing so through utilizing native political forces. This profoundly modified the traditional concept of war between nation-states or between cohesive multinational empires. It meant that henceforth every war between states would be accompanied by class war within those states and that the war would be ultimately transformed into seizures of power. Naturally, Lenin conceived of this scheme only in relation to "capitalist" states which, in our context, it would be more logical to describe as democratic states. Lenin was aware that this concept could be applied ubiquitously but he expected the Communist states would protect themselves through dictatorship and internal security organs like the Cheka.

Lenin expressed several of his meta-strategic ideas in his *Left Wing Communism: An Infantile Disorder*, which he sub-titled, "A Popular Essay in Marxian Strategy and Tactics." To readers familiar with Lenin's secret operations and conversant with Lenin's Aesopian language, *Left Communism* is almost

---

[d]Clausewitz told the Germans more than one hundred years earlier that a large country like Russia could be defeated only by "political means." We know that Lenin read Clausewitz and that Clausewitz had great impact on him. We do not know whether he caught this particular remark but it is unlikely he overlooked it. Perhaps he did not want to copy it down or his excerpt and comment were not published by the Soviet government.

a textbook on subversion. The booklet was written between February and April of 1920. It was published—deliberately, I am sure—on June 10, on the very day when the League of Nations was formally established. As early as March 1, Lenin had warned that a war with Poland was impending and the war did start on April 25. Subsequently Lenin attempted to exploit the war with Poland for carrying communism into Germany. Thus, the book was written in the gestation period when offensive revolutionary war against the West came under active consideration.

Lenin, of course, did not intend to disclose his meta-strategic and strategic principles in their full meaning. He simply wanted to ensure that the foreign Communist parties would really help Soviet Russia instead of just talking about ideology and theory. The foreign comrades had to be told some of the facts of life.

Lenin stressed the need for the "revolutionary party of the proletariat" to link itself to, and to a certain extent even to merge with, the nonproletarian toiling masses. He objected to "frenzy" which results in instability and barrenness of "revolutionariness." He indicated that Marxists reject individual terrorism, but they do so "only on the grounds of expediency." He insisted that tactics had to be elaborated in connection with "objective situations." It is "obligatory to participate even in the most reactionary parliament and in a number of other institutions." "Compromises" may be necessary. It is also obligatory to combine legal and illegal forms of struggle. It is imperative to work "wherever the masses are to be found," even when they are in organizations that show "reactionariness." Trying to avoid such reactionariness "would be the greatest folly, for it would mean fearing that function of the proletarian vanguard which consists in training, educating, enlightening and drawing into the new life the most backward strata and masses of the working class and the peasantry."

The most dangerous mistake revolutionaries can make is to mistake their desire and their ideological attitude for actual facts. What is obsolete for the Communists is not necessarily obsolete for the proletarian class or for the masses. Hence, reactionary parliaments should be used and, naturally, they must be used "for revolutionary purposes."

It is ridiculous in the extreme, Lenin explained, not to maneuver and to refuse "to utilize the conflict of interests . . . among one's enemies." Powerful enemies can be conquered only

by exerting the utmost effort and by necessarily, thoroughly, carefully, attentively, and skillfully taking advantage of every, even the smallest, 'rift' among the enemies, of every antagonism of interest among the bourgeoisie of the various countries and among the various groups or types of bourgeoisie . . . by taking advantage of every, even the smallest, opportunity of gaining a mass ally . . . Those who do not understand this do not understand even a particle of Marxism, or of scientific, modern socialism in general.

Those who have not proved their ability to apply "this truth in practice have not yet learned to assist the revolutionary class in its struggle . . . "

The whole point lies in knowing how to apply these tactics in such a way as to raise, and not lower, the general level of proletarian class consciousness, revolutionary spirit, and ability to fight and conquer.

The unity of international tactics of the communist working class movement of all countries demands, not the elimination of variety, not the abolition of national differences . . . but such an application of the fundamental principles of communism . . . as will correctly modify these principles in certain particulars, correctly adapt and apply them to national and national state differences.

Victory cannot be won with the vanguard alone. To throw the vanguard alone into the decisive battle . . . before the broad masses have taken up a position either of direct support of the vanguard, or at least of benevolent neutrality toward it . . . would not be merely folly but a crime.

When it is a question of the practical activities of the masses, of the disposition . . . of vast armies, of the alignment . . . for the final and decisive battle, then propaganda habits alone, the mere repetition of the truth of 'pure' communism are of no avail.

Hence, the strictest loyalty to communism "must be combined with the ability to make all the necessary practical compromises, to maneuver to make agreements, zig-zags, retreats and so on," and to "accelerate the inevitable friction, quarrels, conflicts and complete disintegration" among the opponents.

The crucial question is whether the effective forces are aligned in such a way that first

all the class forces hostile to us have become sufficiently entangled, sufficiently at loggerheads with each other, have sufficiently weakened themselves in a struggle which is beyond their strength; that second, all the vacillating, wavering, unstable intermediate elements . . . have sufficiently exposed themselves . . . and have sufficiently disgraced themselves through practical bankruptcy; and that third, among the proletariat a mass sentiment in favor of supporting . . . revolutionary action . . . has risen and begun vigorously to grow, then revolution is indeed ripe.

It is necessary to keep in mind that even when Lenin is talking descriptively, he is actually issuing generalized instructions.

It follows that the revolutionaries must be able "to master all forms or sides of social activity without exception" and must be ready "to pass from one form to another in the quickest and most unexpected manner."

An army which does not train itself to wield all arms, all the means and methods of warfare . . . behaves in an unwise or even in criminal manner. But this applies to politics even more than it does to war. . . . If, however, we master all means of warfare, we shall certainly be victorious . . . even if circumstances do not permit us to use weapons that are most dangerous to the enemy, weapons that are most swift in dealing mortal blows.

Furthermore, revolutionaries must combine "illegal forms of struggle with every form of legal struggle." The work of propaganda, agitation and organization must go on all the time. The bourgeoisie sees only one side of Bolshevism—"insurrection, violence, terror." As soon as Communists in all countries display "the utmost flexibility in their tactics," they will be able to march forward to victory.

Lenin made a specific, albeit veiled reference to Malinovsky who, before World War I, was the second in command of the Party, but also was an Okhrana agent and possibly acted as a double agent working for Lenin. Lenin wrote that Malinovsky betrayed "scores and scores of the best and most loyal comrades," which is exaggerated as to numbers but otherwise correct. Lenin added that Malinvosky did "not cause even more harm . . . because we had established a proper combination of legal and illegal work . . . Malinovsky was forced, in order to gain our confidence, to aid us in establishing legal daily papers" and "to assist in the education of scores and scores of thousands of new Bolsheviks through the medium of the legal press." Then Lenin penned this sentence: "It will not harm those German (as well as British, American, French and Italian) comrades who are confronted with the task of learning how to carry on revolutionary work inside the reactionary trade unions [Lenin, of course, was talking about penetration into the police] to give serious thought to this fact." Since undoubtedly the bourgeoisie is now "sending agents provocateurs into the Communist parties," it should be remembered that "one method of combating this peril is by a skillful combination of legal and illegal work." In other words, the Malinovsky case was a paradigm of subversive technique.

Lenin also made a pointed reference to his "German deal." He wrote: "The party which concluded a compromise with the German imperialists by signing the Brest-Litovsk Treaty had been working out its internationalism in action ever since the end of 1914." The phrase, "internationalism in action," is in the best Aesopian style. Lenin continued: "It was not afraid to call for the defeat of the tsarist monarchy and to condemn 'defense of the fatherland' in a war between two imperialist robbers. . . . The revolution, having overthrown tsardom and established a democratic republic, put this party to a new and tremendous test; this party did not enter into any agreement with 'its' imperialists but worked for their overthrow and did overthrow them." This is a completely correct statement, because the "agreement" was with the *other* imperialists. It is, however, surprising that Lenin was so frank as to use the term, "agreement," which actually may be regarded as an exaggeration.

After seizing political power, Lenin stated, his Party "proposed peace to all nations, and yielded to the violence of the Brest-Litovsk robbers only after the

Anglo-French imperialists had frustrated peace, and after the Bolsheviks had done everything humanly possible to hasten the revolution in Germany and other countries." This alibi is partly incorrect, and partly mendacious. It should be obvious that the time between November 7 and March 3, hardly is enough to do "everything humanly possible" and to hasten *several* revolutions. *Passons*. It is true enough that Lenin was compelled to yield.

And he was right when he maintained against Kautsky that his "internationalist tactics" accomplished "the utmost possible in one country for the development, support and stirring up of the revolution in all countries." He contrasted this with the dreams about "unity" which characterized the Second International.

In *Left Communism*, Lenin was not making abstract statements about a philosophy of strategy and he was not systematizing the principles of meta-strategy. He was drawing lessons from experiences.

Whether Lenin ever wrote down the *summa* of his meta-strategic principles, I do not know; such a *summa* certainly has not been published. I am by no means certain that he ever studied the matter systematically so that he would have all of his meta-strategic principles present in his mind at one time.

Yet, even before World War I, Lenin talked about his idea that "Marxism is distinguished from all primitive forms of socialism by the fact that it does not tie the movement to any particular form of struggle" and that it realizes that "new forms of struggle . . . must inevitably arise as the given social situation changes." He always was interested in "concreteness," he stressed "peculiar features," and asserted that every struggle must be fought "in accordance with the peculiar features" of each country's "economics, politics, culture, national composition . . . colonies, religious divisions, etc." Lenin's mind was completely open for new strategies and stratagems and he was operationally quite inventive; which does not imply that he always was successful. For all theoretical and practical purposes, Lenin covered himself amply by stating that *all* activities, techniques, and weapons must be mastered and that they must be used according to expediency. Although the point is rarely comprehended, this is really the last word on the matter.

Meta-strategy was practiced long before Lenin, for example, by such exceptional captains as Hannibal, Marlborough, Napoleon I, and Wellington; by Imperial Germany from Bismarck to the military and civilian strategists who were in charge during World War I; and by the Romanov dynasty. Lenin probably was not familiar with the historical background, but he had ample opportunity to observe imperial Russian and German operations.

Lenin hardly knew about Benjamin Franklin who wrote eloquently about the subject, but he was not unfamiliar with the history of the American and French revolutions and he may have known that during the War of 1796 Buonarroti advised the French on propaganda in Italy.

As we have seen, Mr. Beilenson considers that Lenin established subversion on a permanent and global basis, and that this was his main innovation. Undoubtedly, this innovation was derived from Marx's notion of "permanent revolution," but Marx failed to spell out this pregnant concept which, in Lenin's time, was variously interpreted.[e] From the seventeenth century until Lenin's death (and beyond) the British frequently practiced political warfare. During Lenin's life time, tsarist Russia had been operating subversion in a semipermanent fashion, especially in the Balkans. Both the British and, to a lesser extent, the Russian efforts were nearly continuous, yet the concrete subversive undertakings were restricted to certain places at certain times. By connecting a permanently functioning worldwide subversive apparatus *to modern political parties*, Lenin created the first instrument which, regardless of its shortcomings, enabled the conduct of permanent and global subversion.

Lenin, of course, did not invent the *concept* of an "International." The credit for this innovation, I think, belongs to the Jesuits whom, long before Lenin's time, Russian revolutionaries credited with having invented the conspiratorial party. During the eighteenth century, the Masons created one or several Internationals, each of which remained "polycentric." The Masons derived some of their effectiveness from the fact that ruling princes and publicists held membership.

During the Napoleonic wars so-called "secret societies" sprang up, notably in Italy and France, but in other countries, too. Those societies usually had multinational membership and systematically attempted to operate on an international scale. When their conspiratorial and terroristic tactics backfired, new groups were founded which were more propagandistic and less terroristic and which were seeking novel ways of international cooperation. Paris and subsequently London were the centers of international contacts and planning.

Allowing for simplification, these groups can be divided into left wing revolutionaries (notably the Babouvistes and Blanquists); nationalists, initially the Carbonaris and later Mazzini's Giovine Europa creations; and more or less open constitutional or democratic-reformist groups usually connected with Masonry.

On September 22, 1845, the Chartists set up the Fraternal Democrats which must be regarded as the forerunner of the three Marxist Internationals. It was George Julian Harney, the founder of the Fraternal Democrats, who drew Marx and Engels into the international movement.[5] The *Bund der Kommunisten* was connected with both the Chartists and the French revolutionaries, and its predecessors, the *Bund der Gëachteten* and *Bund der Gerechten* were linked to the *Babouviste société des saisons* as well as to Etienne Cabet's *Icariens* who supplied the myth. (Cabet coined the term, "communism.")

In 1847, Mazzini set up in England The People's International League which espoused constitutional reform all over Europe and which, though it counted a

---

[e]Lenin's European intellectual ancestry goes back to Babeuf and Buonarrotti, particularly to article 11 of the *Analyse de la Doctrine de Babeuf*. "La révolution n'est pas finie" so long as full equality has not been established.

few Chartists within its ranks, was antisocialist in orientation. The organization was supported by persons close to the British government.

In 1849, Marx and Mazzini forgot about internationalism and concentrated on the affairs of Germany and Italy, respectively. However, in 1850, Mazzini, Ledru-Rollin, Ruge, and Darasq, a Pole, set up the Central European Committee,[6] which was a rump International of nonsocialist republican orientation.

Polish émigrés had established what can only be described as an International *sui generis*. The Poles made every effort to unite the European revolutionaries against Russia and its allies.

In 1864, these various currents plus additional groups like the positivists and the anarchists joined together in the First International which also aroused the interest of Napoleon III and, so it seems, of President Lincoln. The First International brought together too many disparate elements, viewpoints, and interests to be viable. After an interval, it was succeeded by the Second International which, though it was more socialistically cohesive, did not work either. *Au fond* it was little more than an agency coordinating national democratic parties espousing socialist economics and representing the labor movement. It ceased being revolutionary, it lacked political objectives that were applicable to all member parties, and it was unable to design a common strategy.

It is against *this* background that Lenin's Communist International must be viewed: he combined the conspiratorial and propaganda techniques, married both to ideology, tied them to national and social revolutionary movements, and put the whole show on a truly international basis. In addition, he established the International as a worldwide combat Party under a single high command with disciplinary powers.

It may be mentioned that when Lenin was founding the Communist International, he knew the limitations of such organizations, but he attempted to draw practical lessons from historical experiences. The democratic world did not even know that there were experiences in the sphere of common international action which they could have applied to strengthen democratic solidarity.

Lenin may be considered as a successor to Machiavelli, although Lenin probably never studied the Florentine diplomat. In many respects Lenin's thinking parallels that of Machiavelli who was a meta-strategist in his own right. Machiavelli's hero, Cesare Borgia, had died miserably in a ditch years before *The Prince* was written; hence his was not an example to be imitated.[7] The point is that from the viewpoint of political effectiveness, Lenin's advice is superior to that of Machiavelli and that Lenin adapted the general principles of Machiavellism to a modern society. Machiavelli, the Masons, and the plotters of the nineteenth century addressed autocratic and aristocratic rulers. Lenin initially also dealt with an autocracy or pseudo-autocracy. But he then turned his attention to mass movements and to "Machiavellism" as applied to democratically ruled hostile states.

Lenin by no means restricted himself to the Machiavellian approach *sensu proprio*, but combined it with the utopianism of Thomas More who was Machiavelli's contemporary. Lenin's *State and Revolution* is his only semi-utopian sin, but the content of this book does not particularly matter. Throughout most of his writings Lenin was really playing the strings of what could be called a "para-ideology." Such a construct is not an integrated body of thought (although such a body also exists) but a *myth* about what those utopian thoughts *could* be. Lenin's para-ideology creates the impression that the Communists aim at the scientific organization of society and at genuine and lasting equality, and that they will achieve unprecedented progress through abolishing property. The *hint* is that this miracle can be wrought through totalitarianism.

In brief, while meta-strategy as Lenin conceived it, is permanent and global subversion potentially or actually linked to war, that subversion would not work unless it were vaguely based, not on Marxism or Leninism, but on a socialist and utopian para-ideology. This redemptory faith has little to do with the pertinence of socialism as an economic organization, let alone the construction of a workable socialist system. But Lenin knew how to instill that faith and how to commit "masses" to it. The traditional strategist moves troops into battle, the meta-strategist moves the faithful into political conflict.

In Lenin's meta-strategic scheme, propaganda was a vital element. Certainly, it was the *one* operation which was conducted every day in a maximum number of languages and publication media, and at a maximum number of places. Lenin's contribution to the art of propaganda has been denied and his propaganda often has been described as dull and unimaginative. From a literary point of view, this criticism may be justified, as all those who are reading Communist prose will unhappily confirm. But since Communist propaganda has been highly successful, this criticism is strategically without merit.

To illustrate. By 1921 the incredible failure of what was called "War-Communism" became apparent to all, not merely because of the Kronstadt uprising but especially because of the extraordinary famine which threatened the survival of at least one-fifth of the population. There was no choice but to ask the capitalist countries for food and economic assistance. Yet up to that time Soviet Russia had been an outcast and was quite unable to obtain any support. Nevertheless, thanks partly to Maxim Gorky, aid was now organized for humanitarian reasons by Fridtjof Nansen and Herbert Hoover.

A similar calamity would have ruined almost any other state and the record which communism did make would normally have been regarded as convincing proof that this system—which was expected to raise productivity instantly—was unworkable. But exactly the opposite happened: In addition to massive strategic support there suddenly gushed forth a ground swell of sympathy for Soviet Russia. The progressive liberals in the democratic countries, who should have opposed dictatorship, began to agitate in favor of the Soviet regime. Gabriele d'Annunzio, the intellectual father of fascism, went so far as to accuse the governments of the world of murdering the Russian peasants. The strategic significance of this switch needs no elaboration.

What had happened? To be sure, there was sympathy for the starving masses. But this sympathy for the sufferers was not turned into hatred for those who created the suffering, instead it grew into sympathy for the tyrants. This amazing turn did not happen accidentally, but was due to Lenin's strategy which, in the best judo style, was designed to take advantage of the predicament. Under the innocuous label of facilitating and organizing economic aid for Soviet Russia, an international propaganda network was established. Lenin entrusted the task of building this network to Willy Muenzenberg whom he instructed to procure maximum economic assistance, to exert pressure on the bourgeoisie, and to bring about the diplomatic recognition of Soviet Russia. Muenzenberg set up the International Workers Relief which became the first major front organization.

Muenzenberg and Lenin had met early in 1915 at Berne, Switzerland, where Muenzenberg, despite ideological disagreements, proved to be very helpful in publishing Lenin's writings. More or less acting on his own, Muenzenberg organized an international Communist youth conference in opposition to the war. Lenin took personal interest in that conference. Muenzenberg sided with the Zimmerwald Left (i.e., Lenin). He also was one of the promoters of the Kienthal conference, and in 1917 was Lenin's first choice to serve as intermediary between Lenin and the German legation. Since Muenzenberg was a German citizen, Fritz Platten was chosen instead.

The Germans later permitted Muenzenberg to cross Germany to attend the Stockholm Conference and return to Switzerland. Yet Muenzenberg was not *en règle* with the German military authorities.

During the Second Congress of the Comintern in 1920, Muenzenberg resumed close cooperation with Lenin at Moscow. At that time Muenzenberg was the main promoter of the International Communist Youth Movement and he had built up a substantial international propaganda network. Lenin recognized the political importance of youth and hoped the Youth International could be used to split the socialist parties and pull their left wing into the Communist fold.

In earlier years Muenzenberg had been leaning toward anarchism. In 1920-21, he took a position to the left of Lenin and insisted that the Youth International should remain fairly independent from the Comintern: the youth would never allow that the Party dictate its policies. Lenin originally had promised to Muenzenberg a great deal of autonomy, but when the troubles of 1921 arose, he adopted the line that the youth movement should be educational and not political in nature. The Party stalwarts were gunning for Muenzenberg, his political autonomy was cancelled, and Muenzenberg was shifted to the relief operation.

Now a wiser man, Muenzenberg insisted and secured substantial autonomy. On this basis Muenzenberg was able to establish dozens, perhaps hundreds of front organizations all over the world. Through those organizations he made non-Communist "philosophers and horse thieves" work for the Communist cause. In due time Muenzenberg enlisted the permanent or sporadic help of persons like Albert Einstein, Sigmund Freud, Romain Rolland, Martin Anderson

Nexö, Kaethe Kollwitz, Martin Buber, Heinrich Mann, Theodore Dreiser, André Gide, Mary Pickford, many prominent theater directors, and leading book publishers.

Muenzenberg has been called the inventor of the "fellow traveler," but it is more correct to call him the organizer of the predestined fellow traveler.

The general concept of the "front organization" probably must be ascribed to Lenin, though such outfits existed earlier and the fabled wolf who dressed himself in sheep's clothing doubtless was the original inventor. However, Lenin and Muenzenberg were the joint originators of the pro-Soviet front organization and without Muenzenberg the front organization technique hardly would have become operational and in all likelihood never would have become effective.[f]

Muenzenberg's preeminence as a propagandist, i.e., as disseminator of first rate texts, has been attested to by no less an expert than Arthur Koestler, who himself was one of Muenzenberg's close collaborators.[8]

Muenzenberg can be regarded as Lenin's chief international recruitment officer, the activator of sympathizers, and the neutralizer of the uncommitted. By contrast Karl Radek was Lenin's expert at polarization and served as his conduit to nationalists, especially the German nationalists and the Reichswehr who, by ideology and interest, should have been ferocious enemies of Soviet Russia. Yet Lenin and Radek were striving for an operational alliance with those "natural enemies." Lenin was a firm believer in the French idea that is is useful to "faire flèches de tous les bois."

And they succeeded in the improbable task. The interplay between the Muenzenberg and Radek types of propaganda was the basis of the Rapallo Treaty between Soviet Russia and Germany. The purpose of this alliance was explained in 1923 by Bukharin before the Fourth Comintern Congress: "We have grown so much that we are able to conclude a military alliance with one bourgeoisie in order to smash . . . another bourgeoisie." This was classical meta-strategy: Germany's national interests were exploited against Germany and through the use of deceptive propaganda the improbable trick became feasible.

Still, this doesn't yet describe the full scope of Lenin's meta-strategy. During the first three years of the Lenin regime the monetary currency of the country was almost totally destroyed. The financial disaster was at the bottom of the economic disaster, and it also greatly hampered the foreign operations of the Communist state and the Comintern. Late in 1921, Lenin instituted the first measures to stabilize the currency. This work was completed in 1922 when, in essence, the prerevolutionary ruble was resurrected and tied to a 25 percent gold cover. Since then the ruble was devalued several times but, despite endemic inflation, it was consistently managed in an orthodox fashion as a stable currency and regarded as one of the pillars of Soviet international power.

---

[f]Naturally, Muenzenberg attained his major successes under Stalin with whom he broke in the late 1930s. When he was fleeing from the Nazis, he either was murdered or committed suicide in 1940.

Stalin wrote, or presumably wrote, in 1906 that to make a revolution one needs "arms, arms, and arms again." Whether Lenin rediscovered General Montecuccoli who had insisted that to wage war, one needs "money, money, and money again," is questionable. But the insight was driven home forcefully that gold had better uses than to be made into chamber pots. The evidence shows that the Swedish banker Olof Aschberg, who played a role in Parvus's smuggle operations during World War I and in the financing of the Bolsheviks, in short, the "German Deal," clarified for Lenin the importance and basic procedures of international finance.

Aschberg organized the first sales of Russian gold in 1919. In 1920, he organized Russian trade. Again it was Aschberg who in 1921 persuaded Lenin and Finance Commissar Grigory Sokolnikov, a passenger on the famed "sealed train," that the currency had to be stabilized and be backed by gold.[g] N.N. Kutler, a prominent financial adviser to the tsar, was given the task of reestablishing monetary order. The State Bank was reorganized and placed under Sheinman, a friend of Aschberg's, while the newly formed Commerce Bank was entrusted to Tarnowsky, a prerevolution banker; Aschberg became chairman of the board. Lenin asked: "Why does it follow that the 'great, victorious, global' revolution can and should apply only revolutionary methods?" Why, indeed!

I said before that Lenin was a poor "resource strategist," but it should now be added that in the end, he recognized his mistake. He finally understood that international financial power, in a very basic way, is the key to resource strategy, to defense and war, and to meta-strategy. At the point of gold and currency stability, Lenin's break with the infantile disease that is communism, was the most dramatic.

The meta-strategy which we have described is a meta-strategy of power accumulation, conquest, and control. But for a theoretical Communist, imperialism and world dictatorship are not proper objectives. At best they could be regarded as transitory goals or phases and they have in fact been sold in this manner. If the need for conquistadorial and dictatorial transitions be granted, there still would be an urgent need for a strategy constructing socialism. Lenin thought he had such a strategy and believed the construction of a socialist economy and a nonbureaucratic state was a straightforward task of changing property relationships, managerial practices, and political institutions, not to mention his quaint idea that socialism would result if Soviet power and electric power were combined. The socialist economy which he introduced was patterned after the German war economy and had been modelled by Walter Rathenau, president of German General Electric. Lenin opposed the system of centralized planning which Stalin later introduced, but he was not sure he had an alternative. He dis-

---

[g]It took Lenin almost four years to get the point. By contrast, Napoleon established his autocracy on November 9, 1799 (18 Brumaire) and the Banque de France which was to stabilize the French currency and finance Napoleon's strategy, was founded on February 13, 1800.

covered he had misunderstood the problem and began—in economics, though not in politics—to move in a new direction.

He recognized the need for a "cultural revolution" but he conceived this requirement in a rather elementary way as the rapid improvement of educational standards and behavior patterns. It was too late. Whether or not, if he had lived longer, he could have freed himself from his habit of thinking in terms of conflict, he sensed that the building of socialism required a constructive approach. This was precisely what Rosa Luxemburg had told him and what before 1921-1922 he did not believe. He never got close to conceiving something like a strategy of problem-solving.

So, in the end, Lenin was a first-rate strategist and he may well be considered as the master of meta-strategy. But Lenin did not change the world in the way he wanted and set out to do. The class society remained: there are now in the USSR over 3000 millionaires, which is a good accomplishment by capitalist standards, but a poor result in terms of the socialist myth. The ruling class has grown four- or five-fold over that under the tsar. There is bureaucratic dictatorship of a totalitarian character. The multiple national problems have remained unsolved. There is no democracy. Soviet imperialism turned out to be the biggest imperialism of all history. Naturally so, because Lenin did not bequeath a tradition of building freedom but a tradition of destructive conquest. As a result, the frequency of war has risen and the danger that there will be ever more devastating wars in the future is steadily growing.

This deplorable historical situation has emerged because totalitarianism found in Lenin a superb strategic innovator. By contrast, the forces which want freedom, democracy, and peace, so far have been unable to devise an effective strategy and, for that matter, have yet to learn that there is such a thing as meta-strategy.

To sum it all up: Much of Lenin's life was characterized by almost obsessive insistence on "splitting tactics." Lenin was a "splitter" of his own Party and he resorted to splitting whenever he felt he needed more freedom from his impinging comrades. Splitting also can be applied to opponents for the purpose of weakening them, and he was a master at splitting his enemies. Splitting is the very essence of subversion, as it is the secret of imperialist domination. Hence Lenin's strategy can be simplified:

against enemy morale—agitate and deceive;
against enemy organizations—infiltrate and split;
against enemy strength—outarm, disarm, paralyze, fight, and destroy;
against enemy strategy—provoke, surprise, and entrap.

As Lenin himself put it: "The whole is politics."

Notes

1. *Leningradskaia Pravda*, February 13, 1956.

2. Leonard Schapiro and Peter Reddaway, eds., *Lenin, The Man, The Theorist, The Leader: A Reappraisal* (New York, 1967). Erickson's chapter contains an excellent survey of the literature. All subsequent quotations in this chapter are from this volume.

3. D. Grinishin, *Die Militärische Tätigkeit Wladimir Iljitsch Lenins* (Berlin, 1958).

4. The concept was explained by Trotsky in *The History of the Russian Revolution* (New York, 1932), III, 207.

5. Oscar J. Hammen, *The Red '48ers, Karl Marx and Friedrich Engels* (New York, 1969), pp. 141, 156.

6. Peter Cadogan, "Harney and Engels," *International Review of Social History*, X (1965), 75.

7. For a pertinent criticism of Machiavelli see Gaetano Mosca, *Ciò che lla storia potrebbe insegnare* (Milano, 1958), pp. 673-718.

8. For all the foregoing information, see Babette Gross, *Willy Muenzenberg, Eine Politische Biographie* (Stuttgart, 1967), chapters I-IV.

17 The Influence of Lenin on the History of Our Times: The Question of Totalitarianism

Bertram D. Wolfe

Our Time of Troubles

The century in which I was born has gone into the history books as *la belle époque,* the "Grand Century of Peace and Progress." Our own century, I think, will be recorded as our *smutnoe vremya,* our time of troubles.

From the fall of Napoleon in 1815 to the First World War in 1914 there was no general war in Europe. My generation was taught to believe that the twentieth century would be too civilized for war. And look at it now!

We have had two total wars, in which every man, not excluding criminals and crackpots, has learned to use a rifle with a telescopic sight, to make bombs, to throw grenades, to try to persuade men and settle issues by assassinating a John F. or a Robert Kennedy, or a Martin Luther King. A new generation of well-to-do young terrorists is fouling its nest by tossing bombs into libraries and university buildings, by cutting off power from laboratories, classrooms and hospitals, as it did in Berkeley recently. In the thirties storm troopers smashed all the shop windows of Berlin belonging to Jews in the Night of Crystal. Similar violent minorities are satisfying their passions and trying to force their views upon our universities by smashing thirty-four windows under cover of darkness in a single night, as occurred in Stanford.

The Age of the Dictators

Ours is an age of force and violence, of barbed wire running through the heart of a great city from which sentries shoot to kill their own countrymen going from one part of their own land to another.

The first cause of this brutalization and dehumanization of man is the crisis in the civilization of Europe during which the ancient continent stumbled, all unconsciously, into the age of total wars. In my own lifetime I have seen two such total wars followed by two periods of false peace. The First World War broke down into lesser wars, civil and national. Then the lesser wars built up into the second total war. Today we hold our breaths lest they now beget a third. If the First World War can be ascribed to men's blunders, the second was unleashed by the pact for the redivision of the world entered into by the two giant totalitarian states born in the fiery womb of the First World War.

The heroes or antiheroes of our age are the *men of might* produced by an age of blood and death: Lenin, Mussolini, Hitler, Stalin, Khrushchev, Brezhnev, Mao Tse-tung and lesser two-bit dictators over their own peoples, like Franco and Castro and Ho Chi-Minh. Total war has been their progenitor and their opportunity. The war which Wilson proclaimed would make the world safe for democracy begot the age of dictatorships. For this first total war that opened our age's Time of Troubles, neither Lenin nor his disciples and imitators can be blamed. True, he was the only leading socialist who felt so little apprehension at the war clouds gathering in the Balkans that he did not trouble to attend the two emergency sessions of the Socialist International, the Congress on War in Basle in 1912, and the special session of the International Socialist Bureau in London in 1913. In 1913 he could coolly write to Gorky: "A war between Austria and Russia would be a useful trick for the revolution in all of Eastern Europe, but it is not likely that Franz Joseph and Nikolasha will give us that pleasure...."[1] Lenin instinctively recognized that a general war originating in the Balkans might be "a useful trick" for him but this does not give him any responsibility for the crisis in European civilization that gave him his opportunity.

Given this opportunity, however, Lenin used it to initiate the manners and morals, and the machinery of power, that coastitute the second factor in the formation of our Time of Troubles. It is this factor which I shall now examine as my contribution to the observance of Lenin's centenary.

The Selfless Egoist

What kind of man was this "event-making man," V.I. Lenin?

He was—I have written elsewhere—a selfless egoist. We never catch him glancing into the mirror of history. He lived austerely. He was selfless, too, in that he never sought either the perquisites and privileges, or the cult of adoration that often go with the absolute power he sought and achieved.

But this selflessness was only the outer shell. At the core of Lenin's spirit was an abnormally powerful, unquestioning belief in himself, and an absolute certitude that the Marxism he believed in was an infallible doctrine, and that he was the only true master and expounder of this science.

The Infallible Doctrine

"Out of every hundred Bolsheviks," he wrote in the margins of a book he was reading, "70 are fools and 29 rogues, and only one a real socialist."

And in his *Philosophical Notebooks:* "After half a century, not a single

Marxist has understood Marx." Implicit but unspoken is the thought that there was the one exception.

He possessed a certitude of his rightness in every controversy, large or small. Indeed, given his dogmatic, domineering temperament, there were no small controversies. When you differed with him, you were cast into outer darkness, both intellectually and morally. When he spoke, it was Marxism, Science, and History that spoke, the working class, the vanguard, the Party, the infallible interpreter of the infallible science that teaches its high priest what history wants man to do, to think and feel, to be, and to become.

From this belief followed the conviction that he must have authority and power in whatever sphere he happened to be operating: the troika, the editorial board, the Central Committee, the Party, power in Russia; power in the international movement, power in the world. Whatever organization he could not control, he split. "Split, split, and again split," was the order he gave the faithful. The Russian word he used in his command was *raskol*, a word which signifies both split and sect. Both meanings fit perfectly for he was both an inveterate splitter and an inveterate sectarian.

The Dictator

When did Lenin become a dictator? There is reason to answer: As soon as he became a "Leninist."

In 1902 when he was still one of the six editors of *Iskra*, to the other five he sent a memorandum explaining that "we should show every kindness to the peasantry" but "not yield an inch" in "our maximum program." "If the peasants do not accept socialism when the dictatorship comes, we shall say to them: 'It's no use wasting words when you have got to use force.' " On the margin of this memorandum Vera Zasulich wrote, "Upon millions of people? Just you try!" When he came to power, that is just what he tried. In the end he shrank back from the consequences, but his disciple and successor, Joseph Stalin, fulfilled his injunction.

Also in 1902 he wrote:

The committee should lead all aspects of the local movement and direct all local institutions, forces and resources. . . . Discussion of all party questions, of course, will also take place in the local circles, but the deciding of all general questions of the local movement should be done only by the committee. The independence of local groups would be permitted only in questions of the technique of transmitting and distributing. The composition of the local groups should be determined by the committee which designates delegates to such and such a district and entrusts these delegates with setting up the district group, all the members of which must in turn be confirmed in their positions by the committee. The district group is a local branch of the committee that receives its powers only from the latter.

In 1903, when at last a Congress met to unify the splintered Social Democratic Party under the aegis of *Iskra*, at the first defeat he suffered (on a strict definition of the word *member* in the by-laws), Lenin split the unity congress in two. He called an *Iskra* caucus to consolidate the split but posted guards to keep all the other *Iskra* editors except Plekhanov out of the *Iskra* caucus. Soon he would split with Plekhanov too for it was from his first clash with Plekhanov that he derived his guiding motto: "To regard all persons without sentiment, to keep a stone in one's sling. . . ."[2]

At the same Congress, when a delegate spoke in liturgical language of the projected Central Committee as a "Spirit omnipresent and one," Lenin cried out from his seat, "*Ne dukh, a kulak!* " (Not spirit, but fist—the whole of Lenin's organization philosophy is in that cry, always providing the "Fist" is his.)

If splitting with Plekhanov gave him a wrench because Plekhanov had been his master, splitting with Martov wounded his heart because, even on his deathbed, Lenin showed that he still felt affection for Martov.

Down with All Softheartedness

But to Krzhizhanovsky he sent instructions: "Write to Martov, appealing for the last time to reason . . . and prepare for war with the Martovites. Do not look on Martov as before. The friendship is at an end. Down with all softheartedness."

Down with All Softheartedness could be posted over the laboratory in which Lenin was to make his living experiment to impose his blueprint on the Russian people.

At the Party Court of Honor, where he was put on trial for slandering his own comrades during the electoral campaign of 1906, Lenin coolly admitted that he had chosen "obnoxious terms calculated to evoke hatred, aversion, contempt . . . calculated not to convince but to break up the ranks of the opponent, not to correct the opponent's mistake but to destroy him, to wipe this organization off the face of the earth." His excuse? He had taken it for granted that a difference on how to nominate candidates for Duma Deputy would become a "splitting point." Since he expected a split, that meant war, and in war one acted as if one were at war. "And I shall always act in that way whenever a split occurs . . . in the event of the development of a split, I shall always conduct a war of extermination." When Lenin said extermination he meant it. When the occasion arose, it must be said that he was faithful to his pledge.

Lenin was thus the organizer of his own faction and party. He was its self-chosen leader, he personally selected his own lieutenants in high places and low, he was its commander-in-chief exacting from his followers the discipline of an army. He defined and redefined its doctrines and its tactics. He instilled into it his own total rejection of all existing institutions. He was its will and its intellect. I would be tempted to say its heart as well, were he not by grave and serious conviction opposed to all sentimental considerations, all emotions save the emotion of class hatred, all general moral rules applying to the treatment of one's fellow man merely because he is human. To the Young Communist League he would say in 1920:

Our morality is completely subordinated to the interests of the class struggle. . . . For Communists, morality consists entirely of compact united discipline and conscious mass struggle against the exploiters. We do not believe in a timeless morality and we expose all fairy tales about such a morality.[3]

This ruthlessness and cynicism were partly natural to Lenin, partly the result of a blueprint he had devised for himself in accord with what he thought a revolutionist should be like. It was this amorality that made it possible for him to arrange the counterfeiting of Russian rubles and direct holdups by his followers to obtain funds for his action, though public opinion was shocked and a congress of his Party had expressly forbidden such acts. This it was that made it possible for him to use such unscrupulous lieutenants as Victor Taratuta, Joseph Stalin, and Roman Malinovsky and defend them against exposure. This it was that made it possible for him to use the funds and physical aid made available to him by the German General Staff from 1915 to 1918, so long as the source was properly disguised.[4]

Lenin's Centralism

The first striking peculiarity in Lenin's organization doctrine is its extreme centralism, coupled with an extreme distrust of the rank and file of his party and the local organizations. When Lenin was in control of the central organ of the Party, he asked defiantly: "What is bad about the complete dictatorship of the central organ? "[5] Chided with suppressing party democracy, Lenin answered for himself and his band of professional revolutionaries: "They have no time to think of the toy forms of democracy . . . but they have a lively sense of their *responsibility* and they know by experience that to get rid of an undesirable member, an organization of real revolutionaries will stop at nothing."[6]

This is surely one of the most unresponsive answers in political literature. Lenin argues that under the conditions of police spying in Russia, party democracy is a "useless and harmful toy." But the context reveals that even in a free country the chief function of party "democracy" to him is to provide "the general control, in the literal sense of the term, that the Party exercises over every member," a control which enables the Party to decide whether to assign to a member one function or another, or to get rid of him altogether as unfit. He believes that, in the context of illegality, democracy can be replaced completely by the mutual trust of Socialists in each other, the absolute trust of all in the self-selected leading committee, and faith in the ability of the latter to get rid of those who cannot be trusted.

Even more uncompromising is Lenin's championing of "bureaucratic centralism" as against the democratic autonomy of the primary or local organizations and their control over the center. This bureaucratic centralism he considers as appropriate to a Socialist party in any country. The language of his celebration of "bureaucratism" is prickly and rough-hewn, but its meaning is startlingly clear:

Bureaucratism *versus* autonomy, such is the principle of revolutionary social democracy as against that of the opportunists. . . . The organization of revolutionary social democracy strives to go from the top downward and defends the enlargement of the rights and plenary powers of the central body.[7]

Of course it was hard, indeed impossible, for this power-centered man to imagine that he would not be in control of the center. To Lunacharsky he said:

"If we have in the CC or in the central organ a majority, then we will demand the firmest discipline. We will insist on every sort of subordination of the Mensheviks to party unity . . ."

I asked Vladimir Ilyich: "Well, and what if it should turn out after all that we are in a minority? "

Lenin smiled enigmatically and said: "It depends on the circumstances. In any case we will not permit them to make of unity a rope around our necks. And under no circumstances will we let the Mensheviks drag us after them on such a rope."[8]

Not until Lenin had been chided by his opponents for more than half a decade for his rejection of Party democracy did he finally seek to conceal somewhat his arch centralism and aversion to any local autonomy or to control from below. For the purposes of his concealment, he coined his celebrated term, *democratic centralism*! Even after he was in power and no longer could give as his justification the tsar's police, in the third year of his rule he defined that self-contradictory term as "meaning only that representatives from the localities gather and choose a responsible organ. . . . The responsible organ must do the administering."

When Lenin's concept of democratic centralism was transplanted to the Communist International, it was formulated this way:

The main principle of democratic centralism is that of the higher cell being elected by the lower cell, the absolute binding force of all directives of a higher cell to a cell subordinate to it, and the existence of a commanding [*vlastnogo*; i.e., endowed with, or clothed with, power] Party center [the authority of which] is unchallengeable for all leaders in Party life, from one congress to the next.[9]

Lenin's division of spheres between what should be "centralized" and what "decentralized" would be comical were it not for its tragic implications for Russia and for communism. In his "Letter to a Comrade on Our Organizational Tasks," Lenin wrote:

We have arrived at an extremely important principle of all Party organization and Party activity. In regard to ideological and practical *direction* the movement and the revolutionary struggle of the proletariat need the *greatest possible centralization*, but in regard to *keeping the center informed* concerning the movement and concerning the Party as a whole, in regard to *responsibility* before the Party, we need the *greatest possible decentralization*. The movement must be led by the smallest possible number of the most homogeneous groups of trained and experienced revolutionaries. But the largest possible number of the most varied and heterogeneous groups drawn from the most diverse layers of the proletariat (and of other classes) should take part in the movement. And in regard to each such group the center of the Party must have always before it not only exact data on their activities but also the fullest possible knowledge of their composition.[10]

If we add to this the rule prescribing that the "committee should lead *all* aspects of the local movement and direct *all* local institutions, forces . . . decide all general questions" and leave "independence of the district groups . . . only in the questions of the technique of transmitting and distributing," then Lenin's conception of hierarchical centralism becomes terrifyingly clear. All power, all command, all decision should be with the center ("the district group receives its powers only from the latter"), but the duty to carry out, obey and report should be "decentralized" and accorded as a "privilege" to every local organization and individual member, and even to party sympathizers.

Afraid that his readers might not get its full implications, Lenin repeated it all again, as was his wont, with only slight variations and different underscorings:

We must centralize the direction of the movement. We must also (and we must *for this reason*, for without the informing of the center its leadership is impossible) decentralize as much as possible the *responsibility before the Party* of each circle which forms part of the Party or inclines to it. This decentralization is the necessary condition for revolutionary centralization and *its necessary corrective*. In order that the center may not only give advice, persuade, and argue (as has been done up to now), but may really direct the orchestra, it is essential to know exactly who is playing which fiddle and where; who, where, is learning to master which instrument or has mastered it; who, where and why, is playing out of tune (when the music begins to grate on the ear); and who, how, and where should be transferred to correct the dissonance, and so on.[11]

From the outset Lenin's "center" was self-appointed. He began with himself, then gathered around him those who agreed with him. Again and again he removed players from his orchestra when their playing grated on his ears, gathering others more in harmony with his directing. Thus his "Leninist" center was self-perpetuating.

The same ideas reappeared in the years of comparatively open activity between 1907 and 1914, when *Zvezda* and *Pravda* were legal journals and the Bolsheviks could campaign openly and elect deputies to the Duma. They continued during the six months of 1917 when Russia, in Lenin's words, was "the freest country in the world." And they continued when Lenin held power in party and country. At first he sought to justify his centralism before its critics by pointing to the harsh conditions of a conspiratorial underground movement, but in time it became clear that his centralism sprang from the deepest necessities of his temperament, his confidence in himself, and his pessimistic view of his fellow men. He has been compared to a schoolmaster commanding his pupils (by Edmund Wilson) and to a general commanding an embattled army (in his own figures of speech on military discipline). Here, in any case, is a revolutionary of a rare type: a revolutionary with a military-bureaucratic mind, to whom the complete centralization and control of all activities is—of all things—the road to a stateless, partyless utopia!

Hence Lenin's Archimedean cry for an organization of revolutionaries "to turn Russia upside down" did not cease when Russia was turned upside down. As before, Lenin continued to repeat the cry for "organization, organization, organization." In power, as when fighting for power, he said: "Our fighting method is organization." But now he had something new to add. To the old dream of centralized organization of the Party, which he did not for a moment abandon, he added the new dream of total organization by the Party. Of what? Why, of Russia. Its industries and its agriculture, its feelings and its thoughts, its habits, even its dreams—total organization of slackness, of the waywardness of will, of all deeds and desires. "We must organize everything," he said in the summer of 1918, "take everything into our hands."[1][2]

The Nature of Totalitarian Dictatorship

When Lenin said class war, he meant war. It would, of course, be a war for the good of humanity, but for the good of humanity, a good part of humanity would have to be dealt with according to the rules of war. Even on fellow socialists, when they differed with him, he waged "a war of extermination."

When we get power [Lenin wrote in 1916] we will establish a dictatorship of the proletariat, although all evolution moves toward the elimination of rule by force of one part of society over another. Dictatorship is the rule of a part of society over the whole of society, and, moreover, a rule basing itself directly on force.

This he wrote in 1916 when he was but dreaming of his possible dictatorship. But on December 5, 1919, after he had been dictator in fact for two years, he wrote: "Dictatorship is a harsh, heavy, and even bloody word." And on October 10, 1920, near the end of the third year of his rule, he bade advocates of democracy remember: "The scientific concept of dictatorship means neither more nor less than unlimited power, resting directly on force, not limited by anything, not restricted by any laws, nor any absolute rules. Nothing else but that."

This formulation is beautiful in its pedantic clarity, for the first giant step in the establishment of a totalitarian power is the destruction of all the restraints that limit power, the restraints of religion, morality, tradition, institutions, constitutions, and laws, that may place any restrictions upon the atomization of a people. The history of all totalitarian regimes has proved the rightness of Lenin's "scientific definition." If one adds to that Lenin's total rejection of the existing world and his conviction that he was the infallible interpreter of an infallible doctrine that told him what mankind should be like, to what blueprint it must be made to conform, and what "history" wants man to do; and further the ambition expressed by Lenin in the summer of 1918, "We must organize everything, take everything into our hands," we have a fair definition of totalitarianism.

This ambition to organize everything tidily, accurately, and totally was actually inherent in Lenin's doctrine from the start. We have only to read attentively his outburst against the first and chief of the cardinal sins in his Decalogue: *stikhiinost* (elementalness, spontaneity, initiative from below). To him it was the opposite of *soznatelnost* (consciousness, the instruction or direction that comes from above from the "vanguard" or "center"). In his first characteristic credo of 1902, he declared war on *stikhiinost*. In early 1918, when he was already in power, he pronounced the elemental, uncontrollable spontaneity of the "million-tentacled hydra" of the "petty bourgeois" peasantry and the workers affected by them to be "the main enemy." And in 1922 and 1923, after he had been four years in power and was discovering that the great "machine refuses to obey the driver's hand," he reiterated the denunciation, adding the grim corollary: "Petty bourgeois spontaneity is more terrible than all the Denikins, Kolchaks, and Yudeniches put together."

Lenin's Idea of the Class War

The operative word in what Lenin called the class war was not class but war. This involved not merely an acceptance of terror and a loving concern with the idea of its application but also a pedantic elaboration of terroristic methods that distinguished him from other socialist leaders.

In 1901, he wrote in the Marxist theoretical journal, *Zarya*, an apostrophe to lynch law: "Trial by the street breathes a living spirit into the bureaucratic formalism that pervades our government institutions."

In 1905, he did not hurry back to Russia while tsarism was reeling, as did Martov, Leon Trotsky, and Rosa Luxemburg, but he showered his followers with detailed and bloody instructions from afar. In January 1905, he wrote his "Plan of the Battle of Saint Petersburg": "Revolution is war. . . . The workers will arm themselves. . . . Each will strain with all his might to get himself a gun, or at least a revolver."

Subtly he recalled the cry of Zaichnevsky: "To the Axe! No, with axes you won't be able to do anything against sabres. With an axe you can't get to him; perhaps with a knife, but that is even less. No, what we need is revolvers . . . still better, guns."

In a call for a Congress of his party, he suggested as the order of business: "Organization, relation to the periphery, uprising, arming of the workers—setting up workshops for making dynamite." Workshops for making dynamite on the order of business of a socialist Congress—who but Lenin could write that? and his draft "Resolution on Armed Uprising" said: "The Congress resolves . . . that by preparation of the uprising it understands not only the preparation of weapons and creation of groups, etc., but also the accumulation of experience by means of . . . individual armed attacks on the police and army . . . on prisons, government institutions, etc."

For these armed groups he exceeded himself in the ardor of his incitements and the detailed pedantry of his instructions: "The bomb is a necessary part of the equipment for arming the people. . . . Bombs can be prepared everywhere and in all places. . . . In this, frenzied energy is needed, and yet more energy. With consternation, by God, with consternation, I see that there has been talk of bombs for more than a half year, and not a single bomb has been made. . . ."

In his "Tasks of the Detachments of the Revolutionary Army," written at the moment when the tsar was promising a constitution and large sections of the opposition were calling off their activities to see what the promise meant, Lenin instructed his revolutionary detachments to "engage in actions on their own and assume leadership over mobs." They must:

arm themselves as best they can (guns, revolvers, bombs, knives, brass knuckles, cudgels, rags soaked in kerosene to start fires, rope or rope ladders, spades for erecting barricades, barbed wire, tacks against cavalry, etc., and so forth). . . . Select leaders or officers, work out signals . . . cries, whistles, passwords, signs to know each other in darkness or in tumult. . . . Attack a policeman or cossack who has gotten separated and take away his weapons. . . . Climb on roofs or upper floors to shower stones on troops, boiling water, etc. [Always there was that etc. for fear that they would do nothing without his instructions, and perhaps he had forgotten something.]

He gave directions for securing the help of friendly officers, for procuring explosives, learning the layout of prisons, police stations, ministries, arms deposits, banks, instructions for employment of the aged, the weak, women, and children. These directives, and the train of thought they bespoke, are unique in the history of modern socialism. The ruthlessness of Nechayev, the romantic exaltation of criminals and barricades by Bakunin, the call of Zaichnevsky to the axe, are mere violent posturing in comparison.

Up to August 1914, the overwhelming majority in every socialist party and of Russian workingmen and revolutionary intellectuals rejected both Lenin's view of dictatorship over the working class and other classes, his methods of organization, and his prescriptions for waging the class war. They were outraged by his quarrelsome splitting, his bank holdups, his money counterfeiting. Had they understood more fully what he was saying and believed he meant it literally, they would have been still more outraged. These methods isolated him and reduced his following to a little band of "rockhards"—a word he loved to echo— of men who admired him for his ruthlessness and cynicism, plus men in key posts, who, as it turned out when the police files were opened, were agents of the police.

Total War was Lenin's Opportunity

But in August 1914 began the terrible years—four long years of a frozen war of position, brutalizing years in which statesmen and generals treated their male citizens as so much human materiel to be expended without stint or calculation in the pursuit of undefinable and unattainable objectives. Men learned to accept as commonplace the mud and blood of the trenches and the ruthless logic of mutual extermination. They learned to master their fear of death and their revulsion against inflicting it. They developed a monstrous indifference to suffering, their own as well as that of others. Universal military discipline made Lenin's vision of military discipline in his party and public life seem less alien. Total war, which saw in entire nations a total enemy, made Lenin's idea of exterminating entire "hostile classes" less shocking. Universal war so brutalized European man that, as Reinhold Niebuhr wrote, "It became possible to beguile men into fresh brutalities by the fury of their resentment against brutality." Now that all things were being subjected to the arbitrament of bullet and bayonet, why not war and peace and the "system" that was declared to have made the sterile carnage possible and, according to Lenin, "inevitable." (It would take Lenin's disciples fifty years and an awareness of the atomic stalemate before they would grudgingly admit that universal war might not be inevitable.)

"Since it was a time of horrors," Raymond Aron would write in retrospect, "at least violence might have peace as its objective." If Lenin still rejected peace in favor of prolonging war until it could be transformed into a universal civil war,[a] this fine point of distinction was now less noticeable, for was he not "rejecting" the imperialist war and declaring war on "the system that begot it"?

Thus, war was Lenin's opportunity, since it made his fantastic prescriptions on military discipline and class war seem less unnatural. For, before there could come the reign of what Churchill would one day call "the bloody-minded professors of the Kremlin," there had first to be the bloody mess of Flanders Field, in which, as England's wartime leader, Lloyd George, himself would write, "Nothing could stop Haig's compulsion to send thousands and thousands to their death against the enemy's guns in the bovine and brutal game of attrition."

The Beginnings of Total Power

The completeness of Lenin's belief in himself was matched by the completeness of his distrust of everybody else, from the proletariat to his own lieutenants, local bodies, and rank and file. Once in power he tried to define and prescribe everything, give detailed orders and write detailed decrees and instructions on everything, check upon everything's execution. His correspondence is filled with such detailed prescriptions and reports.

Uncomfortable as always in the presence of spontaneity, complexity, ambiguity, partial truths, shadings, pluralism, openness, the not-yet-known, the imperfectly known, or the unknowable, Lenin treated all questions of government and human conduct as if they had only one right answer, one simple, definite solution. The striking exception was his retreat in 1921 from the complete nationalization of everything down to the last bit of wool out of which a housewife might otherwise have knitted a sock or sweater, the last typewriter, scrap of paper, and inkwell, and the last exchange of rural grain for city-made hammers or nails, an impossible procedure partly brought on by the exigencies of civil war and partly by the primitive and credulous nature of Lenin's orginal "Marxist" dogmas. The retreat gave Russia Lenin's "New Economic Policy," or N.E.P., from which Stalin was to return to all-out nationalization.

Apart from this, Lenin's answer to whatever failures and irrationalities arose from his fantastic blueprint and his excessive centralization and control was yet more control and yet more administrative machinery.

A "terrible simplifier" in his remedies, he tended to cut through any com-

---

[a]Actually, when Lenin got back to what he pronounced "the freest country in the world in wartime" and sought to overthrow its new freedoms, for the first time in his life he found himself face to face with mass meetings of real peasants and workingmen in uniform. Then he found it convenient to urge peace and not prolongation of the war, and limited his slogans to suggestions of fraternizing in the trenches, grounding arms, turning arms on your own officers, desertion of the imperialist war to seize land in one's native village. The transforming of the imperialist war into universal civil war proved so impractical for the seizure and holding of power that within two months of his *coup d'état* he was threatening to "appeal to the sailors of Kronstadt" against his own Central Committee if they continued to vote for "revolutionary war" in place of a separate peace with Germany.

plexity or muddle with the simplest of remedies: *arrest*! Set up another overseer committee to oversee the remiss or defective one, and "arrest a few scoundrels as an example."

A perpetual conspirator himself, before he came to power one of his weapons of confusion and demagogy was to bombard the Provisional Government with demands for the arrest of the "wealthy conspirators," the "ten capitalist ministers," and a stipulated number of bankers, manufacturers, and millionaires.

When the Provisional Government, simultaneously attacked by Lenin from the "left" and Kornilov from the "right," guiding itself by the false maxim *pas d'ennemi à gauche*, armed the Bolsheviks along with the other socialists and democrats against Kornilov, Lenin privately told his followers, "We will support Kerensky as the rope does the hanged man." But publicly he "supported" Kerensky with the demand, "Arrest Miliukov, arrest Rodzianko." In the "Threatening Catastrophe and How to Combat It," written a little over a month before he seized power, Lenin demanded "the abolition of commercial secrets [Is there any country with more secrets today than the totalitarian regime he founded?] and the firing squad for hiding anything."

But it was after he took power in the state that was "to begin at once to wither away" that his imagination ran riot. On November 18, 1917, he called upon the people of Petrograd and Moscow to show initiative by "arresting and handing over to revolutionary tribunals" all those guilty of "damage, slowing up, undermining production . . . concealment of supplies . . . any sort of resistance to the great cause of peace," to the policies of "land to the peasants" and "workers' control of production and distribution." Every man his own judge!

Then he proposed that every man be his own executioner, too, provided only that he was one of the mob and not one of the "scoundrels, loafers, rich." The instruction came in a draft article entitled, with unconscious irony, "How to Organize Competition." Each commune, each village, each town, should show "initiative and inventiveness" in devising ways of "cleansing the Russian land of all noxious insects, scoundrel fleas, bedbug rich, and so forth and so forth."

When I read this passage afresh with its "insects, fleas, and bedbugs," it gave me a start. I had always imagined that the vocabulary for the dehumanizing of men to make them easier to kill had been invented by Vishinsky in the great purge trials. There the former Menshevik took special pleasure in denouncing the Old Bolsheviks who only yesterday had looked down on him. He called them "a foul-smelling pile of human garbage, vultures, serpents in human form, jackals, the last scum and filth of the past. . . . They must be shot like dirty dogs," he said. "Our people are demanding one thing: Crush the accursed reptiles."

Vishinsky's choice vocabulary and the grim and depressing study of the trials had made me sensitive to this device. Hence, when I read one day, that a group of Americans had chosen for themselves the name, Black Panthers, I exclaimed, "These people are resigning from the human race. They are giving notice that they will spring from ambush, shoot from behind shrubs and trees, and from the rooftops of buildings." Alas, I was correct. And when they chose to call the police and administrators and other officials "pigs" I knew that they were dehumanizing their intended targets. But it has astonished me to learn that Lenin, too, invented this, and gave to his successors from Stalin to Vishinsky, the inhuman terms, "noxious insects, scoundrel fleas, bedbug rich."

"In one place they will put into prison a dozen rich men, a dozen scoundrels, a half-dozen workers who shirk on the job. . . . In another place they will set them to cleaning outside toilets. In a third they will give them yellow tickets [as identity cards] after a term in prison . . . so that the entire people . . . will act as the overseers of them as harmful people (wreckers). In a fourth they will shoot on the spot one out of every ten guilty of sloth . . . the more varied, the better . . . for only practice can work out the best measures and means of struggle."

Clearly, Lenin was being unjust to himself when he wrote: "We will suppress the resistance of the possessing classes by the methods they used," since "other means have not been invented." In the speech in which he thus belittled his own inventiveness, he invented the term "enemies of the people" for an entire political party, the Kadets, and outlawed them and their elected Deputies to the Constituent Assembly. In three weeks he had invented the Extraordinary Commission (*Cheka*) along with the experimental "shooting of one in ten."

On January 27, 1918, he demanded that the entire working class join the terror. Workers who did not want to join in the hunt against "speculators" must be "forced to . . . under threat of the deprivation of their bread cards." Every factory and every regiment must pitch in to set up "several thousand raiding parties of ten to fifteen people each." "Regiments and workshops that do not accurately set up the required number of detachments [the word accurately is typical of this pedant of terror] will be deprived of bread cards and subject to revolutionary measures of persuasion and punishment. . . . Speculators caught with the goods . . . will be shot on the spot by the detachments. The same punishment for the members of the detachments convicted of bad faith."

As a socialist, Lenin had voted for the resolution of the parties of the Second International in favor of abolishing the death penalty for any crime. No one dreamed then that in the twentieth century the death penalty would be restored for theft, crimes against property, or "speculation."

But Lenin was furious with his lieutenants for abolishing the death penalty in October 1917. Even before the civil war began—a war provoked largely by such arbitrary acts as are here described, by Lenin's insistence on one-party rule and the outlawing of other parties, and by his dispersal by force of the Constituent Assembly when he found that the Russian people in their first (and last) free election had not given him a majority—he had restored the death penalty and was calling for "shooting on the spot." "As long as we do not apply terror—shooting on the spot—" Lenin told the representatives of organizations for procuring food on January 14, 1918, "we won't get anywhere." When the civil war ended, the death penalty was abolished (on January 17, 1920) but restored in

May of the same year. The first Criminal Code of the RSFSR provided the death penalty for seventy crimes. With ebbs and flows, the regime Lenin set up, returning now to "Leninist norms," has once more restored the death penalty for the various types of "aggravated speculation," theft, forgery, and crimes against the one real property, state-owned property.

C'est ne que le provisoire qui dure. Lenin did not intend this "accurate" application of terror to chaos to be more than temporary. But there is an embarrassment of riches in Lenin's subsequent writings and speeches in the same vein. Let us skip to the Eleventh Congress, held during the gentler age of the N.E.P., in April 1922, the fourth and last year of his rule, when Lenin was talking of the problem of "purchasing canned goods in a cultured manner." Then he said: "One must think of this elementary culture, one must approach a subject thoughtfully. If the business is not settled in the course of a few minutes on the telephone, collect the documents and say: 'If you start any of your red tape, I shall put you in prison.' "

C'est ne que le provisoire qui dure. Perhaps Lenin was in earnest when he wrote: "As soon as the new order has been stabilized, all administrative restrictions [on the press] will be abolished and a complete liberty of the press, subject only to the limitations of juridical responsibility, will be instituted in conformity with the most liberal and progressive legislation."[13]

The decree promised that each group of citizens would get printing plants and a supply of newsprint according to its numbers of adherents.

But after more than a half century the monopoly of the press continues, and even the Party is by Lenin's fiat denied the right to organized discussion and groupings to advance proposals or correct errors.

The one-party state is owner of all the means of communication, all printing plants, all journals, all bookstores, all libraries, all critics, and all criticism, decides what should be published and in how many copies, and what censored, what rewritten, what falsified over the author's signature, what should be sold, and what destroyed.

It is possible that Lenin's promise is not mere demagogy nor an attempt to silence critics. Lenin carried with him some of the intellectual baggage of nineteenth century socialist humanism and democracy and it took some little time to shake it off. But his heirs began without the encumbrance of this heritage from the nineteenth century. They were born and forged in the age of iron totalitarianism. All they need is to find some quote from Lenin to justify any dictatorial act and those quotations exist in abounding profusion to make pious and infallible their deeds.

On the International Arena

When Lenin entered the international arena, he carried the same methods with him. Thanks to the persuasiveness of power and victory, he felt that everything he had done in Russia in his war with the Mensheviks, the "Economists," and the Socialist Revolutionaries, all his unending splits on matters large and small, his rigid "night watchman" organization principles (as Rosa Luxemburg had ironically called them), his extreme centralism—had been legitimatized by victory and proved correct by history. Now he prepared to enforce on every party which approached his "Holy of Holies," all these views and procedures, in order to banish "Menshevism" from the ranks of the new International from the out-set.

At this moment he was completely possessed by the legends or myths within which he lived his political life. He was sure that the world war was the *"final crisis of capitalism"*; that the Russian Revolution and his *coup d'état* which that Revolution had made possible were but the first act in the *"world revolution"* which must now spread swiftly through Europe and the world.

"A quite small party is sufficient to attract the masses," Lenin told the great Italian Party when he was naming the leaders and groups that it must expel. "In certain moments there is no need for a large organization.... You are in a preparatory period. The first stage of that period is a break with the Mensheviks like that we carried out in 1903." Lenin had his way with the Italian Party, splitting open the powerful workers' front in Italy; through the breach, Mussolini "marched" triumphantly on Rome, traveling all but the last few miles in a Pullman sleeping car. The same pattern was repeated by Lenin's "best disciple," Joseph Stalin, at the end of the twenties, enabling Hitler's storm troopers to march through the breach Stalin created between Socialists and Communists by his dogma that the main enemy was not the fascists but the "social fascists," the "Mensheviks" of the period.

Thus, V.I. Lenin, and his disciple and successor, Joseph Stalin, were the mid-wives of the birth of Mussolini's incomplete totalitarianism, and of Hitler's ruthless totalitarian rule. "The revolution is an idea that has found bayonets," Mussolini said. And Mao, more crudely, stressed power rather than ideology with his "Power comes out of the barrel of a gun." Indeed, the ideology Lenin had devoutly borrowed from Marx, he had already hammered thin. His classless elite, recruited from students and intellectuals who are children of the possessing classes, might well seize power not, as Marx expected, where the economy was most advanced and the working class most "conscious," cultured, organized, numerous, and politically most active; it might seize power just as easily, nay, even more easily, where the economy was backward, the workers neither mature nor conscious nor politically active, and all political parties of all classes rudimentary or nonexistent. Indeed, the more fragmented and the less organized and educated a society, the easier for a little classless band of the discontented to seize power in the name of socialism and the proletariat.

This vanguard-elite theory would later make it possible for restless students, officers, or intellectuals to seize power in the name of the proletariat even where the proletariat was in its infancy. In the name of this doctrine, Mao could seize power "for the proletariat" by means of peasant armies. Ho Chi-Minh might do the same in a land where the only workers were plantation hands and handicraftsmen plying their ancient trades. All that was needed was a power vacuum; a supply of arms (the Second World War took care of that); a supply of malcontents (and where are there no malcontents?); an *apparat* to seize power; some fragments of Lenin's doctrine; and Stalin's example. Once in power they can do as Lenin, Stalin, and Khrushchev have done: use the "proletarian power" to rule society as a whole, to put all industry, all weapons, all means of communication, into the hands of the ruling "party," to develop a power as total as the wayward spirit of man and the development of technology and controls permit.

The trouble with this system is that permanent dictatorship spells permanent illegitimacy. History has known several types of legitimacy: hieratic or religious legitimacy, monarchical hereditary legitimacy, constitutional democratic legitimacy. When a given type of legitimacy is ruptured by revolution, the only wholesome government that can issue from the breakdown is a prelegitimate government, one that has the grace to call itself *provisional* and to recognize that its chief task is to summon the nation to elect a constitutional or constituent assembly to write a new constitution and provide a new legitimacy. In our age, this is most likely to be a democratic legitimacy.

But permanent dictatorship does not provide for an expression of the popular will. Such a regime can last for fifty years and yet not dare to submit its acts to its subjects for approval or correction. Every time a dictator dies, it faces a new crisis of succession, for there is no legitimate procedure to determine a successor. As Rosa Luxemburg tried to tell Lenin in her friendly warning:

Dictatorship, certainly! But this dictatorship consists in *the manner of applying democracy*, not in its *elimination*, it means resolute attacks upon the well-entrenched rights and economic relations of bourgeois society without which a socialist transformation cannot be accomplished. But this dictatorship must be the work of a *class*, and not of a little leading minority in the name of the class. Freedom for the supporters of the government alone [she wrote in a truly memorable passage of her criticism of Lenin's revolution], freedom only for the members of one party—however numerous they may be—that is no freedom at all. Freedom is always freedom for the one who thinks differently. Not because of any fanatical conception of "justice" but because all that is instructive, wholesome, and purifying in political freedom depends on this essential characteristic, and its effectiveness vanishes when "freedom" becomes a special privilege.

. . .with the repression of political life in the land as a whole, life in the soviets must also become more and more crippled. Without general elections, without unrestricted freedom of press and assembly, without a free struggle of opinion, life dies out in every public institution, becomes a mere semblance of life, in which only the bureaucracy remains as the active element. Public life gradually falls asleep, a few dozen party leaders of inexhaustible energy . . . direct and rule . . . an élite of the working class is invited from time to time to meetings where they are to applaud the speeches of the leaders, and to approve proposed resolutions unanimously—at bottom then a clique affair . . . not the dictatorship of the proletariat but the dictatorship of a handful of politicians. . . . Such conditions must inevitably cause a brutalization of public life: attempted assassinations, shooting of hostages, etc.[14]

After fifty years, she is a prophet still.

As we review the hundred years of Lenin's life and the seven decades of our century, it seems to me that we must begin with a mea culpa. Our age has been brutalized by the psychology and habits of total war. Totalitarianism is only one byproduct of this brutality. Its practitioners forgot that man, being capable of evil, cannot be trusted with unrestricted power.

We must learn afresh a sense of man's limitations, of the precariousness, uncertainties and mysteries of life, the unexpected possibilities of our every act, the disorderliness and irrationality and discontinuity of history. The attempt to remake the world totally by force has manifestly collided with insuperable obstacles. Our boasted technological progress, too, is coming into a collision with what seems to be a stone wall at the end of a blocked street.

Saint-Just rises from the ashes of his dream to remind us that "when all the stones are cut to build the structure of freedom, from the self-same stones you can build a palace or a tomb," even as economically "from one cross, two scaffolds can be made."

However, since today we are reviewing Lenin's life and work and not our age as a whole, I shall give the last word to a fellow historian in England, Max Beloff, who has written in *Encounter* "The world has been a poorer and bleaker and more dangerous place because Lenin lived."

Notes

1. V.I. Lenin and A.M. Gorkii, *Pisma, vospominaniia, dokumenti* (Moscow, 1958), p. 91.

2. Lenin, *Collected Works*, English Translation from the Fourth Russian Edition (Moscow, 1960), IV, 342.

3. Address to the Young Communist League, October 2, 1920.

4. The scope of the present analysis prevents the documentation of these matters. On aid from the German government and General Staff, see George Katkov, "German Foreign Office Documents on Financial Support to the Bolsheviks in 1917," *International Affairs* (London, April 1956), pp. 181-89; Werner Hahlweg, *Lenins Rückkehr nach Russland, 1917* (Leiden, 1957); Z.A.B. Zeman, *Germany and the Revolution in Russia, 1915-1918* (Oxford, 1958). On the revolutionary holdups, see the chapter "Arms and the Man," in this writer's *Three Who Made a Revolution*. On Lenin's blueprint for his own spirit, see my

"Leninism," in *Marxism in the Modern World*, ed. Milorad M. Drachkovitch (Stanford, California, 1965), pp. 51-54.

5. Leon Trotsky, *Lenin* (New York, 1925), p. 43.

6. *Sochineniia*, 4th ed., V, 448.

7. Ibid., VII, 365-66.

8. *Vospominaniia o Lenine* (Moscow, 1956), p. 313.

9. Lenin to the Ninth Party Congress in April 1920; and *II Kongress Kommunishcheskogo Internatsionala*, p. 576.

10. *Sochineniia*, VI, 221-23; VII, 355-56.

11. Ibid.

12. *Sochineniia*, XXVII, 477.

13. Decree issued on November 10, 1917, by Lenin: "On the Press of the Party and the Soviets," *Collection of Documents* (Moscow, 1954), p. 173.

14. Rosa Luxemburg, *The Russian Revolution* and *Leninism or Marxism?* (Both in one volume) (Ann Arbor, 1961), pp. 69-78.

About the Contributors

Bernard W. Eissenstat, Ph. D., is professor of history and chairman of the East European and Russian Area Studies Program at Oklahoma State University. Born in the state of New York, he holds degrees from the University of Rochester, the University of Iowa, and the University of Kansas. For the past eight years he has directed an institute on radicalism at Northern Arizona University and is currently director of a similar institute at Oklahoma State University. He has been a participant in a number of ETV programs and has published in a number of journals such as the *Slavic Review* and *Soviet Studies*. He is also co-editor of *Western Civilization* (3 vols.).

Lewis S. Feuer, Ph.D., is professor of sociology at the University of Toronto. Born in New York City, he holds degrees from the City College of New York, Vassar College, and the University of Vermont. He has been the recipient of both the Cromwell Medal in history and the Bowdoin Medal and Prize. He also was a Fellow for the Advancement of Education and Exchange Scholar to the Institute of Philosophy of the Soviet Academy of Sciences in Moscow. Professor Feuer's publications include: *Karl Marx and Frederick Engels, Basic Writing on Politics and Philosophy, Marx and the Intellectuals*, and numerous articles appearing in *Survey, Western Political Quarterly, New Politics, Pacific Sociological Review, Philosophy of Science, The Journal of Philosophy, American Quarterly*, and *Journal of the History of Ideas*.

Gregory Guroff, Ph.D., is assistant professor of history at Grinnell College. He was born in Chicago, and received his degrees from Princeton University. Dr. Guroff has carried on research within the Soviet Union where he participated in the Soviet American Exchange Program. He has held NDFL Fellowships and served as Research Associate at the Center of International Study at Princeton University. The paper appearing in this volume is part of a larger study on the origins of Soviet economic planning. Professor Guroff has made a number of contributions to scholarly journals both in the United States and abroad.

Darrell P. Hammer, Ph.D., is an associate professor of political science at the University of Indiana. He was born in Iowa and holds degrees from Wichita State University, the University of Washington, and Columbia University. He also did research at Leningrad University for two years, among other grants. Professor Hammer has held a Ford Foundation Foreign Area Fellowship, and a Social Science Research Council Fellowship. His publications include numerous articles in *Slavic Review, Soviet Studies, American Political Science Review, Problems of Communism*, and *The New Republic*.

John L.H. Keep, Ph.D., is at present professor of history at the University of Toronto. For a number of years he taught Russian History at the School of Slavonic and East European Studies, the University of London. Professor Keep has carried on research inside the Soviet Union on three different occasions, and has been a Research Fellow at Osteuropa-Institute, the Free University of Berlin. His publications include: *The Rise of Social Democracy in Russia*, editor of *Contemporary History in the Soviet Mirror*, "Lenin as Tactician," in *Lenin, the Man, the Theorist, the Leader: a Reappraisal*, "October in the Provinces," in *Russia in Revolution*, and various articles in *The Slavonic and East European Review, Soviet Studies, Survey*, and *Problems of Communism*.

Roy D. Laird, Ph.D., is professor of political science and a member of the staff of the Slavic and Soviet Area Center at the University of Kansas. He was born in Blue Hill, Nebraska, and received degrees from Hastings College, the University of Nebraska, and the University of Washington. Professor Laird is a founder of both the Conference on Soviet Agricultural and Peasant Affairs, and the International Symposium of Soviet Agriculture. He has also served as a Research Analyst for the United States Government. He is the author of *Collective Farming in Russia, The Rise and Fall of the M.T.S. As An Instrument of Soviet Rule*, and has edited *Soviet Agricultural and Peasant Affairs*, and *Soviet Agriculture: The Permanent Crisis*. Professor Laird has also contributed numerous articles to academic journals.

Alfred Levin, Ph.D., is a professor of history at Kent State University. He was born in Colchester, Connecticut, and received degrees from Brown University and Yale University. Among Professor Levin's awards are a Fulbright Research Grant to Helsinki University Library, an Inter-University Travel Grant to the USSR. In 1970 he received a grant from IREX to continue his research in the Soviet Union. His publications include: *The Second Duma, The Dynamics of Soviet Society*, and *Essays in Russian History: A Collection Dedicated to George Vernadsky* which he co-edited with Alan D. Ferguson. He has published articles in the *Journal of Modern European History*, the *Slavonic and East European Review, Slavonic Encyclopedia*, and *Slavic Review*, as well as in a number of other journals both here and abroad.

Robert H. McNeal, Ph.D., is professor of history at the University of Massachusetts. He received degrees from Yale University and Columbia University, and taught at the University of Alberta, Princeton University, McMaster University, and the University of Toronto. Professor McNeal is the author of *The Bolshevik Tradition: Lenin, Stalin, Khrushchev, International Relations among Communists*, and is currently working on a biography of Krupskaya. He also edited *Stalin's Sochineniia* (Vols. XIV-XVI) and *Stalin's Works*.

Jacob Miller is presently at the Institute of Soviet and East European Studies at the University of Glasgow, Glasgow, Scotland. He received his degree in economics and spent research time in the Soviet Union at the State Planning Commission's Institute of Economic Research. He was the founder of *Soviet Studies*, which he served as editor for twenty-one years (1949-1969). His special interest is the social, mental and emotional factors of the Soviet politico-economic situation, and he has published a number of articles and two books on this subject.

Alec Nove was born in Scotland and holds degrees from King Alfred School and the London School of Economics. He has served as Reader in Russian Social and Economic Study at the University of London, director of the Institute of Soviet and East European Studies at the University of Glascow, and visiting professor of economics at the University of Kansas and the University of Pennsylvania. Professor Nove edited *Soviet Studies* and *Journal of Development Studies*, and served as First Secretary to the British Embassy in Moscow. His publications include: *The Soviet Economy, Economic Rationality and Soviet Politics, Trade with Communist Countries* (co-author), *The Soviet Middle East* (co-author), and *Economic History of the USSR*. Professor Nove has also made contributions to various journals in the United States and Great Britain.

Michael S. Pap, Ph.D., is professor of history at John Carroll University and serves as director of the Institute for Soviet and East European Studies. He was born in Carpatho-Ukraine, and acquired American citizenship in 1952. He received his Ph.D. from Heidelberg University, and has studied also in Czechoslovakia and Vienna. He is the recipient of the Shevchenko Freedom Award (1966). Dr. Pap is also a Counselor in the International Refugee Organization and a Research Associate on the Committee of International Relations, University of Notre Dame. His publications include: *Soviet Education, Soviet Concept of National State, Communist Challenge to America, World Communism in Crisis*, and numerous articles.

Stefan T. Possony is presently director of the Political Studies Program at the Hoover Institution on War, Revolution and Peace. He was born in Vienna, Austria, and educated in Austria, Germany, France, and the United States. He has served as a psychological warfare specialist to both the French and American governments. His publications include: *Lenin: The Compulsive Revolutionary, Strategie des Friedens, Lenin: A Reader*, and *The Legality of U.S. Action in Vietnam*.

Bernard A. Ramundo, LL.B., Ph.D., is assistant director, Office of International Cooperation, Department of Transportation, dealing with industrial cooperation with countries of Eastern Europe and the Soviet Union. He holds degrees from the City College of New York, Columbia Law School, Columbia University, and American University. Dr. Ramundo served as Liaison Officer with the Group of Soviet Forces during the Potsdam Mission, and political advisor to the Chief of the Potsdam Mission. He is the author of *The (Soviet) Socialist Theory of International Law, Peaceful Coexistence: International Law in the Building of Communism*, and various articles on Soviet Law.

Peter Scheibert, Ph.D., is professor of Eastern European history at Marburg University. He was born in Berlin, and completed his doctorate in 1939. Professor Scheibert lectured at the University of Cologne, and served as research assistant to the German Foreign Office. Among many other scholarly studies he is the author of *Von zu Lenin*.

Harry Schwartz, Ph.D., is a professor at State University College, and the specialist on Soviet Affairs and member of the Editorial Board of the *New York Times*. He received his degrees from Columbia University, and taught at Syracuse University, Columbia University, American University and Brooklyn College. Dr. Schwartz served as a specialist on Soviet economic intelligence with the Office of Strategic Services, and with the Department of State. His publications include: *Introduction to the Soviet Economy; Prague's 200 Days: The Czechoslovak Democratic Experiment in Action; The Soviet Economy Since Stalin; Tsars, Mandarins, and Commissars: A History of Chinese-Russian Relations; Russia's Soviet Economy; The Red Phoenix; Russia Since World War II; Russia Faces the 1960's: Russia's Postwar Economy*, and numerous scholarly articles on the Soviet economy and society.

Albert L. Weeks, Ph.D., is associate professor of political science at New York University. He received his degrees from the University of Chicago and Columbia University, and holds a Certificate from the Russian Institute of Columbia University. Professor Weeks served as editorial assistant on Newsweek Magazine, and also was a Soviet political analyst to the United States Department of State. His publications include: *The First Bolshevik: A Political Biography of Peter Tkachev*, and *The Other Side of Coexistence: An Analysis of Russian Foreign Policy*. He has also contributed articles to *The New Republic, The New Leader, Survey, The American Slavic and East European Review, The Russian Review*, and *The Annals*.

Bertram D. Wolfe was born in Brooklyn, and educated at the College of the City of New York, the University of New Mexico, and Columbia University. He was a personal acquaintance of Stalin, Trotsky, Bukharin, Molotov, Manuilsky, Kerensky and many other important figures in Russian history. He received an honorary doctorate from the University of California in 1962, and has been awarded three Guggenheim Fellowships. He is presently Senior Research Associate at the

Hoover Institution for the Study of War, Revolution and Peace. He is the author of *Khrushchev and Stalin's Ghost, Communist Totalitarianism*, and *Strange Communists I Have Known*. Professor Wolfe has contributed articles to *Foreign Affairs, The Slavic Review, The Russian Review*, and is presently working on a series of volumes on the history of the Russian Revolution.

Zigurds L. Zile, S.J.D., is a professor at the University of Wisconsin Law School. He was born in Riga, Latvia, and became an American citizen in 1953. Professor Zile received his degrees from the University of Wisconsin and Harvard University, and has served as a Graduate Fellow at the Harvard Russian Research Center. His publications include: *The World of the Soviet Serviceman: Selections from the Red Star, Ideas and Forces in Soviet Legal History: Statutes, Decisions and Other Materials on the Development and Process of Soviet Law,* and *Legal Aspects of Verification in the Soviet Union*. He has also contributed to the *Wisconsin Law Review,* the *Washington University Law Quarterly, American Journal of International Law* and the *Cornell Law Quarterly*.

Index of Persons